Sheffield Hallam University
Learning and IT Services
Adsetts Centre City Campus
Sheffield S1 1WS

101 899 198 0

D1138063

THE ECONOMICS
OF BANKING

ONE

THE ECONOMICS OF BANKING

SECOND EDITION

Kent Matthews
and
John Thompson

JOHN WILEY & SONS, LTD

Copyright © 2008   John Wiley & Sons, Ltd
                    The Atrium, Southern Gate, Chichester,
                    West Sussex PO19 8SQ, England

                    Telephone +44 (0) 1243 779777

                    Email (for orders and customer service enquiries): cs-books@wiley.co.uk
                    Visit our Home Page on www.wiley.com

First edition published 2005, © John Wiley & Sons, Ltd.

Reprinted September and October 2008.

All Rights Reserved. No part of this publication may be reproduced, stored in a retrieval system or transmitted in any form or by any means, electronic, mechanical, photocopying, recording, scanning or otherwise, except under the terms of the Copyright, Designs and Patents Act 1988 or under the terms of a licence issued by the Copyright Licensing Agency Ltd, 90 Tottenham Court Road, London W1T 4LP, UK, without the permission in writing of the Publisher. Requests to the Publisher should be addressed to the Permissions Department, John Wiley & Sons Ltd, The Atrium, Southern Gate, Chichester, West Sussex PO19 8SQ, England, or emailed to permreq@wiley.co.uk, or faxed to +44 (0) 1243 770620.

Designations used by companies to distinguish their products are often claimed as trademarks. All brand names and product names used in this book are trade names, service marks, trademarks or registered trademarks of their respective owners. The Publisher is not associated with any product or vendor mentioned in this book.

This publication is designed to provide accurate and authoritative information in regard to the subject matter covered. It is sold on the understanding that the Publisher is not engaged in rendering professional services. If professional advice or other expert assistance is required, the services of a competent professional should be sought.

Other Wiley Editorial Offices

John Wiley & Sons Inc., 111 River Street,
Hoboken, NJ 07030, USA

Jossey-Bass, 989 Market Street, San Francisco,
CA 94103-1741, USA

Wiley-VCH Verlag GmbH, Boschstr. 12,
D-69469 Weinheim, Germany

John Wiley & Sons Australia Ltd, 42 McDougall Street,
Milton, Queensland 4064, Australia

John Wiley & Sons (Asia) Pte Ltd, 2 Clementi Loop #02-01,
Jin Xing Distripark, Singapore 129809

John Wiley & Sons Canada Ltd, 6045 Freemont Blvd,
Mississauga, ONT, L5R 4J3

Wiley also publishes its books in a variety of electronic formats. Some content that appears in print may not be available in electronic books.

Cover image courtesy of James Fletcher.

Library of Congress Cataloging-in-Publication Data

Matthews, Kent.
    The economics of banking / Kent Matthews and John Thompson. – 2nd ed.
        p. cm.
    Includes bibliographical references and index.
    ISBN 978-0-470-51964-6
    1. Banks and banking.   2. Microeconomics.   I. Thompson, John L.   II. Title.

HG1601.M35 2008
332.1–dc22   2007052384

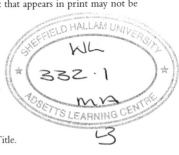

A catalogue record for this book is available from the British Library

ISBN: 978-0-470-51964-6 (P/B)

Typeset by Thomson Digital, India
Printed and bound in Great Britain by CPI Antony Rowe, Chippenham, Wiltshire

Contents

Preface   vii

CHAPTER 1   Trends in Domestic and International Banking   1

CHAPTER 2   Financial Intermediation:
The Impact of the Capital Market   21

CHAPTER 3   Banks and Financial Intermediation   35

CHAPTER 4   Banking Typology   51

CHAPTER 5   International Banking   61

CHAPTER 6   The Theory of the Banking Firm   77

CHAPTER 7   Models of Banking Behaviour   93

CHAPTER 8   Credit Rationing   115

CHAPTER 9   Securitization 证劵化   131

CHAPTER 10   Banking Efficiency and the Structure of Banking   147

CHAPTER 11   Banking Competition   171

CHAPTER 12   Bank Regulation   187

CHAPTER 13   Risk Management   209

CHAPTER 14   The Macroeconomics of Banking   243

References   265

Index   273

Preface to the Second Edition

'Learning by doing' and 'error correction' are mechanisms in economic models for the dynamic propagation of impulses. The creation of this second edition is no different. We have learnt by doing, and the second edition updates the data that underpin the trends in banking. We have also revisited sections of the book with the aim of expanding on specific issues while maintaining the objectives set out in the preface to the first edition.

In Chapter 1 we have added a section on the future of retail banking and constructed a theoretical framework to explain the development of international banking. In Chapter 6 we show how the Cournot imperfect competition model is derived and how the monopoly and the perfect competition models of the banking firm can be obtained as special cases of the Cournot model. The Northern Rock banking crisis exploded on the scene while we were revising the text for the second edition, thus providing useful example material. The Northern Rock crisis, together with its implications for liquidity management, are analysed in Chapter 7. The subprime problem and its transmission from the USA to global banking markets are examined in Chapter 9. A revised Chapter 10 introduces the benchmarking of bank performance and the measurement of bank efficiency, and a new chapter on competition in the banking market is developed as Chapter 11. The discussion on bank regulation is expanded in Chapter 12 to include more material on Basel II. A major revision of risk management in Chapter 13 includes more material on credit risk management and operational risk. Finally, the global credit crunch of 2007–2008 provides good material for the context of the creditist models of Bernanke and Gertler in the macroeconomics of banking in Chapter 14.

Error correction has taken the form of correcting typographical and formulaic errors frequently picked up by our students and adopters, as well as more careful explanation and presentation of material.

As usual, continuing innovation in banking means that the dynamics propagated by the forces of 'learning by doing' will never run out, and there will always be new material that will require interpretation within the context of existing models and theories of banking. Hopefully, the mechanism of error correction has produced a second edition that has fewer errors than the first edition. We thank all our sharp-eyed students and adopters who have pointed out the shortcomings in the first edition.

Preface to the First Edition

There are a number of good books on banking in the market; so, why should the authors write another one and, more importantly, why should the student be burdened with an additional one? Books on banking tend to be focused on the management of the bank and, in particular, management of the balance sheet. Such books are specialized reading for students of bank management or administration. Students of economics are used to studying behaviour (individual and corporate) in the context of optimizing behaviour subject to constraints. There is little in the market that examines banking in the context of economic behaviour. What little there is, uses advanced technical analysis suitable for a graduate programme in economics or combines economic behaviour with case studies suitable for banking MBA programmes. There is nothing that uses intermediate level microeconomics that is suitable for an undergraduate programme or nonspecialist postgraduate programmes.

This book is aimed at understanding the behaviour of banks and at addressing some of the major trends in domestic and international banking in recent times using the basic tools of economic analysis. Since the 1950s great changes have taken place in the banking industry. In particular, recent developments include:

(i) Deregulation of financial institutions including banks with regard to their pricing decisions, though in actual fact this process has been accompanied by increased prudential control.

(ii) Financial innovation involving the development of new processes and financial instruments. New processes include new markets such as the Eurocurrency markets and securitization as well as the enhanced emphasis of risk management by banks. Certificates of Deposit, Floating Rate Notes and Asset Backed Securities are among the many examples of new financial instruments.

(iii) Globalization so that most major banks operate throughout the world rather than in one country. This is evidenced by statistics reported by the Bank for International Settlements (BIS). In 1983 the total holdings of foreign assets by banks reporting to the BIS amounted to $754,815bn. In 2003 this figure had risen to $14,527,402bn.

(iv) All the above factors have led to a strengthening in the degree of competition faced by banks.

This text covers all these developments. Chapters 1–3 provide an introduction surveying the general trends and the role of the capital market, in general, and banks, in particular, in the process of financial intermediation. Chapters 5 and 6 cover the different types of banking operation.

Discussion of theories of the banking firm takes place in Chapters 6 and 7. Important recent changes in banking and bank behaviour are examined in Chapters 8 and 9. These include credit rationing, securitization, risk management and the structure of banking. Finally, the relationships between banks and macroeconomic policy are analysed in Chapter 13.

The exposition should be easily accessible to readers with a background in intermediate economics. Some algebra manipulation is involved in the text but the more technical aspects have been relegated to separate boxes, the detailed understanding of which are not necessary to follow the essential arguments of the main text.

Our thanks for help go to our colleagues Professor Chris Ioannidis of Bath University, Professor Victor Murinde of Birmingham University, Professor C. L. Dunis and Jason Laws of Liverpool John Moores University for helpful discussions at various stages of the writing, and to Tianshu Zhao of the University of Wales Bangor for comments on the final draft. The year 3 students of the Domestic and International Banking Module at Cardiff University made a number of useful (and critical!) comments, as did students from the postgraduate module on International Banking. They are all, of course, exonerated from any errors remaining in the text, which are our sole responsibility.

Kent Matthews   *John Thompson*
Cardiff University   Liverpool John Moores University

CHAPTER 1

Trends in Domestic and International Banking

MINI-CONTENTS

1.1 Introduction
1.2 Deregulation
1.3 Financial innovation
1.4 Globalization
1.5 Profitability
1.6 The future
1.7 Conclusion
1.8 Summary

1.1 INTRODUCTION

The main thrust of this chapter is to introduce the major changes that have taken place in the banking sector and to set the context for later discussion. Aggregate tables and statistics are employed to highlight the nature of the changes. It should also be noted that many of these changes are examined in more detail later on in the book. It is also necessary at this stage to explain the nature of various ratios that we will use throughout this text. The relevant details are shown in Box 1.1.

Banking is not what it used to be. In an important study, Boyd and Gertler (1994) pose the question, 'Are banks dead? Or are the reports grossly exaggerated?' They conclude, not dead, nor even declining, but evolving. The conventional monotask of taking in deposits and making loans remains in different guises, but it is not the only or even the main activity of the modern bank. The modern bank is a multifaceted financial institution, staffed by multi-skilled personnel, conducting multitask operations. Banks have had to evolve in the face of increased competition both from within the banking sector and without, from the non-bank

BOX 1.1   Illustration of the derivation of key ratios

Simple stylized examples of a bank's profit and loss (income) account and its balance sheet are shown below. Note in these accounts, for the purpose of simplicity, we are abstracting from a number of other items such as bad debts and depreciation and taxation.

Stylized Balance Sheet

Assets	£	Liabilities	£
Cash	100	Sight deposits	3000
Liquid assets	1000	Time deposits	2500
Loans and advance	6000	Bonds	1000
Fixed assets	200	Equity	800
Total	7300		7300

Stylized Profit and Loss (Income) Account

	£
Interest income	700
+Non-interest (fee) income	600
Less interest expenses	600
Less operating expenses	500
= Gross profit	200

The key ratios are easily derived from these accounts as demonstrated below:

Return on assets (ROA)	$= (200/7300) \times 100 = 2.7\%$
Return on equity (ROE)	$= (200/800) \times 100 = 25\%$
Net interest margin (NIM)	$= ((700 - 600)/7000) \times 100 = 1.4\%$
	(the denominator is interest-earning assets)
Operating expense (OE) ratio	$= (500/7300) \times 100 = 6.8\%$

financial sector. In response to competition, banks have had to restructure, diversify, improve efficiency and absorb greater risk.

Banks across the developed economies have faced three consistent trends that have served to alter the activity and strategy of banking. They are (i) deregulation, (ii) financial innovation and (iii) globalization. We will see that the forces released by each of these trends are not mutually exclusive. The development of the eurodollar market[1] arose out of a desire to circumvent regulation in the USA (eurocurrency banking is examined in Chapter 5). Deregulation of the interest ceiling on deposits led to the financial innovation of paying variable interest rates on demand deposits. Deregulation has also allowed global forces to play a part in the development of domestic banking services which were thought to have barriers to entry.

---

[1] The term 'eurodollar' is a generic term for deposits and loans denominated in a currency other than that of the host country. Thus, for example, both euro and dollar deposits in London are eurodollars.

There have been a number of comprehensive surveys of the process of financial innovation and deregulation in developed-economy banking systems.[2] This chapter describes the trends in banking that have arisen as a result of the forces of deregulation, financial innovation and globalization over the last two decades of the twentieth century. What follows in the remainder of this book is an attempt to demonstrate the value of economic theory in explaining these trends.

1.2 DEREGULATION

The deregulation of financial markets and banks in particular has been a consistent force in the development of the financial sector of advanced economies during the last quarter of the twentieth century. Deregulation of financial markets and banks has been directed towards their competitive actions, but this has been accompanied with increased regulation over the soundness of their financial position. This is called 'prudential control' and is discussed further in Chapter 12. Consequently, there is a dichotomy as far as the operations of banks are concerned: greater commercial freedom (i.e. deregulation) but greater prudential control (i.e. more regulation).

Deregulation consists of two strands: removal of impositions by government bodies such as the Building Societies Act, discussed below, and removal of self-imposed restrictions such as the building society cartel whereby all the societies charged the same lending rates and paid the same deposit rates. The process of deregulation across the developed economies has come in three phases but not always in the same sequence. The first phase of deregulation began with the lifting of quantitative controls on bank assets and the ceilings on interest rates on deposits. In the UK, credit restrictions were relaxed, starting with competition and credit control[3] 1971. In the USA it began with the abolition of regulation Q in 1982.[4] In the UK, the initial blast of deregulation had been tempered by imposition of the 'corset'[5] during periods of the 1970s to constrain the growth of bank deposits and, thereby, the money supply. By the beginning of the 1980s, exchange control had ended in the UK and the last vestige of credit control had been abolished.[6] Greater integration of financial services in the EU has seen more controls on the balance sheets of banks being lifted.[7]

The second phase of deregulation was the relaxation of the specialization of business between banks and other financial intermediaries, allowing both parties to compete in each other's markets. In the UK this was about the opening up of the mortgage market to

[2] See, in particular, Baltensperger and Dermine (1987), Podolski (1986) and Gowland (1991).

[3] The policy termed 'competition and credit control' removed direct controls and encouraged banks to compete more aggressively.

[4] Regulation Q set a ceiling on the interest rate that banks could pay on time deposits. The object was to protect savings and loan associations (roughly the equivalent of UK building societies) from interest rate competition.

[5] This was a policy whereby banks were compelled to lodge non-interest-bearing deposits at the Bank of England if the growth of their interest-bearing deposits grew above a specified level. The basic idea was to prevent banks from competing for funds.

[6] In the UK, hire purchase control had been abolished by 1981.

[7] For a review, see Vives (1991).

competition between banks and building societies in the 1980s. The Building Societies Act 1986 in turn enabled building societies to provide consumer credit in direct competition with the banks and specialized credit institutions. In the USA, the Garn−St Germain Act 1982 enabled greater competition between the banks and the thrift agencies. A further phase came later in 1999 with the repeal of the Glass−Steagall Act (1933)[8] which separated commercial banking from investment banking and insurance services.

The third phase concerned competition from new entrants as well as increasing competition from incumbents and other financial intermediaries. In the UK, new entrants include banking services provided by major retail stores and conglomerates (Tesco Finance, Marks & Spencer, Virgin) but also the new financial arms of older financial institutions that offer online and telephone banking services (Cahoot − part of Abbey National, Egg − 79% then owned by Prudential). In the USA, new entrants are the financial arms of older retail companies or even automobile companies (Sears Roebuck, General Motors). Internationally, GE Capital owned by General Electrical is involved in industrial financing, leasing, consumer credit, investment and insurance. In 2002 this segment of General Electric accounted for over one-third of its total revenue of $132bn.[9]

1.3 FINANCIAL INNOVATION

'Financial innovation' is a much overused term and has been used to describe any change in the scale, scope and delivery of financial services.[10] As Gowland (1991) has explained, much of what is thought to be an innovation is the extension or imitation of a financial product that already existed in another country. An example is the introduction of variable-rate mortgages into the USA when fixed rates were the norm and of fixed-rate mortgages into the UK where variable rates still remain the dominant type of mortgage.

It is generally recognized that three common but not mutually exclusive forces have spurred on financial innovation. They are (i) instability of the financial environment, (ii) regulation and (iii) the development of technology in the financial sector. Financial environment instability during the 1970s was associated with volatile and unpredictable inflation, interest rates and exchange rates and, consequently, increased demand for new instruments to hedge against these risks. Regulation that tended to discriminate against certain types of financial intermediation led to regulatory arbitrage whereby financial institutions relocated offshore in weakly regulated centres. It was the regulation of domestic banks in the USA that led to the development of the eurodollar market offshore. At the same time, technological development has created a means of developing a wide range of bank products and cost reductions, thus meeting the demand for new instruments mentioned above. The advance of technology can be viewed in the same way as Schumpeter's waves of technological innovation and adaptation. The first wave can be thought of as the application of computer

---

[8] The Financial Services Competition Act (1999) allows commercial banks to have affiliated securities firms in the USA.

[9] Annual Report *www.ge.com*

[10] A dated but excellent survey of financial innovation in banking can be found in the Bank for International Settlements (BIS, 1986) report.

technology in the bank organization. This would not only be bank specific but also be applicable to all service-sector enterprises that are involved in the ordering, storing and disseminating of information such as, for example, rating agencies. The second wave involves the application of telecommunication and computer technology to the improvement of money management methods for the consumer. The third wave involves the customer information file, which enables financial institutions to gather information about the spending patterns and financial needs of their clients so as to get closer to the customer. The fourth wave is the further development of electronic payment methods, such as smart cards, e-cash and online and home banking services.

Technological financial services are spread through competition and demand from customers for services provided by other banks and financial intermediaries. Figure 1.1 describes the process of financial innovation.

The three forces of financial instability, regulation and technology put pressure on banks to innovate. Innovation also creates a demand for new financial products which feed back into the banking system through customer reaction and demand. The influence of the three factors and the feedback from customer demand for financial services are shown in Figure 1.1.

Goodhart (1984) identified three principal forms of structural change due to financial innovation. They are in turn:

1. The switch from asset management to liability management.
2. The development of variable-rate lending.
3. The introduction of cash management technology.

Asset management fitted easily into the post-war world of bank balance sheets swollen with public sector debt and quantitative controls on bank lending. The basic idea behind the concept of asset management is that banks manage their assets regarding duration and type of lending subject to the constraint provided by their holdings of reserve assets. The move to liability management (namely their ability to create liabilities by, for example, borrowing in the interbank market) came in the USA by banks borrowing from the offshore eurodollar

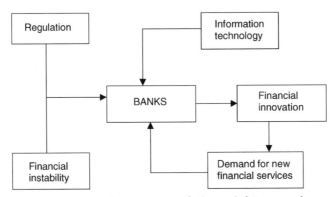

FIGURE 1.1 The Process of Financial Innovation.

market (often from their own overseas branches) in an attempt to circumvent the restrictions of regulation Q. The ceiling on the rate payable on deposits drove savers to invest in securities and mutual funds. In the UK, liability management was given a boost with the Competition and Credit Control Act 1971. With asset management, the total quantity of bank loans was controlled by restriction, and deposits were supplied passively to the banking system.

Volatile inflation and interest rates during the 1970s led to the further development of variable-rate lending. Blue-chip customers always had access to overdraft facilities at variable rates, but during the 1970s more and more companies switched to variable-rate loans (linked to the London interbank offer rate – LIBOR). Banks were able to lend to customers subject to risk, competitive pressure and marginal costs of lending. The total stock of bank loans became determined by the demand for bank credit (this implies a near-horizontal supply of bank loans curve). The development of liability management and variable-rate lending led to the rapid expansion of bank balance sheets. Banks managing their liabilities by altering interest rates on deposits and borrowing from the interbank market satisfied the demand for bank loans. Thus, the simplest type of financial innovation was the development of interest-bearing demand deposits which enabled banks to liability-manage.

The pace of technological innovation in banking has seen the development of new financial products that have also resulted in a decline in unit costs to their suppliers – the banks. Credit cards, electronic fund transfer (EFT), automated teller machines (ATMs) and point-of-sale (POS) machines have had the dual effect of improving consumer cash management techniques and reducing the costs of delivery of cash management services. A good example is the use of debit cards over cheques. The costs of clearing a cheque are 35p per item, compared with 7p per debit card transaction.[11]

1.4 GLOBALIZATION

The globalization of banking in particular has paralleled the globalization of the financial system and the growth in multinational corporations in general. To some extent, banking has always been global. The internationalization of banking in the post-war world has resulted from the 'push' factors of regulation in the home country and the 'pull' factors of following the customer.[12] This explanation of the internationalization of banking fits particularly well with the growth of US banking overseas. Restrictions on interstate banking[13] impeded the growth of banks, and restrictions on their funding capacities drove US banks abroad. The byproduct of this expansion was the creation of the eurodollar market in London – the most liberally regulated environment at the time. The 'pull' factor was provided by the expansion of US multinationals into Europe. US banks such as Citibank and Bank of America expanded into Europe with a view to holding onto their prime customers. Once established in Europe, they recognized the advantages of tapping into host-country sources of funds and of offering investment-banking services to new clients.

---

[11] Association of Payment Clearing Services information office, *www.apacs.org.uk*

[12] An overview of the determinants of the internationalization of financial services is given by Walter (1988).

[13] The Bank Holding Act 1956 effectively prohibited interstate banking.

Canals (1997) typifies the globalization process in terms of three strands. The first is the creation of a branch network in foreign countries. The most notable example of this strategy has been Citigroup and Barclays. The second strand is merger or outright takeover. The third strand is an alliance supported by minority shareholding of each other's equity. The 1980s and 1990s saw a raft of strategic alliances and takeovers in the EU, beginning with Deutsche Bank's purchase of Morgan Grenfell in 1984.[14]

The trend towards harmonization in regulation has also facilitated the globalization process. Initially this stemmed from the attempt to create a 'level playing field' through the 1988 Basel Accord. The creation of a single market in the EU and the adoption of the Second Banking Directive 1987–8 was done with a view to creating a single passport for banking services. The second directive addressed the harmonization of prudential supervision, the mutual recognition of supervisory authorities within member states and home-country control and supervision. The result of further integration of the EU banking market will see a stronger urge to cross-border financial activity and greater convergence of banking systems in Europe.[15]

Further impetus for the globalization of banking comes from the WTO General Agreement on Trade in Services (GATS). The provisions of GATS include (a) removal of capital account restrictions, (b) allowing market access, (c) ensuring equivalent regulatory treatment for foreign banks as domestic banks and (d) a move towards harmonizing regulatory practice with international best practice. While there have been great inroads made into formerly protected banking markets by the large developed-economy banks, frictions in the process have been caused by judicial and administrative impediments that hinder foreign banks from expanding too fast in domestic markets.[16]

The progressive relaxation of capital controls has added to the impetus for globalization in banking. Table 1.1 shows the increasing foreign currency position of the major banking economies since 1983. Foreign claims refer to claims on borrowers resident outside the country in which the bank has its headquarters.[17] The rapid growth of foreign asset exposure is particularly striking in the case of the UK, which has seen foreign currency assets increase their share from under 20% of total assets in 1983 to over 30% in 2003.

The pace of globalization in banking was intensified by the increasing trend to securitization (securitization is examined in greater detail in Chapter 9). 'Securitization' is a term that describes two distinct processes. Firstly, it can be thought of as the process by which banks unload their marketable assets – typically mortgages and car loans – onto the securities market. These are known as asset-backed securities (ABSs). Secondly, it can be thought of as the process of disintermediation whereby the company sector obtains direct finance from the international capital market with the aid of its investment bank. Large companies are frequently able to obtain funds from the global capital market at more favourable terms than they could from their own bank. Banks have often led their prime customers to securitize, knowing that, while they lose out on their balance sheets, they gain on fee income.

---

[14] For a recent review of trends in the EU, see Dermine (2003).

[15] For an analysis of convergence of banking systems, see Mullineux and Murinde (2003).

[16] See Murinde and Ryan (2003).

[17] The figures include the foreign currency loans of the branches of domestic banks located in foreign countries.

TABLE 1.1 Total foreign claims ($bn)

Country	1983	1988	1993	1998	2003	2006
France	70.8	97.8	115.5	189.7	1353.4	2614.6
Germany	33.7	93.2	179.6	399.5	2576.8	3541.9
Japan	61.1	338.9	405.9	295.9	1238.2	1854.3
Switzerland	16.7	36.5	51.8	83.9	1565.0	2462.4
UK	85.8	99.4	184.9	338.5	1637.4	3094.6
USA	21.4	162.3	179.3	305.0	838.3	1333.7

Source: BIS.

1.5 PROFITABILITY

The forces of competition unleashed by the deregulatory process have had stark implications for bank profitability. Banks faced competition on both sides of the balance sheet. Table 1.2 shows the evolution of bank profitability measured by the return on assets (ROA) – see Box 1.1. The effect of financial innovation and globalization has been to expand banks' balance sheets in both domestic and foreign assets. Profits as a percentage of assets declined in most cases both as balance sheets expanded and as competition put pressure on profitability. However, the banks of some countries have been successful in reducing costs and restoring ROA, but the pressure on profits has been a consistent theme.

Table 1.2 shows that ROA tends to be procyclical (vary positively with the business cycle), but in general it has been declining. Figures for 2006 show that the USA has been singularly successful in maintaining profitability, while ROA in the UK has declined sharply. Banks in Switzerland have been able to maintain their position over the past 25 years. In the case of France and Japan, the ROA for the year 2006 is higher than that for 1979. But in most cases the corresponding figures are lower. Taking out the effects of the cycle tends to confirm the common pattern of declining ROA except in the case of the USA.

TABLE 1.2 Return on assets (%)

Country	1979	1984	1989	1994	1999	2001	2003	2006
France	0.3	0.2	0.3	0.0	0.5	0.7	0.5	0.6
Germany	0.5	0.7	0.7	0.5	0.4	0.2	−0.1	0.4
Japan	0.4	0.5	0.5	0.1	0.0	−0.7	0.1	0.6
Switzerland	0.6	0.7	0.7	0.4	0.9	0.5	0.6	0.5
UK	1.8	0.9	0.2	1.1	1.4	1.1	1.0	0.5
USA	1.1	0.8	0.8	1.7	2.0	1.8	1.4	1.0

Source: OECD and Bankscope.

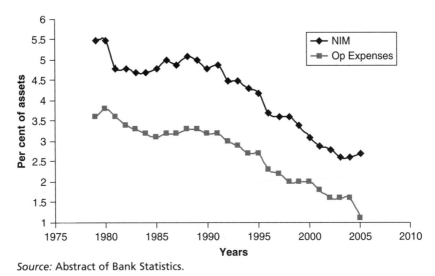

Source: Abstract of Bank Statistics.

FIGURE 1.2 NIM and Operating Expenses, Barclays Group UK 1979–2005.

Figure 1.2 illustrates a similar decline in net interest margin (NIM) for the Barclays Group in the UK. At the end of the 1970s the consolidated NIM of the Barclays Group was 5.5%, but by 2005 it had fallen to 3.0%.

Prior to the major deregulatory forces of the 1980s, bank margins were relatively wide and also influenced by the level of interest rates. The rise in interest rates that accompanied a rise in inflation increased margins because a significant proportion of deposits (i.e. sight deposits) paid no interest, whereas all assets except the minimal deposits at the Bank of England earned interest linked to the official bank rate. This was known as the *endowment effect*, which comprises two components – the net interest margin and the net interest spread:

$$\text{Endowment effect} = \text{net interest margin} - \text{net interest spread}$$
$$\text{Net interest margin} = \text{net interest income/interest-earning assets}$$
$$\text{Net interest spread} = \text{rate received in interest-earning assets}$$
$$- \text{rate paid on interest-earning deposits}$$

The innovation of interest-bearing demand deposits reduced the endowment effect during the early 1980s. Competition from within the banking system and from non-bank financial intermediaries (NBFIs) saw spreads declining in the late 1980s. Table 1.3 shows the general trend in net interest margins for selected economies. Except for the USA, where there has been a rebuilding of interest margins up to 1994, most countries show a low, cyclical but declining margin. It is also noticeable that the net interest margin is substantially higher in the USA than in the other countries listed. The same applies to a lesser extent to the UK.

A clearer picture can be seen in Figure 1.3, which shows the net interest margin for domestic and international lending for the Barclays Group. The steepest decline in the net interest margins is in the domestic sector where competition from incumbents and new entrants was the fiercest. The slower decline in net interest margins on international balances

TABLE 1.3 Net interest margins

Country	1979	1984	1989	1994	1999	2001	2003	2006
France	2.6	2.5	2.0	1.4	0.7	1.0	0.9	0.8
Germany	2.0	2.5	2.0	2.2	1.5	1.2	1.3	0.8
Japan	1.8	1.2	1.0	1.3	1.4	1.3	1.2	1.1
Switzerland	1.1	1.3	1.4	1.4	0.9	11	1.2	0.5
UK	3.9	3.0	3.2	2.4	1.2	1.8	1.7	1.1
USA	1.3	3.3	3.3	3.8	3.5	3.4	3.3	2.3

Source: OECD and Bankscope.

indicates the strength of competition that already existed in this arena. The traditional bank faces competition on both sides of the balance sheet. On the assets side, banks are faced with competition from specialist consumer credit institutions, NBFIs and the forces of disintermediation. On the liability side, banks face competition from mutual funds and an array of liquid savings products offered by NBFIs. The economics of the competitive process can be described by Figure 1.4, which shows equilibrium at point A for bank services. The demand for bank services is a bundled entity of balance sheet services like loan advances and deposit-taking, and off-balance sheet services like guarantees, credit lines and insurance. The price of the bundled service is P_B and the total quantity is Q_B (not illustrated on the axes). The demand for bank services falls from D to D' in response to competition from NBFIs and the forces of disintermediation. Normally, a new equilibrium would be defined at point B, but banks are unable to exercise the same exit strategies as other commercial firms. Banks cannot just close down without causing problems to the banking system and, ultimately, the

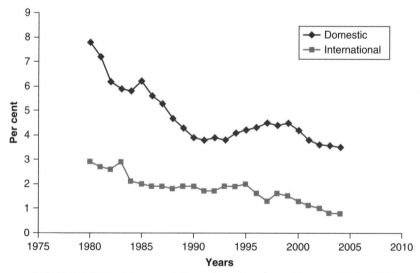

FIGURE 1.3 Net Interest Margins, Barclays Group 1979–2004.

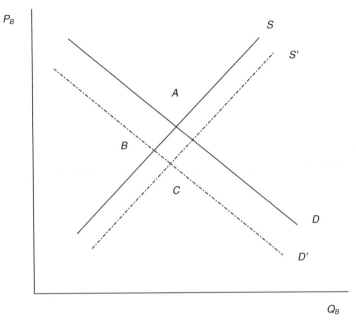

FIGURE 1.4 Competition from NBFIs.

payments system. Hence, the banks have to lower their cost structure so as to reach equilibrium at a point such as *C*.

This is further demonstrated in Figure 1.5 which shows that, faced with a fall in demand for its services resulting in a fall in the price of its services from P_B to P'_B (not shown on the axis), an individual bank can only restore profitability by reducing its costs. Both fixed costs

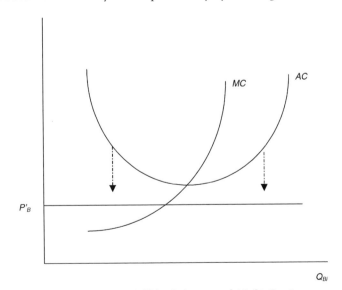

FIGURE 1.5 Fall in Prices and Unit Costs.

TABLE 1.4 Bank restructuring (number of institutions*)

Country	1980	1992	1995	2001	2003	2004	2005
France	1033	1701	1453	1068	959	830	801
Germany	5355	3517	3500	2521	2226	2147	2089
Japan	—	141	149	133	131	n/a	n/a
Switzerland	478	434	382	327	301	299	295
UK[a]	796	665	560	385	356	346	335
USA[a]	14 423	12 370	10 062	8175	7851	7701	7598

* Including savings, mutual and cooperative banks. [a] Commercial banks only
Source: OECD.

and variable costs have to be reduced to move the AC schedule down so that the cost falls to P'_B where price equals marginal and average total costs.[18]

Restructuring of the banking system to lower operational costs has taken the form of downsizing through defensive merger and staff shedding. Table 1.4 shows the extent of this trend internationally. Where merger has resulted in economies of scale, unit costs have been reduced through consolidation, branch closures and labour shedding. Figure 1.6 shows how merger results in lower costs through exploiting economies of scale. The merged bank is able to close branches and concentrate branch business on surviving branches. The increased business of the joint bank shown by the increase in quantity of bank activity from Q_{B1} to Q_{B2} is conducted at a lower unit cost shown by the fall in price from P_{B1} to P_{B2}.

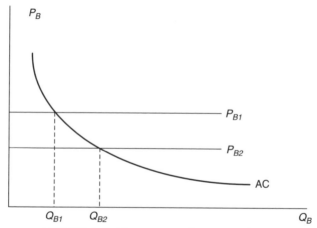

FIGURE 1.6 Mergers and Cost Reduction.

[18] Note in this exposition we are assuming the existence of perfect competition.

TABLE 1.5 Operational costs (%) as a percentage of total assets

Country	1979	1984	1989	1994	1999	2001	2003	2006
France	1.2	2.0	1.6	1.5	1.2	1.6	1.3	0.9
Germany	2.0	2.2	1.2	1.9	1.7	1.7	1.3	0.7
Japan	1.4	1.1	0.8	1.0	1.0	0.9	1.5	0.7
Switzerland	1.5	1.4	1.6	1.8	1.8	1.4	1.5	0.9
UK	3.6	3.2	3.3	2.6	1.9	1.8	1.8	0.6
USA	2.6	3.0	3.4	3.8	3.8	3.6	3.4	1.2

All banks, *source:* OECD and Bankscope.

In the UK, cost reduction has been conducted by branch closure, staff shedding and, in some cases, merger or takeover. Table 1.5 shows the evolution of operational costs, as a percentage of assets, for the banks of different countries. Figure 1.2 also shows the decline in operating costs for the Barclays Group. The extent of branch closures in the UK can be seen in the decline in the total number of branches of five major banks – Barclays, National Westminster, Lloyds, HSBC and TSB[19] – shown in Figure 1.7.

In most countries, operational costs have declined as the pressure on profitability has driven banks to increase productivity by using technology intensively (online and telephone banking) and force down unit costs. This is seen clearly in the case of the UK, Germany and Japan. Note that the changes for the USA are significantly different from those experienced by the other countries in Table 1.5. Operating expenses are much higher and have actually risen during some of this period.

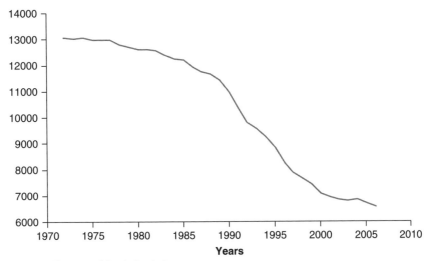

Source: Abstract of Bank Statistics.

FIGURE 1.7 Bank Branches, Top 5 Banks UK 1970–2006.

[19] The merger of Lloyds and TSB to form Lloyds-TSB led to the closure of a number of joint branches.

Competition is generally viewed as a good thing as it generates allocative, productive and dynamic efficiency. However, competitive pressure has driven banks to consolidate, with the threats that concentration has for market power and consumer welfare. However, consolidation is not necessarily anticompetitive. Banks have seen increased competition from incumbents, non-bank financial firms and even non-financial firms. They have seen an erosion of their monopoly power because deregulation combined with technology has lowered entry barriers. Comparative advantage has been eroded with new disclosure laws that have struck at the heart of the confidentiality advantages of banking. In particular, the Know Your Customer (KYC) laws associated with money laundering activity have placed banks in the invidious position of policing their own clients, counter to the traditional confidentiality qualities associated with the bank–customer relationship. The development of unit trusts and money-market mutual funds has enabled consumers to diversify their portfolios even with relatively small investments rather than tie them up in low-yielding-time deposits. So, in terms of the banks' core business of balance sheet activity, technology and financial innovation has made competition more real from the threat of entry. Technology has lowered the barriers to entry, which makes banking markets contestable. The threat of entry ensures that incumbent banks will behave in a competitive manner.

One of the products of competition on the balance sheet has been diversification. Banks have diversified into non-intermediary financial services, ranging from investment brokerage to insurance. One of the results of this has been the spectacular growth in off-balance-sheet (OBS) activity. OBS activity as a percentage of gross income has grown in all developed-economy banks. In many banks, OBS activity accounts for nearly half of gross income. Table 1.6 provides a representative list of OBS activity undertaken by banks, and Table 1.7 shows how it has grown internationally. The share of OBS activity has grown dramatically in most countries. It has particularly grown in France. The increase in the share of OBS activity in the UK and USA has been only moderate and highlights the strength of competition for other financial services between banks, other financial intermediaries and non-financial companies offering financial services (Sears, GE, Virgin, Marks & Spencer, etc.). Non-interest income makes up nearly half of total income for banks in the developed economies.

With the lifting of quantitative controls on lending and deposit-taking, and faced with increased competition and the loss of prime clients to the capital markets, banks have taken greater risks in expanding their balance sheets.

Deregulation has been replaced with re-regulation with prudential regulations on capital adequacy (regulation and systemic risk are examined in Chapter 12). The safety net of the lender of last resort raises problems of creating moral hazard. An often-heard argument is that the climate of competition and deregulation has led to adverse incentives, with banks taking on excessive risk and making imprudent loans.

1.6 THE FUTURE

While banks have opened their doors to sell new products, they also let in a myriad of new risks associated with this activity. Risks on the balance sheet remain, but risk management systems have been developed that have ushered in an age of technocracy. Credit ratings are available from the many rating agencies, but internal models such as credit scoring and the

TABLE 1.6 Summary of OBS activities

Contingent claims	Financial services

Loan commitments
  Overdraft facilities
  Credit lines
  Back-up lines for commercial paper
  Standby lines of credit
  Revolving lines of credit
  Reciprocal deposit agreements
  Repurchase agreements
  Note issuance facilities
	Loan-related services
	  Loan origination
	  Loan servicing
	  Loan pass-throughs
	  Asset sales without recourse
	  Sales of loan participations
	  Agent for syndicated loans

Guarantees
  Acceptances
  Asset sales with recourse
  Standby letters of credit
  Commercial letters of credit
  Warranties and indemnities
  Endorsements
	Trust and advisory services
	  Portfolio management
	  Investment advisory services
	  Arranging mergers and
	    acquisitions
	  Tax and financial planning
	  Trust and estate management
	  Pension plan management
	  Trusteeships
	  Safekeeping
	  Offshore financial services

Swap and hedging transactions
  Forward foreign exchange contracts
  Currency futures
  Currency options
  Cross-currency swaps
  Interest rate swaps
  Interest rate caps, collars and floors
	Brokerage/agency services
	  Share and bond brokerage
	  Mutual fund brokerage
	  General insurance brokering
	  Real estate agency
	  Travel agency

Investment banking activities
  Securities and underwriting
  Securities dealership/distribution
  Gold and commodities trading
	Payment services
	  Data processing
	  Network arrangements
	  Cheque clearing house services
	  Credit/debit cards
	  Point-of-sale machines
	  Home and online banking
	  Cash management systems

Export–import services
  Correspondent bank services
  Trade advice
  Export insurance services
  Counter-trade exchanges	

Source: Lewis, M. (1991), Theory and practice of the banking firm, *Surveys in Monetary Economics*, vol. 2, edited by Green, C. J. and Llewellyn, D. T. Blackwell, Oxford.

TABLE 1.7 Net non-interest income as % of gross income

Country	1979	1984	1989	1994	1999	2001	2003	2004	2005
France	17.0	13.0	21.4	48.0	67.0	72.0	65.3	70.2	69.2
Germany	27.2	25.9	36.0	25.4	42.7	48.7	36.4	26.0	45.6
Switzerland	44.0	38.7	38.3	54.6	64.4	60.5	54.4	61.4	63.8
UK	41.3	40.0	37.6	42.8	40.7	43.5	46.4	56.5	57.6
USA	34.7	34.2	30.0	34.4	43.1	43.3	44.6	42.9	42.7

Commercial banks, *source:* OECD.

use of proprietary models such as Creditmetrics™ have reduced the judgemental influence of the branch manager. Securitization is used as a capital-raising and risk-managing strategy. The recognition of market risk has spawned an industry of internal model application such as Value-at-Risk, and organizational, fraud and dominance risk has created the relatively new area of operational risk management (see Allen *et al.*, 2004).

However, there are risks associated with consolidation. If there are large social costs of bank failure, the trend towards consolidation could create conditions of 'too big to fail', which enables the bank to exploit unpriced risk from the hidden subsidy of the central bank and financial authorities, creating additional risks associated with moral hazard. Weak regulatory authorities may find themselves captured by the very banks they hoped to control by opening the banking system to external competition.

Risks will also emerge from greater interaction of the banks with capital markets. Hedge fund and private equity fund activity is often debt financed, with banks taking a significant position. As the collapse of LTCM has shown, the role of lender of last resort has been extended to non-bank financial institutions simply because the banks have a significant stake in the hedge funds.

It is also claimed that competition can be excessive in banking. Market power may moderate risk-taking activity (Vives, 2001). A bank with more market power enjoys higher profits and has more to lose from excessive risk taking. The erosion of monopoly power has seen increased risk taking, which it has been argued has resulted in increased financial fragility following deregulation and liberalization. However, we can be relatively sanguine about the negative effects of excess competition. Firstly, the banks that threaten entry will bid margins down to the point where monopolistic competition is sustained. No external bank would want to enter a market that exhibits conditions of perfect competition. Secondly, the empirical evidence shows that within continental Europe and even in the UK, where the banking market is relatively open, the market has remained largely under conditions of monopolistic competition relating to its balance sheet activity throughout the deregulatory period of the 1980s and 1990s.[20]

At the beginning of this chapter we stated that banking is not dead but evolving. The question is, evolving into what? Llewellyn (2006, 1996) provides us with a glimpse into banking in the twenty-first century. The banks have faced competition in specific financial

---

[20] See Matthews *et al.* (2007) for a study of the UK, and Casu and Girardone (2006) for a study of continental Europe.

products, where competitors have cherry-picked the most profitable areas of banking. This has forced the banks to unbundle the complete service they previously provided in bundled form. The traditional bundling of financial services has enabled the banks to conduct cross-subsidization with an opaque pricing strategy. The obvious example is cost-free cheque accounts. The bank in the future may be forced into unbundling its services and providing a more transparent pricing strategy.

The twenty-first century bank might include the following features:

1. Deconstruction – the process of decomposing services into their component parts which can then be priced and provided separately.
2. Overcapitalization – many banks in the developed economies find themselves with excess capital, meaning too much capital necessary to support the existing or expected level of assets. In response, banks can do one or all of the following: expand the balance sheet by taking on more risky loans; make an acquisition; share buy-backs. It should be borne in mind that some banks find that they are undercapitalized as a result of the 2007 'credit crunch'.
3. Cross-subsidization will be eroded as new entrants pick out the services that are the most profitable.
4. Banks will separate core competencies from delivery. The banking firm has advantages in information gathering and confidentiality, risk analysis, monitoring of loans, enforcement of loan contracts and brokerage. These will be separated from delivery in that the bank would act as a vessel to service customer needs from in-house and outsourced venues.
5. Banks will gravitate towards delivery of financial services for which the capital market would be a greater source of funds than the traditional deposit (securitization).
6. A higher proportion of the bank's income will come from off-balance sheet business.
7. The structure of the bank will change and will move in the direction of what Llewellyn (1996) terms 'contract banking'.

What contract banking means is that the bank will have a contract to deliver financial services to its customer. In the same way as a car manufacturer has a contract to deliver a car to a client and will source the components from all over the world, a bank will do the same. Figure 1.8 illustrates the concept of the contract bank. The contract bank will deliver financial services to the customer and will source certain services from other banks, other financial services from non-bank financial institutions (NBFIs) and the capital market. The contract bank will absorb the risks of dealing with multiple sources and supply a range of financial services to its customers consistent with a 'one-stop-shop' or universal bank where all financial services are produced under one entity.

It is tempting to say that the shift from bricks and mortar to online and e-banking will presage a move towards the 'virtual bank', but that would be too simplistic. The anonymity of virtual banking destroys customer loyalty. While offering the convenience of e-banking to many customers, branches would possibly redefine their services to capture a growing wealthy clientele.[21]

---

[21] The *Economist*, 16 June 2007, had a report on the Umpqua Bank in western USA that has replaced the traditional bank teller with 'universal associates' who earn their salary from commission on sales of financial products. The branch has a budget to spend on flowers for unwell clients, ice cream on a hot day, plush sofas, books and free internet surfing.

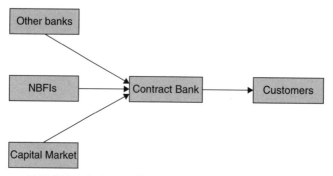

FIGURE 1.8 Organization of the Contract Bank.

1.7 CONCLUSION

This chapter has reviewed the major trends in international banking during the latter quarter of the twentieth century. As noted at the beginning of the chapter, the major trends were (i) deregulation, (ii) financial innovation and (iii) globalization. These were common to banks in most countries, although there were some intercountry differences, and are explicable in terms of the forces of deregulation, financial innovation and globalization. As a result, banks have faced pressure on profits and interest rate margins. In response, they have downsized, diversified, restructured and expanded balance sheets. In the remaining chapters of this book, we aim to use economic theory to explain the response of banks to increasing competitive pressure and to examine the question as to whether there is something special about banks that needs a protective belt not afforded to other commercial enterprises.

1.8 SUMMARY

- Banks across the developed world have faced three consistent trends: (a) deregulation, (b) financial innovation and (c) globalization.
- Deregulation has three phases:
  - It began with the removal of legal and quantitative restrictions on bank activity.
  - The second phase was the abolition of artificial barriers between types of financial intermediary and financial services.
  - The third phase was the encouragement of greater competition from non-bank financial intermediaries, non-intermediary financial firms and conglomerate organizations.
- Financial innovation was the outcome of three specific forces: (a) financial instability, (b) financial regulation and (c) technological innovation. The three principal forms of structural change due to financial innovation are:
  - The switch from asset to liability management.
  - The further development of variable-rate lending.
  - The introduction of cash management technology.

- Globalization of banking has paralleled the globalization of the financial system and the growth in multinationals.
- The forces of competition unleashed by deregulation have seen banks fighting to maintain profitability.
- Across most of the developed economies there has been a decline in net interest margins, reduction in unit costs, restructuring through downsize and merger and increase in diversification as banks have moved into traditionally non-banking financial services.
- The bank of the future is very likely to be a financial institution like the current universal banks that provide all types of banking and financial service. Unlike the modern universal bank, the bank of the future may be a contract bank that will supply all financial services but source individual services from other financial institutions.

QUESTIONS

1   What have been the principal trends in international banking during the last two decades of the twentieth century?

2   What have been the three phases of bank deregulation during the 1980s and 1990s?

3   It has been suggested that financial innovation has been the result of three interacting forces. What are these?

4   What are the three principal forms of structural change in banking owing to financial innovation, as identified by Goodhart (1984)?

5   What are the three strands in the globalization of banking identified by Canals (1997)?

6   What has been the long-term trend in net interest margin and bank profitability? Why has this occurred?

TEST QUESTIONS

1   Examine the international trends in commercial banking in the past two decades. Analytically account for the trends and, on the basis of your account, comment and make a projection on the future of banking in the next decade.

2   Are banks dead or are the reports grossly exaggerated?

2

Financial Intermediation: The Impact of the Capital Market

MINI-CONTENTS

2.1 Introduction
2.2 The role of the capital market
2.3 Determination of the market rate of interest
2.4 Summary

2.1 INTRODUCTION

In this chapter we examine how the introduction of a capital market improves the welfare of agents in the economy. The capital market can be defined as a market where firms and individuals borrow on a long-term basis as opposed to money markets where funds are lent and borrowed on a short-term basis. The two parties involved in the capital market are (a) deficit units who wish to spend more than their current income and (b) surplus units whose current income exceeds their current expenditure.

In its broadest sense, the capital market includes both the issue and sale of securities such as bonds and shares and dealings through financial intermediaries. In this chapter we are concerned with the impact of the capital market on the cost of raising funds, and in Chapter 3 we consider the role of financial intermediation in general and banks in particular in the capital market.

We show that the welfare of an individual agent is increased if the savings and investment decisions are improved with the existence of a financial intermediary as compared with the situation where no intermediation takes place. In this world the individual agent accepts the rate of interest − in other words, he/she is a price taker. We then move on to show how the rate of interest is determined by savers and investors in the capital market as a whole. The theory elaborated in this chapter is a theory of financial intermediation that does not explain the existence of banks. The purpose of developing a capital market theory of intermediation in this chapter is to allow the explanation of the existence of banks developed in Chapter 3.

2.2 THE ROLE OF THE CAPITAL MARKET

The role of the capital market in the economy can best be illustrated by making use of standard microeconomic theory within an intertemporal maximizing process.[1] The example of two-period analysis is adopted in this text for ease of exposition, but the predictions still hold for multiperiod analysis. Additional assumptions in the model are:

(i) The existence of a perfect capital market. This implies that (a) the individual can borrow/lend whatever he/she wishes at the ruling rate of interest, (b) the individual possesses perfect knowledge of the investment/borrowing opportunities open to him/her and (c) access to the capital market is costless.
(ii) There are no distortionary taxes.
(iii) The agents maximize their utility.
(iv) Investment opportunities are infinitely divisible. This is not a realistic assumption but is made to develop the theory of the capital market.
(v) Investment is subject to diminishing returns.

We are dealing with a two-period model where the agent has an initial endowment of income equal to Y_1 in period 1 and to Y_2 in period 2. First of all, we will assume that there is no capital market. Hence, the initial building block is the physical investment opportunities line (PIL). This specifies the investment opportunities open to the individual in period 1. This is shown in Figure 2.1, where we assume for the sake of convenience of exposition that $Y_1 = Y_2$. Hence, consumption in period 2 (C_2) may be augmented by saving goods in period 1 and investing them and consuming the resultant output in period 2. However, it is not possible to borrow goods from future income to increase consumption in period 1. The shape of the PIL represents assumption (v), i.e. diminishing returns to investment.

The individual's utility function is represented by the indifference curves such as U. These represent the individual's time preference for current consumption in period 1 over period 2. The steeper the slope of the indifference curve, the greater is the time preference for consumption in period 1.

The initial endowment is shown at point Z in Figure 2.1. At this point, consumption in periods 1 and 2 is equal to the individual's initial endowments − i.e. Y_1 and Y_2 respectively. Alternatively, the agent can move to the left of point Z, say at point Q, by saving $Y_1 - C_1$ in period 1 to augment consumption in period 2 from Y_2 to C_2. This investment creates output and consumption of C_2 in period 2. Note, however, that the agent cannot move to

---

[1] This analysis follows Hirschleifer (1958).

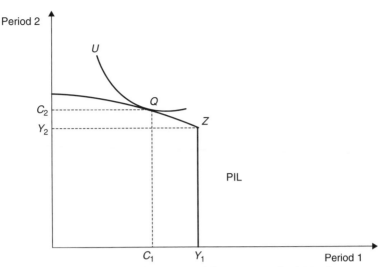

FIGURE 2.1 Equilibrium Without a Capital Market.

the right of Y_1 because there is no mechanism for him/her to borrow from his/her future endowment without some form of capital market. This accounts for the vertical section of the PIL at point Z.

At point Q, the agent's rate of time preference is equal to the marginal return on investment.

The key point to note in this analysis is that the individual agent's consumption pattern is constrained by his/her own production possibilities, and the individual is doing the business of saving and investment on his/her own – a process known as *autarky*.

However, at this point we can introduce the capital market. This is represented by the financial investment opportunities line (FIL). Financial investment opportunities are defined for a given level of wealth, which is conditional on the initial endowment for this agent. The maximum possible consumption in period 2 occurs where the agent saves all his/her income from period 1 to finance consumption in period 2 (consumption in period 1 is zero). Likewise, the maximum possible consumption in period 1 occurs where the agent's borrowings in period 1 exhausts his/her period-2 income (consumption in period 2 is zero). Here, r represents the rate of interest obtained through financial investment, and the slope of FIL is equal to $-(1 + r)$. This shown in Box 2.1.

There are an infinite number of financial investment opportunities lines – one for each different level of wealth.

Introduction of the capital market alters both the real investment and consumption possibilities open to the agent. The optimum production plan will be that which maximizes the present value of output. This occurs at the point of tangency of FIL and PIL (i.e. point T in Figure 2.2) where the marginal rate of return on investment is equal to the capital market rate of interest. The individual agent is now not constrained to consume output in the two

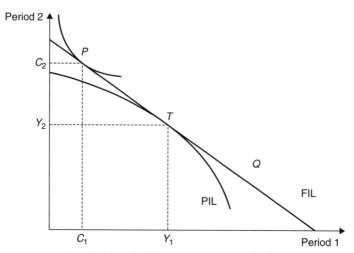

FIGURE 2.2 Equilibrium With a Capital Market.

periods as specified by point T. He/she can borrow or lend output via the capital market to secure the desired pattern of consumption over the two periods. The optimum consumption pattern will be given where the agent's rate of time preference is equal to the capital market rate of interest. In Figure 2.2, we have shown the position for the agent who lends funds in period 1 to augment his/her consumption in period 2. As before, the agent's initial endowment is Y_1 and Y_2, with the optimum level of production at point T. The agent's utility is maximized at point P, the tangency point of FIL and the agent's best indifference curve (i.e. the one furthest from the origin, thus offering the highest level of utility so that the rate of time preference equals $1 + r$). $Y_1 - C_1$ represents saving, which is invested in the capital market, and, in period 2, $C_2 - Y_2\{= (1 + r)(Y_1 - C_1)\}$ is the increase in consumption in period 2 attributable to the investment in the capital market. In the case of a borrower, the equilibrium point would be to the right of point T in Figure 2.2, with consumption being increased above output in period 1 but falling below the period-2 output as the loan has to be repaid.

The key point to note is that the production consumption process has been split into two separate stages. In stage 1 the optimum level of production is determined, and in stage 2 the optimum level of consumption is obtained independently of the production decision made in stage 1. As a result of the introduction of the capital, market utility has increased. This must be so for the saver because his/her equilibrium is at point P above the PIL.[2] This contrasts with the situation under autarky in Figure 2.2, where the point T lies on the PIL. Similarly, the borrower can move to the right of the initial endowment, which was not possible under conditions of autarky, thus increasing his/her utility.

---

[2] This assumes that the real investment opportunities in the rest of the economy offer a higher return than additional investment by the agent in his/her own firm.

BOX 2.1

The individual's utility function is given by

$$U = U(C_1, C_2)$$
$$dU = U_1 dC_1 + U_2 dC_2 = 0$$

where C_1 and C_2 are consumption in periods 1 and 2 respectively. Consumption in period 2 is given by

$$C_2 = F(Y_2; Y_1 - C_1)$$

where Y_1 and Y_2 are the fixed initial endowments in periods 1 and 2. With Y_2 and Y_1 fixed as the initial endowments:

$$dC_2 = -F' dC_1$$

so that the marginal return on investment is

$$\frac{dC_2}{dC_1} = -F'$$

The agent's rate of time preference (i.e. the preference for consumption in period 1 as against that in period 2) is then

$$\frac{dC_2}{dC_1} = -\frac{U_1}{U_2}$$

Hence, equilibrium is given by

$$\frac{U_1}{U_2} = F'$$

where the agent's rate of time preference is equal to the marginal return on investment, i.e. at point Q in Figure 2.1.

Note here that allocation of consumption between the two periods is constrained by the initial endowments and technology. The introduction of a capital market alters the situation by providing a third alternative, i.e. that of borrowing or lending by way of financial securities.

Hence, the individual's consumption possibilities are now given by

$$C_2 = Y_2 + (1 + r)Y_1$$
$$C_1 = Y_1 + \frac{Y_2}{(1 + r)}$$

where, as before, Y_1 and Y_2 represent the initial fixed endowments in periods 1 and 2 respectively, and r represents the capital market rate of interest.

(continued)

As defined in the main body of the text, the capital market is defined by the FIL with a slope of $-(1 + r)$. The slope is easily demonstrated using Figure 2.3.

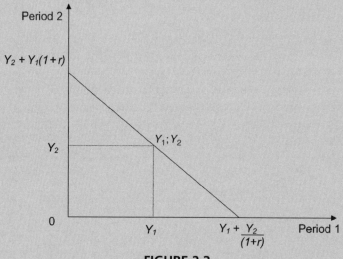

FIGURE 2.3

Select any point on Figure 2.3, say $Y_1; Y_2$. The slope is then given by

$$\frac{Y_2 - 0}{Y_1 - \left(Y_1 + \dfrac{Y_2}{(1 + r)}\right)}$$

After simplifying and cancelling out Y_1 in the denominator

$$= \frac{Y_2}{-Y_2/(1 + r)}$$
$$= -(1 + r)$$

The solution comes in two steps. Firstly, select the optimum level of production. Output in period 2 is given by

$$O_2 = F(Y_2, Y_1 - O_1)$$

where O_2 is the output in period 2, O_1 is the output in Y_1, noting that $O_1 = Y_1$ minus investment in period 1, Y_1 and Y_2 as before.

With Y_2 and Y_1 fixed as the initial endowments:

$$dO_2 = -F' \, dO_1$$

so that the marginal return on investment is

$$\frac{dO_2}{dO_1} = -F'$$

(continued)

The highest valuation of output for the two periods is given by

$$F' = (1 + r)$$

and is independent of consumption.

The optimal allocation of consumption between the two periods is given by equality between the individual's time preference and the capital market rate of interest, i.e.

$$\frac{U_1}{U_2} = (1 + r)$$

noting that the optimal consumption pattern is independent of the allocation of output between the two periods.

Clearly, the assumptions made at the outset of the analysis are overly restrictive. The capital market is not perfect since borrowers have to pay a higher rate of interest than lenders (depositors). Taxes are discriminatory. Nevertheless, we would contend that, while these assumptions are not likely to be met completely, the analysis still provides a useful basis for evaluating the role of the capital market. The analysis is demonstrated more formally in Box 2.1.

This theory explains how financial intermediation improves an individual's welfare by enabling him/her to save and increase his/her utility in the future or borrow from his/her future resources so as to increase his/her utility in the current period above what was available under autarky. But where does this interest rate come from? Who decides what is the market rate of interest? These questions can only be answered when we move from the individual analysis to the market as a whole.

2.3 DETERMINATION OF THE MARKET RATE OF INTEREST

We saw how savers can increase their welfare by moving along the FIL and how borrowers can also increase their welfare by doing the same. These savers and borrowers have to come together in a market so as to intermediate. Through the process of the capital market, savers are able to channel their surplus resources to borrowers who have deficit resources. Savers make saving decisions so as to increase their consumption in the future. Borrowers make investment decisions to enable them to create or produce a higher level of output than under autarky so that they are able to repay their borrowing in the future and improve their welfare at the same time.

The separation of the investment–production decision from the savings–consumption decision allows us to develop the classical (pre-Keynes) theory of saving and investment in the form of the loanable funds theory. The loanable funds theory explains how the rate of

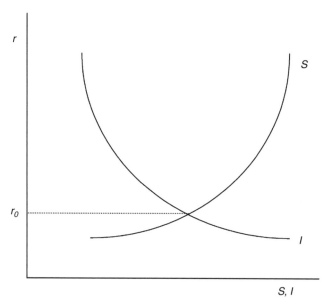

FIGURE 2.4 Determination of the Equilibrium Rate of Interest.

interest is determined by the interaction of savers and investors. Figure 2.4 illustrates the equilibrium rate of interest determined by the interaction of savings and investment decisions by agents in the economy. Investment varies inversely with the rate of interest, and saving varies positively with the rate of interest. The higher the rate of interest, the higher is the level of saving induced by agents prepared to sacrifice current consumption for future consumption. The equilibrium rate of interest is the point where investment equals savings, shown as point r_0 in Figure 2.4, in other words where

$$S(r) = I(r)$$
$$S_r > 0$$
$$I_r < 0$$

The theory was criticized by Keynes (1936) both as a theory of interest rate determination and as a theory of savings. Because this theory enabled the classical economists to argue that investment was equal to savings at all times, the macroeconomy was always at full employment. Whatever the merits or otherwise of Keynes's critique, we can show how the theory can be used to explain how a market can produce financial intermediation. Nowadays, savers have a myriad of savings instruments offered to them: mutual funds and PEPs are but two of a number of such savings instruments. We can use the loanable funds theory to examine the modern-day equivalent in the form of savings instruments that act as alternatives to the conventional bank deposit.

In the loanable funds theory, the financial counterpart to the savings and investment decision is the flow supply and demand for financial securities. The flow supply is the
increase/decrease in supply of securities, and, correspondingly, the flow demand is the
increase/decrease in demand for securities. Investors borrow by supplying securities that act
as claims to capital goods. We can think of investors as firms that wish to borrow funds to
invest in projects that yield a positive rate of return. They borrow funds by issuing new securities (equity, bonds, commercial paper), which represent liabilities to the firm. Households
(and even other firms and non-bank financial institutions such as pension funds and insurance companies) will channel savings by demanding new securities to add to their portfolio
of assets. So, savings represent the flow demand for securities (ΔB^d) and investment represents the flow supply of securities (ΔB^s), where Δ is the change in the level of stock, B represents the stock of bonds as a proxy for all securities and the superscripts represent demand
and supply. In other words

$$S = \Delta B^d$$
$$I = \Delta B^s$$

The flow demand for securities is positively related to the rate of interest because the flow
demand is negatively related to the price of securities. Hence, as the rate of interest rises, the
price of securities falls and the flow demand increases. Box 2.2 explains why the price of a
security and the rate of interest are inversely related. The flow supply of securities is negatively related to the rate of interest because supply is positively related to the price of securities. Hence, the demand and supply equations can be specified formally as

$$\Delta B^d = f(r)$$
$$\Delta B^s = g(r)$$
$$f' > 0; g' < 0$$

Figure 2.5 illustrates the case.

Consider what happens if there is an increased desire to invest by firms. The investment
schedule shifts up to the right from I_0 to I_1 and the equilibrium rate of interest increases
from r_0 to r_1, as shown in Figure 2.6. To attract funds for investment, firms will increase
the flow supply of securities. At every level of the rate of interest, the flow supply of securities would increase, shifting the ΔB^s schedule to the right. The increase in the flow supply of securities will drive down the price of securities and drive up the rate of interest
from r_0 to r_1.

Consider what happens when there is an increased desire to save by savers. How is the
message that savers wish to save more transmitted to investors? The change in savings preference shifts the saving schedule in Figure 2.7 from S_0 to S_1 and the rate of interest falls
from r_0 to r_1. The increased desire for savings is translated into an increase in the flow
demand for securities. The ΔB^d schedule shifts to the right for every given level of the rate
of interest. The increase in the flow demand for securities drives up the price of securities
and drives down the rate of interest from r_0 to r_1.

BOX 2.2

The yield (r) on a security is given by its dividend yield and expected capital gain. If the dividend is denoted by D and the price of the security is denoted by P, the yield at a point in time is described by

$$r = \frac{D_t}{P_t} + \frac{{}_tEP_{t+1} - P_t}{P_t}$$

where ${}_tEP_{t+1}$ is the rational expectation at time t for the price of the security in period $t + 1$. Rearranging this equation and solving for P_t, we have

$$P_t = \frac{D_t}{(1 + r)} + \frac{{}_tEP_{t+1}}{(1 + r)}$$

Taking expectations of this expression and pushing the time period one stage forward:

$$_tEP_{t+1} = \frac{{}_tED_{t+1}}{(1 + r)} + \frac{{}_tEP_{t+2}}{(1 + r)}$$

Substituting this expression into P_t, we have

$$P_t = \frac{D_t}{(1 + r)} + \frac{{}_tED_{t+1}}{(1 + r)^2} + \frac{{}_tEP_{t+2}}{(1 + r)^2}$$

By continuous forward substitution, the expression for P_t becomes

$$P_t = \sum_{i=0}^{n} {}_tE\frac{D_{t+i}}{(1 + r)^i} + \frac{{}_tEP_{t+n}}{(1 + r)^n}$$

We don't know the true value of future dividends, and the best guess for them is the current value of dividends. So, the expected value for D_{t+1} and all future values of D is simply D_t. Let's assume, for argument's sake, that the maturity of the security is infinite, meaning that it is an irredeemable asset. Then the second term on the right-hand side of the equation goes to zero as $n \rightarrow \infty$. After substituting D_t for expected future values of D, the first term on the right-hand side can be expressed as

$$P_t = \frac{D_t}{(1 + r)}\left(1 + \frac{1}{(1 + r)} + \frac{1}{(1 + r)^2} + \cdots\right)$$

(continued)

The term in parentheses is nothing other than the sum of a geometric series, which can be expressed as

$$P_t = \frac{D_t}{(1 + r)}\left(\frac{1}{1 - \dfrac{1}{(1 + r)}}\right)$$

$$\Rightarrow \frac{D_t}{(1 + r)}\left(\frac{1 + r}{r}\right) = \frac{D_t}{r}$$

So, at any point in time, the price of a security is inversely related to its yield or rate of return. In an efficient capital market, the yield on the security will represent the rate of interest in the economy. The price will change only if the rate of interest changes or if the expected future dividend stream changes.

The loanable funds theory is self-contained. For financial intermediation to exist, it would appear that all that is needed is an efficient capital market. So, why do we need financial intermediaries and banks?

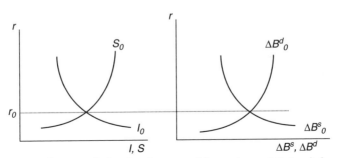

FIGURE 2.5 Equivalence of the Savings and Investment Schedules to the Flow and Demand for Securities.

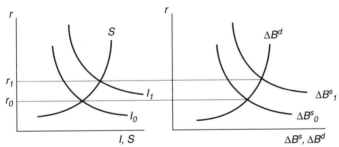

FIGURE 2.6 Increased Desire to Invest by Firms.

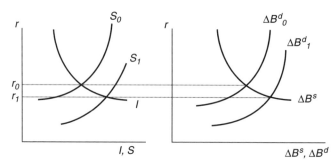

FIGURE 2.7 Increased Desire to Save by Households.

We have so far established that the introduction of a capital market increases welfare, but the question still remains as to why funds flow through a financial intermediary rather than being transferred directly from the surplus units. In a Walrasian world of perfect frictionless markets, there would be no need for financial intermediaries, as lenders and borrowers would be able to contact each other to arrange for loans. Patently, the view does not accord with the world we observe, so we must be able to provide sensible reasons for the existence of financial intermediaries and, in particular, banks. This is the subject of Chapter 3.

2.4 SUMMARY

- Financial intermediaries are superior to autarky.
- Borrowers and savers are brought together in a capital market, which enhances the utility of both parties, i.e. it is welfare superior.
- The loanable funds theory provides a theory of interest rate determination, which provides the equilibrium rate in the capital market.
- The loanable funds theory is a theory of capital market intermediation but does not satisfy the preferences of all borrowers and savers.

QUESTIONS

1 What is the role of the capital market in a modern economy?

2 Using the Hirschleifer (1958) model, show how financial intermediation improves the performance of an economy compared with financial autarky.

3 Show how the loanable funds theory of interest rates depends on the behaviour of savers and investors.

4 How far does the view that the existence of financial intermediation benefits an economy depend on the assumptions underlying the Hirschleifer model?

5 Trace out the way in which a reduction in the desire to invest will lead to a reduction in interest rate.

TEST QUESTIONS

1   What is 'financial intermediation'? Demonstrate the welfare superiority of the introduction of financial intermediation.

2   Outline the effects on the market rate of interest and the welfare implications for borrowers and savers of (a) an increase in desired savings and (b) an increase in desired investment.

3

Banks and Financial Intermediation

MINI-CONTENTS

3.1 Introduction

3.2 Different requirements of borrowers and lenders

3.3 Transaction costs

3.4 Liquidity insurance

3.5 Asymmetry of information

3.6 Operation of the payments mechanism

3.7 Direct borrowing from the capital market

3.8 Conclusion

3.9 Summary

3.1 INTRODUCTION

In this chapter we examine the role of financial intermediation in general and banks in particular. Financial intermediation refers to borrowing by deficit units from financial institutions rather than directly from the surplus units themselves. Hence, financial intermediation is a process that involves surplus units depositing funds with financial institutions that in turn lend to deficit units. This is illustrated in Figure 3.1. In fact, the major external source of finance for individuals and firms comes from financial intermediaries – Mayer (1990) reports that over 50% of external funds to firms in the USA, Japan, the UK, Germany and France were provided by financial intermediaries.

Financial intermediaries can be distinguished by four criteria:

1. Their liabilities, i.e. deposits, are specified for a fixed sum that is not related to the performance of their portfolio.
2. Their deposits are of a short-term nature and always of a much shorter term than their assets.

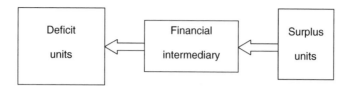

FIGURE 3.1 Financial Intermediation.

3. A high proportion of their liabilities are chequeable.
4. Neither their liabilities nor their assets are in the main transferable. This aspect must be qualified by the existence of certificates of deposit (see Chapter 4 for a description of these assets) and securitization (see Chapter 9 for a full discussion of securitization).

At the outset it is useful to make the distinction between financial intermediaries who accept deposits and make loans directly to borrowers and those who lend via the purchase of securities.[1] The former category includes banks and building societies whose operating methods are so similar that they can be classified under the heading 'banks'. The second category includes institutions such as insurance companies, pension funds and the various types of investment trust that purchase securities, thus providing capital indirectly via the capital market rather than making loans. These do not meet the first criterion noted above. Hence, our discussion is limited to the first group, the dominant institutions of which are banks.

3.2 DIFFERENT REQUIREMENTS OF BORROWERS AND LENDERS

The utility functions of borrowers and lenders differ in a number of ways. Borrowers often require quite large quantities of funds, whereas the lender generally will only have smaller amounts of surplus funds; in other words, the capacity of the lender is less than the size of the investment project. For example, the purchase of a house is likely to require more funds than can be provided by any individual lender. Thus, the bank will collect a number of smaller deposits, parcel them together and lend out a larger sum. This is called 'size transformation'.

Secondly, the lender usually wants to be able to have access to his/her funds in the event of an emergency; that is, he/she is wary of being short of liquidity. This results in the lender having a strong preference for loans with a short time horizon. Conversely, the borrower wishes to have security of his/her funds over the life of the project or investment. Consider the example of investment in new plant and machinery with a life of 15 years. Assume also that funds are required for the full life of the plant, but loans are only available with a maturity of 3 years. This would necessitate the borrower having to renew the loan or find alternative lending facilities every 3 years, or 5 times over the life of the project. Banks can fill

---

[1] A third category of financial intermediary is a broker who acts as a third party to arrange deals but does not act as a principal. This type of financial intermediary, while important, is also not relevant to our discussion.

this gap by offering short-term deposits and making loans for a longer period. The extreme example of this process is housing loans, which have a typical life of 25 years,[2] whereas the financial intermediary will support this loan by a variety of much shorter deposits. This is called 'maturity transformation'. An illustration of the degree of maturity transformation carried out by banks can be gleaned from the balance sheets of UK-owned banks. As at 31/12/06,[3] their aggregate balance sheets showed that sterling sight deposits, i.e. repayable on demand, were 33% of total sterling assets. This is in contrast to the fact that 50% of sterling assets were for advances, i.e. a much longer term.[4] Banks are able to carry out maturity transformation because they have large numbers of customers and not all customers are likely to cash their deposits at any one particular time. An exception to this occurs in the case of a run on the bank, where large numbers of depositors attempt to withdraw their funds at the same time.

The final type of transformation carried out by banks is 'risk transformation'. Lenders will prefer assets with a low risk, whereas borrowers will use borrowed funds to engage in risky operations. In order to do this, borrowers are willing to pay a higher charge than that necessary to remunerate lenders where risk is low. Two types of risk are relevant here for the depositor: default and price risk. Default risk refers to the possibility that the borrower will default and fail to repay either (or both) the interest due on the loan or the principal itself. Deposits with banks generally incur a low risk of default. This is not completely true as there have been a number of bank bankruptcies, but even here in most countries the depositor will regain either the total or a substantial proportion of the deposit in the event of bank bankruptcy because deposits are insured. Price risk refers to variation in the price of the financial claim. Bank deposits are completely free from this risk as their denomination is fixed in nominal terms. Consequently, lenders are offered assets or financial claims that attract a low degree of price risk[5] in the absence of the failure of the bank.

On the asset side of banks' balance sheets, price risk is mainly absent except in the case of the failure of the firm or individual, i.e. default. In such instances the value of the loan depends on how much can be obtained when the firm is wound up. Similarly, in the case of securitization of loans, the market value may differ from the value of the loans on the books of the financial intermediary. Hence, the main risk for the banks is default. How do banks deal with the risk of default of their borrowers? One important method for retail banks is by pooling their loans. This is feasible since retail banks will have a large number of loans and they will endeavour to spread their loans over different segments of the economy such as geographical location, type of industry, etc. By diversifying their portfolio of loans in this way, banks are able to reduce the impact of any one failure. They are able to reduce

[2] 25 years is the normal length of the mortgage when taken out, but, in fact, the average real life of a mortgage is considerably less owing to repayment following purchase of a new house or just to refinance the mortgage by taking out a new one.

[3] *Source:* Bank of England statistics. *www.bankofengland.co.uk*

[4] It may be objected that some bank lending is by way of overdraft, which is also of a short-term nature. On the other hand, most overdrafts are rolled over. In any case there are serious problems involved in recalling overdrafts, not least of which is the potential bankruptcy of the borrower and consequent loss for the bank.

[5] Note, however, that bank deposits are subject to real-value risk since variations in the general price level will alter the real value of assets denominated in nominal terms.

the risk in their portfolio. Banks will also obtain collateral[6] from their borrowers, which also helps to reduce the risk of an individual loan since the cost of the default will be borne by the borrower up to the value of the collateral. Banks can also screen applications for loans and monitor the conduct of the borrower – this aspect is considered more fully in Section 3.4. Banks will also hold sufficient capital to meet unexpected losses, and in fact they are obliged to maintain specified ratios of capital to their assets by the regulatory authorities according to the riskiness of the assets. By all these means, the bank can offer relatively riskless deposits while making risky loans.[7] Wholesale banks will also reduce risk by diversifying their portfolio, but they have one additional weapon to hand. They will often syndicate loans so that they are not excessively exposed to one individual borrower.

As we have seen above, banks can engage in asset transformation as regards size, maturity and risk to accommodate the utility preferences of lenders and borrowers. This transformation was emphasized by Gurley and Shaw (1960), and we need to consider whether this explanation is complete. In fact, immediately the question is raised as to why firms themselves do not undertake direct borrowing. Prima facie, it would be believed that the shorter chain of transactions involved in direct lending/borrowing would be less costly than the longer chain involved in indirect lending/borrowing. This leads to the conclusion that, in a world with perfect knowledge, no transaction costs and no indivisibilities, financial intermediaries would be unnecessary.

In fact, these conditions/assumptions are not present in the real world. For example, uncertainty exists regarding the success of any venture for which funds are borrowed. Both project finance and lending are not perfectly divisible, and transaction costs certainly exist. Hence, it is necessary to move on to consider the reasons why borrowers and lenders prefer to deal through financial intermediaries. One of the first reasons put forward for the dominance of financial intermediation over direct lending/borrowing centres on transaction costs – Benston and Smith (1976) argue that the '*raison d'être* for this industry is the existence of transaction costs', and this view is examined in Section 3.3. Other reasons include liquidity insurance (Diamond and Dybvig, 1983), information-sharing coalitions (Leyland and Pyle, 1977) and delegated monitoring (Diamond, 1984, 1996). These are dealt with in Sections 3.4 to 3.5.

3.3 TRANSACTION COSTS

As a first stage in the analysis of the role of costs in an explanation of financial intermediation, we need to examine the nature of costs involved in transferring funds from surplus to deficit units.[8] The following broad categories of cost can be discerned:

1. Search costs – these involve transactors searching out agents willing to take an opposite position, e.g. a borrower seeking out a lender(s) who is willing to provide the sums

---

[6] 'Collateral' refers to the requirement that borrowers deposit claims to one or more of their assets with the bank. In the event of default, the bank can then liquidate the asset(s).

[7] Risk is often measured by the variance (or standard deviation) of possible outcomes around their expected value. Using this terminology, the variance of outcomes for bank deposits is considerably less than that for bank loans. In the case of bank deposits, the variance of price risk is zero and that for default risk virtually zero.

[8] A general analysis of transaction costs in the theory of financial intermediation can be found in Benston and Smith (1976).

required. It would also be necessary for the agents to obtain information about the counterparty to the transaction and then negotiate and finalize the relevant contract.

2. Verification costs – these arise from the need of the lender to evaluate the proposal for which the funds are required.

3. Monitoring costs. Once a loan is made, the lender will wish to monitor the progress of the borrower and ensure that the funds are used in accordance with the purpose agreed. There is a moral hazard aspect here as the borrower may be tempted to use the funds for purposes other than those specified in the loan contract.

4. Enforcement costs. Such costs will be incurred by the lender should the borrower violate any of the contract conditions.

The role of costs can be examined more formally. In the absence of a bank, the cost/return structure of the two parties is depicted below, denoting the rate of interest as R, the various costs incurred by the borrower as T_B and those incurred by the saver as T_S:

$$\text{The return to the saver } (R_S) = R - T_S$$
$$\text{The cost to the borrower } (R_B) = R + T_B$$
$$\text{Then the spread} = R_B - R_S = T_B + T_S$$

The spread provides a profit opportunity, which can be exploited by the introduction of a bank. The bank has a transactions cost denoted by C. For the sake of ease of exposition, we will assume that this cost is borne solely by the borrower. Following the introduction of a bank, the cost/return structure of the two parties will be amended to

$$\text{The return to the saver } (R_S) = R - T'_S$$
$$\text{The cost to the borrower } (R_B) = R + T'_B + C$$
$$\text{Then the spread} = R_B - R_S = T'_B + T'_S + C$$

where the prime indicates the costs after the introduction of a bank.

The introduction of the bank will lower the cost of the financial transaction provided the borrower's and saver's costs fall by more than the amount of the charge raised by the intermediary, i.e. provided

$$(T_B + T_S) - (T'_B + T'_S) > C$$

This analysis can also be illustrated graphically using the model developed in Chapter 2 via an adaptation of Figure 2.3. As in Chapter 2, in Figure 3.2 we again assume a two-period analysis with a saver being repaid in period 2. The initial endowment is given as Z providing income of Y_1 and Y_2 in periods 1 and 2 respectively.[9] The financial investment opportunities line (FIL) is given by the dotted line OK based on the assumption that there are no transaction costs (i.e. $T_S = T_B = 0$) so that the slope is $-(1 + R)$. A saver will consume less than Y_1 in period 1 so that his/her equilibrium position will be along OK to the left of Z. Conversely, for the borrower the equilibrium will also be on OK, but to the right of Z.

---

[9] For the sake of ease of exposition, this initial endowment is assumed to be the optimum level of production.

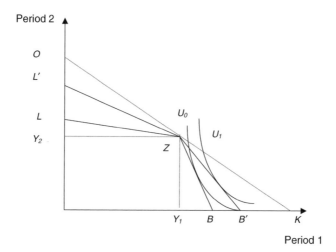

FIGURE 3.2 Equilibrium with Transaction Costs.

The existence of transaction costs alters the shape of FIL.[10] For a borrower faced with transaction costs of T_B, the slope of FIL alters to $-(1 + R + T_B)$, i.e. it becomes steeper. In other words, a borrower attracts fewer goods by borrowing, so that the segment of FIL below point Z rotates inwards to B, with the degree of rotation depending on the magnitude of T_B. Similarly, for the saver the slope of FIL becomes $-(1 + R - T_S)$, i.e. it becomes flatter. Consequently, FIL to the left of Z shifts inwards to L. This leaves the new budget line L, Z, B kinked at Z, with the magnitude of the kink depending on the size of T_B and T_S. If the introduction of the intermediary lowers aggregate transaction costs, then the kink in the budget line will be smaller than that given by L, Z, B. In Figure 3.2 we have labelled the FIL as L', Z, B' on the assumption of lower transaction costs after the introduction of the intermediary. This lies above the no-intermediary FIL but below the no-transaction-cost FIL. The gap between these two kinked FILs reflects the size of the cost reduction, i.e. $(T_S + T_B) - (T'_S + T'_B + C)$, following the introduction of the intermediary. Since the points L', Z, B' lie above L, Z, B, a higher level of utility is gained by both lenders and borrowers as compared with the situation of no financial intermediary. For example, the maximum utility of the borrower in the absence of a financial intermediary is U_0, whereas the existence of the financial intermediary improves his/her welfare position and the utility position shifts up to U_1. The points L', Z, B' dominate L, Z, B and represent welfare superiority. But this statement is subject to the qualification that transaction costs decrease after the introduction of a financial intermediary. In fact, it would be expected that costs would fall because of competition between financial institutions to serve as financial intermediaries. However, it would not be expected that the FIL would be a straight line such as OK in Figure 3.2 because the financial intermediary(ies) would require a profit from their operations. This means a gap will exist between the saving and borrowing rates so that the interest rate charge for borrowing would always be higher than that paid to savers.

We now consider the grounds for believing that the fall in the total costs incurred by borrowers and lenders will be greater than the charge levied by the bank. As far as search costs are

[10] This argument is adapted from Niehans (1978, Chapter 6).

concerned, UK banks are located in the high streets of towns and/or the City of London. The growth of IT has also permitted direct access to financial institutions, as, for example, in Internet and telephone banking. There is therefore no need to search for them – their location is well known, thus lowering costs for both borrowers and lenders. The contractual arrangements are easily carried through standard forms of contract, which again lowers transaction costs as a new contract does not have to be negotiated with each loan. Costs are also lowered for borrowers through size and maturity transformation – consider the scale of costs likely to be incurred nego-tiating a series of small loans and their subsequent renegotiation as and when each individual loan matures. In fact, economies of scale are likely to be present, particularly in the banking sphere.[11] Costs of monitoring n loans carried out by q investors are likely to be far more than the costs if monitoring were carried out by one financial intermediary. We return to this topic in Section 3.5, where we examine the potential for cost reduction where information is 'asymmetric'.

In addition to economies of scale, scope economies are also likely to be present. Scope economies arise from diversification of the business. Thus, for example, one office can process the acceptance of deposits and the construction of the corresponding asset portfolio includ-ing loans. Clearly, given the geographical dispersion of agents and the resulting transport costs, some economies can arise from the concentration of lending and deposit acceptance facilities. Pyle (1971) argues that scope economies can be explained within a portfolio frame-work. Deposits earn a negative return, and loans and advances earn a positive return. If these two returns were positively correlated (which would be expected), then the financial inter-mediary would hold a short position in the first category and a long position in the second. In other words, the financial intermediary will issue deposits and make loans.

It is therefore fairly certain that the introduction of banks (financial intermediaries) lowers the costs of transferring funds from deficit to surplus units. Nevertheless, a word of caution is appropriate here for two reasons. Firstly, economies of scale seem to be exhausted relatively early – see Chapter 10 for a discussion of this point. Secondly, a number of large firms with high-class reputations find it cheaper to obtain direct finance through markets for equity, bonds and commercial paper. This aspect, i.e. disintermediation, is considered in Section 3.5.

In spite of the clear evidence that banks do generally lower the aggregate cost of finan-cial intermediation, this appears to be an incomplete story of why financial intermediation occurs. In particular, it seems to suggest that the level of transaction costs is exogenous with-out examination as to why these costs vary between direct and indirect borrowing/lending. Further analysis is therefore required as to the nature of these costs.

3.4 LIQUIDITY INSURANCE

In the absence of perfect information, consumers are unsure when they will require funds to finance consumption in the face of unanticipated events. Hence, it is necessary for con-sumers to maintain a pool of liquidity to offset the adverse effects of these shocks to the economic system. Provided these shocks to individual consumers are not perfectly correlated, portfolio theory suggests that the total liquid reserves needed by a bank will be less than the aggregation of the reserves required by individual consumers acting independently. This is

---

[11] See Chapter 10 for a full discussion of the presence of economies of scale in the banking industry.

the basis of the argument put forward by Diamond and Dybvig (1983) to account for the existence of financial intermediaries, i.e. banks. In other words, the existence of banks enables consumers to alter the pattern of their consumption in response to shocks compared with the pattern that would have existed otherwise. The value of this service permits a fee to be earned by the financial intermediary.

Diamond and Dybvig present their model as a three-period model. Decisions are made in period 0 to run over the next two periods, i.e. periods 1 and 2. Technology is assumed to require two periods to be productive. Any interruption to this process to finance consumption provides a lower return. Consumers are divided into two categories: those who consume 'early' in period 1 and those who consume 'late' at the end of period 2. Clearly, early consumption imposes a cost in the form of lower output, and hence consumption, in period 2. The introduction of a bank offering fixed money claims overcomes this problem by pooling resources and making larger payments to early consumers and smaller payments to later consumers than would be the case in the absence of a financial intermediary. Hence, the financial intermediary acts as an insurance agent.

It should be noted that the key point is that the existence of uncertainty provides the underlying rationale for the model. There is also the critical assumption that the division of agents between the two classes of consumers is certain. Finally, the explanation is not independent of transaction costs as the role of the bank does depend on it possessing a cost advantage, otherwise individuals would introduce their own contracts which would produce a similar outcome.

3.5 ASYMMETRY OF INFORMATION

The basic rationale underlying the asymmetry of information argument is that the borrower is likely to have more information about the project that is the subject of a loan than the lender. The borrower should therefore be more aware of the pitfalls of any project and, in particular, the degree of risk attached to the project than the lender. Asymmetry of information between borrower and lender raises two further problems: moral hazard and adverse selection. In the context of finance, moral hazard is the risk that the borrower may engage in activities that reduce the probability of the loan being repaid. Moral hazard may arise both before and after the loan is made. Prior to the loan being granted, the borrower may well have inflated the probable profitability of the project either by exaggerating the profit if the venture is successful or minimizing the chance of failure. It is difficult for the lender to assess the true situation. After the loan is negotiated, moral hazard may occur because the borrower acts in a way detrimental to the repayment of the loan; for example, engaging in other, more risky, activities. Adverse selection may occur because the lender is not sure of the precise circumstances surrounding the loan and associated project. Given this lack of information, the lender may select projects that are wrong in the sense that they offer a lower chance of meeting the outcomes specified by the borrower than loans for other more viable projects that are rejected.

The results of the existence of asymmetric information between a borrower and lender and the associated problems of moral hazard and adverse selection reduce the efficiency of the transfer of funds from surplus to deficit units. In which ways can the introduction of a bank help to overcome these problems? Three answers are given in the literature: (i) the banks are subject to scale economies in their borrowing/lending activity so that they can be considered information-sharing coalitions; (ii) the banks monitor the firms that they finance, i.e. they operate as delegated monitors of borrowers; (iii) the banks provide a mechanism for commitment to a long-term relationship. In all these cases a bank may be able to overcome the twin problems of moral hazard and adverse selection.

3.5.1 Information-Sharing Coalitions

The seminal contribution to this literature is Leyland and Pyle (1977). As we have discussed above, the assumption is made that the borrower knows more about the risk of a project than the lender. Hence, it is necessary to collect information to try to redress the balance. One problem is that information is costly to obtain and is in the nature of a 'public good'. Any purchaser of information can easily resell or share that information with other individuals so that the original firm may not be able to recoup the value of the information obtained. A second aspect is that the quality of the information is difficult to ascertain, so that the distinction between good and bad information is not readily apparent. Leyland and Pyle argue that, because of this difficulty, the price of information will reflect its average quality, so that firms that search out high-quality information will lose money.

They further argue that these problems can be resolved through an intermediary that uses information to buy and hold assets in its portfolio. Thus, information becomes a private good because it is embodied in its portfolio and, hence, is not transferable. This provides an incentive for the gathering of information.

Furthermore, Leyland and Pyle argue that one way a firm can provide information about its project is to offer collateral security, and so a 'coalition of borrowers' (i.e. the bank) can do better than any individual borrower. This can easily be demonstrated. Assume N individual borrowers each have an identical project yielding the same expected return, say R. The variance of each individual return is given by σ^2. The 'coalition' does not alter the expected return per project, but the variance is now σ^2/N because of diversification.

Leyland and Pyle also put forward the view that their analysis offers an explanation for the liability structure of a bank's balance sheet. They propose that the optimal capital structure for firms with riskier returns will be one with lower debt levels. Provided a bank has reduced the level of risk, the structure of liabilities observed with high debt in the form of deposits is quite logical.

3.5.2 Role of Banks in Delegated Monitoring

Defined broadly, 'monitoring' refers to the collection of information about a firm, its investment projects and its behaviour before and after the loan application is made. Examples of monitoring include:

1. Screening the application of loans so as to sort out the good from the bad, thus reducing the chance of financing excessively risky loans.
2. Examining the firm's creditworthiness.
3. Seeing that the borrower adheres to the terms of the contract.

A bank has a special advantage in the monitoring process as it will often be operating the client's current account and will therefore have private information concerning the client's flows of income and expenditure.

This factor is very important in the case of small- and medium-sized companies and arises from the fact that banks are the main operators in the payments mechanism.

A bank will require a firm to produce a business plan before granting a loan. Given the number of such plans examined, a bank will have developed special expertise in assessing such plans and will therefore be more competent in judging the validity of the plan and separate the viable from the non-viable projects. A similar process will be required for domestic loans, and the bank will scrutinize the purpose of such loans. Further controls exist in the form of 'credit-scoring' whereby a client's creditworthiness is assessed by certain rules. A very simple example of this is in respect of a house purchase where the maximum amount of a loan is set with reference to the applicant's income. It should be admitted that other more public information is available in respect of firms. Specific rating agencies exist that provide credit ratings for firms and also sovereign debt. The most well-known examples are Standard & Poor and Moody. This information becomes available to the general public because of reports in the media. Nevertheless, the existence of rating agencies augments rather than detracts from the role of banks in the assessment of creditworthiness of prospective borrowers. The final example concerns monitoring after the loan has been granted. Banks will set conditions in the loan contract that can be verified over time. For a firm these typically will include the adherence to certain accounting ratios and a restraint over further borrowing while the loan is outstanding. The bank is able to check that such conditions are being adhered to. In addition, collateral security will often be required. Failure to adhere to the terms of the agreement will cause the loan to be cancelled and the collateral forfeited.[12]

The information obtained from borrowers is also confidential, which is not the case when funds are obtained from the capital market. In the latter situation, the firm raising funds must provide a not inconsiderable amount of detail to all prospective investors. There is a second advantage to firms raising bank loans. The fact that a firm has been able to borrow from a bank and meet its obligations regarding repayment provides a seal of approval as far as the capital market is concerned. It shows that the firm has been satisfactorily screened and absolves the capital market from repeating the process. The role of banks, in particular, provides a means for the problems associated with asymmetric information to be ameliorated. For monitoring to be beneficial, it is necessary to show that the benefits of monitoring outweigh the costs involved in gathering the information. As noted in Section 3.3, banks have a comparative advantage in the process of monitoring the behaviour of borrowers both before and after the loan is granted. This gives the lenders an incentive to delegate the monitoring to a third party, thus avoiding duplication of effort. Any bankruptcy cost will be spread over a large number of depositors, making the average cost per depositor quite small. This contrasts with the situation where each lender is concerned with few loans. In such cases the failure of one borrower to service the loan according to the agreement would have a major impact on the lender.

---

[12] This argument abstracts from the dilemma facing banks in the case of loans at risk. Should they lend more and hope to regain the outstanding amount of the loan at some time in the future or should they cancel the loan now? The first option entails the risk of a larger loss in the future and the second a loss now.

Diamond (1984, 1996) presents a more formal model of intermediation reducing the costs of outside finance under conditions of imperfect information. Diamond considers three types of contracting arrangement between lenders and borrowers: (a) no monitoring, (b) direct monitoring by investors and (c) delegated monitoring via an intermediary. In the case of no monitoring, the only recourse to the lender in the case of a failure by the borrower to honour his/her obligations is through some form of bankruptcy proceedings. This is an 'all or nothing' approach and is clearly expensive and inefficient. Direct monitoring can be extremely costly. The example given by Diamond (1996) assumes there are m lenders per borrower and a single borrower. If K is the cost of monitoring, then the total cost of monitoring without a bank is mK. The introduction of a bank changes the situation. Assume a delegation cost of D per borrower. Then the cost after delegation will be $(K + D)$ as against (mK) without a bank.[13] It is readily apparent that $(K + D)$ will be less than mK, so that the introduction of a bank has lowered the cost of intermediation. This process is illustrated in Figure 3.3.

The analysis so far assumes that the monitoring cost per loan remains the same, but, as noted earlier, the monitoring cost per transaction would be expected to fall because of the existence of economies of scale and scope. There is still the problem for the lenders/depositors of monitoring the behaviour of the bank, as the depositors will not be able to observe the information gleaned by the bank about the borrowers. They can, however, observe the behaviour of the bank, so that it could be argued that the process has merely led to a transfer of the monitoring of the behaviour of the borrower to that of the bank. The second prop to the analysis is that it is assumed that the bank maintains a well-diversified portfolio so that the return to the investors in the bank, i.e. the ultimate lenders, is almost riskless (but not completely so given the fact that banks do fail, e.g. BCCI) and therefore not subject to the problems associated with asymmetric information. The depositors also have the sanction of withdrawing deposits as a means of disciplining the bank. Furthermore, in addition to the diversification of its portfolio, depositors receive further protection because of the supervision of banks carried out by a regulatory authority, the precise nature of which depends on the institutions of the country concerned. Consequently, the bank is able to issue fixed-interest debt and make loans to customers with conditions significantly different from those offered to the depositors.

3.5.3 A Mechanism for Commitment

The third reason given for the existence of banks given asymmetric information is that they provide a mechanism for commitment. If contracts could be written in a form that specifies all possible outcomes, then commitment would not be a problem. However, it is quite clear that enforceable contracts cannot be drawn up in a manner that specifies all possible outcomes; in other words, there is an absence of complete contracts. Mayer (1990) suggests that, if banks have a close relationship with their borrowers, then this relationship may provide an alternative means of commitment. It is argued that, in particular, Japanese and German banks do have a close relationship with their clients and in many cases are

---

[13] If there were N rather than a single borrower, then the two costs without and with a bank would be nmK and $(K + nD)$ respectively. This leaves the analysis intact.

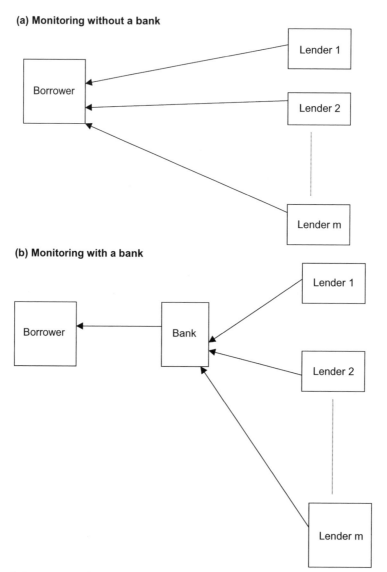

FIGURE 3.3 Financial Intermediation as Delegated Monitoring.

represented on the firms' governing bodies. This enables the bank to have good information about investment prospects and the future outlook for the firm, and to take remedial actions other than foreclosure in the event of the firm experiencing problems. This close relationship may help, then, to ameliorate the twin problems of moral hazard and adverse selection. Hoshi *et al.* (1991) provide supportive evidence that firms with close banking ties appear to invest more and perform more efficiently than firms without such ties. On the other hand, there is the danger of 'crony' capitalism, and the close ties may inhibit banks from taking action.

3.6 OPERATION OF THE PAYMENTS MECHANISM

As we have noted above, operation of the payments mechanism provides banks with an advantage over other financial intermediaries. In this section, we therefore examine the operation of the payments mechanism.

The role of banks in the UK economy dates back to the seventeenth century when gold-smiths accepted deposits of gold for safe custody and a 'gold deposit' receipt was given to the depositor. The depositors could settle accounts by transferring ownership of the gold deposited with the goldsmith. At the same time the goldsmiths quickly found that not all gold was likely to be withdrawn at the same time, so that they could issue receipts for more gold than they held in their vaults, i.e. a fractional reserve banking system existed. This emphasizes the two main purposes money serves in the economy. It is both a medium of exchange and a store of value. Bank deposits provide both of these functions, but it is interesting to note that the store-of-value function preceded their role as a medium of exchange. Bank deposits are unique in the financial system because they serve both purposes at the same time; in other words, they are a 'bundle' of services. Clearly, bank deposits are just one of many instruments that can serve as a store of value where savings can be warehoused. The crucial difference between bank deposits and other assets serving as a store of value is that bank deposits also serve as a medium of exchange. Most payments are effected by a book-keeping entry moving a balance from one account to another rather than by transferring actual cash. This can be carried out using a cheque or, alternatively, by a debit card (i.e. electronically). Hence, it is always necessary for the public to keep money balances, i.e. bank deposits, to finance their transactions. This fact gives banks a great advantage over other financial institutions because they can then use these funds held on deposit as a means to purchase interest-earning assets so as to earn profits. Banks also go to considerable lengths to protect this advantage; for example, by providing a free or nearly free service of transferring funds from one agent to another. Banks are virtually alone in offering a service in which payments are guaranteed by cheque guarantee card. Nevertheless, this service is expensive to provide so, as we have explained in Chapter 1, banks are trying to reduce costs by measures such as branch closure and greater operational efficiency.

To sum up this section, the operation of the payments mechanism by banks gives them a great advantage over rivals in the role of financial intermediaries.

3.7 DIRECT BORROWING FROM THE CAPITAL MARKET

Banks have an important role to play in the economy even in respect of direct borrowing by deficit units. This role takes the following forms of guarantee:

1. Loan commitments by way of note issuance facilities consisting of promises to provide the credit in the event of the total issue not being taken up by the market.
2. Debt guarantees – one obvious example of this activity is the guarantee of bills of exchange on behalf of its customers.
3. Security underwriting whereby banks advise on the issue of new securities and also will take up any quantity of the issue not taken up in the market.

TABLE 3.1 Fee or commission income as a percentage of net interest income (Barclays Group)

1980	1984	1988	1990	1994	1996	1998	2000	2002	2003	2006
29	41	52	64	84	80	70	65	63	65	78

Source: Barclays Bank Annual Reports and Accounts.

For all these activities the bank earns fee income rather than interest receipt. This type of business is referred to as 'off-balance-sheet business' because it does not appear on the balance sheet, unless the guarantee has to be exercised.

One measure of the importance of such business can be derived by dividing a bank's income between: (i) net interest income (i.e. the gap between interest paid out on deposits and interest received from lending) and (ii) fee or commission income. Clearly, the latter component includes far more than the banks' role in direct lending, but, nevertheless, it does provide a guide to the importance of banks in activities outside traditional financial intermediation. Table 3.1 shows the growth in importance of fee income for the Barclays Group[14] over the period from 1980 to 2006. We therefore believe that banks are and will continue to be an important component of the financial intermediation process.

3.8 CONCLUSION

In this chapter we have discussed the reasons why banks continue to exist and, also, the purpose served by them. Broadly, our discussion has followed the historical development of the subject. Initially, the literature concentrated on the existence of transaction costs involved in the mobilization of funds, thus leading on to why economies of scale and scope may exist in this process. Subsequently, the discussion centred on the possible asymmetries of information, with perhaps the most important contribution being the role of banks as 'delegated monitors' as put forward by Diamond.

In the real world we see direct and indirect borrowing (via an intermediary) existing side by side. This requires an explanation. Firms[15] that have a good reputation because of their success in the past will be able to borrow directly from the market, whereas the less successful firms will be constrained to borrow through banks. A similar argument has been put forward by Holmström and Tirole (1993). The constraint in this case is the amount of capital possessed by the firm. Firms with insufficient capital to permit additional direct borrowing will be forced to borrow through financial intermediaries.

---

[14] There is no reason to believe that the figure for other banks will be wildly different from those quoted for Barclays.

[15] This is one reason disintermediation has occurred. The question of reputation also affects banks. In some cases, banks have attracted lower credit ratings from the agencies, so that first-class companies may be able to borrow at lower rates of interest than banks have to pay on deposits. This is just one reason why banks have moved into the off-balance-sheet business.

3.9 SUMMARY

- Savers and borrowers have different requirements, which favours financial inter-mediation.
- Financial intermediaries carry out size, risk and maturity transformation.
- Operation of the payments mechanism affords the banks advantages in the process of financial intermediation.
- The existence of economies of scale and scope provides a boost to financial inter-mediation through lowering transaction costs.
- Banks provide liquidity insurance.
- Asymmetry of information between savers and borrowers provides banks with an advantage over their competitors in the process of financial intermediation.
- Banks also act as information-sharing coalitions.
- Banks operate as delegated monitors of the behaviour of the borrower.
- Banks are involved when firms go directly to the capital market for funds.

QUESTIONS

1   How do borrowers and lenders differ in their requirements? Can banks reconcile these differences?
2   What are the distinguishing features of financial intermediaries?
3   What are the sources of economies of scale and scope in banking?
4   What are the sources of transaction costs in the transfer of funds from surplus to deficit units?
5   What problems does 'asymmetry of information' create in the loan market? Can banks help to reduce the impact of this problem?
6   Can rating agencies overcome the problem of asymmetry of information?

TEST QUESTIONS

1   Why do banks exist?
2   What is 'special' about a bank?

4

Banking Typology

MINI-CONTENTS

4.1 Introduction
4.2 General features of banking
4.3 Retail banking
4.4 Wholesale banking
4.5 Universal banking
4.6 Summary

4.1 INTRODUCTION

In this chapter we describe the different types of banking operation so as to provide a background to the more analytical material examined later. The basic operation of all types of bank is the same. They accept deposits and make loans. Since the main medium of our analysis is the balance sheet, we reproduce in Table 4.1 a simple stylized bank balance sheet before proceeding to more detailed balance sheets in the following sections.

Definition of the items set out in Table 4.1 is quite simple. Sight deposits are those that can be withdrawn without notice, whereas time deposits are deposits made with a bank for a fixed period of time. Capital represents a shareholder's interests in the firm and comprises equity, reserves, etc. Balances at the central bank are those required to finance interbank transactions and required reserves to meet ratios specified by the central bank. Other liquid reserves consist of assets that can be converted into cash quickly and without loss. Investments consist of holdings of securities issued by the government and in some cases firms. Loans generally form the main component of banks' earning assets.

This simple stylized balance sheet brings out the essence of banking operations:

1. Banks accept deposits and make loans. As noted in Chapter 2, their deposits are of a shorter duration (maturity transformation) and less risky (risk transformation) than their loans.
2. Capital is required so that shareholders bear the risk of failure rather than stakeholders. Capital requirements are the heart of prudential control, as discussed in Chapter 12.
3. The degree of leverage as the capital forms a small fraction of total assets.

TABLE 4.1 Stylized bank balance sheet

Assets	Liabilities
Cash balances (including balances at the Central Bank and notes and coins in the bank)	Sight deposits
Other liquid assets	Time deposits
Investments	Capital
Loans	

In principle, four types of banking operation can be distinguished: (i) retail banking; (ii) wholesale banking; (iii) universal banking; (iv) international banking. We reserve discussion of international banking to Chapter 5. In practice, individual institutions can rarely be classified unambiguously to one of the four categories. Reference to Barclays website (*www.barclays.co.uk*) shows that they offer a range of products including personal banking, banking for business, international banking and a wide range of services apart from the traditional banking services of accepting deposits and making loans. These include other services such as stockbroking, asset management and investment banking. Consequently, banks can be classified according to a spectrum, with a number of banks providing mainly or only retail banking services (e.g Tesco Finance) and, at the other end of the spectrum, mainly wholesale services (e.g. JP Morgan). Most banking firms operate a wide range of services and are therefore universal banks falling in the middle of the spectrum. Nevertheless, it is useful to discuss the structure of banking under the classifications indicated above so as to gain greater insight into the different types of banking operation.

4.2 GENERAL FEATURES OF BANKING

4.2.1 Maturity Transformation

In Chapter 2 we drew attention to the degree of maturity transformation carried out by banks. In Tables 4.2A and B we report details of the maturities of loans made by and the type of deposits held by UK residents at British banks.[1] The figures run from 1999 to 2006 but show little variation, with the exception of the increase in time deposits towards the end of the period. The point that is highly significant about the figures is the maturity length of the loans, especially the high proportion of those over 5 years, probably partly reflecting bank operations in the housing mortgage market. In contrast, some 40% of the deposits are sight deposits, and this indicates a significant degree of maturity transformation by banks in their role as financial intermediaries.

---

[1] Note that the figures have a slightly different coverage from the figure for the proportion of sight deposits quoted in that chapter.

TABLE 4.2A Maturity of sterling advances to UK residents (%)

	1999	2000	2001	2002	2003	2004	2005	2006
Overdrafts	6.6	6.9	7.3	7.2	7.3	7.3	7.4	7.3
Next day to 1 year	21.9	21.8	24.0	24.0	24.2	24.0	24.8	25.4
Over 1 year to 3 years	8.1	8.3	7.7	7.4	7.6	7.6	7.3	7.3
Over 3 years to 5 years	5.8	5.8	5.4	5.5	6.3	5.7	6.2	6.4
Over 5 years	57.6	57.2	55.6	55.9	54.6	55.4	54.3	53.6
Total	*100*	*100*	*100*	*100*	*100*	*100*	*100*	*100*

Source: Abstract of Banking Statistics 2003, Table 2.07, British Banking Association.

TABLE 4.2B Maturity of UK residents' deposits (%)

	1999	2000	2001	2002	2003	2004	2005	2006
Sight Deposits	43.0	44.5	47.3	49.8	50.3	47.9	40.2	37.8
Time Deposits	57.0	55.5	52.7	50.2	49.7	52.1	59.8	62.2

Source: Abstract of Banking Statistics 2005, Table 2.04, British Banking Association.

4.2.2 Reserve Asset Ratios

In most countries, banks are required to hold at their central bank a specified balance as a proportion of the level of their deposits. This proportion is termed the 'reserve ratio', which varies widely between countries. Details for a number of countries are shown in Table 4.3.

UK banks are compelled to maintain non-interest-bearing deposits at the Bank of England equal to 0.15% of eligible sterling liabilities (roughly approximated by deposits). This is not a reserve ratio as operated in other financial systems, but is rather intended to finance the operations of the Bank of England, since these deposits will be invested in interest-bearing

TABLE 4.3 Reserve ratios – various countries

Central bank	Ratio	Interest-bearing
European Central Bank	2%	Yes
Bank of Japan	Varies between 0.05 and 1.3%	No
Bank of England	0.15% and reserve level agreed with individual banks	Yes
Swiss National Bank	0.25%	No
Federal Reserve USA	Varies between 0 and 10%	No

government securities and the interest receipts used to defray operating costs. In addition, the banks agree reserve balances with the Bank of England and adhere to these on average over the monthly account period. Interest is earned on these balances provided they remain within the agreed amounts. This contrasts with the Eurosystem where the banks have to keep a reserve (2%) of specified short-term liabilities of the institutions at the European Central Bank (ECB), and this requirement has to be met on average over a 1 month maintenance period. These banks earn interest on these compulsory balances at a rate equal to the average rate of the weekly tenders over the maintenance period. In the USA the position is different again. A reserve has to be maintained at the central bank equivalent to between 0 and 10% on deposits depending on their nature and size. These are non-interest-bearing balances. In Japan and Switzerland the banks are required to keep reserves equal to between 0.05 and 1.3% and 2.5% respectively. It can be seen therefore that wide differences exist between individual banking systems as regards the application of reserve ratios.

4.2.3 Risks Faced by Banks

Banks face a number of risks in their day-to-day operations. These include:

Liquidity risk The risk that the demand for repayment of deposits exceeds the liquid resources of banks. This arises from the maturity transformation carried out by banks, as discussed in Section 4.2.1. Not only are the maturities of their assets longer than those of their deposits but also a high proportion of assets comprises loans and advances which are not readily realizable. See Box 7.3 for the Northern Rock example.

Asset risk The risk that assets held by banks may not be redeemable at their book value. This can be the result of market price changes of investment securities or non-repayment, i.e. default. Asset risk not only refers to the capital value but also to the interest paid on the assets.

Foreign currency risk The risk that exchange rates may move against the bank, causing the net value of its foreign currency assets/liabilities to deteriorate.

Payments risk Risk that arises from operation of the payments mechanism and the possibility of failure of a bank to be able to make the required settlements. This risk has been reduced by the move from end-of-day net settlement of interbank balances to real-time gross settlement, whereby all interbank transactions are recorded in the central bank accounts as they occur. This reduces the time lags between settlements and, therefore, payments risk.

The **risk of settlement** has come to be known as **Herstatt risk** after the closure of Bankhaus Herstatt on 26 June 1974 by the West German authorities during the banking day but after the close of the German interbank payment system. Some of Herstatt's counterparties had paid deutschmarks to the bank before its closure in the expectation of receiving US dollars before the end of the banking day in New York. At 10.30 a.m. New York time, US dollar payments from Herstatt's account were suspended, leaving the counterparties exposed to the deutschmark values paid to Herstatt. The definition of Herstatt risk is the loss in foreign exchange trading where one party delivers foreign exchange but the other party fails to meet its end of the bargain.

Off-balance-sheet risk The risk that business that is fee earning, such as offering guarantees, will lead to losses through the failure of the counterparties to carry out their obligations.

These risks have a different impact on different types of bank. Liquidity and asset risk apply to all banks, whereas foreign currency and off-balance-sheet risks apply mainly to wholesale banks and payment risk to retail banks. Bank risk management practices are discussed more fully in Chapter 13.

4.3 RETAIL BANKING

Retail banking can be characterized as providing the services of accepting deposits and making loans to individuals and small businesses, i.e. the banks act as financial intermediaries. These transactions are typically of small value per transaction but large in volume. Normally, the payments system is operated by banks heavily involved in retail banking. Use of retail banks for payments extends to wholesale banking operations where working balances are kept at retail banks. The number of payment transactions in any one year is extremely large, as Table 4.4 shows. In addition, payments are affected by smartcards, with money balances contained on chip-and-pin and credit cards.

We mentioned above that retail banking involves liquidity and asset risks. These are overcome by attracting large numbers of customers, both depositors and borrowers. This means that the chance of large numbers of deposit withdrawals is remote as long as the bank can maintain confidence in its ability to repay depositors on demand. Banks do this by maintaining sufficient notes and coins to meet all demands for cash by customers. A second line of defence exists in their holdings of liquid assets with a portfolio of gradual maturing securities. A further defence is possible through bank holdings of UK government securities, which can be easily sold on the gilt-edged market. Finally, banks are subject to prudential control so as to protect the public—see Chapter 12 for a full discussion of prudential control of banks.

With respect to asset risk, the large number of borrowers also acts as a protection, since it is unlikely that a small number of loan failures will cause the banks great financial distress. A further defence against loan failure is obtained by screening loan applications prior to granting the loan. As we noted in Chapter 3, these banks have a special advantage in this respect as they probably operate the borrower's bank accounts and, therefore, have a fair idea of the pattern of his/her receipts and payments. This is apart from any collateral security or loan conditions imposed by the bank. Furthermore, after the loan has been granted, the bank will have expertise in monitoring the loan.

The opening sentence in Chapter 1 posed the question as to whether banks were in decline. We argued that they were evolving, and one reason for their evolution is the increased competition, in particular in retail banking. We discussed in Chapter 1 that

TABLE 4.4 Clearing statistics annual volume 2004

	000 items
Paper clearance	2 091 546
Automated clearance	4 637 433

Source: Abstract of Banking Statistics 2005, Table 7.01, British Banking Association.

increased competition led to a search for lower operating costs. One form of cost reduction came from the introduction of cash dispensers and automated teller machines. In Chapter 1 we noted that the costs of clearing a cheque are 35p per item compared with 7p per debit card transaction (Association of Payment Clearing Services Information Office, *www.apacs.org.uk*). Because of the choice of a number of building societies to adopt banking status, a better measure of the increase over time in the numbers of such machines is given by looking at the statistics for a single banking firm rather than banks in general. In 1973, Barclays had 253 cash and automated teller machines, but by 2006 this figure had risen to 3729 (Abstract of Banking Statistics (2007), Table 5.03, British Banking Association). Given that cash withdrawals cost less by automated methods than at branches, this transformation represents a major source of operating cost reduction. A further component of cost reduction arises from the closure of branches, which is itself aided by automated cash withdrawal facilities. While it is true that branch closure reduces costs, it also reduces the barriers to entry of new firms, thereby increasing competition in retail banking. Thus, in recent years, as noted in Chapter 1, a number of non-banking firms have entered retail banking in the UK; for example, the supermarkets Sainsbury and Tesco.

4.4 WHOLESALE BANKING

In contrast to retail banking, wholesale banking deals with a smaller number of customers but a larger size of each account. Typically, the minimum size of a deposit is £250 000, and that for a loan is £500 000, although the size of both transactions is generally significantly larger. Furthermore, for very large loans, groups of banks will operate as a syndicate, with one bank being denoted the lead bank. Syndication has two advantages for the bank from the risk management point of view. Firstly, risk from exposure to an individual customer is reduced. Secondly, risk reduction through diversification can be achieved through extending the range of types of customer to whom loans are made.

The balance sheets in wholesale banking differ from those in retail banking in a number of important ways:

1. Because they do not operate the payments mechanism, their holdings of cash and balances at the central bank are lower than those in retail banking.
2. The greater importance of off-balance-sheet assets. The off-balance-sheet activities are those listed in Table 1.6, and the growth of non-interest income recorded is shown in Table 1.7. Relating specifically to income earned in 2006, interest income was 61.8% of total operating income for the Cooperative Bank but only 43.9 and 9.5% respectively for Citicorp and Morgan Stanley (Bankscope Stats).
3. A much greater use of foreign currency business than in retail banking.
4. A smaller proportion of sight deposits. A greater volume of trading assets such as securities.
5. Wholesale banks make greater use of the interbank market than retail banks to obtain their funds.

It is sometimes thought that wholesale banks do not carry out maturity transformation because, in view of the smaller number of large deposits and loans, they could match the maturity distribution of their assets and liabilities. The absence of any maturity transformation would reduce the role of wholesale banks to that of brokering loans, so that the sole rationale for their existence would be cost reduction, as discussed in Chapters 2 and 3. In fact, they do carry out maturity transformation. While the figures recorded in Tables 4.2A and B refer to both retail and wholesale banks, the Bank of England (1987) reported details for retail and wholesale banks separately. For example, it was revealed that British non-retail banks held 52.8% of their liabilities in liabilities with a maturity of 0–7 days, but only 14% of their assets in this category (the corresponding figures for the retail banks were 83.5 and 3.5%). Again at the longer end of the spectrum, liabilities over 3 years came to 2.0% of total liabilities, contrasting with the figure for assets of 41.9% (again, the figures for retail banks were 65.7 and 0.4%). It must be admitted that these figures are dated, but we would not expect the current situation to be drastically different from that depicted by these statistics. Clearly then, wholesale banks do engage in maturity transformation, but to a lesser degree than the retail banks.

Wholesale banks manage the associated liquidity risk through the interbank market (see Box 4.1). If wholesale banks are short of funds, they can raise money through borrowing in the interbank market. Surplus funds will be deposited in the interbank market. This is called 'liability management' and is less costly than raising the rate of interest on their deposits, as this would apply to all deposits and the interbank market borrowing cost only applies to the extra funds.

BOX 4.1   Money markets

The most important money markets in London are the interbank market and the market for certificates of deposit (CDs). Together they represented roughly 60% of the total money markets (*Bank of England Quarterly Bulletin,* autumn 2002, Markets and Operations). All the money markets are wholesale markets where large-size deposits and the borrowing of money take place. Individual transactions will not be less than £500 000.

As the name suggests, the interbank market is where banks lend and borrow funds. Nowadays, large industrial and commercial firms also place funds in the market. The term 'maturity of funds borrowed or deposited' can vary from overnight to longer periods but with a usual maximum of 3 months. The rates of interest charged in the money markets are the result of keen competition, and one rate in particular, the London interbank offer rate (LIBOR), serves as a reference rate for floating-rate loans so that they are adjusted periodically in line with the movement of LIBOR.

The CD market is similar, but the deposit is backed by a certificate, which can be traded in a secondary market, thus offering an advantage to the holder that he/she can liquidate their holdings if he/she is short of cash. They are usually issued with an original maturity of between 3 months and 5 years and a minimum value of £50 000. The advantage of these markets is that they offer a convenient and short-term outlet for surplus funds. This is clearly better than holding non-interest-bearing deposits at the central bank. Similarly, banks that are short of funds can raise money through these markets. Hence, banks can use these markets to manage their liabilities and assets. For further theoretical discussion of asset and liability management, see Chapter 7.

Asset risk is managed in the same way as for the retail banks but without the advantage of maintaining the client's payments account. We now turn to universal banking.

4.5 UNIVERSAL BANKING

Universal banks are banks that operate the entire range of financial services ranging through the normal banking service of accepting deposits and making loans, insurance, security services, underwriting and owning shares in client companies. As we noted in the introduction to this chapter, most if not all banking firms now operate a wide range of services, so that in one sense they are all one-stop or universal banks. However, as discussed below, the term 'universal banking' tends to have a more specialized meaning when applied, in particular, to German and Japanese banks. Before developing this argument, we will discuss briefly the organizational structure of universal banks.

Saunders and Walter (1993)[2] listed four different types of universal bank organization:

1. A fully integrated bank providing all services within a single firm. No examples of this structure currently exist.
2. A partially integrated universal bank that undertakes commercial and investment banking under the same roof but that provides the other services through specialized subsidiaries. Deutsche Bank AG is one example of this structure.
3. A bank whose core business is not only accepting deposits and making loans but also providing a wide range of financial services through subsidiaries. Barclays plc provides an example of this category.
4. A holding company that controls separate subsidiaries set up to provide banking, investment banking and other financial services. Citigroup illustrates this formation.

Universal banking in continental European countries (especially Germany) and Japan goes further than just providing a wide range of financial services. In Germany, banks are widely represented on supervisory boards—see Cable (1985) for further discussion of this point. In Japan the standard structure consists of groups of firms ('keiretsu') consisting of financial and non-financial firms with cross-shareholdings, shared directorships and fairly close cooperation.

The value of universal banks as against smaller but specialized banks is the subject of much discussion (see Benston, 1994, for a good survey of the issues). It is probable that, by offering a wide range of financial services, universal banks are more able to attract and keep customers. On the other hand, greater specialization may bring its own rewards, especially with regard to greater flexibility to meet changing market conditions.

The separation of ownership and management in modern corporations has created an agency problem in that the managers, i.e. the agents, will operate to serve their own interests which may not be in the best interests of the owners. It is argued that universal banking provides scope for improved monitoring and control of the non-financial firms—see Stiglitz (1985)—as compared with the 'stand-off relationship' that tends to exist in the UK and USA.

---

[2] See also Walter (2003).

In a way, it is similar to a retail bank operating like the payments bank of a small customer where the bank can observe closely the behaviour of the borrower. This helps to resolve the agency problem. However, it may also be argued that the close relations between lenders and borrowers lead to an incestuous relationship detracting from firm action when it becomes necessary. The problems of the Japanese banks at the current time may be evidence of such a defect.

Another advantage of universal banks concerns the size and the ability to obtain economies of scale and scope. With regard to economies of scale, it seems to be generally agreed that the long-run cost curve is rather flat and that economies of scale are exhausted at a fairly low scale, i.e. in the region of $100m–$500m of assets/liabilities. This evidence is surveyed more fully in Chapter 10. In respect of economies of scope, the extension of the field of business may well induce lower operating costs as well as operating as a diversification of the portfolio, thus leading to a reduced overall risk. Naturally, this argument depends critically on the absence of correlation coefficients equal to $+1$ between the returns on the various activities. The conclusion in Benston (1994) is that 'both theory and evidence support the expectation that risks should be reduced rather than increased should banks be permitted to engage in securities, insurance and other products and services'.

One countervailing argument from the point of view of size concerns regulation of banks. Universal banks may become 'too large to fail' and therefore be rescued in the event of insolvency. This question of the size of banks and bank regulation is discussed more fully in Chapter 12.

Finally, we come to the way firms raise finance. It is often argued that the discipline of the stock market is imperative to provide stimulus for corporate efficiency. The force of the argument also depends on the belief that universal banking will lead to the raising of excessive levels of finance through banks rather than the market and therefore result in a suboptimal allocation of capital. This could arise in two ways. Firstly, when a firm goes to the market to raise new finance, the cost of capital will depend on the market's view of that firm. Secondly, the share price will reflect the market's view of the firm as to whether or not new finance is desired. Poor performance will induce falls in the share prices and potential takeover bids. Two qualifications apply to this belief, namely that (a) the stock market conforms to the efficient markets hypothesis and (b) the takeover mechanism is an efficient mechanism to allocate corporate control.

4.6 SUMMARY

- All banks undertake maturity transformation.
- Banks face liquidity, asset, foreign currency, payment and off-balance-sheet risks.
- Retail banks have a large number of customers with a small value per transaction. This permits them to use the 'law of large numbers' to manage risk.
- Wholesale banks have a small number of customers with a large value per transaction. Wholesale banks make greater use of the interbank money market to manage liquidity risk.
- Universal banks provide all financial services to customers.
- The distinctions are becoming blurred, but there are differences between the types of bank with respect to sources of income and their engagement in ancillary services.

QUESTIONS

1 What risks do all banks face in their operations?

2 What are retail banks? What are the main features of their balance sheets?

3 What are wholesale banks? How do they differ from retail banks in their operating methods?

4 What are the four different types of universal bank organization identified by Saunders and Walter?

5 What advantage does a system of universal banks have relative to other types of banking?

6 How far are the differences between the various types of bank diminishing over time?

TEST QUESTIONS

1 What are the main features of the different types of banks that operate in the developed economies?

2 It is argued that the trend to universal banking will leave no room for bank specialization. Critically evaluate this argument and comment on the risks associated with the increased tendency towards universal banking.

5

International Banking

MINI-CONTENTS

5.1 Introduction
5.2 The nature of international banking
5.3 Growth of international banking
5.4 The eurocurrency markets
5.5 Summary

5.1 INTRODUCTION

In this chapter we look at the nature of international banking and how it differs from normal domestic banking. It is worth pointing out that international banking has a long history dating back to well before Christ. More recently – for example, in the fourteenth century – Italian bankers lent heavily to the ruling English King Edward III and in fact were not repaid. However, since the early 1970s international banking has grown rapidly (as evidenced by Figure 5.1).

Any theory of international banking needs to answer four questions:

1. Why banks choose particular locations for their operations.
2. Why banks maintain a vertical organizational structure and yet at the same time a horizontal structure with facilities in different countries. This is of particular interest given the speed with which banking services can be transmitted electronically.
3. Why international and global banking has developed.
4. The impact of the development of the eurocurrency markets on macroeconomic variables.

This chapter addresses these four questions.

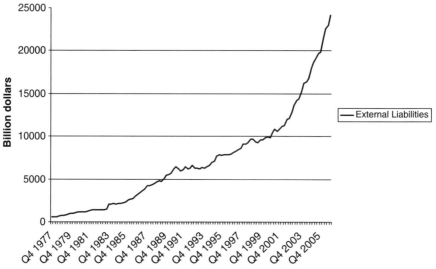

FIGURE 5.1 International Banking: External Liabilities 1977 Quarter 4 to 2006 Quarter 4.

5.2 THE NATURE OF INTERNATIONAL BANKING

Following the taxonomy set out by Kim (1993), Figure 5.2 illustrates the framework of international banking activity. At the centre is the multinational bank with branches and offices in many countries but a parent organization and head office located in a particular country (i), the banking centre. The customers in any country (k) can obtain services from

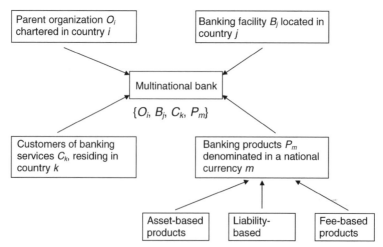

FIGURE 5.2 A Framework for Understanding International Bank Activity.

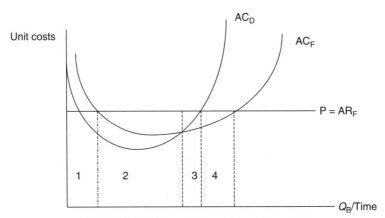

FIGURE 5.3 Four-Phase Location Cycle.

the multinational bank denominated in any currency (m). This figure brings out the salient features of international banking, namely that the locations, services and currencies are diverse.

The decision to locate a banking facility in a foreign country will depend on a combination of home-country factors, host-country factors and the cost and benefits of location. For example, home-country factors could be restrictive regulation that imposes costs on the bank, or increasing resource costs such as the cost of skilled personnel. Host-country factors could include light regulation, monopoly characteristics in the host country, low resource costs and following the customer. Empirical research on the factors that determine foreign entry of international banks suggests that banks locate in areas where expected profits are larger because of high expected economic growth and development or because of similar legal origins, institutions and banking regulations.[1] Kim (1993) typifies a four-phase location cycle theory in terms of the dynamic comparative advantage framework illustrated in Figure 5.3. Figure 5.3 shows a dynamic cost curve that has unit costs on the vertical axis and scale of bank activity over a period of time on the horizontal axis.

The average cost curve over time in the home country is described by AC_D and the average cost curve in the host country is described by AC_F. The average revenue in the host country is given by AR_F (we are assuming perfect competition for expositional purposes). The cycle is distinguished by four phases. In phase 1, $AC_{Fv} > AR_F > AC_D$, the bank produces banking services in the home country and exports to the host country. In phase 2, $AR_F > AC_F > AC_D$, the bank sets up facilities in the host country and produces banking services at home and abroad. In phase 3, $AR_F > AC_D > AC_F$, because home costs are higher than host-country costs, the bank concentrates its banking activity in the host country. In phase 4, $AC_D > AR_F > AC_F$, the bank relocates in the host country and imports bank services to the home country. Such a characterization is a simplification but highlights the argument that location is driven ultimately by the profit motive. While there are

---

[1] Focarelli and Pozzolo (2000) and Galindo *et al.* (2003). For a recent study of international bank location based on competitive advantage, see Claessens and Van Horen (2007).

few examples of phase 4 occurring in reality, phases 2 and 3 explain the growth of London as an international banking centre in terms of lower regulatory costs than in many other economies.

Further clarification of international banking comes from the Bank for International Settlements (BIS), which splits total international banking into two distinct categories (see McCauley *et al.*, 2002). Firstly, there is international banking whereby funds are raised in domestic markets to finance its claims on borrowers in foreign markets. In the second category (i.e. global banking), the bank uses funds raised in the foreign market to finance claims in that foreign market. As McCauley *et al.* point out, the essential difference is that international banking is cross-border banking, whereas global banking concentrates on serving local markets by raising funds locally. In the remainder of this chapter, the term 'international banking' will be used to mean the first and more narrow definition. Another aspect of international banking in the broad sense is eurocurrency business. A eurocurrency can be defined as a deposit or loan denominated in a currency other than that of the host country where the bank is physically located. Thus, for example, a deposit of yen in London is a eurocurrency, whereas a deposit of yen in Tokyo is not. It should be appreciated that eurocurrencies have nothing to do with the euro (the currency of the majority of the Eurozone countries). The term 'eurocurrency' is misleading in a second way, as the markets are not confined to Europe – see Section 5.3 for a discussion of the various international banking centres. The eurocurrency markets account for about 80% of international banking, so we concentrate on these markets later on in the chapter.

The differences between the various types of international business can be further explained with reference to Table 5.1, which is adapted from McCauley *et al.* (2002, table, p. 42). The bank has its head office (HO) in the UK and has foreign assets comprising loans to borrowers in the EU. The bank can finance these loans in five ways. The first two consist of taking deposits in the UK and lending the funds on to the EU borrower via its EU banking affiliate. Most international banking is of this form or a variation whereby the funds pass through a third country. In the third case a depositor in the EU lends to a UK bank that in turn lends to a EU firm. These three categories are classified as 'international lending'. Eurocurrency lending will fall into this category. Categories 4 and 5 are forms of global banking as the funds are deposited in the EU and lent in the EU.

TABLE 5.1 Categories of banking business

Banking type	UK resident			Cross-border		EU resident		
1. International	saver: deposit	→	HO	loan	→		→	borrower
2. International	saver: deposit	→	HO	deposit	→	bank loan affiliate		borrower
3. International			HO	← deposit			←	saver
				loan	→		→	borrower
4. Global						bank affiliate	← deposit → loan	saver borrower
5. Global	saver	→		deposit		bank loan affiliate	→	borrower

One way of measuring the relative importance of global versus international banking is to measure the ratio of locally funded foreign assets to the total foreign (cross-border + local) assets. This ratio will be 1 for a purely global bank and 0 for a purely international bank. Clearly, banks are usually mixed – global and international – and the average ratio for all banks reporting to the BIS was 0.39 at the end of September 2001 (see McCauley *et al.*, 2002, Table 1). This conceals quite wide differences between the various countries: for example, the figures for the UK, the USA and Japan are roughly 0.9, 0.8 and 0.3 respectively.

The character of the operations of wholesale banks in international and global banking is similar to their domestic operations, so no further comment is necessary.

5.3 GROWTH OF INTERNATIONAL BANKING

As mentioned earlier, the volume of international banking has grown significantly over recent years, and this is worthy of further comment. One measure, i.e. the stock of external liabilities of banks reporting to the Bank for International Settlements (BIS), has grown at just over 5% per annum over the period 1977 to 2006. This growth is illustrated in Figure 5.1. The following reasons can explain this growth:

1. The general relaxation of controls on international capital movements permits banks to engage in overseas business.
2. Banks seek to maximize profits, so it is quite natural for them to seek additional profit opportunities through dealing in foreign currency deposits and overseas transactions. This would be particularly relevant if the banks themselves faced strong competition in their domestic markets.
3. Some banks may themselves have (or perceive themselves to have) superior techniques, so that expansion in multinational business offers them the chance to exploit their comparative advantage in other countries. The flipside of this is that some other banks may perceive that overseas banks have superior techniques and that they can acquire the relevant techniques through overseas acquisitions. Hence, overseas banking is carried out by banks with the express intention of increasing their competitive edge in domestic markets.
4. Banks desire to follow their clients, so that, if important clients have overseas business, the banks will also engage in such business. Furthermore, by establishing its own overseas operations, a bank may be able to monitor more thoroughly the overseas operations of clients.
5. As will be discussed in Chapter 10, it is generally believed that the long-run cost curve of banks is relatively flat and that economies of scale are quite quickly eliminated. This reduces or eliminates the advantage of having one large office as against dispersed offices. This is reinforced by the relatively low salaries accompanied with satisfactory levels of expertise in certain overseas countries. The migration of banking services to Asia and India, in particular, is an illustration of this phenomenon.
6. Regulation. One of the main reasons for the development of the eurocurrency business was the regulations imposed on US banks operating in the USA. They found that the

regulatory environment in London was more favourable, and this led to the further development of London as an international banking centre. The importance of this factor has probably reduced over recent years, with the desire of the regulators to create a 'level playing field', as exemplified by the Basel agreements – see Chapter 12 for a discussion of bank regulation in general and the Basel agreements in particular. Nevertheless, once a centre has attracted banking facilities, they will tend to remain in that centre even after the initial benefit has been eliminated because of the acquired advantages, such as expertise, qualified staff, etc.

7. Portfolio theory suggests that diversification leads to lower risk. Applied to banking, this suggests that banks should diversify their operations both as to currency type and geographical area.

Point 6 above suggests that we should expect some centres to be more important than others as international banking centres. This is true, as international banking is carried out in a number of centres, the importance of which varies considerably. Table 5.2 reports the stock of total external liabilities for banks located in a variety of countries. Clearly, London is by far the most important international banking centre, with some 23% of all external bank liabilities originating from banks located in the UK. The next largest figure is for banks located in the USA, which follows some way behind with 12% of the total of external liabilities. As far as Europe is concerned, banks located in Germany and France account for 7.1 and 8.8% of the total respectively. It is also interesting to note that the Cayman Isles account for virtually the same total as Germany.

Finally, the relative importance of the different currencies in the external claims of banks can be seen in Table 5.3. The type of currency is dominated by the euro and US dollar, which between them accounted for roughly 78% of total cross-border claims.

TABLE 5.2 Selected international banking centres, December 2006 (total outstanding external liabilities of banks in reporting countries)

	Billion dollars	Percentage of all countries
Belgium	753.9	3.1
Cayman Isles	1620.0	6.7
France	2122.9	8.8
Germany	1722.2	7.1
Japan	681.7	2.8
Luxembourg	607.0	2.5
Switzerland	1001.0	4.1
UK	5432.1	22.5
USA	2819.1	11.7
All countries	*24175.7*	

Source: BIS Quarterly Review, September 2007, Table 2A.

TABLE 5.3 Total cross-border claims by BIS-reporting banks, stocks at end December 2006, by currency

Currency	Billion dollars	Percentage of total
US dollar	10571.5	40.4
Euro	9889.3	37.8
Yen	835.2	3.2
Other currencies	4884.8	18.6
Total	*26180.8*	*100.0*

Source: *BIS Quarterly Review,* September 2007, Table 5A (Assets).

5.4 THE EUROCURRENCY MARKETS

5.4.1 Reasons for the Growth of the Eurocurrency Markets

The eurocurrency markets started in the 1960s with a market for dollars deposited outside the USA. A variety of reasons are given for this phenomenon. One suggestion is that, during the Cold War, Russia and China wished to hold dollars because of the importance of the dollar in international finance. On the other hand, these two countries did not wish to deposit dollars in the USA for fear that they could be blocked in times of dispute. Holding dollar deposits at a bank in London removed this fear because these deposits could not be distinguished by the US Federal Reserve from any other dollar deposits held by the bank concerned. A second reason was the existence of interest rate ceilings placed on deposits at banks in the USA (regulation Q – see Chapter 1, footnote 4, for an explanation of regulation Q). This restriction became more onerous as interest rates rose worldwide. Furthermore, the impact of this restraint was enhanced by the more onerous reserve requirements and deposit insurance costs imposed on banking in the USA as compared with London where prudential control was more relaxed. The net effect of these restraints induced a wider spread between the lending and deposit rate in the USA. Consequently, by moving dollar operations to London, international banks could offer higher deposit rates and lower borrowing rates on dollar transactions in London than in New York. This is demonstrated in Figure 5.4.

These restraints have since been lowered by the repeal of regulation Q, with the consequent removal of the interest rate constraints and the international adoption of the Basel I prudential control rules lowering the regulatory difference between countries. Nevertheless, once the changes had taken place, there was considerable inertia in the system, so that London today remains the largest international banking centre.

A second important factor in the growth of the eurocurrency markets is the growth of international banking itself. The reasons for this growth have been discussed in Section 5.3, so no further comment is necessary.

We now move on to consider the institutional aspects of the eurocurrency markets.

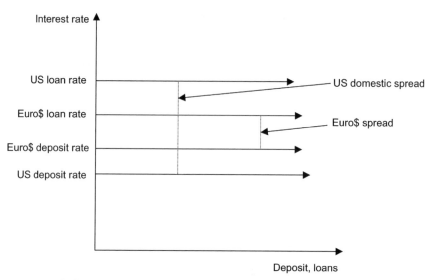

FIGURE 5.4 Eurocurrency Lending and Deposit Rates.

5.4.2 Institutional Aspects of Eurocurrency Markets

The first point to note about these markets is that they are wholesale markets with transactions of typically $1m or more. The second point to note is that there is a large amount of bank lending, so the gross size of the market is much larger than the net size when interbank transactions are netted out. This can be clearly seen from the detail in Table 5.4, which refers to total cross-border claims of the banks reporting to the BIS[2] where nearly two-thirds of the claims represent interbank transactions. Interest rates in the eurocurrency markets should be closely aligned with the corresponding domestic rates of interest, otherwise arbitrage potential exists. For example, in London the link between domestic and eurodollar interest rates of the same maturity is represented by the following relationship:

$$R_\pounds = R_\$ + E(\Delta ER) \tag{5.1}$$

where $R_\pounds$ is the nominal sterling rate of interest, $R_\$$ is the nominal eurodollar rate of interest on the corresponding eurodollar security and $E(\Delta ER)$ is the expected appreciation/depreciation on the dollar versus sterling.

Note that the relationship above is expressed in terms of expectations and therefore involves some uncertainty. However, this can be removed by taking the appropriate actions in the forward market to buy or sell sterling according to whether the initial transaction involved purchase of sterling or eurodollars. Arbitrage will ensure that this relationship holds. For example, if the return in London is higher than, say, that in New York, then funds will

---

[2] Note that the figures refer to total claims rather than eurodollar claims. Figures are not available for eurodollar markets alone, but, as eurodollar markets are the largest component of external claims, the figures in Table 5.4 should be reasonably representative of eurodollar markets.

TABLE 5.4 Interbank transactions: cross-border claims, end December 2006

Source of claim	Billion US$	Percentage of total
Banks	16545.6	63.2
Non-banks	9635.2	36.8
Total	*26180.8*	*100.0*

Source: BIS Quarterly Review, September 2007, Tables 5A and 5B (Assets).

flow to London from New York. In terms of equation (5.1), the movement of funds will cause $R_\pounds$ to fall and the spot sterling rate to rise (the dollar to fall) and the forward rate of sterling to fall (dollar to appreciate) as agents buy dollars (sell sterling) forward to hedge against any adverse movement in the exchange rate. The converse would apply if the return in New York were higher than that in London. This would cause the equality depicted in equation (5.1) to hold in the two markets or more generally in all markets.

Turning now to the balance sheets: on the liability side, the deposits are short term, typically less than 3 months, with depositors consisting of banks (as we have seen in Table 5.4), government bodies and multinational corporations.

On the asset side – the lending side–a large proportion of eurocurrency lending is by way of syndicated loans. These consist of a loan made by a large number of banks that subscribe to the total. Details of the ratio of syndicated-to-total eurocurrency lending are not available, but some guide can be obtained by comparing the increase in non-bank external assets of the reporting BIS banks with the volume of announced syndicated lending over the same period. For the fourth quarter of 2006, the percentage of syndicated lending amounted to 60.3% of the change in volume of non-bank external assets (see *BIS Quarterly Review*, September 2007, Tables 2a and 10). The term of syndicated loans is usually between 3 and 15 years, so that the loans can be classed as medium-term loans. This contrasts with the short-term nature of deposits and indicates a degree of maturity transformation taking place. Because of the large number of banks engaged in any one syndicated loan, one bank will act as the lead bank and organize the detail of the loan. For this the lead bank will receive a fee in addition to the normal interest rate charged on the loan which is generally linked to a reference rate, such as the London interbank offer rate (LIBOR). Consequently, the loans are at floating rates, limiting the interest-rate risk exposure of the banks.

What is the advantage of syndicated loans from the point of view of the borrower compared with raising funds directly from the capital markets? Two advantages seem to be present – size and speed. Borrowers can generally raise large sums. For example, in 1989 a $13.6bn credit was organized for Kohlberg Kravis Roberts to finance the leveraged takeover of R.J.R. Nabisco. An additional advantage is that such loans can be arranged more quickly than going directly to the capital market, where various formal procedures need to be implemented. For example, a syndicate led by Morgan Guarantee took just 5 days to arrange a $15bn loan for BP. From the point of view of the lender, syndicated credits offer the opportunity of engaging in lending while at the same time limiting the exposure to any one particular company.

We now move on to the next aspect of the eurocurrency markets, which is the impact they have on the financial system in general.

5.4.3 Consequences of Eurocurrency Markets

Three consequences are apparent from our discussion so far. Firstly, it is obvious that a degree of maturity transformation takes place. Borrowing is by way of deposits of less than 3 months, whereas lending is for longer periods. Secondly, a degree of risk transformation takes place. Low-risk deposits are placed with banks, and these are lent onwards in the form of more risky loans. These two functions are relatively uncontroversial, although the degree of interbank lending may give rise to concern because the failure of one bank would have repercussions on the rest of the banking system. The third potential consequence is in relation to macroeconomic variables.

Do the banks operating in the eurocurrency markets act more as financial intermediaries redistributing liquidity or are they acting like banks in the domestic economy, increasing the money supply but on a worldwide basis? If the latter is the case, the eurocurrency markets serve as a vehicle for the propagation of inflation. It may seem to be intuitive that, given the degree of interbank lending, eurocurrency banks operate more like non-bank financial intermediaries and redirect credit rather than create money.

We illustrate the operation of the eurocurrency market (in this case the currency is dollars) with a simple stylized example. In this example the US banking system is consolidated to simplify the exposition by avoiding interbank transfers. The banks in the eurocurrency markets, i.e. the eurobanks in our example, keep their balances with US domestic banks in the form of a normal bank account. A UK trader receives payment for exports to the USA to the value of $10m. Instead of converting the dollars into sterling, the UK trader deposits the dollars with eurobank A. Since this bank has no immediate use for the dollars, it redeposits the dollars via the money market with eurobank B, which lends the $10m to its customer. Table 5.5 illustrates the effect of these transactions on the balance sheet of the various operators. In scenario 1 there is no net effect on the US banking system because the dollars have merely been transferred from the US company to the UK trader and then to eurobank A by the UK customer. This leaves aggregate liabilities of the consolidated US banking system constant. It is merely the ownership of the deposits that has changed. However, eurobank deposits have increased by $10m. Scenario 2 shows the transfer of the funds to eurobank B. Again there is no net effect on the US banking system because the transfer has only led to a change in ownership of the demand deposit from eurobank A to eurobank B. In contrast, the liabilities of the eurobank deposits have increased by a further $10m as there is now the new deposit with eurobank B, while the UK trader still holds the original $10m deposit with eurobank A. The final entries in the balance sheets shown in scenario 3 occur when eurobank B lends the dollars to the ultimate borrower, i.e. the customer. Again, there is no effect on the US banking system because the demand deposit has merely been transferred from eurobank B to the customer without any alteration in their liabilities. The net effect on the assets and liabilities of eurobank B is also zero, because on the asset side the demand deposit with the US banking system has been exchanged for a loan with no effect on its liabilities.

Note that the effect on the aggregate assets and liabilities of the US banking sector is zero, and all that has happened is that there has been a redistribution of the ownership of assets and liabilities. This suggests that the eurosystem merely redistributes rather than creates extra liability, but the liabilities of the eurobanks have risen by $20m. If, on the other hand, the money supply in the USA rose, then it would be expected that dollar deposit balances held

Table 5.5 Operation of eurocurrency markets

Scenario 1	Assets ($m)	Liabilities ($m)
Consolidated US banking system		
US resident deposit	0	−10
Eurobank A demand deposit	0	+10
Net change	0	0
Eurobank A		
UK company time deposit	+10	+10
Net change	+10	+10

Scenario 2	Assets ($m)	Liabilities ($m)
Consolidated US banking system		
Eurobank A demand deposit	0	−10
Eurobank B demand deposit	0	+10
Net change	0	0
Eurobank A		
Demand deposit with US bank	−10	0
Time deposit with eurobank B	+10	0
Net change	0	0
Eurobank B		
Time deposit with eurobank A	0	+10
Demand deposit with US bank	+10	0
Net change	+10	+10

Scenario 3	Assets ($m)	Liabilities ($m)
Consolidated US banking system		
Customer	0	+10
Eurobank B	0	−10
Net change	0	0
Eurobank B		
Loan to customer	+10	0
Demand deposit with US bank	−10	0
Net change	0	0

by the eurobanks would increase, and this would represent an increase in the money supply both in the USA and overseas.

In reality, a shift from dollar deposits to eurodollar deposits creates a small amount of additional liquidity because the eurocurrency banks operate on a lower reserve ratio. This conclusion is demonstrated more formally in Box 5.1.

BOX 5.1 The operation of the eurocurrency markets

The simple model used below is based on banks with assets consisting of loans and reserves assumed to be held with the central bank. The liabilities consist of deposits, with no distinction being made between time and sight deposits.[3] Hence

$$L + R = D + R_E \qquad (5.1.1)$$

where L = loans, R = reserves, D = domestic deposits and R_E = deposits from eurobanks.

Eurobanks operating in the eurocurrency markets hold deposits (R_E) with US banks as additional reserves. Assume these amount to a fraction ρ of eurodollar deposits EU so that

$$R_E = \rho EU \qquad (5.1.2)$$

Domestic US banks hold reserves with the central bank in the proportion σ to their total deposits, so that

$$R = \sigma(D + R_E) \qquad (5.1.3)$$

We specify the demand for eurodollar deposits as a function of total liquidity (M^*), so that

$$EU = \varepsilon M^* + \alpha \qquad (5.1.4)$$

where α is a shift parameter allowing for an increase/decrease in the demand for eurodollar deposits. For example, an increase in α shifts the demand curve upwards for the same level of M^* and

$$M^* = C + D + EU \qquad (5.1.5)$$

The money base (B) is defined as

$$C + R = B \qquad (5.1.6)$$

where C = currency.

(continued)

---

[3] Note that, for the sake of convenience, we are omitting bank capital, which is assumed to be given.

Hence, using (5.1.5) and (5.1.6) yields

$$M^\star = B - R + D + EU \tag{5.1.7}$$

and using (5.1.3) yields

$$M^\star = B - \sigma(D + R_E) + D + EU \tag{5.1.8}$$

Rearranging and using (5.1.2) gives

$$M^\star = B + (1 - \sigma)D + (1 - \sigma\rho)EU \tag{5.1.9}$$

specifying the demand for domestic US dollar deposits as a function of $M^\star$, so that

$$D = \gamma M^\star + \beta \tag{5.1.10}$$

where β is a shift parameter allowing for an increase/decrease in the demand for domestic deposits.

Substituting (5.1.10) into (5.1.9) produces

$$M^\star = B + (1 - \sigma)(\gamma M^\star + \beta) + (1 - \sigma\rho)EU$$

Rearranging gives

$$M^\star = \frac{B + (1 - \sigma)\beta + (1 - \sigma\rho)EU}{1 - (1 - \sigma)\gamma} \tag{5.1.11}$$

Substituting for $M^\star$ in the demand for eurodollar deposits (5.1.4) gives

$$EU = \varepsilon\left(\frac{B + (1 - \sigma)\beta + (1 - \sigma\rho)EU}{1 - (1 - \sigma)\gamma}\right) + \alpha \tag{5.1.12}$$

so

$$EU = \frac{\varepsilon B + \varepsilon(1 - \sigma)\beta + \alpha(1 - (1 - \sigma)\gamma)}{(1 - (1 - \sigma)\gamma - \varepsilon(1 - \sigma\rho))} \tag{5.1.13}$$

Noting that the preference shift from US dollars to eurodollars is given by $d\alpha$, which equals by definition $-d\beta$, because a rise in eurodollar deposits is matched by a fall in domestic dollar deposits, then

$$\frac{dEU}{d\alpha} = \left(\frac{1 - (1 - \sigma)\gamma - \varepsilon(1 - \sigma)}{1 - (1 - \sigma)\gamma - \varepsilon(1 - \sigma\rho)}\right) \tag{5.1.14}$$

(continued)

The key point is to note that (5.1.14) is very close to unity, showing that a shift in preferences, such as an increased demand for eurodollars at the expense of US dollars, should not have any great effect on the financial system. This strongly suggests that eurocurrency operations act more akin to non-bank financial intermediaries than banks and merely rearrange rather than create liquidity.

However, it is also true that eurodollar deposits themselves are ultimately layered on base money. This can be shown by differentiating (5.1.1 3) with respect to B to produce

$$\frac{dEU}{dB} = \frac{\varepsilon}{1 - (1 - \sigma)\gamma - \varepsilon(1 - \sigma\rho)} \qquad (5.1.15)$$

Consequently, an increase in the US monetary base will lead to an increase in both the US money supply and eurodollar deposits. For a full analysis of this subject, see Niehans and Hewson (1976).

5.5 SUMMARY

- Total international banking consists of cross-border (traditional international banking) and global banking.
- Eurocurrency banking forms the major part of the narrow definition of international banking.
- Banks choose to operate in a particular location because of home-country factors, host-country factors and the cost and benefits of location.
- The precise organizational structure can be explained by the four-phase location cycle theory in terms of the dynamic comparative advantage framework set out in Section 5.2 and illustrated in Figure 5.3.
- The development of the eurocurrency markets can be explained by a number of factors including cost advantages due to regulation arbitrage and inertia once these advantages had been diminished.
- International banking centres have been developed, among which London is the largest.
- About two-thirds of eurocurrency lending is between banks.
- Eurocurrency markets distribute rather than create additional liquidity.

QUESTIONS

1   What are the types of international banking identified by the Bank for International Settlements and McCauley?

2   What are the reasons for the growth in international banking?

3   What are the eurocurrency markets? Why have they grown in recent years?

4   What are the main assets and liabilities of a bank operating in the eurocurrency markets? To what extent is syndicated lending important?

5   What are the consequences of the growth of the eurocurrency markets for the international financial system?

6   Why would the following relationship be expected to hold in the eurocurrency markets:

$$R_{\pounds} = R_{\$} + E(\Delta ER)$$

where $R_{\pounds}$ is the nominal sterling rate of interest, $R_{\$}$ is the nominal eurodollar rate of interest on the corresponding eurodollar security and $E(\Delta ER)$ is the expected appreciation/depreciation of the exchange rate?

TEST QUESTIONS

1   Explain the growth of international banking during the second half of the twentieth century. Regulatory avoidance has been claimed to be one of the reasons for this growth. Why has the growth in international banking continued in spite of a reduction in regulatory constraints?

2   What is the role of eurocurrency banking? Discuss the implications for the supply of eurodollars of a portfolio switch from domestic dollar deposits to eurodollar deposits.

ANNUAL REPORT

6

The Theory of the Banking Firm

MINI-CONTENTS

6.1 Introduction
6.2 The textbook model
6.3 The perfectly competitive bank
6.4 The monopoly bank
6.5 The imperfect competition model
6.6 Summary

6.1 INTRODUCTION

This chapter examines the contribution of the economics of the firm in order to further our understanding of the behaviour of banks. Chapter 3 examined the question as to why banks exist? This is no easy question to answer, but the why banks exist question is separate from why we need a special theory of the banking firm. There are no specific economic theories of the steel firm or the car components firm, so why do we feel that there should be a specific theory of the banking firm? The answer to this question is the same as in the case of theories of monetary exchange. Banks are different from other commercial and industrial enterprises because the monetary mechanism enables them to attract deposits for onward investment. By taking part in the payments mechanism and by emphasizing the medium of exchange function of money, they are able to encourage the store of value functions.[1]

Banks also have a leverage that is quite different from ordinary firms. The debt−equity ratio for conventional commercial firms will be of the order of 0.5−0.6. Banks, however, have debt liabilities sometimes 9 times greater than their equity.[2] The existence of a central bank with a lender-of-last-resort function is an obvious explanation for why banks can get away with this

---

[1] The association of banks with the payments mechanism was also discussed in Chapter 3.

[2] Wholesale banks have debt−equity ratios of the order of 5:1.

type of liability structure. The fact that banks operate with an unusually high debt–equity ratio tells us that the guardians of the payment system – the central banks – think that commercial banks are special. The specialness of banks, examined in Chapter 3, deems that a theory of the banking firm be distinct from the normal economic theory of the firm.

6.2 THE TEXTBOOK MODEL

Intermediate textbooks of economics will typically portray the banking sector as a passive agent in the monetary transmission mechanism. This view stems from the familiar money multiplier approach to the determination of the money supply. Box 6.1 describes the textbook

---

BOX 6.1   The money multiplier

The money multiplier is a non-behavioural relationship between changes in the stock of base money and the stock of broad money. Base money (H) is made up of currency in circulation with the non-bank public (C) and bank reserves (R). The stock of broad money (M) is the sum of currency in circulation with the non-bank public and bank deposits (D). These two statements are as follows:

$$H = C + R \tag{6.1.1}$$

$$M = C + D \tag{6.1.2}$$

Divide (6.1.2) by (6.1.1):

$$\frac{M}{H} = \frac{C + D}{C + R} \tag{6.1.3}$$

Divide the top and bottom of the right-hand side of equation (6.1.3) by D:

$$\frac{M}{H} = \frac{C/D + 1}{C/D + R/D} = m$$

$$\Delta M = m\Delta H$$

The first term of the numerator is the ratio of currency to deposits. The second term of the denominator is the ratio of reserves to deposits. So far this amounts to the manipulation of two identities and does not involve behaviour. However, if it is assumed that the currency–deposit ratio (c) is fixed and the reserve–deposit ratio (k) is fixed, then we can think of m as the money multiplier, which translates changes in base money to changes in broad money through the banking system of deposit creation.

TABLE 6.1 Bank balance sheet

Assets	Liabilities
L Loans	D Deposits
R Reserves	

money multiplier that links the broad measure of money to base money (or high-powered money). The money multiplier can also be translated into a deposit multiplier and an equivalent credit multiplier where the banking system is a passive agent.

The starting point is a primitive type of balance sheet where it is assumed that the bank has no physical capital on its assets and no equity on its liabilities.[3] This simple balance sheet is described in Table 6.1.

Let there be a required reserve ratio k so that $R = kD$. Then the balance sheet can be represented as

$$L = (1 - k)D \tag{6.1}$$

From Box 6.1 we can divide both sides of equation (6.1) by base money H:

$$\frac{L}{H} = \frac{(1 - k)D}{C + R}$$

so that

$$L = \left(\frac{(1 - k)D}{C + R}\right)H \tag{6.2}$$

Dividing the top and bottom of the right-hand side of equation (6.2) by deposits D, assuming that c and k are constant and taking first differences, we can represent the credit multiplier as

$$\Delta L = \left(\frac{1 - k}{c + k}\right)\Delta H \tag{6.3}$$

where $c = C/D$ and, as before, $k = R/D$.

Similarly, the deposit multiplier is given by

$$\Delta D = \left(\frac{1}{c + k}\right)\Delta H \tag{6.4}$$

---

[3] An advanced treatment of the material in this chapter can be found in Freixas and Rochet (1997, Chapter 3).

The central bank can control the supply of base money by using open-market operations to fund the government budget deficit, which is given by the financing constraint[4]

$$G - T = \Delta H + \Delta B \tag{6.5}$$

where G is government spending, T is tax receipts and ΔB is the sales of government debt. By eliminating the increase in base money from the credit and deposit multipliers in (6.3) and (6.4), we can see that there is a direct link between the financing of the government budget deficit and the increase in bank lending and deposit supply:

$$\Delta L = \left(\frac{1 - k}{c + k}\right)([G - T] - \Delta B)$$

$$\Delta D = \left(\frac{1}{c + k}\right)([G - T] - \Delta B) \tag{6.6}$$

The above set of expressions says that the banking system supplies credit and takes deposits according to a fixed coefficient relationship to the government financing condition.

The familiar criticism applied to the money multiplier model can be applied to the credit and deposit multipliers. The ratio of currency to deposits (c) is a choice variable to the non-bank public, dictated largely by the bank's interest-rate-setting behaviour. Similarly, in the absence of regulation, k is a choice variable to the banks.[5] Finally, the supply of base money is not exogenous but usually supplied on demand by the central bank to the banking system.

In developing a framework for the analysis of the banking firm, Baltensperger (1980) sets the objective function of the bank as a profit function (π):

$$\pi = r_L L - r_D D - l - s - c \tag{6.7}$$

where r_L is the rate of interest charged on loans, r_D is the interest paid on deposits, L is the stock of loans, D is the stock of deposits, l is the cost of illiquidity, s is the cost due to default and c^6 is the real resource cost. The main task of a theory of the banking firm is to provide analytical substance to the components on the right-hand side of the equation by specifying their determinants. In Section 6.3 we follow this approach to examine the interest-setting behaviour of a perfectly competitive bank.

6.3 THE PERFECTLY COMPETITIVE BANK

We can begin by adding a small element of realism to the simple balance sheet stated in Table 6.1. We can introduce a market for a risk-free, short-term, liquid asset such as government Treasury bills (T) or deposits in the interbank market that pay a rate of interest (r_T),

---

[4] Note that, for the sake of ease of exposition, we are ignoring any financing requirements attributable to intervention in the foreign exchange markets.

[5] Note that, even in the case where a reserve ratio is imposed as a legal restraint, it is a minimum ratio, so that k is at least a partial choice variable for the banks.

[6] Note that in this case c refers to costs, not to the cash ratio as in (6.6) and previous equations.

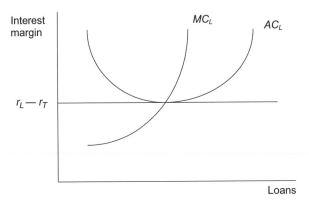

FIGURE 6.1 The Competitive Model.

which is given to the firm, i.e. a constant. We can also introduce a cost function that describes the bank's management costs of servicing loans and deposits $\{C(D, L)\}$.[7] The cost function is separable in deposits and loans and exhibits positive marginal costs of servicing both. In the competitive model of the banking firm, the individual bank is a price taker, so that r_L and r_D are constants as far as the individual firm is concerned. The bank's objective is to maximize profit (π):

$$\max \pi = r_L L + r_T T - r_D D - C(D, L) \tag{6.8}$$

such that

$$L + T = (1 - k)D \tag{6.9}$$

The equilibrium conditions (see Box 6.2) are

$$r_L = r_T + C'$$
$$r_D = r_T(1 - k) - C'_D \tag{6.10}$$

We have the result that a competitive bank will adjust its volume of loans and deposits in such a way that the interest margin between the risk-free rate and the loan rate will equal the marginal cost of servicing loans, and the margin between the reserve-adjusted risk-free rate and the deposit rate will equal the marginal cost of servicing deposits. Given the assumption of reparability of the cost function noted above, the equilibrium for loans for a single bank is shown in Figure 6.1. The average cost of loans curve is shown by AC_L (this is given by $C(L, D)/L$) and the marginal cost curve by MC_L (this is C'_L in the algebra).

From (6.10) we can substitute for r_T and obtain

$$r_L = r_D + kr_T + C'_L + C'_D \tag{6.11}$$

---

[7] $C\{(D, L)\}$ represents the items l, s and c in equation (6.7).

BOX 6.2   The perfectly competitive bank

The bank's objective is to maximize profit. The profit function of the bank is described by

$$\pi = r_L L + r_T T - r_D D - C(D, L) \qquad (6.2.1)$$

(6.2.1) is maximized subject to the balance sheet constraint

$$L + T = (1 - k)D \qquad (6.2.2)$$

Substituting the balance sheet constraint into the objective function means that the bank's profit function can be rewritten as

$$\pi = r_L L + r_T[(1 - k)D - L] - r_D D - C(D, L) \qquad (6.2.3)$$

The first-order conditions are

$$\frac{\partial \pi}{\partial L} = r_L - r_T - C_L' = 0 \qquad (6.2.4)$$

$$\frac{\partial \pi}{\partial D} = r_T(1 - k) - r_D - C_D' = 0$$

The margin of intermediation (the difference between the loan rate and the deposit rate) is given by rearranging (6.11) to obtain

$$r_L - r_D = C_D' + C_L' + k r_T \qquad (6.12)$$

This result demonstrates a basic result: namely that the margin of intermediation is given by the product of the reserve ratio and the risk-free rate and the sum of the marginal costs of loan and deposit production by the bank.

The competitive model is clearly restrictive, but we will see that this result carries through to the case of a monopoly.

6.4 THE MONOPOLY BANK

The competitive model is only a partial economic analysis, and the assumption of price taker makes it an overly restrictive model. At the other extreme is the monopoly model of banking based on Klein (1971) and Monti (1972). The existence of monopolistic features is taken as something characteristic of financial intermediaries. Banks are usually the source of funding for enterprises in the early stages of development. It can be argued that the information role of banks gives them some monopolistic discretion in the pricing of loans according to risk characteristics.

Initially, to appreciate the role of monopoly, we can abstract from the costs of producing loans and deposits and assume that the bank faces fixed costs of operation. As in the competitive model, the balance sheet is given by

$$L + T + R = D \tag{6.13}$$

with the reserve ratio condition $R = kD$. The monopoly bank represents the banking industry as a whole and will face a downward-sloping demand for loans with respect to the loan rate and an upward-sloping demand for deposits with respect to the deposit rate. So

$$
\begin{aligned}
L^d &= L(r_L) \\
D^d &= D(r_D)
\end{aligned}
\tag{6.14}
$$

with the conditions $L_r < 0$ and $D_r > 0$.

The assumptions of this model are that:

1. The bank faces a scale as well as an allocation decision, and scale is identified by the volume of deposits.
2. The market for bills is perfectly competitive and the bank is a price taker, so that r_T is a constant as far as the monopolist is concerned. (We assume that the monopoly bank is one of an infinite number of other operators in the bill market.)
3. The loan and deposit markets are imperfectly competitive.
4. Loans are imperfect substitutes for bills.
5. Reserves earn no interest.
6. The bank maximizes profit.
7. The bank faces a fixed cost schedule.

The bank maximizes $\pi = r_L L(r_L) + r_T \big(D(1 - k) - L\big) - r_D D(r_D) - C$.

Box 6.3 details the derivation of the interest-setting equations by the monopoly bank, which are as follows:

$$r_L = \frac{r_T}{\left(1 - \dfrac{1}{e_L}\right)} \tag{6.15}$$

$$r_D = \frac{r_T(1 - k)}{\left(1 + \dfrac{1}{e_D}\right)} \tag{6.16}$$

Equations (6.15) and (6.16) should be familiar from the well-known result relating price to marginal revenue.[8] These equilibrium conditions are described in Figures 6.2 and 6.3.

[8] From your intermediate microeconomics you should be familiar with the expression $P = MR/(1 + 1/e)$, where P is price, MR is marginal revenue and e is price elasticity.

BOX 6.3   The profit-maximizing exercise for the monopoly bank

The bank max.imizes $\pi = r_L L (r_L) + r_T(D(1 - k) - L) - r_D D(r_D) - C.$

Being a monopoly, the bank can set prices or quantities but not both. In this exposition we assume that the bank sets the rate of interest on loans and deposits and the market determines the stock of loans and deposits. Ignoring costs, the first-order conditions are

$$\frac{\partial \pi}{\partial r_L} = L + L_r r_L - r_T L_r = 0 \tag{6.3.1}$$

$$\frac{\partial \pi}{\partial r_D} = r_L(1 - k)D_r - D - D_r r_D = 0$$

Rearranging (6.3.1), we have the following expressions:

$$r_L + \frac{L}{L_r} = r_T \tag{6.3.2}$$

$$r_D + \frac{D}{D_r} = r_T(1 - k)$$

The expressions for the interest elasticity of demand for loans (e_L) and the interest elasticity of demand for deposits (e_D) are as follows:

$$e_L = -\frac{L_r}{L/r_L} > 0$$

$$e_D = \frac{D_r}{D/r_D} > 0 \tag{6.3.3}$$

Using (6.3.2) in (6.3.3), we obtain the following expressions for the loan rate and the deposit rate:

$$r_L = \frac{r_T}{\left(1 - \dfrac{1}{e_L}\right)} \tag{6.3.4}$$

$$r_D = \frac{r_T(1 - k)}{\left(1 + \dfrac{1}{e_D}\right)} \tag{6.3.5}$$

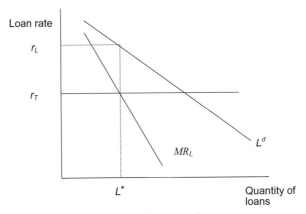

FIGURE 6.2 Equilibrium for Loans.

Figure 6.2 shows that the monopoly bank extends loans until the marginal revenue on loans, described by the MR_L curve, equals the opportunity cost, the rate of interest on bills. Thus, the monopoly bank produces L^* loans.

Figure 6.3 shows that the bank sells deposits up to the point where the marginal cost of deposits equals the marginal return from its investment (recall that only a fraction $(1 - k)$ of deposits can be reinvested). Hence, the bank supplies D^* deposits.

Superimposing Figure 6.2 on Figure 6.3 shows how the scale of bank activity is obtained. Figure 6.4 shows the equilibrium level of loans L^* and deposits D^* for the bank.

The monopoly model has the following useful properties:

1. A rise in the bill rate raises the loan rate and the deposit rate.
2. A rise in the loan rate reduces the equilibrium quantity of loans and increases the equilibrium quantity of deposits. The bank substitutes loans for bills at the margin.

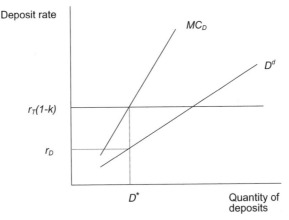

FIGURE 6.3 Equilibrium for Deposits.

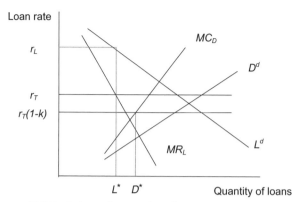

FIGURE 6.4 The Scale of Banking Activity.

However, the model does have a number of weaknesses:

1. Profit is earned exclusively from monopoly power.
2. There is no analysis of the costs of supplying loans and deposits.
3. The volume of loans and deposits (and in turn the loan rate and deposit rate) are determined independently of each other.
4. The assumption of price maker in the loan and deposit market and price taker in the bill market is questionable.

The treatment of costs is easily rectified by including the cost function of (6.8) in the profit function of the monopoly bank. Representing the loan rate as a function of loans and the deposit rate as a function of deposits, we can express the objective function of the bank as:

$$\pi = r_L(L)L + r_T(D(1 - k) - L) - r_D(D)D - C(D, L) \text{ with } r'_L < 0 \text{ and } r'_D > 0$$

Box 6.4 shows the derivation of the two key equations below:

$$\frac{r_L - r_T - C'_L}{r_L} = \frac{1}{e_L} \tag{6.17}$$

$$\frac{r_T(1 - k) - C'_D - r_D}{r_D} = \frac{1}{e_D} \tag{6.18}$$

Equations (6.17) and (6.18) describe the equivalence of the Lerner index (adapted to the banking firm) to the inverse of the elasticity.[9] A monopoly bank sets loans and deposits such that the price margin of loans and deposits over costs is equal to the inverse of the elasticity.

---

[9] The Lerner index is given by $(P - MC)/P$, where MC is marginal cost. Substituting $MR = MC$ in footnote 8 gives the condition $(P - MC)/P = 1/e$. See Lerner (1934).

BOX 6.4   The monopoly model with costs of servicing deposits and loans

The bank maximizes $\pi = r_L(L)L + r_T(D(1 - k) - L) - r_D(D)D - C(D, L)$.

In this exercise we have the bank setting the quantity of loans and deposits and the market determining the rate of interest in the loan and deposit markets.

The first-order conditions are:

$$\frac{\partial \pi}{\partial L} = r_L'L + r_L - r_T - C_L' = 0 \tag{6.4.1}$$

$$\frac{\partial \pi}{\partial D} = r_T(1 - k) - r_D'D - r_D - C_D' = 0 \tag{6.4.2}$$

The interest elasticity of loans is given by $e_L = -\frac{r_L}{r_L'L} > 0$ and the interest elasticity of deposits is given by $e_D = -\frac{r_D}{r_D'D} > 0$. Substituting these terms in (6.4.1) and (6.4.2) yields

$$\frac{r_L - r_T - C_L'}{r_L} = \frac{1}{e_L} \tag{6.4.3}$$

$$\frac{r_T(1 - k) - C_D' - r_D}{r_D} = \frac{1}{e_D} \tag{6.4.4}$$

6.5 THE IMPERFECT COMPETITION MODEL

The Klein–Monti model can easily be extended to the case of Cournot imperfect competition. To enable aggregation, assume that there are n banks (indexed by $i = 1, 2, \ldots, n$), all facing the same linear cost function of the type

$$C_i(D, L) = \gamma_D D_i + \gamma_L L_i$$

Each bank maximizes its profits, taking the volume of deposits and loans of other banks as given. We show in Box 6.5 that there is a unique equilibrium where each bank sets its deposits $D_i^* = D/n$ and loans as $L_i^* = L/n$. The equivalent conditions for equations (6.17) and (6.18) are as follows:

$$\frac{r_L - (r_T + \gamma_L)}{r_L} = \frac{1}{ne_L} \tag{6.19}$$

$$\frac{r_T(1 - k) - \gamma_D - r_D}{r_D} = \frac{1}{ne_D} \tag{6.20}$$

The important thing to note about expressions (6.19) and (6.20) is that the response of the loan rate and the deposit rate to changes in the bill rate will depend on the intensity of competition given by the number of banks:

$$\frac{\partial r_L}{\partial r_T} = \frac{1}{1 - 1/ne_L} \tag{6.21}$$

$$\frac{\partial r_D}{\partial r_T} = \frac{1 - k}{1 + 1/ne_D} \tag{6.22}$$

BOX 6.5   The Cournot imperfect competition model

Let there be n identical banks in the market, all facing the same loan rate and deposit rate of interest. The level of loans supplied by each bank is L_i and the level of deposits taken by each bank is D_i ($i = 1, 2, 3, \ldots n$).

By assumption, the aggregate stock of loans L and the aggregate stock of deposit D are given by

$$L = \sum_{i=1}^{n} L_i = nL_i$$

$$D = \sum_{i=1}^{n} D_i = nD_i \tag{6.5.1}$$

Each bank faces the same market rate of interest for loans and deposits. The respective rate of interest on loans and deposits is given by the market demand and the aggregate supply in each market.

The objective function of each bank $\{i\}$ is described by

$$\pi_i = r_L(L)L_i + r_T(D_i(1 - k) - L_i) - r_D(D)D_i - C(D_i, L_i) \tag{6.5.2}$$

Note that the rate of interest for loans and deposits in (6.5.2) is determined by the market for loans and deposits.

Substituting the linear cost function $C_i(D, L) = \gamma_D D_i + \gamma_L L_i$ in (6.5.2) and recognizing the conditions given by (6.5.1), we have

$$\pi_i = r_L\left(\frac{1}{n}\sum_{i=1}^{n} L_i\right)L_i + r_T(D_i(1 - k) - L_i) - r_D\left(\frac{1}{n}\sum_{i=1}^{n} D_i\right)D_i - \gamma_D D_i - \gamma_L L_i \tag{6.5.3}$$

(continued)

Each bank maximizes profit independently of the actions of the other banks in the market:

$$\frac{\partial \pi_i}{\partial L_i} = \frac{r'_L}{n}L_i + r_L - r_T - \gamma_L = 0 \tag{6.5.4}$$

$$\frac{\partial \pi}{\partial D_i} = r_T(1 - k) - \frac{r'_D}{n}D_i - r_D - \gamma_D = 0 \tag{6.5.5}$$

Defining the interest elasticity of loans as $e_L = -\dfrac{r_L}{r'_L L_i} > 0$ and the interest elasticity

of demand for deposits as $e_D = \dfrac{r_D}{r'_D D_i} > 0$, (6.5.4) and (6.5.5) can be expressed as

$$r_L\left(1 - \frac{1}{e_L n}\right) = r_T + \gamma_L \tag{6.5.6}$$

which is

$$\frac{r_L - (r_T + \gamma_L)}{r_L} = \frac{1}{e_L n} \tag{6.5.7}$$

and as

$$r_D\left(1 + \frac{1}{e_D n}\right) = r_T(1 - k) - \gamma_D \tag{6.5.8}$$

which is

$$\frac{r_T(1 - k) - \gamma_D - r_D}{r_D} = \frac{1}{e_D n} \tag{6.5.9}$$

A more rigorous derivation of the above results can be found in Freixas and Rochet (1997).

Equations (6.21) and (6.22) describe a range of responses of the loan rate and deposit rate to changes in the bill rate. At one end we have $n = 1$, which is the monopoly case described by (6.15) and (6.16). At the other end we have the perfect competition case when $n = +\infty$, which gives the results implied by the set of equations (6.10).[10] The prediction of the

[10] This result is derived from equation (6.11). Differentiating with respect to r_T, note that the linear specification of the cost function implies that $C''_L = C''_D = 0$.

imperfect competition model is that the margin of intermediation (the spread between the loan rate and the deposit rate) narrows as competition intensifies. In the special case of equivalent fixed costs faced by each bank, the spread is given from (6.19) to (6.20) to obtain

$$r_L - r_D = \frac{r_T}{\left(1 - \dfrac{1}{ne_L}\right)} - \frac{r_T(1 - k)}{\left(1 + \dfrac{1}{ne_D}\right)}$$

as $n \to \infty$, $r_L - r_D \to r_T k$ which is the result implied by (6.12) when $C'_L = C'_D = 0$.

The main result of the oligopolistic model is that competition leads to narrowing spreads. In terms of Figures 6.2 and 6.3, what this means is that the slope of the demand for loans and the slope of the demand for deposits gets flatter as competition increases. The spread narrows until at the limit the demand for loans and the demand for deposits is horizontal (the case of perfect competition) and the spread falls to $r_T k$. The number of banks in the market measures competition in the oligopolistic version of the model of the banking firm. In reality, competition can be strengthened even if the number of banks in a market declines because of restructuring and defensive merger. The threat of entry can result in incumbent banks behaving competitively. Generally, it can be argued that the market imperfections that the monopoly and oligopolistic competition model aims to capture are not sensible. Imperfections exist in the markets that banks operate in, but these imperfections are rarely in terms of restrictive practices. The imperfections associated with banking are:

(a) Incomplete or imperfect information.
(b) Uncertainty.
(c) Transactions costs.

For its many faults, it is surprising the extent to which the Monti–Klein model is used to analyse the banking sector.[11] The reason is partly because of its simplicity and powerful analytical capability, but also because it enables economists to analyse the banking sector as a single representative bank. The separability result that loans and deposits are independently set turns out to be non-robust. Once risky loans are introduced into the model, reserve requirements and other liquidity constraints on the bank faced with recourse to the central bank or the interbank market result in loans being dependent on deposit decisions.[12] Interdependence is also restored if the cost function for loans and deposits is non-separable (see Freixas and Rochet, 1997).

---

[11] The most recent empirical paper that looks at the passthrough of the official rate of interest to loan and deposit rates uses the Monti–Klein model as the starting point for analysis (Bruggeman and Donnay, 2003).

[12] See, for example, Prisman et al. (1986) and Dermine (1986).

6.6 SUMMARY

- A model is not reality, but for an economic model to be useful it has to address reality in its conclusions.
- The model of the banking firm makes a number of unrealistic assumptions, but it makes a strong empirical prediction.
- Competition drives down the margin of intermediation (spread between the loan rate and deposit rate).
- In the limit, the margin is given by the reserve ratio and the marginal costs of supplying loans and deposits.

QUESTIONS

1   Outline the effects of a decrease in the desired ratio of currency to deposits on bank lending and deposit creation.

2   What are the implications of an increase in the reserve–deposit ratio on the interest rate spread between loans and deposits?

3   Explain the effects of an increase in the interest elasticity of loans and deposits on the interest rate spread between loans and deposits.

4   What are the potential effects on UK banks if (or when?) the UK joins the European Monetary Union?

5   What is the implication of an increase in the bill rate of interest on the loan rate and deposit rate in the Monti–Klein model of banking?

TEST QUESTIONS

1   We do not have theories of the steel-producing firm or the automobile firm. Why do you think we need a theory of the banking firm?

2   Let the balance sheet of the bank be described by $L + R + T = D + E$, where L is the stock of loans, R is reserves, T is the stock of liquid assets, D is deposits and E is equity capital. Let the required return on bank capital be given by ρ. Let the reserve–deposit ratio be given by k and the capital–loan ratio be given by b. If the demand for loans is given by the equation $r_L = \alpha - \beta L$ and the rates of interest on loans, deposits and liquid assets are given by r_L, r_D and r_T respectively, ignoring costs, derive the profit-maximizing expression for the loan rate. What is the effect of an increase in the required return on capital? What is the effect of an increase in the capital–loan ratio?

CHAPTER 7

Models of Banking Behaviour

MINI-CONTENTS

7.1 Introduction

7.2 The economics of asset and liability management

7.3 Liquidity management

7.4 Loan pricing

7.5 Asset management

7.6 The real resource model of asset and liability management

7.7 Liability management and interest rate determination

7.8 Summary

7.1 INTRODUCTION

Chapter 6 examined the theory of the banking firm with a model borrowed specifically from the industrial organization (I-O) literature of economics. This chapter continues with this theme by looking at alternative approaches to the banking firm and tries to redress some of the criticisms of the I-O approach.

One of the main criticisms of the Monti–Klein model is its failure to incorporate risk associated with the lending decision. This chapter makes an attempt to incorporate uncertainty of yields on assets by appealing to portfolio theory, as developed along the lines of the Tobin–Markowitz model. It will be shown that the assumption of risk aversion produces a risk premium in the margin of intermediation and explains the role of diversification in the asset management of banks.

7.2 THE ECONOMICS OF ASSET AND LIABILITY MANAGEMENT

In one sense, asset and liability management is what banking is all about. The business of taking in deposits that are liquid and convertible on demand and transforming them into medium/long-term loans is the core activity of a bank. The management of risk on the balance sheet is the function of asset and liability management. The two fundamental risks a bank faces on its balance sheet are:[1]

1. Default risk.
2. Withdrawal risk.

The allocation of the liabilities of the bank to earning assets so as to minimize the risk of default and the maintenance of sufficient liquid assets so as to minimize the risk of withdrawal are the proper functions of asset and liability management. This chapter will examine the management of the items on both the asset and liability side of the bank's balance sheet. We begin with the asset side. A bank will aim to maximize returns on earnings assets with a mind to minimizing the risk of default. On the one hand, it handles a portfolio of assets that is a mixture of risky loans and low-earning but low-risk bills and cash reserves that usually earn little or no return. The purpose of holding cash reserves is to minimize withdrawal risk and for the bank not to face cash reserve deficiency.

7.3 LIQUIDITY MANAGEMENT

Liquidity management involves managing reserves to meet predictable outflows of deposits.[2] The bank maintains some reserves and it can expect some loan repayment. The bank can also borrow funds from the interbank market or at the discount window from the central bank. The management of the asset side of the bank's balance sheet can be considered as part of a two-stage, decision-making process. At the first stage the bank decides the quantity of reserves to hold to meet the day-to-day withdrawals of deposits. The remainder of assets can be held as earnings assets. At the second stage the bank decides how to allocate its earnings assets between low-risk, low-return bills and high-risk, high-return loans.

A simple model of liquidity management will have the bank balancing between the opportunity cost of holding reserves rather than earning assets and the adjustment costs of having to conduct unanticipated borrowing to meet withdrawals. This is a typical trade-off, which requires the bank to solve an optimization problem under stochastic conditions. Let the balance sheet of the bank be described by loans (L) plus reserves (R) and deposits (D):

$$L + R = D \tag{7.1}$$

---

[1] There are, of course, many other types of risk that, although not fundamental, are significant for a bank's operations. These are examined in more detail in Chapter 13.

[2] This section of the chapter borrows heavily from Baltensperger (1980). See also Poole (1968).

The bank faces a continuous outflow of deposits over a specific period of time before new deposits or inflows replenish them at the beginning of the new period. If the withdrawal outflows are less than the stock reserves, the bank does not face a liquidity crisis. If, on the other hand, the bank faces a withdrawal outflow that is greater than its holding of cash reserves, then it faces a liquidity deficiency and will have to make the deficiency up by raising funds from the interbank market or the central bank. The opportunity cost of holding cash reserves is the interest they could have earned had they been held as an earning asset. Let the deposit outflow be described by a stochastic variable x. A reserve deficiency occurs if $(R - x) < 0$.

Let the adjustment cost of raising funds to meet a reserve deficiency be proportional to the deficiency by a factor p. Then it can be shown that a bank will choose the level of liquid reserves such that the probability of a reserve deficiency is equal to the ratio of the rate of interest on earning assets (r) to the cost of meeting a reserve deficiency (p). The bank chooses the level of reserves such that the marginal benefits (not having to incur liquidation costs) equal the marginal costs (interest income foregone). See Box 7.1.

If the stochastic process describing the deposit outflow in terms of withdrawals is a normal distribution with a given mean, so that at the end of the period the expected withdrawal is $E(x)$, the optimal stock of reserves held by a bank is described in Figure 7.1. If the cost of obtaining marginal liquidity increases (p rises), the ratio r/p declines and more reserves are held. If the return from earnings assets rises (rise in r), fewer reserves are held. If the probability of outflows increases (shift in distribution to the right), more reserves are held. In Figure 7.1 the ratio r/p falls from 0.6 to 0.4 and cash or liquid reserves rise from 28 to 31.

BOX 7.1   The optimal reserve decision

Let x denote the outflow of deposits, $f(x)$ denote the probability distribution function of x and r be the interest earned on the bank's earnings assets. The balance sheet of the bank is as described by equation (7.1.1). Let the expected adjustment cost of a reserve deficiency be denoted by A. This would be the cost of funding a reserve shortfall. The opportunity cost of holding reserves is rR. For simplicity, assume that the expected adjustment cost is proportional to the size of the reserve deficiency and the pr. Then

$$A = \int_R^\infty p(x - R)f(x)\,dx \qquad (7.1.1)$$

For a given set of parameters, the bank can optimize its holding of reserves by minimizing the expected net cost function:

$$C = rR + A$$

$$\Rightarrow rR + \int_R^\infty p(x - R)f(x)\,dx \qquad (7.1.2)$$

(continued)

Minimizing (7.1.2) with respect to R yields

$$\frac{\partial C}{\partial R} = r - p\int_{R}^{\infty} f(x)\,dx = 0$$

$$\Rightarrow \frac{r}{p} = \int_{R}^{\infty} f(x)\,dx \qquad (7.1.3)$$

The bank chooses the level of reserves such that the probability of a reserve deficiency is just equal to the ratio r/p.

When the adjustment cost is proportional to the absolute size of the adjustment, the optimal position for the bank is given by

$$TC = C \pm v(R - R_0)$$

$$\frac{\partial TC}{\partial R} = \frac{\partial C}{\partial R} \pm v = 0$$

$$\Rightarrow r - p\int_{R^*}^{\infty} f(x)\,dx \pm v = 0$$

$$\therefore \frac{r \pm v}{p} = \int_{R^*}^{\infty} f(x)\,dx$$

The final equation defines a lower and upper bound for R. As long as R is bounded by upper and lower limits $R_L < R < R_U$, no adjustment takes place.

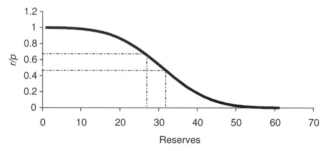

FIGURE 7.1 Cumulative Distribution of Deposit Outflow.

The model says that, in the absence of regulatory reserve ratios, a bank will decide on the optimal level of reserves for its business on the basis of the interest on earnings assets, the cost of meeting a reserve deficiency and the probability distribution of deposit withdrawals. However, in reality many central banks operate statutory reserve ratios. But the model is robust to the imposition of a reserve ratio. Box 7.2 shows that the major effect of imposing a reserve ratio is to reduce the critical value of the deposit withdrawals beyond which a

BOX 7.2   Reserve requirements

Without legal reserve requirements, the critical level of deposit outflow x is the beginning-period level of reserves R. Let the reserve requirement be that the end-period reserves $(R - x)$ should be a fraction k of end-period deposits:

$$R - x = k(D - x) \tag{7.2.1}$$

A reserve deficiency occurs when:

$$R - x < k(D - x) \tag{7.2.2}$$

Solving the inequality for x gives a critical value, which defines a new critical outflow that marks a reserve deficiency:

$$x > \frac{R - kD}{1 - k} \equiv \hat{x} \tag{7.2.3}$$

The size of the reserve deficiency is given by:

$$x(1 - k) - (R - kD) = (x - \hat{x})(1 - k) \tag{7.2.4}$$

The expected value of the adjustment cost is now defined as

$$\widetilde{A} = \int_{\hat{x}}^{\infty} p(x - \hat{x}) f(x) dx$$

$$\Rightarrow \int_{\hat{x}}^{\infty} p(x(1 - k) - (R - kD)) f(x) dx \tag{7.2.5}$$

The optimality condition gives

$$\frac{r}{p} = \int_{\hat{x}}^{\infty} f(x) dx \tag{7.2.6}$$

The difference with the result obtained in Box 7.1 is that the probability gives the likelihood of x exceeding $\hat{x}$ rather than R.

reserve deficiency occurs. What this means is that the optimality decision relates to free reserves (reserves in excess of the reserve requirement) rather than total reserves.

If adjustments for reserve deficiency were costless, the bank would always adjust its portfolio so that it started each planning period with the optimal reserve position, which would be independent of the level of reserves inherited from the previous period. If adjustment costs exist, an adjustment to the optimal level of reserves R^* will be profitable only if the resulting gain more than offsets the cost of the adjustment itself. Suppose that the adjustment cost C is proportional to the absolute size of the adjustment, so that

$$C = v|R - R_0| \qquad (7.2)$$

where R_0 represents the beginning-period reserves before adjustment and R represents the beginning-period reserves after adjustment.

This type of model (shown in Box 7.1) allows for reserves to fluctuate within a range and triggers an adjustment only if the level of reserves goes above or below the limits. When $R < R^*$, an increase in reserves lowers costs. The marginal gain from a reserve adjustment is greater than the marginal cost defined by the parameter v. In other words, when $\partial C/\partial R - v > 0$, it is profitable to make an adjustment. When the marginal gain from an adjustment is equal to the marginal cost, in other words, when $\partial C/\partial v - v = 0$, a further adjustment in R is no longer profitable. Although C is reduced, it would do so only by an amount smaller than v. When $R < R^*$, a reduction in R is profitable because that also lowers costs. Again, when $\partial C/\partial v - v = 0$, any further adjustment does not cover marginal net adjustment costs. When $R_0 > R_L$, reserves increase to R_L. Similarly, when $R_0 > R_U$, reserves decrease to R_U. Figure 7.2 illustrates.

As a postscript to this section and a test of the predictive power of economic theory to explain liquidity management of banks, we can use the results of Box 7.1 to examine the implications of the Northern Rock banking crisis in the UK during the summer of 2007. Box 7.3 describes the liquidity shortage faced by Northern Rock bank.

During the summer of 2007, the Northern Rock bank faced a run on its deposits, leaving it short of liquidity to meet withdrawals. The Bank of England did not at first respond by lending to individual banks. The run ended only after the Bank of England and the

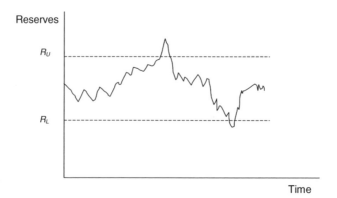

FIGURE 7.2 Reserve Adjustment.

BOX 7.3   The Northern Rock liquidity crisis

Northern Rock bank, a former building society, faced a liquidity problem and had to borrow emergency funds from the Bank of England. The bank funded 77% of its lending operations from the interbank market (see Chapter 9). Traditionally, solvent but illiquid banks would be able to borrow from the central bank at a penal rate of interest. Box 7.1 shows how a bank balances the cost of borrowing from the central bank against the opportunity cost for holding liquid reserves. The UK banking system operates on near cash ratios agreed with the banks (apart from the 0.15%, see Chapter 4, Section 4.2.2, for a description of the ratios) and no required liquidity ratios. The implicit assumption is that there is a type of unwritten contract between the Bank of England and the banking system that a solvent but illiquid bank could always get funds from the central bank. In practice the option was never exercised as any solvent bank could raise funds on the interbank market. However, the interbank market in the UK seized up during the summer of 2007 when not only did the spread between the London interbank offer rate (LIBOR) and the Bank of England base rate rise at one point beyond 100 basis points, but banks were not lending to each other. The commercial banks looked to the Bank of England to inject liquidity into the banking system. On 12 September the Bank argued that providing greater short-term liquidity might unblock the interbank market and ease the liquidity problems of individual banks but would also undermine the efficient pricing of risk by providing insurance ex post to banks for taking risky positions. Such action would sow the seeds of a future financial crisis. In other words, the Bank of England was using the moral hazard argument (see Chapter 8). According to the Bank of England, the provision of liquidity would occur only if withholding it would be more costly to the economy than the moral hazard cost of supplying funds. On 19 September the Bank had changed its mind and announced an injection of £10bn.

Treasury guaranteed the deposits of Northern Rock. The vacillation of the Bank of England in providing funds will have affected the commercial banks' expectation of the cost of borrowing from the central bank. In terms of Box 7.1, the ratio $\{r/p\}$ will have fallen. The prediction of the model is that banks in the UK will in future operate on higher cash and liquidity ratios.

7.4 LOAN PRICING

We have seen how competitive conditions have helped to determine the spread between the loan rate and the deposit rate. But this is not the only factor that determines the margin of intermediation. The rate of interest on loans will depend on a variety of individual borrower characteristics, but one common characteristic is an allowance for the risk of default combined with the degree of risk aversion by the bank.

The risk aversion model of portfolio selection of the Tobin (1958) and Markowitz (1959) type can be applied to the issue of asset allocation in banking (see Section 7.5). The same model can also be used to obtain some general conclusions about intermediation, the existence of the banking firm and loan pricing. The question posed by Pyle (1971) was: 'Under what conditions would a bank sell risky deposits in order to buy risky loans?' Another way of asking this question is: Under what conditions will intermediation take place?

Consider a bank that faces a choice of three assets: one riskless asset and two assets (loans and deposits) with uncertain yield. We can think of deposits as a negative asset. Let the profit function for the bank be given by:

$$\pi = r_L L + r_T T - r_D D \qquad (7.3)$$

and the balance sheet by

$$L + T = D \qquad (7.4)$$

where T is the stock of risk-free bills, L is the stock of (risky) loans and D is the stock of deposits (risky negative assets).

Pyle (1971) shows that a necessary and sufficient condition for intermediation to exist given independent loan and deposit yields is a positive risk premium on loans

$$E(r_L) - r_T > 0 \qquad (7.5)$$

and a negative risk premium on deposits

$$E(r_D) - r_T < 0 \qquad (7.6)$$

which means that all that is required is that there be a positive spread:

$$E(r_L) - E(r_D) > 0 \qquad (7.7)$$

If the correlation between the yield on loans and the interest on deposits is zero, then the spread is given by

$$E(r_L) - E(r_D) = \beta(\sigma_{rL}^2 L + \sigma_{rD}^2 D) \qquad (7.8)$$

The interest rate spread, or margin of intermediation as it is sometimes referred to, depends on the volatility of yields on assets and deposit liabilities of the bank and the coefficient of risk aversion β — see Box 7.4.

Basically, what is involved here is an arbitrage process that is exploiting the interest rate differential. We may ask why there is no infinite arbitrage that drives down the differential to zero? The check on the differential is the existence of risk aversion. So it is the existence of risk aversion that ensures that the spread does not fall to zero.

The model of a risk-averse bank provides an insight into the pricing of loans as a mark-up on the risk-free rate of return. The mark-up is a function of the volatility of the yield on assets and the coefficient of risk aversion. However, it is not a general model. A model that

BOX 7.4 The conditions for the existence of intermediation

Let the expected utility function of the bank be described by:

$$E\{U(\pi)\} = E(\pi) - \frac{1}{2}\beta\sigma_\pi^2 \tag{7.4.1}$$

where

$$E(\pi) = E(r_L)L + r_T T - E(r_D)D \tag{7.4.2}$$

and $E(r_L) = E(r_L + \varepsilon_L)$, $\varepsilon_L \sim N(0,\sigma_L^2)$, $E(r_D) = E(r_D + \varepsilon_D)$, $\varepsilon_D \sim N(0,\sigma_D^2)$ and β is the coefficient of risk aversion.

Substituting (7.3.2) into (7.3.1) and noting that

$$Cov(r_L, r_D) = \rho_{r_L r_D}\sigma_{r_L}\sigma_{r_D}$$

$$E\{U(\pi)\} = E(r_L)L + r_M M - E(r_D)D - \frac{1}{2}\beta\{\sigma_{r_L}^2 L^2 + \sigma_{r_D}^2 D^2 - 2\rho_{r_L r_D}\sigma_{r_L}\sigma_{r_D}(L)(D) \tag{7.4.3}$$

where $\rho_{r_L r_D}$ is the correlation coefficient between the stochastic yield on loans and deposits. Substituting for M from the balance sheet of the bank, the first-order conditions for utility maximization are as follows:

$$\frac{\partial E\{U(\pi)\}}{\partial L} = E(r_L) - r_M - \frac{1}{2}\beta[2L\sigma_{r_L}^2 - 2\rho_{r_L r_D}\sigma_{r_L}\sigma_{r_D}D] = 0 \tag{7.4.4}$$

$$\frac{\partial E\{U(\pi)\}}{\partial D} = r_M - E(r_D) - \frac{1}{2}\beta[2D\sigma_{r_D}^2 - 2\rho_{r_L r_D}\sigma_{r_L}\sigma_{r_D}L] = 0 \tag{7.4.5}$$

$$E(r_L) - r_T = \beta\sigma_{r_L}(\sigma_{r_L} - 2\rho_{r_L r_D}\sigma_{r_L}\sigma_{r_D}L) \tag{7.4.6}$$

$$E(r_D) - r_T = -\beta\sigma_{r_D}(\sigma_{r_D} - 2\rho_{r_L r_D}\sigma_{r_L}\sigma_{r_D}L) \tag{7.4.7}$$

If the yields of loans and deposits were independent $E(r_L, r_D) = 0$, then the correlation coefficient between the yields on loans and deposits would be zero. We can see that (7.3.6) is positive and (7.3.7) is negative. We can also see that intermediation is impossible if the correlation is unity – the bracketed parts of (7.3.6) and (7.3.7) cannot both be positive. Notice that a negative correlation enables intermediation to take place and creates the condition for a risk-averse bank to conduct asset transformation. However, a zero or negative correlation is too restrictive a condition for the existence of intermediation or a risk mark-up on the risk-free rate. If the correlation between the loan rate and deposit rate is positive (as is likely in reality), by subtracting (7.3.7) from (7.3.6) we can see that the condition for a positive spread (margin of intermediation) of the correlation coefficient can be positive but small:

$$\rho_{r_L r_D} < \frac{(\sigma_{r_L}^2 + \sigma_{r_D}^2)}{\sigma_{r_L}\sigma_{r_D}(D + L)}$$

incorporates risk characteristics will also have to explain why a bank is able to bear greater risks than private individuals.

In reality, the pricing of loans will not only consider risk characteristics but also the return on assets that shareholders expect from the business of banking.

7.5 ASSET MANAGEMENT

Analysis of Section 7.4 also helps us to arrive at some general principles on how a bank manages its assets. We can pose two questions. Firstly, how does a bank allocate its assets between high-risk, high-return loans and low-risk, low-return assets? Secondly, how does a bank allocate its assets between a risk-free asset and risky assets? These questions can be answered by appealing to portfolio theory and the Markowitz separation theorem. Portfolio theory tells us that we can separate the asset allocation decision into two stages. The first stage involves the construction of a composite asset made up of an optimal combination of risky assets. The second stage involves a comparison between the composite risky asset and the risk-free asset.

The optimal combination of risky assets is a unique combination that cannot be improved upon, either in terms of higher return or lower risk. Consider two assets A and B with two different risk return characteristics as shown in Figure 7.3. On the vertical axis we have expected return and on the horizontal we have a measure of risk. Asset A has a low-risk, low-return characteristic. Asset B has a high-risk, high-return characteristic.

It would be difficult to choose between A and B without knowing something about the risk preferences of the bank manager. However, we know that an asset such as C would be preferable to both A or B, because it has a higher return than A for the same level of risk and the same return as B but for lower risk. The question is, can we combine A and B in such a way as to generate a position C that would be superior to both? By appealing to portfolio theory, we can construct a superior position to A and B on the basis of the covariance of the relative stochastic returns. Box 7.5 shows how this is done.

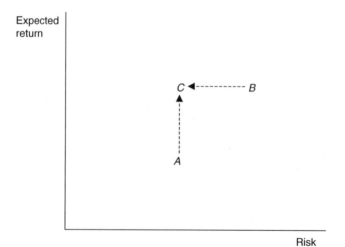

FIGURE 7.3 Optimal Combination of Assets.

BOX 7.5   A primer on portfolio theory

Let R_A and R_B be the rates of return on assets A and B respectively, and σ_A^2 and σ_B^2 be their respective variances. The return on a portfolio that holds a proportion α of A and $(1 - \alpha)$ of B is given by

$$R = \alpha R_A + (1 - \alpha)R_B \tag{7.5.1}$$

The variance of R is

$$\sigma_R^2 = Var(R - E(R))$$
$$\Rightarrow \alpha^2 Var(R_A) + (1 - \alpha)^2 Var(R_B) + 2\alpha(1 - \alpha)Cov(R_A, R_B)$$
$$\Rightarrow \alpha^2 \sigma_A^2 + (1 - \alpha)^2 \sigma_B^2 + 2\alpha(1 - \alpha)\rho_{A,B}\sigma_A\sigma_B \tag{7.5.2}$$

Recall that

$$\rho_{A,B} = \frac{Cov(R_A, R_B)}{\sigma_A\sigma_B}$$

Minimizing (7.4.2) with respect to α:

$$\frac{\partial \sigma_R^2}{\partial \alpha} = 2\alpha\sigma_A^2 - 2(1 - \alpha)\sigma_B^2 + 2\rho_{A,B}\sigma_A\sigma_B - 4\alpha\rho_{A,B}\sigma_A\sigma_B = 0$$
$$\Rightarrow \alpha\sigma_A^2 - (1 - \alpha)\sigma_B^2 + \rho_{A,B}\sigma_A\sigma_B - 2\alpha\rho_{A,B}\sigma_A\sigma_B = 0$$
$$\Rightarrow \alpha(\sigma_A^2 + \sigma_B^2) - \sigma_B^2 - 2\alpha\rho_{A,B}\sigma_A\sigma_B = -\rho_{A,B}\sigma_A\sigma_B$$
$$\Rightarrow \alpha(\sigma_A^2 + \sigma_B^2 - 2\rho_{A,B}\sigma_A\sigma_B) = \sigma_B^2 - \rho_{A,B}\sigma_A\sigma_B$$

Collecting terms and solving for α gives

$$\alpha = \frac{\sigma_B(\sigma_B - \rho_{A,B}\sigma_A)}{[\sigma_A^2 + \sigma_B^2 - 2\rho_{A,B}\sigma_A\sigma_B]}$$

The proportion α can be chosen to minimize the risk of the total portfolio. The choice of the optimal value of α will depend on the correlation between asset A and asset B. Let $\rho_{A,B} = -1$. Then

$$\alpha = \left(\frac{\sigma_B}{\sigma_A + \sigma_B}\right)$$

(continued)

You should be able to confirm that substituting this value into (7.5.2) produces a value for the variance of zero. The figure below shows the three cases of the correlation coefficient being $-1, 1$ and in between.

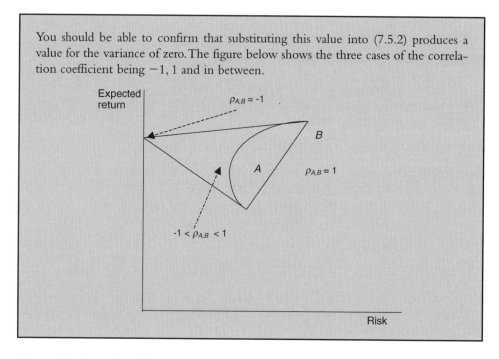

Figure 7.4 shows the efficient frontier that describes the risk-minimizing combination of assets for varying coordinates of expected return and risk measured by the variance.

The composite asset is made up of the optimal combination of loans that minimizes the risk associated with the stochastic returns. The expected return from the total portfolio will include the allocation of assets between the risk-free asset and the risky composite asset. The expected return of the total portfolio is

$$E(\tilde{R}) = \omega E(R) + (1 - \omega)r_T \tag{7.9}$$

where ω is the proportion of the bank's assets that are risky and r_T is the risk-free asset. Given that the returns on the risk-free asset are deterministic, the variance of the returns on the total portfolio is

$$\sigma_{\tilde{R}}^2 = \omega^2 \sigma_R^2 \tag{7.10}$$

Equation (7.9) can also be expressed as

$$E(\tilde{R}) = \left(\frac{E(R) - r_T}{\omega}\right)\omega^2 + r_T \tag{7.11}$$

Substituting for ω^2 in (7.10) into (7.11), we have

$$E(\tilde{R}) = \left(\frac{E(R) - r_T}{\omega\sigma_R^2}\right)\sigma_{\tilde{R}}^2 + r_T \tag{7.12}$$

$$\Rightarrow \theta\sigma_{\tilde{R}}^2 + r_T$$

Equation (7.12) defines the opportunity locus giving the trade-off between expected return and risk for the portfolio, as shown in Figure 7.6. To make the choice of asset allocation

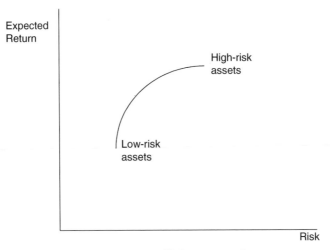

FIGURE 7.4 Efficient Frontier.

between the risk-free asset and the composite risky asset (the proportion ω), we need to know the risk preferences of the bank. This is shown in Figure 7.5 by the utility function that is tangential to the opportunity locus.

Now let us consider how the allocation alters when the composite asset becomes more risky.

Figure 7.6 shows the opportunity locus shifting down from AC to AC'. We can think of the ray from the origin AC and AC' as unit lengths, and any point on the line defines a proportion $(0 < \omega < 1)$. The initial allocation to risky assets is given by the ratio AB/AC and the proportion of assets held in the risk-free asset is shown by BC/AC. The increase in the riskiness of the portfolio is shown by a shift in the opportunity set to AC'. Point C' is to the right of C and shows the same expected return as C but with a higher level of risk. The new equilibrium is shown as B'. The share of the composite risky asset will have fallen to AB'/AC' and the share of the risk-free asset will have increased to BC'/AC'. We have

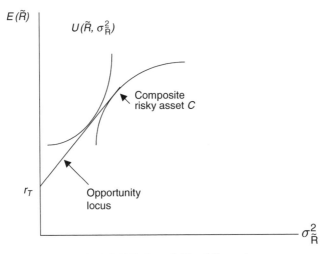

FIGURE 7.5 Portfolio Allocation.

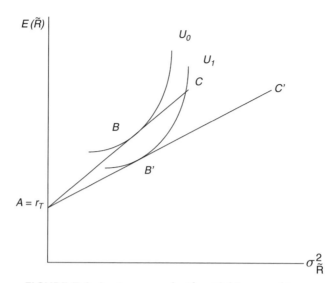

FIGURE 7.6 An Increase in the Riskiness of Loans.

shown that an increase in the riskiness of the portfolio drives the bank to reduce its exposure in the composite risky asset (loans) and hold a higher share of the risk-free asset. Notice
that from equation (7.12) a fall in the yield of loans as a whole has qualitatively the same
effect as a rise in the riskiness of loans.

Consider what happens if the risk-free rate rises (Figure 7.7) but there is no change in the
overall composite loan rate. The opportunity locus shifts from AC to $A'C$. The proportion of
the portfolio held in the risk-free asset increases from BC/AC to $B'C/A'C$. This clearly follows from the preceding analysis, but is it at all realistic? In reality a rise in the risk-free rate
of interest will raise interest rates generally and the allocation will depend on the relative rate

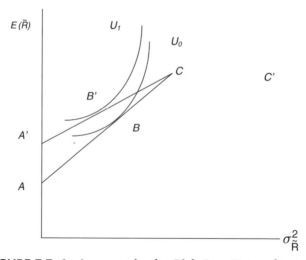

FIGURE 7.7 An Increase in the Risk-Free Rate of Interest.

of interest or the margin between the risk-free rate and the composite risky rate. A general rise in interest rates will have the opportunity locus shift up to the left in parallel to *AC*.

The portfolio model yields the following conclusions:

1. A bank tries to diversify its loan assets between high-risk, high-return lending (new ventures, SMEs,[3] etc.) and low-risk, low-return lending (blue-chip companies, secured lending to households, etc.).
2. The bank holds a proportion of its assets in risk-free liquid assets.
3. An increase in riskiness on the asset portfolio (ceteris paribus) will see banks moving into the risk-free liquid asset.
4. An increase in the return on loans (ceteris paribus) will see banks moving away from the risk-free asset.
5. An increase in the risk-free rate of return (ceteris paribus) will result in banks increasing their holding of the risk-free asset.

While the conclusions of the portfolio model seem like common sense in the practice of banking, there are a number of deficiencies in the model that need to be borne in mind. The results are sensitive to the specification of the utility function. We have implicitly assumed a quadratic or negative exponential utility function in terms of the return on the portfolio. This means that the utility function can be expressed in terms of the first two moments (mean and variance) of the distribution of the returns on assets. This also implies that the distribution of returns is normal. But, in reality, returns on a loan portfolio are not normally distributed. The standard loan contract calls for the repayment of principal and interest. The interest return is not normally distributed. Borrowers may be delinquent and pay less or even default, but they do not pay more than what is specified in the contract. So, there is only downside risk and no equivalent compensating upside risk.

The portfolio model cannot accommodate the customer–loan relationship. The bank will often lend without collateral with the aim of building up a long-term relationship with a customer. A bank may be willing to provide an unsecured loan to an impoverished student on the grounds that it would be useful to gain the loyalty of the student for the future when he or she has graduated and is handling a company account. The customer–loan relationship ensures that lending and overdraft facilities exist in bad times as well as good.

The portfolio model also does not incorporate the intricate bilateral determination of lending terms. The reason being that individual loans have different characteristics of interest to a bank other than return and risk. Lending characteristics would include maturity, collateral and credit rating. Such characteristics are difficult to capture in the simple portfolio model.

7.6 THE REAL RESOURCE MODEL OF ASSET AND LIABILITY MANAGEMENT

The real resource model of Sealey and Lindley (1977) explains the size and structure of bank liabilities and assets purely in terms of the flows of the real resource costs of maintaining balance sheet items. These models start with a production function relating different combinations of liabilities and assets to corresponding feasible combinations of inputs.

---

[3] SME = small- to medium-sized enterprises.

Let the balance sheet of the bank be described by

$$L + R = D \qquad (7.13)$$

Reserves are given by a fixed reserve ratio k, and inputs to production are made up of labour, capital, buildings, etc., and denoted by a resource index I. A production function describes the use of inputs I to produce L and D:

$$f(L,D,I) = 0 \qquad (7.14)$$

The application of resources I to deposit maintenance and loan maintenance is via individual production functions that satisfy the usual conditions of positive marginal productivity and diminishing marginal productivity of resource input. In other words:

$$D = d(I) \quad d' > 0, d'' < 0$$
$$L = l(I) \quad l' > 0, l'' < 0$$

This model is used to explain the allocation of resources to the management of liabilities and assets, but also explains the spread (margin of intermediation) as a function of operating or staff expenses. Box 7.6 derives this formally.

BOX 7.6   Margin of intermediation as a function of operating expenses

Given that the reserve ratio is k, we can write the balance sheet condition as:

$$L = (1 - k)D \qquad (7.6.1)$$

Let there be only one input resource, that is, labour (N). Labour is used to service the number of deposit accounts:

$$D = f(N) \quad f' > 0, f'' < 0 \qquad (7.6.2)$$

The objective function of the bank is to maximize profit. The only factor of production in the servicing of deposits is labour N at a cost w, which is the wage rate:

$$\pi = r_L L - r_D D - wN \qquad (7.6.3)$$

Substituting (7.6.1) and (7.6.2) into (7.6.3) and maximizing with respect to N, we have:

$$\pi = r_L(1 - k) f(N) - r_D F(N) - wN$$

$$\frac{\partial \pi}{\partial N} = r_L(1 - k) f' - r_D f' - w = 0$$

$$\Rightarrow r_L - r_D = kr_L + \frac{w}{f'}$$

(continued)

The elasticity of deposit service to labour input is given by $\varepsilon_N = (f'N/D)$ (the ratio of the marginal product of N to the average product). Substituting this into the margin of intermediation above, we have the following expression:

$$r_L - r_D = kr_L + \left(\frac{1}{\varepsilon_N}\right)\left(\frac{wN}{D}\right) \tag{7.6.4}$$

Equation (7.6.4) says that, for a constant elasticity, the interest rate margin will vary positively with the ratio of staff costs to deposits. The ratio of staff costs to deposits is closely measured by the ratio of staff costs to assets. The figure below shows the path of the average interest rate margin for the UK (top line) and staff costs as a proportion of assets (bottom line). The figure confirms that the interest rate margin (spread) follows the same trend as the ratio of staff costs to assets. In other words, equation (7.6.4) above is empirically confirmed.

Net Interest Margin and Staff Costs (UK)

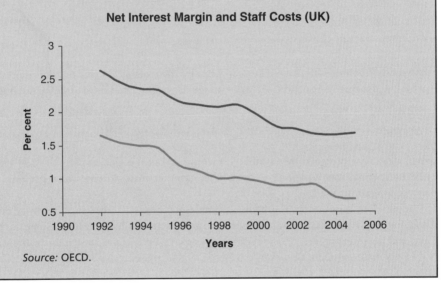

Source: OECD.

The real resource model can be used to explain the scale of bank activity in the form of deposit production to meet a given supply of loans. The model explains the margin of intermediation in terms of operating costs, but, like the portfolio model or the monopoly model, it is a partial explanation.

7.7 LIABILITY MANAGEMENT AND INTEREST RATE DETERMINATION

Liability management involves the active bidding for deposits to meet loan demand. The competitive pricing of deposits in terms of the rate of interest on sight and time deposits is the direct result of liability management. The Monti–Klein model of Chapter 6 is a good starting point for the examination of deposit supply by the banks to meet a deposit demand as part of a general demand for money by the non-bank public. The result that loan and deposit rate settings are independent of each other can be relaxed by assuming that the costs of producing loans and deposits described by the cost function are non-separable. If it is assumed that the marginal cost of producing loans increases the marginal cost of deposits, it can be argued that the monopoly bank needs an increase in the margin of intermediation to compensate it for a marginal increase in deposits.

The competitive bank conducts liability management by funding the additional demand for loans by borrowing from the interbank market. Since the competitive bank is a price taker, the relative rates of interest will be given and the relative positions of loans and liquid assets will be predetermined. The profit function for the competitive bank is given by

$$\pi = r_L L + r_T T - r_D D - r_I I \tag{7.15}$$

where r_I and I are the borrowing rate of interest on the interbank market and the stock of borrowed interbank funds respectively.

The marginal funding condition is that an increase in assets caused by an exogenous increase in demand for bank loans is matched by an increase in interbank borrowing. So

$$dL + dT = dI \tag{7.16}$$

If the ratio of liquid assets T to loans L is given by the existing relative rates of interest, then $T = \alpha L$ and, using (7.16) and (7.15), the marginal profit gained from an increase in loans is

$$\frac{\partial \pi}{\partial L} = r_L + \alpha r_T - (1 + \alpha) r_1 > 0 \tag{7.17}$$

which states that, provided the combined earning on assets is greater than the cost of interbank borrowing, the competitive bank will have recourse to interbank funding of an increase in loan demand.

The problem arises when the banking industry as a whole faces an increase in demand for loans. If all banks have funding deficits and there are no banks with funding surpluses, there will be an excess demand for loanable funds. To understand the industry implications of liability management, we develop a model based on Niehans (1978) and De Grauwe (1982).

The supply of deposits will be positively dependent on the margin of intermediation:

$$D^S = h(r_L - r_D) \quad h' > 0 \tag{7.18}$$

The balance sheet constraint of the bank is

$$L + T + R = D \quad \text{with } R = kD$$

Substituting (7.18) into the balance sheet constraint gives a loan supply function:

$$L^S = g(r_L - r_D, k, r_T) \quad g'_1 > 0, g'_2 < 0, g'_3 < 0 \tag{7.19}$$

The demand for deposits and the demand for loans are given by the following:

$$D^d = D(r_D, X) \tag{7.20}$$

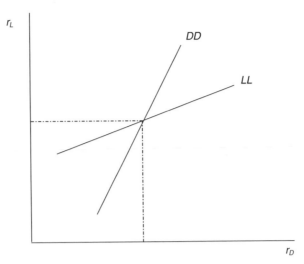

FIGURE 7.8 Equilibrium in the Loan and Deposit Markets.

where $D_r > 0$ and X is a vector of other variables that influence the demand for deposits. The demand for loans is

$$L^d = L(r_L, Z) \tag{7.21}$$

where $L_r < 0$ and Z is a vector of other variables that influence the demand for loans. Equilibrium in the loan market is given by

$$L(r_L, Z) = g(r_L - r_D, k, r_T) \tag{7.22}$$

and equilibrium in the deposit market is given by

$$D(r_D, X) = h(r_L - r_D) \tag{7.23}$$

Figure 7.8 shows the combination of loan and deposit rates that describes equilibrium in the loan and deposit markets. The LL schedule describes equilibrium in the loan market and the DD schedule describes equilibrium in the deposit market. Box 7.7 examines the comparative statics of the model and shows why the slope of the LL schedule is flatter than that of the DD schedule. The intersection of the two schedules gives the loan and deposit rates that equilibrate both markets.[4]

An exogenous increase in the demand for loans shifts the LL schedule up to LL' and increases the loan rate. The bank (or banking system in the case of a non-monopoly bank) will respond by supplying more loans and deposits. To attract more deposits, the bank (banking system) will bid for deposits by increasing the deposit rate. However, because the

---

[4] But note that, if the marginal cost of supplying a marginal unit of deposit to fund a marginal unit of loans is zero, then deposit supply function (and loan supply function) will be perfectly elastic and the LL and DD schedules will have the same slope at unity. The loan rate will be equal to the interbank borrowing rate. This would be the case when the banking industry faces a perfectly elastic supply of loanable funds from the global interbank market.

BOX 7.7　Equilibrium in the loan and deposit markets

Totally differentiating equation (7.22) and collecting terms:

$$L_r dr_L + L_Z dZ = g_1'(dr_L - dr_D) + g_2' dk + g_3' dr_T$$
$$\Rightarrow (g_1' - L_r)dr_L = g_1' dr_D + L_Z dZ - g_2' dk - g_3' dr_T \tag{7.7.1}$$

The slope of the LL schedule is less than unity and given by

$$\left.\frac{\partial r_L}{\partial r_D}\right|_{LL} = \left(\frac{g_1'}{g_1' - L_r}\right) < 1$$

The remaining comparative statics show that an increase in the reserve ratio (k) or a rise in the bill market rate (r_M) or an exogenous increase in the demand for loans has the effect of raising the loan rate for every given deposit rate:

$$\frac{\partial r_L}{\partial k} = \left(\frac{-g_2'}{g_1' - L_r}\right) > 0; \quad \frac{\partial r_L}{\partial r_T} = \left(\frac{-g_3'}{g_1' - L_r}\right) > 0; \quad \frac{\partial r_L}{\partial Z} = \left(\frac{L_Z}{g_1' - L_r}\right) > 0$$

Totally differentiating equation (7.23) and collecting terms:

$$D_r dr_D + D_X dX = h'(dr_L - dr_D)$$
$$h' dr_L = (D_r + h')dr_D + D_X dX \tag{7.7.2}$$

The slope of the DD schedule is greater than unity and given by

$$\left.\frac{\partial r_L}{\partial r_D}\right|_{DD} = \left(\frac{D_r + h'}{h'}\right) > 1$$

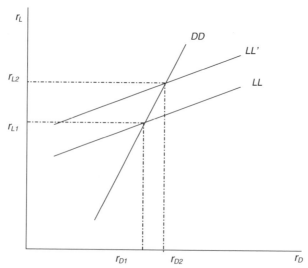

FIGURE 7.9　An Exogenous Increase in the Demand for Loans.

increase in loans has increased the marginal cost of supplying deposits, the rise in the loan rate will be greater than the rise in the deposit rate to compensate the bank in terms of a higher margin of intermediation. Figure 7.9 shows the new equilibrium.

An increase in the reserve ratio or an increase in the bill market rate has the same qualitative effect on the loan and deposit rate as an exogenous increase in loan demand.

7.8 SUMMARY

- The optimal amount of reserves a bank will hold is a trade-off choice based on the cost of meeting an unexpected reserve deficiency and the opportunity cost of holding reserves as a non-earning asset.
- The margin between the loan rate and deposit rate will among other things depend on the degree of risk aversion of the bank.
- The pricing of loans above the risk-free rate will depend on the degree of risk aversion and the riskiness of the loan measured by the volatility of the yield.
- A risk-averse bank will hold a diversified portfolio of assets consisting of risk-free liquid assets and risky illiquid loans.
- An increase in the return on loans will increase the proportion of assets held as loans.
- An increase in the riskiness of loans will result in a decrease in the proportion of assets held as loans.
- The servicing of deposits and loans uses up real resources such as labour, capital, buildings, etc.
- The margin between the loan rate and deposit rate will among other things also depend on the operating costs of the bank.
- Liability management implies that the bank will bid for deposits to meet an increase in demand for loans.
- An exogenous increase in the demand for loans raises both the loan rate and the deposit rate.

QUESTIONS

1   What is liability management? What is asset management?

2   What factors influence a bank's holding of reserves?

3   What is the evidence that a bank behaves like a risk averter?

4   What are the conditions for bank intermediation to take place in the portfolio balance model of banking?

5   What does the portfolio balance model of banking predict on a bank's balance sheet if there is an increase in (a) the yield on loans and (b) the riskiness of loans?

TEST QUESTIONS

1 Discuss the contributions of the theories of the banking firm to our understanding of bank behaviour.

2 How does a bank react to an increase in the demand for loans under conditions of liability management? What are the implications for the banking system as a whole of an increase in the demand for loans?

8

Credit Rationing

MINI-CONTENTS

8.1 Introduction
8.2 The availability doctrine
8.3 Theories of credit rationing
8.4 Asymmetric information and adverse selection
8.5 Adverse incentive
8.6 Screening versus rationing
8.7 The existence of credit rationing
8.8 Summary

8.1 INTRODUCTION

The notion of credit rationing developed as a side product of the view that monetary policy has strong direct effects on the economy through the spending mechanism. The view in the 1950s was that monetary tightness could have strong effects on reducing private sector expenditure even though interest rate changes were likely to be small. The reasoning behind this was that banks restrict credit to borrowers. This was the basis of the so-called 'availability doctrine' which roughly stated says that spending is always in excess of available loanable funds. Indeed, it was noted by Keynes (1930) that 'there is apt to be an unsatisfied fringe of borrowers, the size of which can be expanded or contracted, so that banks can influence the volume of investment by expanding and contracting the volume of their loans, without there being necessarily any change in the level of bank rate'.

The question that troubled the economist was: Could credit rationing be consistent with the actions of a profit-maximizing bank, as it appeared to be inconsistent with basic demand and supply analysis, which postulates the existence of an equilibrium rate at which all borrowers, who are willing to pay that rate, obtain loans? The principal aim of this chapter is to address this question. However, at the outset we should distinguish between two types of credit rationing. *Type 1* credit rationing occurs when a borrower cannot borrow all of what he or she wants at the prevailing price of credit, although he or she is willing to pay the prevailing price. *Type 2* credit rationing occurs when out of a pool of identical borrowers some individuals have their credit demands satisfied while others do not, again when they are willing to pay the prevailing price.

The remainder of this chapter discusses the validity of various theories that have been put forward to explain the existence of credit rationing.

8.2 THE AVAILABILITY DOCTRINE

The 'availability doctrine' loosely states that it is not the price of credit that is the important determinant of credit but the availability of credit. The doctrine arose out of the post–World War II observation of a weak relationship between the rate of interest and the aggregate demand for loans. This apparent inelasticity fitted in with the dominant view that fiscal policy was the driving force of economic stabilization and that monetary policy played only a supporting role.

The reality was that commercial banks emerged from the Second World War with swollen holdings of government debt. The prevailing method of bank management was 'asset management'. Banks switched assets on their balance sheets between overrepresented government bonds and underrepresented private loans as and when open-market operations made it possible. Government and central banks were able effectively to control the flow of credit through open-market operations at the prevailing rate of interest. A tightening or loosening of monetary policy was obtained by appropriate open-market operation, which either increased or decreased commercial bank holdings of government debt which in turn mirrored an increase or decrease in bank lending to the private sector. Additionally, many economies placed quantitative controls on bank lending. The result was that the rate of interest was unable to satisfy the aggregate demand for credit, as described by Figure 8.1.

Figure 8.1 shows that, because of quantitative controls on the ability of the banks to make loans to the private sector, they were limited to OA. Because banks were underweighted on loans in their portfolio, the supply curve of loans was horizontal (i.e. perfectly elastic) at the official lending rate R_L^*. This caused there to be an unsatisfied demand for loans at R_L^* equal to OB minus OA.

A mixture of regulatory restrictions, usury laws and asset management methods employed by banks provided the backdrop for the availability doctrine. From a microeconomic perspective the availability doctrine highlighted the role of non-price factors in the determination of a loan contract. However, rationing in any form that was not exogenously determined by government control and regulation was considered to be inconsistent with profit-maximizing bank behaviour.

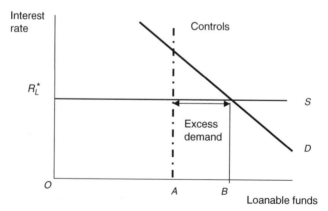

FIGURE 8.1 Exogenous Credit Rationing.

8.3 THEORIES OF CREDIT RATIONING

Early theories of credit rationing were based on the notion of sticky interest rates caused by institutional, legal or cultural factors such as usury laws, transactions costs, inertia or inelastic expectations. These approaches are tantamount to assuming the existence of credit rationing, or it exists because of governmental controls rather than showing that it comes out of optimizing behaviour. Later theories concentrated on the risk of default. The main thrust of this argument is that the financial intermediary could not be compensated for an increase in risk by an increase in the rate of interest. Beyond some specific loan exposure by the bank, the risk will always outweigh the rate of interest and the expected profit will decline as the rate of interest increases beyond some given point, as shown in Figure 8.2.

Figure 8.2 shows that expected profit for the bank increases as the rate of interest rises. This arises because a rising rate of interest will have two opposing effects on the bank's loan revenue. Firstly, expected revenue increases because of the increase in price (assuming loan demand is interest inelastic), and, secondly, expected revenue falls as the risk of default increases. After a certain point the second factor will outweigh the first factor and total expected revenue/profits will decline. Hence, expected profit increases at a declining rate because the increase in the rate of interest also increases the risk of default. Beyond some particular rate of interest $\{R^*\}$, the risk of default will reduce expected profit faster than the rise in the rate of interest will increase expected profit. The result is that there will be a maximum expected profit given by $E(\pi^*)$ at the rate of interest $\{R^*\}$, and beyond this point a higher rate of interest will reduce expected profit.

Hodgman (1960) was one of the first to develop a theory of endogenous credit rationing that was consistent with profit-maximizing behaviour. In this framework, which remains at the heart of the credit-rationing literature, is the notion that the bank's risk of loss (risk of default) is positively related to loan exposure.

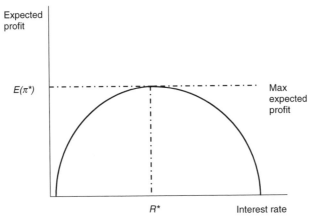

FIGURE 8.2 The Interest Rate and Expected Profit.

The bank's expected return therefore consists of two components, the minimum return in the event of default and, in the absence of default, the full return given by the loan rate less the cost of raising deposits on the money market. This analysis is set out more formally in Box 8.1.

Each of these two components has an attached probability. For very small loans the probability of default is virtually zero. As the loan size increases after a certain point, the probability of default rises so that the expected profit on the loan starts to decrease such that the loan offer curve bends backwards. This is demonstrated in Figure 8.3.

In the range A, loans are small and risk free. In this range $L < l/(1 + \delta)$, the project yields the minimum outcome discounted by the interest cost of funds. In the range B, the probability of default rises with loan size. The maximum loan size is given by L^*. When the demand for loans is D_2, the equilibrium rate of interest is r_2 and loan supply is region B with no excess demand. When the demand for loans is given by D_1 the rate of interest is r_1 and the loan offered is L^*, which is less than the demand at the rate of interest r_1. At D_1 the size of the loan demanded would always exceed the maximum offered, so that credit rationing occurs.

Even if the demand curve lies between D_1 and D_2 and does intersect the loan offer curve but at a higher interest rate than r_1, the loan offered will still be L^*. The Hodgman model is able to explain the possibility of type 1 rationing but is unable to explain type 2 rationing. There is a group demand for credit but at a group interest rate.

Models of limited loan rate differentiation were developed in an attempt to extend the Hodgman analysis, but ended up raising more questions than answers. In Jaffee and

---

BOX 8.1   The Hodgman model

A risk-neutral bank is assumed to make a one-period loan to a firm. The firm's investment project provides outcome $\{x\}$, which has a minimum $\{l\}$ and maximum $\{u\}$ value; so $l < x < u$. The probability distribution function of x is described by $f(x)$. The contracted repayment is $(1 + r)L$, where L is the loan and r is the rate of interest. The bank obtains funds in the deposit market at a cost δ. Expected profit is given by the following function:

$$E(\pi) = \int_{l}^{(1+r)L} xf(x)\, dx + \int_{(1+r)L}^{u} (1 + r)Lf(x)\, dx - (1 + \delta)L \qquad (8.1.1)$$

If default occurs $(x < (1 + r)L)$ the bank receives x. The first term is the income the bank receives if $x < (1 + r)L$; that is, if there is a default. The second term represents bank income if the loan is repaid. The first two terms represent the weighted average of expected revenue from the loan. The weights are probabilistic outcomes. The third term is the bank's cost of funds.

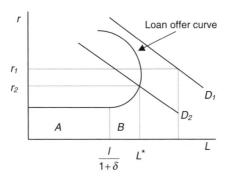

FIGURE 8.3 Type 1 Rationing.

Modigliani (1969) a monopolistic bank is assumed to face rigidities in the setting of differential loan rates. The question that arises in such models is: When is it optimal for a bank to set a rate of interest such that the demand exceeds supply, as in the case of D_1? The problem is that, by assuming constraints to setting interest rates, it should not be surprising that a non-market clearing outcome for the credit market could arise. The more interesting issue is the reasoning and origin for the constraints.

The origin of the practice of limited loan rate differentiation is to do with custom and practice, goodwill, legal constraints (such as usury laws) and institutional rigidities. Interest rates are kept at below market rates as a preferential price to blue-chip customers, emphasizing the customer–loan relationship. Such explanations recognize the fundamental nature of the loan market as being made up of heterogeneous customers. The lender is a price setter and the borrower is a price taker. Different borrowers have different quality characteristics. If the lender is a perfectly discriminating monopolist, it would lend according to the borrower's quality characteristics; hence, there would be no rationing. But the underpinnings of this approach remain ad hoc and not founded in theory.

8.4 ASYMMETRIC INFORMATION AND ADVERSE SELECTION

The move to an endogenous model that exhibits similar properties, using information, costs and costly screening, can be accommodated in the context of rational maximizing behaviour. The development of imperfect-information, endogenous rationing models includes elements of:

(1) *Asymmetric information.* This refers to the possibility that both sides to the transaction do not possess the same amount or quality of information. For example, it may be reasonable to assume that the borrower may have more information about the possible success of the project financed by a loan than the bank.

(2) *Adverse selection.* When the bank may select the wrong candidate, in the sense of the person more likely to default out of a series of loan applications.

(3) *Adverse incentives.* When the contracted interest rate creates an incentive for the borrower to take on greater risk than he/she otherwise would, so that the higher interest rate can be paid.

(4) *Moral hazard.* A situation when one of the parties to an agreement has an incentive to behave in a way that brings benefits to them but at the expense of the counterparty.

The implication of asymmetric information with adverse selection and moral hazard is explored by Jaffee and Russell (1976) to produce a model of type 1 rationing. The model is based on a two-period intertemporal consumption framework. Rationing occurs without the need to appeal to monopoly forces, as in Jaffee and Modigliani (1969). The bank faces two types of borrower: honest borrowers and dishonest borrowers. Honest borrowers will not borrow if they cannot repay, whereas dishonest borrowers will borrow knowing they will not repay. The bank knows that a certain proportion of the borrowers are dishonest but cannot differentiate between the two types (owing to the presence of asymmetric information). One equilibrium is that the bank offers the same interest rate to both types of borrower and rations credit to both. Any attempt to use the rate of interest to separate the two types of borrower could result in instability and a breakdown in the market. Because of adverse selection, in the absence of rationing or collateral requirements, an equilibrium may not even exist. The reasoning is that, if the bank attempts to price the risk of dishonest borrowers into the loan rate, the proportion of dishonest borrowers increases as honest borrowers drop out of the loan market. Adverse selection will have increased the riskiness to the bank which results in a further increase in interest rates and a worsening bout of adverse selection, and so on. The solution is to offer a common contract to both types of borrower, known as a pooling contract. A more formal presentation is presented in Box 8.2.

Honest borrowers have an incentive to set up a separate loan pool as they are subsidizing dishonest borrowers. However, dishonest borrowers will have an incentive to behave like honest borrowers. The optimal outcome is a pooling contract with a smaller loan size than loan demand.

8.5 ADVERSE INCENTIVE

Stiglitz and Weiss (1981) combine adverse incentive with adverse selection to produce a model of type 2 rationing. The interest rate produces not only a direct positive effect on the bank's return but also an indirect negative effect. This negative effect comes in two forms. Firstly, the interest rate charged affects the riskiness of the loan, which is the adverse selection effect. Secondly, the higher the rate of interest charged, the greater is the incentive to take on riskier projects, which is the adverse incentive effect. The relevant analysis is depicted in Figure 8.4.

BOX 8.2   A pooling contract

Each consumer receives current income y_1 and future income y_2, and has consumption c_1 and c_2. A loan is taken out to increase current consumption c_1:

$$c_1 = y_1 + L \qquad (8.2.1)$$
$$c_2 = y_2 - (1 + r)L \qquad (8.2.2)$$

The moral hazard problem occurs because borrower $\{i\}$ defaults on the loan if the cost of default $Z_i < (1 + r_L)L$. The cost of default varies over the population of borrowers. Honest borrowers have a higher Z value than dishonest borrowers. The bank does not know the individual Z values of its borrowers. But it does know that $\mu\%$ will repay loans, so its profit function is given by

$$E(\pi) = \mu(1 + r_L)L - (1 + r_F)L \qquad (8.2.3)$$

where r_F is the cost of funds. Maximizing profit:

$$\frac{\partial E(\pi)}{\partial L} = \mu(1 + r_L) - (1 + r_F) = 0 \qquad (8.2.4)$$

results in a pooling contract:

$$(1 + r_L) = \frac{(1 + r_F)}{\mu} \qquad (8.2.5)$$

All borrowers are offered the same contract.

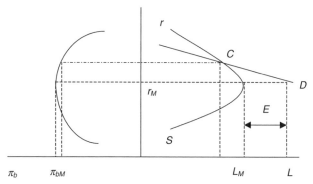

FIGURE 8.4 Type 2 Credit Rationing.

The left-hand side of the figure shows the profit–interest rate combination implied by the fact that profits decline after a particular rate of interest owing to the negative effect of interest rates on bank profits, discussed above. The maximum profit point is shown by π_{bM} and the profit-maximizing rate of interest is shown as r_M. The right-hand side of the figure shows the demand and supply of bank loans. The supply curve reflects the profit function shown on the left-hand side of Figure 8.4 and slopes backwards after the interest rate r_M. The demand for loans intersects the supply at an interest rate above the profit-maximizing rate r_M. For example, if the demand curve intersected the supply curve above r_M there would be no credit rationing. This is a stable equilibrium but is not a profit-maximizing equilibrium because the bank can increase profits by reducing the interest rate to r_M. The maximum loan supply is shown by L_M, which is greater than the loan demanded at the higher rate of interest but less than the loan quantity demanded. There is an excess demand for loans, shown by the range E, so the bank must ration credit between the prospective borrowers. The analysis is presented more formally in Box 8.3.

The weakness of the type 1 and 2 models of rationing is the reliance on the relative ignorance of the bank, i.e. the presence of asymmetric information. This is an odd assumption to make when, at the outset, the theory of banking is based on the notion that banks have a comparative advantage in information gathering. In the context of the rationing framework, it is arguable that the moral hazard (adverse incentives) and adverse selection effects are observable in a dynamic setting. Eventually, the bank, and, ultimately, the banking industry, will become aware of the characteristics of the risky borrowers and devise means of differentiating between the risky and safe borrowers *ex ante* based on past experience.

BOX 8.3   The Stiglitz–Weiss model

The assumptions of the models are as follows:

- There are many investors and each has a project requiring investment k.
- Each investor has wealth $W < k$.
- Each investor borrows to invest.
- All projects yield the same rate of return R but differ in risk.
- Successful projects yield R^*, failures yield 0. Probability of success is p_i.
- The probability density function of p_i is $f(p_i)$.
- So, $R = p_i R_i^*$, where R is the expected return on the project.
- Borrowing is described by $L = W - k$.
- Loans are a standard debt contract $(1 + r)L$.
- $R_i^* > (1 + r)L$.
- The asymmetry of information is that the investor knows the probability of success but not the bank.

The expected return to the individual investor is given by

$$E(\pi_i) = p_i(R_i^* - (1 + r)L) \qquad (8.3.1)$$

(continued)

The expected payoff to the bank is given by

$$E(\pi_b) = (1 + r)L \int_0^p p_i f(p_i) \, dp_i \tag{8.3.2}$$

where p is cutoff probability at which customers come to the bank for loans. The payoff to the investor is

$$E(\pi_i) = R - p_i(1 + r)L \tag{8.3.3}$$

High-risk investors are willing to pay more for the loan. So borrowing occurs if

$$E(\pi_i) \geq (1 + \delta)W$$

where δ is the safe rate of return.

By assumption, the higher the rate of interest, the riskier is the marginal project. This implies that

$$\frac{dp}{dr} < 0$$

The effect of an increase in loan rates to the bank is

$$\frac{dE(\pi_b)}{dr} = L \int_0^p p_i f(p_i) \, dp_i + \left(\frac{dp}{dr}\right)(1 + r)Lpf(p) \tag{8.3.4}$$

The first term of equation (8.3.4) says that a rise in the rate of interest increases repayments for those who repay. The second term says the higher the rate of interest the lower is the quality of the pool of applicants. Profit maximization occurs at

$$\frac{dE(\pi_b)}{dr} = 0 \tag{8.3.5}$$

which is as depicted in Figure 8.4.

8.6 SCREENING VERSUS RATIONING

One method of differentiating between borrower types is by adding the condition of collateral to the loan demanded; for example, deeds to the borrower's house. This provides safety for the bank because, in the case of default, it can sell the house and use the proceeds to pay off the loan. The bank cannot distinguish between the two types of borrower, but it offers alternative combinations of collateral and interest rates that ensure the same expected profit to the bank. Assume that both types of borrower are equally risk averse but the safe borrowers have a preference for a high collateral–low interest rate combination. The risky borrowers, knowing the riskiness of their projects, would be unwilling to commit their own assets as

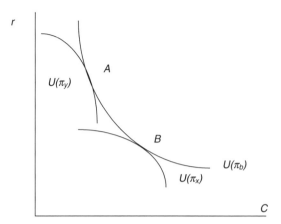

FIGURE 8.5 Screening with Collateral.

collateral and would prefer a low collateral–high interest rate combination. Figure 8.5 illustrates how collateral may be used as a way of screening between borrower types. The bank has an isoprofit curve $U(\pi_b)$, which shows the bank's indifference between collateral $\{C\}$ and interest rate combinations $\{r\}$. The bank has the same expected profit for each point along the isoprofit curve. Borrower X is a safe borrower and borrower Y is a risky borrower. Their respective isoprofit curves (i.e. $U(\pi_y)$ and $U(\pi_x)$) are drawn concave to the axis because both interest rate and collateral appear as costs in their profit functions. Borrower X is willing to provide more collateral for each combination of interest rate than borrower Y. Hence, borrower X's isoprofit curve is lower and to the right of borrower Y's isoprofit curve.

The isoprofit curve $U(\pi_x)$ describes the combination of $\{C, r\}$ that gives the same expected profit for the safe borrower and $U(\pi_y)$ for the risky borrower. The preferred combination for the risky borrower is that shown by the tangency point A, whereas the preferred combination for the safe borrower is B. By revealing their preferences, the bank can price the loan appropriately as a combination of collateral and interest rate for different types of borrower. In the extreme case, as discussed by Bester (1985), the risky borrower would accept a contract that has zero collateral and high interest and the safe borrower would accept a contract with low interest rate and high collateral.

The real-world practice of banks charging higher interest rates for unsecured loans, compared with loans secured on the collateral of property, may be considered as good enough evidence in favour of this model. However, the theory is not complete. Because of decreasing absolute risk aversion, wealthier borrowers would be less risk averse than less wealthy borrowers.[1] Consequently, if the risky borrowers were less risk averse because they were wealthier, they would be able to commit higher levels of collateral, whereas safe borrowers being less wealthy and more risk averse would commit less. While the theory appears sound, as Goodhart (1989) has commented, 'it would be an unusual bank manager in the real world who was seen to seek out poorer clients and refuse loans to wealthier clients',

---

[1] Absolute risk aversion is a measure of the degree of an individual's aversion to small gambles of a fixed absolute size.

on the theoretical assumption that wealthier clients are more risky than poorer ones.[2] In contrast to the theoretical objection to the collateral screening framework, evidence from a study conducted by National Economic Research Associates (1990) shows that collateral is a good signal of project success and, therefore, of the riskiness of a project. The default rate for borrowers who had not offered collateral was 40% compared with 14% for those who had.

The credit-rationing issue has spawned a wide literature that explains the theoretical existence of the phenomenon. Some studies have focused on the customer–loan relationship where traditionally the notion of 'jointness' has been used to explain type 2 rationing. Banks that have a loan relationship with their customers will favour them over others because the granting of favourable loan conditions is expected to generate demand for other bank services in the future. The foundation of the Stiglitz–Weiss model is a principal–agent problem.[3]

An alternative approach based on asymmetric information is suggested by De Meza and Webb (1987), who develop a model in which asymmetric information causes good projects to draw in bad ones. The key to this model is twofold: (a) banks know the average probability of the success of projects but not the probability of specific projects; (b) the success of any project depends on the ability of the borrower, which is not readily apparent. Borrowers are risk neutral and face the same distribution of returns but differ in ability. The bank is assumed to be unable to discriminate by ability. The marginal borrower (i.e. the borrower with low ability) has a lower probability of success than the average and has expected earnings below the opportunity cost of funds supplied by the bank. In this set-up, there is overlending because the bank is subsidizing marginal borrowers by lending to unprofitable projects. Entrepreneurial optimism only worsens the situation and also helps explain the periodic bouts of overlending conducted by banks during boom periods.

8.7 THE EXISTENCE OF CREDIT RATIONING

An important contribution to the controversy is made by Hansen and Thatcher (1983) who question the very existence of credit rationing, as exemplified by the Stiglitz–Weiss approach. Their approach distinguishes between the effect on the loan size of the promised loan contract rate and the loan contract quality or risk class.

The rate charged on the loan (i.e. the loan contract price) depends on the risk quality of the particular loan (or loan class) and shocks to the risk-free rate of interest. The risk quality of the loan is measured by the size of the loan (L) divided by the amount of collateral offered (C). The risk quality of a loan will decrease as either L decreases or C increases. The loan contract price increases with either increases in risk quality or the risk-free rate of interest. The loan contract price is given by $r = r(\phi,\theta)$, where $\phi = L/C$ and θ represents a vector of conditions. The riskless rate of interest is $r = r(0,\theta)$.

The analysis is presented diagrammatically in Figure 8.6, with the size of loan demanded on the horizontal axis and the risk-free rate on the vertical axis. The demand curve for loans

---

[2] Goodhart (1989, p. 175).

[3] An alternative approach is that of Fried and Howitt (1980) who approach the problem as an equilibrium risk-sharing arrangement. In this approach, the risk-averse bank insures the risk-averse borrowers from variable interest rates by offering fixed (or slowly adjusting) rates rather than spot market rates. In the Fried–Howitt set-up, rationing can occur in periods when spot interest rates rise above borrower-contracted rates.

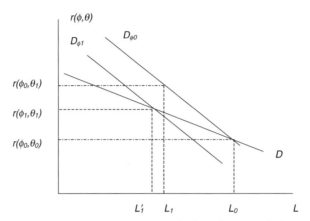

FIGURE 8.6 Hansen and Thatcher Model.

given the quantity of risk category slopes downwards because, as the risk-free rate falls, the loan price also falls, causing an increased demand for loans.

The initial demand curve D_{ϕ_0} is drawn for a given and constant risk category (ϕ_0) and the equilibrium is shown at L_0. The effect of a rise in the risk-free rate for the same quality of loan is shown by $r(\phi_0, \theta_1)$ and the loan size demanded is now L_1. The rise in the interest rate and its effect on loan demand can be decomposed into two effects: a 'pure demand effect' and a 'loan quality effect'. The pure demand effect is shown by a movement along the demand curve from $L_0, r(\phi_0, \theta_0)$ to $L_1, r(\phi_0, \theta_1)$. However, the rise in the loan rate may cause the borrower to alter the quality of the loan by varying the quantity of collateral. Suppose, for example, the rise in the riskless rate causes the borrower to raise the quality of the loan. This is shown in Figure 8.6 by the shift inwards of the demand curve to D_{ϕ_1}. The new equilibrium for loans becomes L_1'. The improvement in the loan quality opted for by the borrower augments the pure demand effect and leads to a lower loan size, giving the impression of being rationed. But this is a self-rationing outcome. The borrower elects a smaller loan size at a lower loan rate. Thus, the finding that banks are unwilling to lend an unlimited amount of funds at a particular rate of interest is not an argument that supports the existence of credit rationing. The analysis is presented more formally in Box 8.4.

The notion that the loan-pricing function is more complicated than the loan interest rate raises all sorts of issues concerning the non-interest elements of the price. It can be argued that the loan-pricing function includes conditions of the loan that vary with the loan size. The promised loan contract rate is the standard loan rate for what appears to be a standard debt contract. For a larger loan size, the contract includes other conditions such as collateral, periodic monitoring, maturity, fee, reporting and, in the extreme case, a representative of the bank on the board of directors. These may be conditions that the borrower is unwilling to meet, in which case the borrower may opt for a lower loan size. The result is that the borrower goes to the bank with a desired loan, as shown in Figure 8.7, of L_0 at a perceived loan price of $r_0 = r(\phi_0, \theta_0)$, where θ describes the conditions of the loan and θ_0 means that there are no conditions except for loan repayment at the specified rate. After realizing the true price of the loan, the borrower chooses a lower loan size, shown as L_1, at a loan price including condition θ_1. This is a self-rationing outcome and could not be viewed as the same type 1 class of credit rationing examined in the literature.

It is clear that the debate on the issue of credit rationing has barely left the theoretical level. The theoretical existence or non-existence of credit rationing does not seem to have influenced the attitudes of policy makers and commissions of enquiry. The Wilson Committee (1979) took the view that the conditions of the loans for small- and medium-sized enterprises (SMEs) were severe and created de facto rationing. The Cruikshank Review (Cruikshank, 2000) examined the overdependence of SMEs on the banks because of the inadequacy of capital market finance. Goodhart (1989), at the time a senior economic adviser at the Bank of England, stated that, although economic theory can devise efficient contracts that may eliminate credit rationing in theory, 'in practice it exists'. This assertion is reminiscent of the old joke that an economist sees something working in practice and asks: Does it work in theory?

BOX 8.4   Hansen and Thatcher

The loan contract price is given by $r = r(\phi, \theta)$, where $\phi = L/C$ (a measure of the risk class) and C is collateral or own equity, and θ represents shocks to the riskless rate. The promised loan rate is a convex function of the loan risk class, so

$$r_\phi = \frac{\partial r}{\partial \phi} > 0, \quad r_{\phi\phi} > \frac{\partial^2 r}{\partial \phi^2} > 0$$

The riskless rate of interest is $r(0, \theta)$, and for any particular riskless rate there is a loan-rate-pricing function that is convex in risk class. The loan-contract-pricing function also has the property that

$$r_\theta = \frac{\partial r}{\partial \theta} > 0$$

The loan-contract-pricing function has the condition that increasing risk premiums are required for increasingly risky loan contracts. Also, the level of the interest rate is higher for higher levels of the riskless rate. Shocks to the riskless rate affect both the loan contract size and the loan contract quality. The total effect of an increase in the riskless rate of interest on the loan size is decomposed into two effects: a 'pure demand effect' and a 'loan quality effect':

$$\frac{dL}{d\theta} = \frac{\partial L}{\partial \theta}\bigg|_{d\phi=0} - \frac{\partial L}{\partial \phi}\bigg|_{d\theta=0} \left(\frac{d\phi}{d\theta}\right)$$

The second part of the right-hand side of this expression is the product of the effect on the loan size of a change in the loan quality risk class at the initial riskless rate and the effect on the loan quality of a change in the riskless rate. The higher riskless rate of interest may cause the loan quality to worsen or improve, based on the ratio of loan to collateral offered by the borrower. Basically, the sign of $d\phi/d\theta$ is ambiguous. Suppose the rise in the riskless rate causes the borrower to raise the quality of the loan, the borrower will demand a lower loan size than that given by the pure demand effect of a rise in the loan rate.

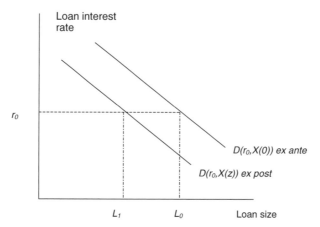

FIGURE 8.7 Loan Price Misperception.

8.8 SUMMARY

- It is taken for granted that credit rationing exists.
- A number of studies for the government and small-business pressure groups testify to its existence.
- The persistent existence of a non-market-clearing outcome in the credit market is hard to explain.
- Economic theory has explained that credit rationing may be an optimal outcome and does not need to appeal to ad hoc explanations or regulation to explain its existence.
- The relevant theory used is not without fault and is not unquestionable.
- The primary role of asymmetric information is hard to sustain in a dynamic setting and in a world where banks continue to gather and process information on their clients.
- Screening via collateral requirements plays a potentially important role in refuting the theoretical case for credit rationing.

QUESTIONS

1 What is the availability doctrine?

2 Explain the difference between exogenous and endogenous credit rationing.

3 What do you understand by type 1 and type 2 rationing?

4 Explain what you understand by the following terms: (a) asymmetric information, (b) moral hazard, (c) adverse selection.

5 Review the implications of adverse incentives for the explanation of credit rationing.

TEST QUESTIONS

1 Critically comment on the argument that profit-maximizing banks would not ration credit because of the many alternative sources of funding available to the borrower.

2 Credit rationing is not really the result of market failure but a failure on the part of the borrower to appreciate the true price of credit'. Discuss.

CHAPTER 9

Securitization

MINI-CONTENTS

9.1 Introduction
9.2 Sales of securities through financial markets
9.3 Asset-backed securitization (ABS)
9.4 The process of asset-backed securitization
9.5 The gains from asset-backed securitization
9.6 Conclusions
9.7 Summary

9.1 INTRODUCTION

In this chapter we consider the role of securitization in banking and we concentrate on the economics of the process rather than the precise administrative detail. It is first of all necessary to distinguish between securitization *per se* and asset-backed securitization (ABS). Cumming (1987) defines securitization as the process of 'matching up of borrowers and savers wholly or partly by way of financial markets'. This definition includes: (i) the issuing of financial securities by firms as opposed to raising loans from banks; (ii) deposits with non-bank financial intermediaries who themselves hold financial securities; (iii) asset-backed securities – i.e. sales of financial securities – which are themselves backed by other financial assets. In Section 9.2 we consider sales of securities through financial markets, which involves a measure of disintermediation, and in Section 9.3 we consider asset-backed securitization. The process of ABS is discussed in Section 9.4 and the gains from the process are considered in Section 9.5. Our conclusions are presented in Section 9.6.

First of all it is useful to consider intermediation as a bundle of separate services, namely:

1. Location of a creditworthy borrower, i.e. *loan origination.*
2. Funds secured through designing securities that are attractive to savers, in the case of bank deposits, i.e. *loan funding.*

3. Administering and enforcing loan conditions, i.e. *loan servicing*.
4. Holding the loan in the lender's portfolio of assets, i.e. *loan warehousing*.

These services can easily be unbundled into their separate components. For example, a bank can check out the creditworthiness of a prospective borrower (loan origination) and pass on the debt by selling it to another institution. This is the process of ABS discussed in Section 9.3. Alternatively, the whole process can be bypassed by selling securities directly on the capital market, and we discuss this process in Section 9.2.

As a prerequisite to the study of securitization, it is instructive to describe the cost to the bank of holding loans on the balance sheet and the cost to the borrower of the loan. As a prerequisite to the study of securitization, it is also instructive to set up a simple model of bank lending describing the cost of holding loans (*CHL*) on a bank's balance sheet and the cost to the borrower of the loan. For a loan to be profitable to the bank, the lending rate must cover the sum of (i) the deposit rate plus any insurance premium, (ii) the return on the capital required by that loan, (iii) administrative costs involved in making and monitoring the loan, (iv) regulatory costs and (v) the expected default rate on loans.[1] This is captured in equation (9.1) and derived from Box 9.1, where the *CHL* represents the cost to the bank of holding loans on its books:

$$CHL = er_E + \left(\frac{1 - e}{1 - k}\right)(r_D + g) + C_L + \rho \tag{9.1}$$

where e is the capital-to-asset ratio, k is the required reserve ratio, r_E is the required rate of return on equity, C_L is the marginal administrative and servicing costs, ρ is the expected rate of loan default, r_D is the deposit rate and g represents the regulatory costs including deposit insurance.

Assuming that the bank is a price taker (i.e. the market is competitive), the price, the loan rate (r_L), will equal the marginal cost of attracting funds, so

$$r_L = er_E + \left(\frac{1 - e}{1 - k}\right)(r_D + g) + C_L + \rho \tag{9.2}$$

Thus, the spread (S_L) between the loan rate and the deposit rate is given by

$$S_L = er_E + \left(\frac{1 - e}{1 - k}\right)(r_D + g) + C_L + \rho - r_D \tag{9.3}$$

Hence, S_L will rise with a rise in r_E, e (provided $r_E > r_D/(1 - k)$), k and g.

From the above expression we can see that more onerous capital requirements (e) and regulatory costs (g) would have tended to raise S_L in the absence of a fall in marginal operating costs (C_L), as discussed in Chapter 1. The influence of these increased costs on firms' borrowing from banks is discussed in Chapter 9, Section 9.2.2.

We now turn to an examination of the sales of securities through financial markets.

---

[1] For the sake of ease of exposition, (i) we assume the expected loss rate is constant across loans at any point of time and (ii) we ignore income taxes and loan fees.

BOX 9.1   Cost to the bank of holding loans on its balance sheet

The balance sheet of the representative bank is given by

$$L + R = D + E \tag{9.1.1}$$

where L is loans, R is reserves, D is deposits and E is equity capital.

Assume that the bank faces a required reserve ratio $k = R/D$ and a capital–asset ratio $e = E/L$. Then the balance sheet can be written as

$$L + kD = D + eL$$

$$L(1 - e) = D(1 - k) \tag{9.1.2}$$

or

$$D = \frac{(1 - e)}{(1 - k)}L$$

Let the required return on equity be denoted by r_E, the expected rate of loan default by ρ, the loan rate by r_L, the deposit rate by r_D, the regulatory costs including insurance by g and the administrative cost function by the function $C(L)$, with $C_L > 0$. The objective of the bank is to maximize expected profit subject to the balance sheet constraint

$$E(\pi) = r_L L - r_D D - r_E E - \rho L - C(L) - gD \tag{9.1.3}$$

Substituting from (9.1.2) above yields

$$E(\pi) = r_L L - r_D\left(\frac{1 - e}{1 - k}\right)L - r_E eL - \rho L - C(L) - g\left(\frac{1 - e}{1 - k}\right)L$$

Optimizing with respect to L and taking the first-order conditions gives

$$\frac{dE(\pi)}{dL} = r_L - r_D\left(\frac{1 - e}{1 - k}\right) - r_E e - \rho - C_L - g\left(\frac{1 - e}{1 - k}\right) = 0$$

Rearranging this expression, we have equation (9.2) in the text:

$$r_L = er_E + \left(\frac{1 - e}{1 - k}\right)(r_D + g) + C_L + \rho$$

9.2 SALES OF SECURITIES THROUGH FINANCIAL MARKETS

This type of securitization can be considered as involving three categories, namely direct replacement of debt claims (Section 9.2.1), direct placement of debt claims underwritten in the financial markets (Section 9.2.2) and holdings of securities by non-banks through deposit replacement (Section 9.2.3). One of the main reasons for this type of securitization is that many large borrowers have had a higher credit rating than the lending banks themselves and can therefore raise finance by tapping financial markets at a lower cost than by borrowing from banks. Secondly, regulatory costs have risen. There are two components to this cost: (1) the cost external to the banks, namely that of the regulator; (2) the costs incurred directly by banks in providing the administrative detail necessary for prudential control and also deposit insurance. It is this latter cost that is represented by g in equation (9.1), and it is argued that this has increased over recent years. This raises the spread between loan and deposit rates, as shown in equation (9.2), and provides an impetus for sales of securities through financial markets. Thirdly, there has been a considerable growth in technology, which permits the development of more sophisticated financial instruments.

9.2.1 Direct Replacement

Direct replacement requires the replacement of bank loans with the sale of securities such as bonds or equity on the financial markets. Most sales of such securities are underwritten by financial institutions, so the banks and other institutions are involved.

9.2.2 Underwritten Replacement

As noted above, most issues of long-term securities, such as bonds and new issues of equity, are underwritten. This involves a financial institution agreeing to buy up any of the securities that are not taken up by the market. Both parties to the agreement benefit. The issuer is guaranteed that the whole issue is taken up and, therefore, certainty regarding the volume of funds raised. From its viewpoint, the financial institution receives a fee for providing the guarantee.

The same is true for short-term lending by way of commercial paper and quasi-short-term lending, such as note issuance facilities (NIFs) and floating-rate notes (FRNs). In the case of NIFs, borrowers issue a stream of short-term notes for a given period underwritten by financial institutions on a rollover basis of 1–6 months, whereby the interest rate is automatically adjusted at each rollover date in accordance with a reference rate, such as the London interbank offer rate (LIBOR). At each stage the underwriter guarantees the issue so that the issue is guaranteed funds for the medium term. FRNs are similar, with maturities of between 5 and 15 years, but are mainly issued by financial institutions.

It can be seen, therefore, that alternatives to bank loans exist. Commercial paper has partially replaced bank loans at the short end of the market, and NIFs have tended to replace bank lending, particularly syndicated lending, for longer-term loans. Nevertheless, banks are involved in view of their underwriting of issues of securities, so that securitization has only partially replaced the role of banks in financial intermediation.

The cost of raising funds in the capital market is defined by

$$r_F = r_I + u \qquad (9.4)$$

where r_F is the cost of funds raised in the capital market, r_I is the return to the investor and u represents issue costs including any credit rating fees expressed as a spread. As shown earlier, the cost of funds raised by deposits (r_L – see equation (9.3)) equals $r_D + S_L$. Firms will be indifferent to raising funds through the capital market and deposits when $r_F = r_L$ or when

$$r_I + u = r_D + S_L \qquad (9.5)$$

This implies that, as the spread rises on bank lending, the cost to firms of raising funds through banks becomes higher and there will be increased recourse to the capital markets. In other words, the total cost of obtaining funds from the capital markets, including underwriting and rating fees (where appropriate), must be less than the costs of borrowing from banks. As we have already stated, this might be the case because of increased costs for banks owing to regulatory factors (g), the development of liability management and higher deposit rates due to competition biting into the 'endowment effect' and also due to a lower credit rating for some banks.[2]

9.2.3 Deposit Replacement

Deposits can be characterized by nominal value certainty and a high degree of liquidity. Certificates of deposit (CDs)[3] do not quite fit this characterization because they are subject to variation, albeit quite small, in nominal value until their maturity. Nevertheless, it seems reasonable to class CDs as a type of deposit in spite of this caveat. Retail savers tend to hold claims on banks in the form of deposits and institutional savers in a wide range of bank claims including subordinated debt and equity as well as deposits. Recently, there has been a marked tendency to hold security claims via other non-bank financial intermediaries. This can be illustrated by the figures shown in Table 9.1, which indicate faster rates of growth of UK non-bank financial intermediaries as compared with the banks themselves, although the absolute value of the outstanding liabilities of the banks (including building societies) is still larger than that of any of the other individual groups of institutions.

A characteristic of the non-bank institutions is that they accept funds and then use these funds to purchase both real and financial securities. Hence, the public is indirectly holding securities, thus bypassing the intermediation role of the banks. It must be admitted that pension fund and life assurance company liabilities are long-term and, therefore, not close substitutes for bank deposits. This is, however, not so for the last category of financial institutions in this table, which are in reality cooperative holders of equity and other financial securities. Furthermore, holders of their liabilities can liquidate their holdings quickly.

---

[2] A good example of a bank with a poor credit rating was BCCI. Because of its low credit standing, BCCI had to have a higher rate of interest in the money market for any funds raised. This enabled institutions with a better credit standing to undertake arbitrage by borrowing funds in the market and on-lending them to BCCI at a higher rate. Obviously, a loss was involved in this arbitrage when BCCI was closed and became bankrupt.

[3] CDs are discussed in Box 4.1.

TABLE 9.1 Liability growth of UK financial institutions, 1987–2006

	Percentage growth
Banks and building societies	266
Pension funds	366
Life assurance companies	561
Unit trusts, OEICs[a] and investment trusts	659

[a] Open-ended investment companies.

Source: Financial Statistics, Office for National Statistics online database.

What has led to the faster rate of growth of the non-bank financial intermediaries? One reason is that, while bank deposits are fixed in nominal terms, their real value and their real return vary with inflation if the rate of interest does not fully compensate for inflation. In contrast, the real return on the liabilities of non-bank financial institutions over the medium term has been higher than that for bank deposits. Secondly, there is probably a wealth effect present with the growth in wealth-favouring securities, which offer long-term benefits in the form of pensions and life insurance.

We now move on to the second broad category of securitization, i.e. asset-backed securitization.

9.3 ASSET-BACKED SECURITIZATION (ABS)

This is a process whereby illiquid assets are pooled together and sold off to investors as a composite financial security that includes the future cash proceeds. The essence of this type of securitization is a present payment in return for future streams of income. The purchaser of the composite financial security finances the purchase through the issue of other financial securities which are termed asset-backed securities.

The types of asset that are securitized are varied, but the concept of securitization can be applied to any asset that has readily ascertainable future streams of income. A wide range of assets meet this criterion and, therefore, have been sold as ABS, particularly by banks but also by other financial institutions and private individuals. One example of this latter category was by David Bowie who raised $55m through the issue of bonds backed by future royalties on previously issued albums. The categories of assets more usually securitized include collateralized debt obligations (CDOs), which include collateralized loan obligations (CLOs) and collateralized bond obligations (CBOs), credit card obligations, auto loans, loans and mortgages. The split-up between the European issues of these various categories for the year 2006 is shown in Table 9.2, from which it can be seen that by far the largest component was mortgage-backed securities (MBSs), roughly 66% (of which roughly 80% consisted of residential mortgages), followed by CDOs[4] at roughly 20%. Residential mortgages are a particularly

---

[4] Collateralized debt obligations (CDOs) are packages of securitized loans issued by banks and other financial institutions.

TABLE 9.2 Composition of European securitization in 2006

Category	Percentage of total
Auto loans	2.5
Credit card	0.7
Loans	3.4
CDOs	19.2
Receivables*	1.3
Other	6.4
MBSs	66.5
Total	*100*

* Includes lease, phone bills, healthcare, train and project receivables.
Source: ESF Securitisation Data Report, Winter 2007.

attractive type of asset to securitize given the large number of different borrowers contained in such an ABS. This spreads the risk if they are genuinely different.[5]

In the case of issues of ABS by banks, their role in the process of intermediation is not eliminated but changed. In other words, some of the bundle of separate activities discussed above are sold separately while still retaining the overall function of intermediation. In particular, ABS removes the fourth function from the banks but still leaves the function of originating the loan with them.

The first issue of an ABS occurred in the US during the 1970s, whereas the first issue in the UK was in 1985. Securitization issues in Europe for 1996 were just short of €40bn but had risen to a total issue during 2006 of €458.9bn, an increase of 580.6% or an average of 28.8% per annum over the whole period. This growth is depicted in Figure 9.1. Note that the European market is dwarfed by that in the USA — comparative figures for 2005 were

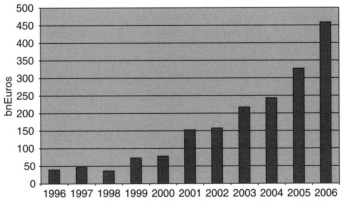

FIGURE 9.1 European Securitization 1996–2006.

[5] The problem in 2007 with subprime mortgages was that they were not intrinsically different and the risk was cumulative rather than diversified.

€327bn as against $3.07trn. The premier European market for ABS was the UK, which accounted for some 50% of the total issues in 2006, with the next highest being Spain and Germany with 11.9 and 10.2% of the total issues.

In Section 9.4 we will look at the process of issuing ABS.

9.4 THE PROCESS OF ASSET-BACKED SECURITIZATION

As we have noted above, the process of securitization involves the issuer pooling together a large number of (typically 100–150) securities into a single asset with a large denomination. For example, the total value of a CDO known as Tullas was $304m, of which the securities of the bankrupt Italian firm Parmalat amounted to $17m (*Financial Times*, 16/1/2004). The securities forming the ABS are grouped together by the source bank (termed the originator) in a range or tranche that is likely to prove acceptable to the ultimate buyers.

A special entity is set up specifically for the transaction. This vehicle is known as a special-purpose vehicle (SPV) or special-purpose entity (SPE) or, if the special entity is a company, a special-purpose company (SPC). This entity is completely separate from the bank and is what is called 'bankrupt remote'; in other words, if the originator becomes bankrupt, no claims can be made against the SPV. Often the form of organization is a trust. The SPV then buys the asset tranche from the originator and finances its purchase by borrowing in the markets against the assets purchased (hence the term asset-backed securities), which it holds in trust on their behalf. Frequently the bank continues to service the loan and passes any receipts on to the SPV.

These securities receive credit enhancement in the form of a guarantee from a bank (this may be the originator) or insurance company. This permits the securities to be rated by a credit agency and then sold on the market in tranches, the composition of which is designed to meet customers' preferences (Box 9.2 illustrates). This part of the process is essential as the key to the whole process is the marketability of the financial claims issued by the SPV. If the claims are not marketable, the whole process fails as the banks will not be able to remove the assets from their balance sheet. In fact, in some cases the asset-backed securities sold may have a higher rating than the originator owing to the credit enhancement process.[6] In contrast, bonds issued by a bank and with a pool of assets acting as collateral would be subject to the credit rating of the originating bank.

This process is illustrated in Figure 9.2.

We now move on to consider the gains from ABS from the banks' point of view.

9.5 THE GAINS FROM ASSET-BACKED SECURITIZATION

Banks gain a number of benefits from ABS. Firstly, issuing ABS is equivalent to raising additional funds since the securitized loans are removed from the balance sheet and are replaced with cash. The decision to engage in ABS by a bank will depend on the cost for the bank

---

[6] For example, in January 2002, Ford Motor Company's credit rating was downgraded but ABS issued by Ford Motor Credit continued to attract a 'Triple A' status.

BOX 9.2   Tranching 分档

The SPV produces the tranches of ABSs by obtaining credit enhancements that raise the ratings granted it by the credit rating agencies. These enhancements are typically provided by the originating bank and can take the form of standby letters of credit to the SPV right through to repurchase agreements of the most junior securities issued by the SPV. The securities issued by the SPV are rated from AAA to unrated debt securities. The bulk of an issue is senior rated debt and is AAA. Unrated debt is often referred to as the 'equity tranche'. It is not equity but, because of its high-risk status, it is thought of as equity because effectively all of the default risk in a particular issue is concentrated in this bottom tranche. An example of a securitization issued in tranches is the Bristol and West issue in 1994 of a £150m securitization of commercial loans on investment property (example taken from an MMF workshop held at the University of Essex on 9 November 2007 – Wolfe (2007)). The issue was through an SPV that issued 15-year floating-rate euro notes in four tranches. Credit rating was provided by Standard and Poor. Table 9.3 provides the details.

TABLE 9.3 Bristol and West Securitization 1994

Tranche	Amount	Spread	Rating
Senior class A	£123.75m	LIBOR + 28 bp	AAA
Class M1	£16.5m	LIBOR + 110 bp	A
Class M2	£5.25m	LIBOR + 130 bp	BBB
Class B	£4.5m	LIBOR + 425 bp	Unrated

Source: Wolfe (2007).

The unrated tranche was not sold and was retained by the originator on its balance sheets. During the mid-1990s the equity tranche retained by the originating bank was of the order of 7% of its capital. However, as investor appetite grew during the late 1990s and into the new century, approximately 1% of the capital structure of the originating banks was assigned to the equity tranche. Much of the unrated debt was taken up by hedge funds.

The unrated debt held by the originating bank attracts a high capital charge (this is examined in Chapter 12), and banks have typically undertaken complex financial transactions to return the debt to the balance sheet disguised as another instrument that attracts a lower capital charge (see Wolfe, 2004).

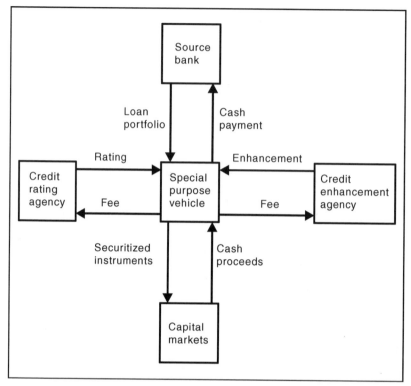

FIGURE 9.2 The Process of Securitization.

of raising funds in this manner being lower than attracting deposits or issuing bonds. The condition necessary for this is:

$$C_P + C_H + C_R < \min(r_D, r_B) \qquad (9.6)$$

where C_P are cash proceeds from ABS, C_H are credit enhancement costs, C_R are credit rating agency fees, r_D is the cost of attracting deposits and r_B is the cost of raising finance through bond issues.

As we have noted, this is often likely to be the case owing to slippages in the banks' own credit rating. It may also help low-rated banks, which have to pay a relatively high rate to raise funds (a high r_D or r_B), to achieve new funds by issuing an ABS at a significantly lower cost. Box 9.3 shows a model linking the theory of bank behaviour and the decision to securitize. It demonstrates that the cost of raising finance through securitization depends positively on a weighted average of the return on reserves and that of bank equity. It also shows that an increase in capital adequacy requirements would lead to an increase in securitization. What Box 9.3 shows is that regulatory capital requirements can be a strong incentive to securitize. If capital requirements on a particular class of loans are greater than that merited by the loan, banks will have an incentive to offload or securitize the loan (see also Pennacchi, 1988). This links directly to the second point listed below.

BOX 9.3 Theory of the banking firm and the decision to securitize

The start for this analysis is a simple bank balance sheet:

$$L + R = D + E \tag{9.3.1}$$

The bank securitizes some of its loan portfolio, so the balance sheet[7] is now changed to

$$L - S + R = D + E$$

or

$$L + R = S + D + E \tag{9.3.2}$$

where S represents asset-backed securities and the other symbols are the same as in Box 9.1. The balance sheet in (9.3.2) implies that the bank can finance its assets by attracting deposits, raising new capital or through securitization.

The capital requirement is now

$$E = e(L - S) \tag{9.3.3}$$

with $0 < e < 1$.

The bank's objective is to maximize profits given by

$$\pi = r_R R + r_L L - r_D D - r_E E - g D - r_S S \tag{9.3.4}$$

where r_S is the return on asset-backed securities. Other interest rates are the same as in Box 9.1.

The demand for bank loans and bank deposits is given by the functions

$$D^d = D(r_D), \quad D' > 0 \tag{9.3.5}$$

$$L^d = L(r_L), \quad L' < 0 \tag{9.3.6}$$

Additionally, the demand for asset-backed securities is given by

$$S^d = S(r_S), \quad S' > 0 \tag{9.3.7}$$

From the balance sheet (9.3.2) we have

$$R = S + D + E - L \tag{9.3.8}$$

Substituting on the right-hand side of (9.3.8) from the definitions above gives

$$R = S(r_s) + D(r_D) + e\{L(r_L) - S(r_S)\} - L(r_L)$$

(continued)

---

[7] We recognize that the values of D and E must have altered following the securitization, but we abstract from this change for the purposes of simplicity.

or

$$R = S(R_S)(1 - e) + D(r_D) - L(r_L)(1 - e) \qquad (9.3.9)$$

Substituting (9.3.5), (9.3.6), (9.3.7) and (9.3.9) into the profit function (9.3.4) gives

$$\pi = r_R\{S(r_S)(1 - e) + D(r_D) - L(r_L)(1 - e)\} + r_L L(r_L) - r_D D(r_D)$$
$$- r_E e\{L(r_L) - S(r_S)\} - g D(r_D) - r_S S(r_S) \qquad (9.3.10)$$

Maximizing with respect to r_D, r_L, r_R and r_S gives the usual optimality conditions. Taking the optimality condition with respect to r_S gives

$$\frac{\partial \pi}{\partial r_S} = r_R(1 - e)S' + r_e e S' - r_S S' - S = 0 \qquad (9.3.11)$$

Solving (9.3.11) for r_S gives

$$r_S = r_R(1 - e) + r_e e - \frac{S}{S'} \qquad (9.3.12)$$

The optimal interest return on ABSs is positively related to a weighted average of the return on reserves and the return on bank equity. By differentiating (9.3.12) with respect to the capital adequacy requirement δ, we can see that

$$\frac{\partial r_S}{\partial e} = r_e - r_R \qquad (9.3.13)$$

An increase in bank capital adequacy requirement (e) leads to a rise in the return on securitization given that the return on bank equity is above the return on reserves, which from (9.3.7) leads to an increase in securitization. A rise in e increases the incentive to remove capital-intensive loans from the balance sheet. Thus, higher capital adequacy will lead to greater securitization.

Secondly, they remove assets from their balance sheet, thus easing pressure from capital regulations. According to the current regulations arising from agreement reached by the Basel Committee on Banking Supervision (1988), a bank must maintain capital equal to at least 8% of the total of its risk-adjusted assets.[8] In this risk weighting, commercial loans carry a weighting of 100% irrespective of the quality of the borrower. Consequently, removal of a tranche of loans eases pressure on capital and permits the bank to engage in other profitable activities, as their capital requirement is restricted to the equity retained by the bank which is clearly lower than the tranche of loans securitized.

[8] The current 'Basel' regulations and proposed amendments are discussed in Chapter 11.

Third, ABSs generally contain high-grade loans that, as noted earlier, are subject to the same capital requirements as lower-grade loans that provide higher yields.[9] Thus, ABS permits the raising of returns for banks by securitizing high-grade loans with relatively low returns and retaining lower-grade loans with higher returns.

Fourthly, securitization provides a means for a bank to manage its risk. By parcelling up asset-backed securities which are then sold on to other institutions, the risk is spread around and is therefore less concentrated. Furthermore, if the bank feels its loans are too heavily directed to a particular borrower or borrowers, or region or industry, it can achieve a greater degree of diversification by removing some loans from its portfolio through the issue of ABS. Another source of risk reduction is that banks can increase their liquidity by selling illiquid loans and replacing them with more liquid assets such as government securities. This claim for risk reduction is subject to a number of caveats. Funds in the money market may be restricted so that renewal of ABS may be difficult, as occurred for the Northern Rock bank (formerly a building society) in the UK during the autumn of 2007 (see Box 7.3 for further discussion of this problem). Consequently, Northern Rock was faced with liquidity problems and was forced to obtain emergency funds from the Bank of England.[10] Additionally, the originating bank may have agreed credit lines with the SPV for support if its money market funding source dries up. If this latter does occur, then the risk is not completely removed from the originating bank. The role of the US subprime mortgage problems in connection with risk management is examined in Box 9.4.

Finally, in this connection securitization has, to some extent, changed the nature of bank lending. Previously, banks used a considerable amount of credit analysis as they would hold the loan on their balance sheets for the full maturity of the loan. With securitization the loan is in fact sold to the capital markets and the credit ratings move to the forefront of the process. This raises the question of the reliability of credit ratings. The *Financial Times* 27/8/2007 reported a study by Bloomberg Markets showing that corporate bonds with a Baa rating had a 2.2% failure rate over 5-year periods from 1983 to 2005. This contrasts with CDOs with the same grade, which were subject to a failure rate of 24%. This suggests that credit ratings may not be fully reliable for derivative securities.

One further problem exists with respect to securitizing loans – the possible requirement of the borrower's permission. Even if this is not the case, the relationship between the bank and the customer may be damaged by the transfer of the loan. A further disadvantage could arise from the costs incurred in the time and expenses involved in designing the issues so that they are attractive to prospective purchasers. This may well make such issues unattractive for banks with low funding costs.

There is also the question as to whether the development of ABS has benefited the economy as a whole. In essence, the process of ABS connects the financial markets with the capital market. This connection should reduce agency and intermediary costs by providing investors with a wider range of securities and enabling cheaper raising of funds. On the other hand, it is sometimes argued that credit facilities have been increased. This is beneficial during

---

[9] Note that this will change under Basel II – see Chapter 12.

[10] It is noteworthy that Northern Rock financed its lending through the capital markets to a far larger extent (77%) than other building societies, whereas on average UK building societies financed 64% of their lending at the end of 2006 through retail shares and deposits.

BOX 9.4 The subprime problem

Before discussing subprime mortgage problems, it is necessary to outline the nature of structured investment vehicles (SIVs). These are similar in nature to the SPVs discussed in Section 9.4 of this chapter and are set up by a range of financial institutions including banks, hedge funds and investment managers. They are created to hold securities and mainly finance themselves by issuing short-term debt[11] with profits being realized by the gap between short- and long-term interest rates (and also by holding risky assets). In the second quarter of 2007, the three main assets held by SIVs in aggregate, according to the *Financial Times* (14/9/07), were (i) corporate financial debt (43%), (ii) residential mortgages (23%) and (iii) CDOs (11%). This indicates their vulnerability to defaults in the mortgage market. It is also relevant that many of the rules of the SIVs specified that the sponsoring institution would provide back-up facilities if the short-term funding sources dried up.

The subprime mortgage problems in the USA arise from lending to house purchasers with a poor credit history. Normally, in a perfect market it would be expected that the interest rate charged for such mortgages and the level of deposit required would include the appropriate risk component so that on average the financial institutions involved would not incur losses. In fact, defaults have become so frequent that the US Federal Reserve estimates that investors will lose between $50bn and $100bn. What went wrong? Interest rates were low, stimulating demand for mortgages. Mortgage providers were competitively searching for borrowers, with the result that risk assessment was virtually zero. This resulted in very risky mortgage loans being made. There is also evidence that fraud and other dubious practices were involved, resulting in the overstating of income.[12] Subsequent rising interest rates meant that borrowers were unable to meet their obligations. The potential problems of default had been passed on to the financial institutions, particularly banks and hedge funds, via SIVs, as the originators of the mortgages had repackaged these loans into securities and sold them on. Consequently, the investment loss had been passed on to these institutions. As indicated above, banks in the USA and Europe have provided back-up facilities to the SIVs and thus become responsible for the assets if the SIVs are unable to raise money in the money markets.

This, in fact, occurred, as SIVs found it difficult to raise loans in the money markets owing to concerns about their riskiness and the difficulty in valuing the complex securities held. This was compounded by the fact that many of these vehicles contain rules requiring them to sell off assets if falls in their market value consume 50% of their capital. Since they are highly leveraged, this has occurred in some cases.

How serious a problem is this for banks? Fitch have calculated that, if the banks were forced to take over all the assets held by 'conduits' (estimated at a staggering

(continued)

[11] They are highly leveraged, so capital only forms a small proportion of their liabilities.

[12] One Californian firm, for a fee of $55, was prepared to employ persons as independent contractors and provide pay slips as proof of income. For a further fee of $25, they would also man telephones to provide glowing references for the would-be borrower if required (*Financial Times*, 9/10/07)

$1400bn), this would only knock off 60 basis points of the average bank's tier 1 capital ratio (*Financial Times*, 10/9/07). However, individual institutions are vulnerable, e.g. IKB (a specialized German lender) which was rescued by other German banks following exposure to the subprime market that exceeded its capital by a big margin. It is also noteworthy that the risk is spread around a wide range of institutions – Singapore's DBS bank announced that its exposure to CDOs could be around $1.6bn. This is, of course, the aim of securitization – to spread the risk around.

The experience of the subprime crisis means that banks will find that securitization will become expensive. The increased risk will be matched with higher yields on securitized assets.

periods of faster growth of an economy but could lead to increased financial distress once a downturn occurs. If this is so, the volatility of the economy may have been increased.

9.6 CONCLUSIONS

In this chapter we have distinguished between securitizations that reduce, at least partially, the role of banks in the process of raising capital and those that represent an unbundling of the financial intermediation process. In the first case, securitization reduces the role of banks significantly as finance would be raised directly from capital markets. The banks also face competition for funds on their liability side from other financial institutions whose liabilities in the UK context have grown more rapidly than those of banks. In the second case, ABS is part of the intermediation process and represents separating the component parts of this process. ABS offers banks the chance of relief from pressures arising from capital shortages as well as offering the opportunity to raise funds at a lower cost than through the normal channels. Banks can also achieve greater portfolio diversification and hence a reduction in risk. However, securitization may provide additional risk to the economy.

9.7 SUMMARY

- Securitization refers to two processes. The first involves the process of disintermediation. The second relates to asset-backed securitization.
- Banks earn fee income from helping firms to issue securities when firms raise funds directly from the capital market.
- Banks conduct securitization as a means of easing the restraints due to imposed capital-to-asset ratios, and as a means of lowering the costs of attracting funds.
- ABS may be beneficial to the economy as a whole through increased liquidity and reductions in the cost of raising funds. On the other hand, the potential for increased financial distress may be increased when a downturn in the economy occurs.

QUESTIONS

1 Financial intermediation can be considered as a bundle of separate services. What are these separate components?

2 What factors explain the growth of securitization?

3 What are (a) NIFs, (b) FRNs and (c) commercial paper? Does the growth of these harm banks?

4 What are the three categories of securitization arranged through financial markets?

5 What is asset-backed securitization? How are the securities issued?

6 How do banks gain from asset-backed securitization?

TEST QUESTIONS

1 Discuss the implications of securitization for the long-term future of banking.

2 What is securitization? Comment on its significance for international banking.

10

Banking Efficiency and the Structure of Banking

MINI-CONTENTS

10.1   Introduction
10.2   Measurement of output
10.3   Performance measures
10.4   Reasons for the growth of mergers and acquisitions
10.5   Motives for mergers
10.6   Empirical evidence
10.7   Summary

10.1 INTRODUCTION

In this chapter we examine the structure of banking and, in particular, the potential for economies of scale and scope together with the related issue as to whether mergers have raised the level of efficiency in banks. We also examine performance measures that indicate the level of efficiency in banks.

Our analysis proceeds with a discussion of the problems of measuring the output of banking firms. Performance measures are examined, and studies of bank efficiency are reviewed. We then proceed to an examination of the motives for mergers and acquisitions and, subsequently, to an examination of the empirical evidence.

10.2 MEASUREMENT OF OUTPUT

A problem exists concerning the measurement of the performance of banking firms, either individually or collectively, as there is no unambiguous measure of the output of banks. An additional difficulty is that output is not measured in terms of physical quantities. Similarly, it is quite difficult to allow for quality improvements. One such example concerns automated teller machines (ATMs). It can be argued that the existence of ATMs improves quality of service since they are available for cash withdrawals at times when bank branches would be closed. They also lead to operating cost reduction per transaction but, on the other hand, may actually lead to a rise in total costs if the number of withdrawals increases significantly. Similarly, closure of branches may lead to increased costs and inconvenience for customers but lower costs for the banks. A further example concerns the role of financial intermediation in offsetting, at least to some extent, the problems arising from the existence of asymmetric information. This was discussed in Section 3.5. The banks provide a valuable role in this respect, but should this role be regarded as a cost or an output? Clearly, the costs involved are an input as far as the bank is concerned, but the services produced can equally be regarded as an output by the customer. This particular example raises a further difficulty, as the monitoring role has no explicit output value.

This contrasts with the position of manufacturing firms where units of output are identifiable, and makes it relatively more difficult to evaluate the pattern of costs before and after a merger of banks.

Bank output can be measured in a number of ways including:

1. The number of accounts.
2. The number of transactions.
3. The average value of accounts.
4. Assets per employee.
5. Average employees per branch.
6. Assets per branch.
7. The total value of deposits and/or loans.
8. The value of income including interest and non–interest income.

Not only is there the difficulty that output can be measured in a number of ways but also there are two approaches to measuring output, namely the intermediation and production methods. It is worthwhile briefly reviewing this debate. The intermediation approach is to view the bank as an intermediary so that its output is measured by the value of loans and investments together with off-balance-sheet income and its input costs are measured by the payments made to factors of production, including interest payments. Within this approach, deposits may be treated as inputs or outputs. From the point of view of bank managers, deposits are inputs essential to obtain profits through the purchase of earning assets such as loans and investments. Conversely, deposits, from the point of view of the customer, are outputs since they create value for the customer in the form of payment, record-keeping and security facilities. Alternatively, this approach may focus on income, with net interest income and non–interest income being defined as output and the corresponding expenses being defined as input.

A second approach is to regard banks as firms that use factors of production (i.e. labour and capital) to produce different categories of loans and deposit accounts. The number of transactions, either in total or per account, is treated as a flow. One problem with this approach is that interest costs are ignored.

A difficulty for both approaches is how to weight the various bank services in the measurement of output. The relative importance of the various services differs widely from bank to bank. This is illustrated in Table 10.1 in the case of three banks selected to represent

TABLE 10.1 Relative importance of balance sheet items as at 31/12/06

	Citigroup	Morgan Stanley	Cooperative Bank
Assets			
Loans	36	0	64
Securities	52	79	33
Other	12	21	3
Total	100	100	100
Liabilities			
Short-term	70	26	81
Other	15	56	11
Non-interest-bearing	9	15	2
Equity	6	3	6
Total	100	100	100

Source: Fitch/Bankscope.

international, investment and retail banks respectively. Clearly, there are major differences in their structure as regards liabilities and assets. Hence, any discussion of the relative efficiency of different banks must be treated with caution.[1]

10.3 PERFORMANCE MEASURES

You were introduced to some basic accounting measures of performance in Chapter 1, which we will repeat here with some modifications. The income statement of a hypothetical bank is set out in Tables 10.2a and b below.

Specific performance measures are:

- Return on assets = profit after tax divided by total assets, $ROA = \frac{24}{1100}(100) = 2.2\%$.

- Return on equity = profit after tax divided by total equity, $ROE = \frac{24}{80}(100) = 30\%$.

- Average earnings on asset = interest income plus non-interest income less provisions divided by total assets, $EOA = \frac{(100 + 30 - 10)}{1100}(100) = 10.9\%$.

- Net interest margin = interest earnings less interest costs divided by interest earning assets, $NIM = \frac{100 - 60}{950}(100) = 4.2\%$.

---

[1] Studies of relative bank efficiency have validity only if the banks in the sample have a more or less common structure.

Table 10.2a Income statement of a hypothetical bank

Component	£m	Definition
Interest income	100	Interest earned on interest-earning assets
Non-interest income	30	Fees and commissions from services
Interest expenses	−60	Interest paid on deposits and interbank borrowing
Provisions for bad debts	−10	Provisions for losses on loans
Operating expenses	−30	Non-interest expenses, wage bill, computers, rent, etc.
Profit before tax	30	
Tax	20%	
Profit after tax	24	

Table 10.2b Balance sheet of a hypothetical bank

Assets		Liabilities	
Cash	50	Sight deposits	500
Liquid assets	250	Time deposit	320
Loans and advances	700	Bonds	200
Fixed assets	100	Equity	80
Total assets	1100		

Interest-earning assets are liquid assets and loans and advances.

- Cost–income ratio = operating expenses divided by operating income (net interest income + non-interest income), $CI = \frac{30}{70}(100) = 42.9\%$.

Banks are frequently compared with each other using some or all of the above performance measures. In many respects, such accounting-based measures are reasonably valid for comparison with similar types of bank operating under common geographical and regulatory conditions. However, they are not necessarily valid for international comparison because of different accounting conventions and differences in the regulatory and risk environments. For example, NIM will reflect risk premia which will differ from country to country depending on the laws of property and the role of collateral in secured lending.

An alternative to the accounting measures approach to assessing bank efficiency is to apply the neoclassical production theory of the firm to the bank. Using the theory of production, clear definitions of technical efficiency and cost efficiency can be obtained. Box 10.1 reviews the theory for a single-output–two-input case.

BOX 10.1   Neoclassical theory of production and technical efficiency

Here we show how cost efficiency can be obtained, and also its decomposition into technical efficiency and allocative efficiency. Figure 10.1 shows an isoquant qq producing a given output q with factor inputs x_1 and x_2 and isocost ww, which traces the ratio of factor prices. Output is described by the production function (10.1.1) and cost function (10.1.2):

$$q = f(x_1, x_2) \tag{10.1.1}$$

$$C = w_1 x_1 + w_2 x_2 \tag{10.1.2}$$

The efficient cost-minimizing position is shown at e, where ww is tangential to qq. Employing a factor combination shown by point c, which is to the right of the isoquant qq, indicates that the firm is technically inefficient because it uses more factors x_1 and x_2 than necessary to produce the output q on the isoquant. Efficiency is decomposed into technical efficiency and allocative efficiency (AE).

A firm that is 100% technically efficient will be producing on the isoquant; for example, point a. A firm at point c will be less than 100% technically efficient. Formally, the measure of technical efficiency (TE) is given by the ratio Oa/Oc. 100% technical efficiency occurs when point c shrinks to point a, so that $TE = Oa/Oc$. One

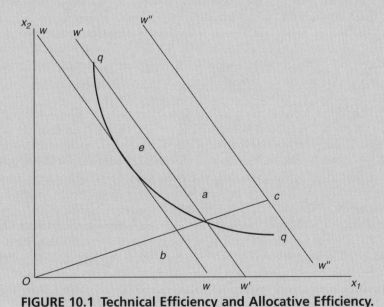

FIGURE 10.1 Technical Efficiency and Allocative Efficiency.

(continued)

hundred per cent cost efficiency is at point e, where the isocost line is tangential to the isoquant. Point e defines the optimal factor mix and the minimum cost position.

However, in Figure 10.1 the firm is using the actual factor mix defined by point c. Thus, the actual cost to the firm is shown by $w''w''$(which is parallel to ww and passes through point c. Therefore, cost efficiency (CE) is measured by Ob/Oc. A firm may be operating with the correct factor mix but using more factors than optimal. At point a, the firm is producing the correct output but using the wrong factor mix and incurring costs defined by the isocost function $w'w'$ parallel to ww that passes through point a. Allocative efficiency (AE) is defined by Ob/Oa. As the firm moves along the isoquant from point a to point e (the minimum cost position), the gap ab shrinks to zero and $AE = 100\%$. Therefore, it can be seen from this decomposition that

$$AE = \frac{CE}{TE} \qquad (10.1.3)$$

The theory of production is straightforward, but the problems arise when it comes to estimating bank efficiency. As stated in Section 10.2, the big problem in performance measurement in banking is the measurement of output. There are two main approaches that can be used to determine what constitutes bank output and commensurately bank input. The most popular method of measuring and assigning inputs and outputs is the intermediation approach. The intermediation approach recognizes that the main function of banks is to act as a financial intermediary. In the intermediation approach, the selection of outputs and inputs is based on the bank's assets and liabilities. The main reason for the use of balance sheet data to measure inputs and outputs is because of the relative availability of the data. Deposits are seen as an input in the production of loans (an output). A typical classification is that of Berger and Mester (1997) where bank inputs are purchased funds, core deposits and labour. Outputs are consumer loans, business loans and securities.

An alternative to the intermediation approach is what is known as the production approach. This approach considers the bank as a producer just like a firm in the product market. Inputs are physical entities such as labour and physical capital. The proponents of the production approach argue that all deposits should be treated as an output since they are associated with liquidity and safekeeping and are involved in generating value added. Other outputs will be net interest income and non-interest income from the profit and loss account.

A popular technology that has been used for measuring bank efficiency is the method of data envelopment analysis (DEA). DEA is a non-parametric approach that constructs an envelope of outputs with respect to inputs using a linear programming method. The advantage of the DEA over parametric methods is that it does not require a functional form for the production function. The drawback of the approach is that it assumes that the data are measured perfectly and therefore there is no random disturbance term associated with the function as in an econometric specification. The general flavour of data envelopment analysis is illustrated in Box 10.2.

The efficiency of the units is measured with the efficiency frontier as the benchmark. Units on the frontier attract a rating of 1 (or 100%), and the inefficient units attract a rating

BOX 10.2   Data envelopment analysis (DEA)

DEA was developed during the 1970s – a seminal article is Charnes *et al.* (1978). It has been applied to a wide range of activities involving multiple objectives and decision-making units. DEA methodology is based on mathematical programming, so it is useful to start with a simple illustrative example of a linear programming problem. Assume that:

1. A firm produces just two products (Y and X) utilizing two inputs (A and B) and, hence, two processes.
2. Process 1 uses two units of A and one unit of B to produce one unit of Y. Process 2 uses one unit of A and two units of B to produce one unit of X.
3. The capacities of A and B are 300 and 400 respectively.
4. Assume the profits per unit for Y and X are both 10.

This can be formulated as a linear programme as follows:

$$2Y + 1X \leq 200$$

$$1Y + 2X \leq 300$$

Maximize $h = 10Y + 10X$ subject to $Y, X \geq 0$.
    The advantage of this simple illustrative model is that it can be solved graphically:

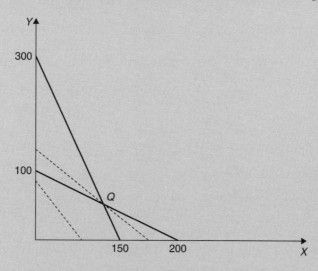

The only region that satisfies both constraints is that given by the frontier 100, Q, 150. The dotted lines represent the profit available from the production process. The object is to move as far outwards as possible so that the most profitable is given by point Q.

(*continued*)

DEA analysis proceeds in a similar manner. Efficiency for the jth firm can be defined as

$$\frac{U_1 Y_{1,j} + U_2 Y_{2,j} + L}{V_1 X_{1,j} + V_2 X_{2,j} + L}$$

where U_1 is the weight given to output 1, Y_{1j} is the amount of output 1 from decision-making unit (DMU) j, V_1 is the weight given to input 1 and X_{1j} is the amount of input 1 to DMU j.

Charnes, Cooper and Rhodes (CCR) formulate the above problem as a linear programming problem, with each DMU representing a bank. The aim is to maximize the ratio of output to inputs for each DMU (i.e. bank) subject to the constraint that this ratio for each other DMU is not greater than unity.

The formulation is as follows (assume three outputs and two inputs). For firm 0:
Maximize

$$h_0 = \frac{U_1 Y_{10} + U_2 Y_{20} + U_3 Y_{30}}{V_1 X_{10} + V_2 X_{20}}$$

subject to

$$\frac{U_1 Y_{10} + U_2 Y_{20} + U_3 Y_{30}}{V_1 X_{10} + V_2 X_{20}} \leq 1 \qquad \text{for firm 0}$$

$$\frac{U_1 Y_{11} + U_2 Y_{21} + U_3 Y_{31}}{V_1 X_{11} + V_2 X_{21}} \leq 1 \qquad \text{for firm 1}$$

$$\frac{U_1 Y_{12} + U_2 Y_{22} + U_3 Y_{32}}{V_1 X_{12} + V_2 X_{22}} \leq 1 \qquad \text{for firm 2}$$

Similarly, for the remaining firms

$$U, V \geq 0$$

More generally, the programme can be formulated as follows:
Maximize

$$h_0 = \frac{\sum_{r=1}^{s} U_r Y_{r0}}{\sum_{i=1}^{m} V_i X_{i0}}$$

(continued)

(where subscript 0 indicates the 0th unit), subject to the constraints that

$$\frac{\sum_{r=1}^{s} U_r Y_{rj}}{\sum_{i=1}^{m} V_i X_{ij}} \leq 1, \qquad U_r \geq 0, \qquad V_i \geq 0$$

for $r = 1, 2, \ldots, n$ and $i = 1, 2, \ldots, m$.

The resulting solution provides, among other information, the efficient frontier, each bank's position relative to the frontier and the scale position (i.e. increasing, decreasing, constant, etc.).

A simple diagrammatic illustration of a trivial production process involving one input and one output is shown in the diagram below. Units A, B, C, D, E and F are efficient in a technical sense as compared with units F and G. For each of the latter units:

(a) Output could be increased with no increase in input – moving from F to E.
(b) Input could be reduced with no reduction in output – moving from G to A.

A simple illustration is shown below:

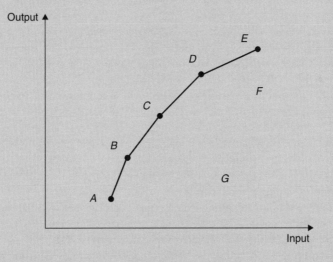

There are two useful features about DEA. Firstly, each DMU is assigned a single efficiency score, hence allowing ranking among the DMUs in a sample. Secondly, it highlights the areas of improvement for each single DMU. For example, since a DMU is compared with a set of efficient DMUs with similar input–output configurations, the DMU in question is able to identify whether it has used input excessively or its output has been underproduced.

(*continued*)

The main weakness of DEA is that it assumes that the data are free from measurement errors (see Mester, 1996). As efficiency is a relative measure, the ranking relates to the sample used. Thus, an efficient DMU found in the analysis cannot be compared with other DMUs outside the sample. Each sample, separated by year, represents a single frontier that is constructed on the assumption of the same technology. Therefore, comparing the efficiency measures of a DMU across time cannot be interpreted as technical progress but rather has to be taken as changes in efficiency (Canhoto and Dermine, 2003).

Most studies using DEA have focused on the USA, but Fukuyama (1993), Berg *et al.* (1993) and Favero and Papi (1995) have done country-specific studies outside the USA. Allen and Rai (1996) have examined banks in 15 countries. Berger *et al.* (1993) conducted a survey of comparative methods of efficiency estimation.

of less than 1 according to their distance from the efficient frontier. Note the potential problem of 'benchmark firms' lying on the efficiency frontier not being efficient in the absolute meaning of technically efficient. Selection of the frontier is via firms that are relatively more efficient than others in the sample. Extension to multiple inputs and outputs is easily achieved through utilization of programming methods.[2] Efficiency frontier methods can also be subdivided into two broad categories, namely non-parametric and parametric approaches.

The main non-parametric approach is data envelopment analysis (DEA), and this imposes no structure on the production process, so that the frontier is determined purely by data in the sample. Utilization of linear programming generates a series of points of best-practice observations, and the efficient frontier is derived as a series of piecewise linear combinations of these points. Often, constant returns to scale are assumed, and the X-inefficiency is measured as the gap[3] between actual and best practice. The problem with this approach is that the total residual (i.e. the gap between best and the firm's actual practice) is assumed to be due to X-inefficiencies, whereas some of it may be attributable to good luck, especially advantageous circumstances and such factors as measurement errors. Hence, it would be expected that efficiency estimates by DEA would be lower than those obtained by the other methods trying to segregate the random error from X-inefficiency.[4]

DEA is essentially a benchmarking exercise that takes the 'best-practice' banks as residing on the frontier and evaluating all other banks against the benchmark set. It is particularly valuable in comparing banks that operate in the same market. A necessary condition for the valid interpretation of DEA is that the banks be reasonably homogeneous. For this reason,

---

[2] Care must be taken to ensure that the number of observations is substantially greater than the number of inputs and outputs, otherwise units will 'self-select' (or near-self-select) themselves because there are no other units against which to make a comparison; e.g. a single observation becomes the most efficient by definition.

[3] Given constant returns to scale, it does not matter whether output is maximized or input minimized.

[4] The overall mean efficiency of US banks in the studies surveyed in Berger and Humphrey (1997) was 0.79%. The mean for the non-parametric studies was 0.72%, and that for the parametric studies 0.84%.

the application of DEA to bank branch efficiency has strong relevance (see, for example, Sherman and Gold, 1985).

An alternative to the non-parametric approach of DEA for evaluating bank efficiency is the parametric approach. Parametric approaches tend to overcome the problem of the error – the gap between the inefficient bank and benchmark being due to good luck (but not the problem of the measurement of the efficient frontier) through the allocation of the residual between random error and X-inefficiency. The cost of this refinement is the imposition of structure necessary to partition the residual. This leaves these approaches open to the same criticism as that applied to the production function approach, i.e. that this structure is inappropriate. Three separate types of non-parametric approach have mainly been used: the stochastic frontier approach (sometimes called the 'econometric frontier approach'), the distribution-free approach and the thick-frontier approach. A brief description of these measures now follows.

10.3.1 Stochastic Frontier Analysis (SFA)

This approach specifies a function for cost, profit or production so as to determine the frontier, and treats the residual as a composite error comprising:

(a) Random error with a symmetric distribution – often normal.
(b) Inefficiency with an asymmetric distribution – often a half-normal on the grounds that inefficiencies will never be a plus for production or profit or a negative for cost.

10.3.2 Distribution-Free Approach (DFA)

Again, a specific functional form is specified and no assumption is made about the distribution of errors. Random errors are assumed to be zero on average, whereas the efficiency for each firm is stable over time:

$$\text{Inefficiency} = \text{average residual of the individual} - \text{average residual for the firm on the frontier}$$

10.3.3 Thick-Frontier Approach (TFA)

A functional form is specified to determine the frontier based on the performance of the best firms. Firms are ranked according to performance and it is assumed that:

(a) Deviations from predicted performance values by firms from the frontier within the highest and lowest quartiles represent random error.
(b) Deviations between highest and lowest quartiles represent inefficiencies.

This method does not provide efficiency ratings for individual firms but rather for the industry as a whole.

10.3.4 The Cost Function Specification

The parametric approach to measuring cost inefficiency is to estimate a cost function for the set of banks in the sample. The assumption is that bank managers aim to minimize bank costs. Consider the following cost function:

$$\ln C_i = f(w_i, q_i, z_i, y) + \ln u_i + \ln \varepsilon_i \tag{10.1}$$

where ln denotes natural logarithm, C represents variable costs, w is a vector of input prices, q is a vector of outputs, z represents bank specific control variables for the ith bank, y represents a vector of common factors (such as the macroeconomic environment), u represents inefficiency and ε is a random error term. Based on the estimation of (10.1), a benchmark bank with the lowest cost is identified and inefficiency is defined in relation to the benchmark bank. Cost efficiency for bank b is defined as the estimated cost needed to produce bank b's output if the bank is as efficient as the best-practice bank. Therefore, cost inefficiency is as follows:

$$\text{Cost inefficiency} = 1 - \frac{\hat{C}^{min}}{\hat{C}^b} = 1 - \frac{\exp \hat{f}(w^b, q^b, z^b, y^b) \exp \ln \hat{u}^{min}}{\exp \hat{f}(w^b, q^b, z^b, y^b) \exp \ln \hat{u}^b} = 1 - \frac{\hat{u}^{min}}{\hat{u}^b} \tag{10.2}$$

where $\hat{u}^{min}$ is the minimum of all the $\hat{u}^b$ of all the banks and b denotes the bank for which the inefficiency is calculated. The cost inefficiency ratio can be thought of as the proportion of costs that are used inefficiently. So a score of 0.3 implies that bank b wastes 30% of its costs relative to the best-practice bank (see Berger and Mester, 1997). Figure 10.2 illustrates the case.

One of the problems associated with the parametric approach is that it requires the specification of a particular functional form. Hence, the measures of inefficiency obtained from the parametric approach will always be open to the charge that the estimates of efficiency could be biased because of misspecification of the functional form. In order to keep as general

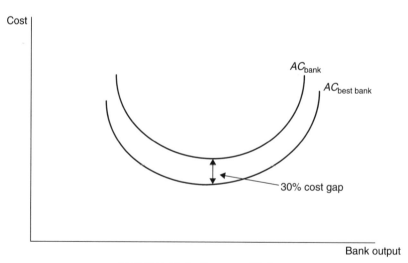

FIGURE 10.2 Cost Inefficiency.

a specification as possible, researchers have used the multi-input, multi-output translog cost function:

$$\ln C = \alpha_0 + \sum_m \alpha_m \ln q_m + \sum_j \beta_j \ln w_j + \frac{1}{2} \sum_m \sum_k \sigma_{m.k} \ln q_m \ln q_k$$

$$+ \frac{1}{2} \sum_j \sum_h \gamma_{j,h} \ln w_j \ln w_h + \sum_m \sum_j \delta_{m,j} \ln q_m \ln w_j + v_m$$

This function is defined for (i) banks with $\{m\}$ outputs and $\{j\}$ input prices. The translog functional form has the following virtues:[5]

1. It accommodates multiple outputs without necessarily violating curvature conditions.
2. It is flexible, in the sense that it provides a second-order approximation to any well-behaved underlying cost frontier.
3. It has a good record of empirical estimation for the decomposition of cost efficiency.

The elasticity of cost with respect to output indicates the existence or otherwise of economies of scale:

$$\frac{\partial \ln C}{\partial \ln q_m} > 1 \text{ if there are diseconomies of scale}$$

$$\frac{\partial \ln C}{\partial \ln q_m} < 1 \text{ if there are increasing returns to scale}$$

$$\frac{\partial \ln C}{\partial \ln q_m} = 1 \text{ if there are constant returns to scale}$$

It would be comforting to report that the various frontier efficiency methods provided results that were consistent with each other. Unfortunately, this is not the case. Bauer *et al.* (1998) applied the different approaches to a study of the efficiency of US banks over the period 1977–1988 using multiple techniques within the four main approaches discussed above. They found that the results derived from non-parametric methods were generally consistent with each other as far as identifying efficient and inefficient firms was concerned. Similarly, parametric methods showed consistent results. Parametric and non-parametric measures were not consistent with each other.

As noted in Table 1.4, there has been a considerable degree of consolidation of the banking industry throughout the world. In Europe, for example, 1024 mergers took place in the period 1997–2004, with 71% between EU-located institutions and 29% involving EU and non-EU institutions (Dermine, 2006).

In the following sections, we examine the reasons for this consolidation and the empirical evidence as to the efficacy of these moves. As most mergers have occurred in the USA, it is natural that most, but not all, of the empirical evidence is based on US experience. For an excellent survey, see Berger *et al.* (1999).

---

[5] See Kumbhakar and Lovell (2000).

10.4 REASONS FOR THE GROWTH OF MERGERS AND ACQUISITIONS

There has been a growth in mergers and acquisitions in recent years. Reference to Table 1.4 illustrates the decline in the number of institutions. As just mentioned, this is further demonstrated by the mergers and acquisitions of credit institutions in Europe during the 1990s, which averaged 380 per year (ECB, 2000). Several reasons have been put forward for this growth. These include (i) increased technical progress, (ii) improvements in financial conditions, (iii) excess capacity, (iv) international consolidation of financial markets and (v) deregulation.

Technical progress has probably increased the scope for economies of scale. Obvious examples include the far greater use of IT, the growth of financial innovation such as the use of derivative contracts and off-balance-sheet business, ATMs and online banking. The larger banking firms can probably derive a greater benefit from these developments than small firms. The second reason is improvement in financial conditions. Reference to Table 1.3 shows that the greatest improvement in the return on assets occurred in the case of the US banks, and Table 10.3 shows that it is in the USA where most mergers have taken place. The rationale underlying this argument is that, owing to increased profitability, firms have extra

TABLE 10.3 Mergers and acquisitions in the international banking sector, 1990–2001[a]

Country	1990–1995		1996–2001	
	Number	Value $ bill	Number	Value $ bill
Australia	53	2.4	91	13.2
Belgium	21	0.8	34	28.1
Canada	52	1.6	112	15.0
France	148	11.8	96	44.6
Germany	123	2.4	229	68.6
Italy	147	19.2	138	80.4
Japan	29	44.4	15	0.8
The Netherlands	36	10.9	24	5.9
Spain	66	5.9	67	31.2
Sweden	44	2.8	38	16.9
Switzerland	81	3.3	43	24.2
UK	140	33.0	279	114.4
USA	1691	156.6	1796	754.9

[a] Includes commercial banks, bank holding companies, saving and loans, mutual savings banks, credit institutions, mortgage banks and brokers.
Source: Reprinted from Amel, C. L., Barnes, C., Panetta, F. and Salleo, C. (2004). Consolidation and efficiency in the financial sector: A review of the international evidence. *Journal of Banking and Finance*, **28**, 2493–2519. With permission from Elsevier.

funds to finance acquisitions. Thirdly, as we have noted in Chapter 1, banks have faced increasing competition from other financial institutions. On the corporate side this has come from direct financing through the capital markets and competition from non-resident banks. This latter aspect is particularly true for US banks (Berger *et al.*, 1999). On the domestic household side, banks face competition regarding the attraction of savings from other financial institutions such as investment trusts. This has probably led to excess capacity in the banking industry, providing an incentive to rationalize via mergers. International consolidation of markets provides the fourth reason for the increasing number of mergers. We examined the globalization of financial services in Section 1.4. It suffices at this stage to point out that increased globalization of financial services provides an incentive for banks to engage in cross-border mergers and acquisitions. Finally, deregulation (discussed in Chapter 1) has provided a strong incentive for banks to merge, particularly in the USA where many restrictions were repealed during the 1980s and 1990s.

10.5 MOTIVES FOR MERGERS

The standard rationale used to justify merger/takeover activity is that well-managed firms will take over poorly managed firms and transform the performance of these firms. There is a reasonable amount of evidence that suggests this is true. For example, Berger and Humphrey (1991) and Pilloff and Santomero (1998) both found for the USA that the acquiring bank was more cost efficient on average than the target banks. In the case of Europe, Vander Vennet (1996) obtained a similar result.

The increased value of banking firms can arise from two potential sources: increased efficiency and increased market power. The first source is beneficial to society and originates from economies of scale and scope (i.e. diversification). Two broad types of efficiency can usefully be distinguished, i.e. output and input. From the output side, scale efficiency denotes the business is operating at the optimum size and also that the scope of the business (i.e. degree of diversification) is appropriate. As most banks offer a quite wide range of services, further large-scope economies are not very likely. As noted earlier, reference to Barclays website (*www.barclays.co.uk*) shows that they offer a wide range of services including personal banking, banking for business and international services apart from the traditional banking services of accepting deposits and making loans. These include other services such as, for example, stockbroking, asset management and investment banking. Furthermore, the potential for scope economies is extremely difficult to measure. The problem is that this requires estimates of cost/revenue functions with and without diversification. Secondly, most banks produce a wide range of products. Originally, there seemed to be quite general agreement that there was little potential for scope economies – see, for example, Mester (1987) and Clark (1988) – but, more recently, a wider range of estimates has been obtained.

From the input side, pure technical efficiency entails the bank using best practice in producing its products, so that a firm can be considered to be technically efficient if it cannot increase any output or reduce any input without increasing other inputs or reducing other outputs. Technical economies occur because the undertaking is not utilizing its resources in the optimum manner. In the literature this is termed 'X-efficiency' or, conversely, the departure from the optimum 'X-inefficiency'. The technical process for banks is not susceptible to analysis from an engineering point of view, so that the production process has to be inferred from such data as the bank's costs or outputs. Allocative efficiency[6] refers to the appropriate combination of inputs given their relative prices.

A second motivation for mergers comes from the separation of ownership and management of firms. Agency theory suggests that managers may pursue their own interests, which may or may not coincide with those of the owners. For example, managers may engage in empire building, particularly as management earnings tend to increase with the size of the firm. Similarly, along the lines argued by Jensen (1986), improved financial conditions might have created 'free cash flow', which was then utilized to finance acquisitions. These considerations suggest that managers may engage in acquisitions that do not maximize shareholder wealth.

A third motive may arise from hubris or arrogance of managers who think that they can identify bargains, maintaining a belief that the market has got the valuation wrong. They thus hope to take over an inefficient bank and improve the situation, thereby making profits for their own bank.

In Section 10.6 we will review the empirical evidence concerning efficacy of mergers and acquisitions in the banking industry.

10.6 EMPIRICAL EVIDENCE

The empirical evidence concerning the evaluation of mergers and acquisitions is based on five different types of analysis, namely studies based on (i) production functions, (ii) cost functions, (iii) use of accounting data, (iv) the efficient frontier approach and (v) event studies. These studies can be divided into two broad categories: (a) static studies, which do not consider the behaviour of the merged firms before and after the merger; (b) dynamic studies, which specifically consider the behaviour of the firms before and after the merger (see Berger *et al.*, 1999). Types (i), (ii) and (iv) above fall into the first category, and types (iii) and (v) into the second category. Note also that this empirical literature also provides evidence about banks per se, as well as the efficacy of mergers. Much of this evidence is derived from the US experience, as the greater numbers of mergers and acquisitions have taken place there. The volume of studies on this topic is large, so we have selected representative studies for the four types which are discussed in the following subsections, but first it is useful to consider whether the acquirers paid excessive prices for the firms acquired.

10.6.1 The Price of Acquisitions

The acquisition of another company through a merger is akin to an option. The would-be acquirer has the choice of acquiring the firm or not doing so. In these circumstances the act of purchase is equivalent to a call option, so that one method of checking whether the purchase price is excessive is to value the 'embedded' option premium and compare this value with the takeover premium in respect of the acquired firm. This is, of course, a 'real' option where there is no underlying that can be traded, as opposed to a financial option where there is a tradable underlying asset. See Dunis and Klein (2005) for an example of this methodology in connection with 15 European bank mergers.

---

[6] Economic efficiency can be defined as the firm's combining its inputs in a manner such that its costs are at a minimum. It is therefore an amalgam of pure technical and allocative efficiencies.

TABLE 10.4 Data for bank mergers modelled as a European call option

Option variable	Data
Share price	Aggregate market value of target and acquirer prior to announcement (4 week average)
Exercise price	Hypothetical future market value of separate entities forecast by their beta value
Standard deviation	Annualized standard deviation of weekly returns after the merger
Dividend yield	Average dividend yield in the year after the merger
Risk-free rate	Domestic 3 month rate to the acquirer
Time to maturity	1 year

Source: Reprinted from Dunis, C. L. and Klein, T. (2005). Analysing mergers and acquisitions in European financial services: An application of real options. *European Journal of Finance*, **11**(4), 339–355. With permission from Taylor and Francis.

We now explain the methodology adopted by Dunis and Klein (2005). The dividend-adjusted Black and Scholes model for a European call option was used to value the implicit option in the case of European mergers. The data required for this valuation are listed in Table 10.4. Note that data are included that were not available at the time of the merger, so the results represent an ex post examination of whether the firm taken over was overvalued at the time of the takeover rather than a forecast of the likely outcome.

The basis of the analysis is then to compare the calculated real-option premium with the actual takeover premium defined as the gap between the share price and the price actually paid. The average option premium for the subsample of 12 cases was 31.5%, with a quite high standard deviation of 27.7%. The average takeover premium was 18.5%. This meant that on average the option premium exceeded the takeover premium, suggesting that, within this subsample, five targets were overpaid and seven cases underpaid. It should, of course, be realized that this result is not necessarily universal and could be specific to the sample.

10.6.2 The Production Function Approach

The production function[7] is a technical expression that depicts output as a function of inputs. One such widely used production function is the Cobb–Douglas version.[8] This production function takes the general form:

$$Y_t = A_t K_t^\alpha L_t^\beta$$

---

[7] This function is termed 'production transformation' in the case of multiple outputs.

[8] Other commonly used versions include the constant elasticity of substitution and translogarithmic forms. Nickell (1996) uses the Cobb–Douglas form and argues that it is a reasonable representation of firms' production processes.

where Y is output, K is capital input and L is labour input. The coefficients α and β are often assumed to sum to 1, so that constant returns to scale are assumed. This function can easily be augmented to include different categories of labour or capital and technical progress (often allowed for by including a time trend). The advantage of this function is that, when transformed into logarithmic specification, it is linear. Comparison before and after mergers can be carried out by the introduction of dummy variables (or 'binary variables' as they are often called)[9] to see if they are positive and significantly different from zero. Given that any benefits of a merger take some time to come through, a series of dummy variables can be used to represent the sequence of years following the merger.

In the UK, building societies are in essence banks with the major proportion of their lending directed towards house purchase. They also raise their funding in a manner similar to retail banks – at the end of 2000, retail funding amounted to 79% of total funding, with the balance coming from wholesale funds. Recent years have seen a large number of mergers among UK building societies. In 1980 there were 273 separate societies with 5684 branches, but by 2000 the numbers had fallen to 67 and 2361[10] respectively (Buckle and Thompson, 2004). The building societies provide a good base to illustrate the use of the production function approach to evaluate the degree of cost reduction.

Haynes and Thompson (1999) studied these mergers in the period 1981–1993 using the production function approach. Within their analysis, the intermediation approach was adopted so that the output was defined as the book value of commercial assets (loans and investments).[11] Inputs were labour and fixed and liquid assets. Dummy variables were introduced to represent years after the merger. The precise function estimated was

$$\ln Q_{it} = \alpha + \beta_1 \ln L_{it} + \beta_2 \ln K1_{it} + \beta_3 \ln K2_{it} + \beta_4 Time + \sum \beta_j Merger_{it-j}$$

where $K1$ and $K2$ represent the division between fixed and liquid assets, respectively, at constant prices, Q is the book value of commercial assets, also at constant prices, L is the labour input (number of full-time employees) and $Merger$ refers to years 1 to 5 after the merger.

Estimation was by ordinary least squares (OLS) using panel data. The study provided evidence of improvements in productivity of approximately 3% in the first year after the merger, rising to 5.5% 5 years later, with a gain of 15% if modelled on a once-and-for-all basis.

The problem with this type of approach is that the estimate of the productivity gains depends critically on the specification of the production function.[12] Haynes and Thompson address this problem by experimenting with differing forms of production functions and report that these revealed results that showed little difference from those reported above. Nevertheless, this caveat remains.

---

[9] Dummy variables assume a value of 1 for a specific period and a value of 0 thereafter. Thus, they can be used to capture the effects of changes after a specific event – mergers in this case.

[10] Note that these figures overstate the number of mergers because some societies have opted to become banks under the 1986 Act.

[11] As noted above, off-balance-sheet items have assumed greater importance in bank profitability, and these will not be captured by the measure of output defined above. This is not likely to be important for this study, as building societies' off-balance-sheet income is quite small.

[12] Haynes and Thompson also estimated a translog functional form for the data and reported that the estimates showed similar results, but without quoting the precise estimates.

10.6.3 The Cost Function Approach

This approach entails estimating a cost function for the banks discussed in Section 10.3 and then examining how the cost function behaves over time. The most frequently used cost function is the translog cost function examined earlier in this chapter (again in Section 10.3). Assuming a simple single output (Q) with two inputs (L and K), the translog cost function can be defined in general as

$$\ln(TC) = \alpha + \beta_1 \ln Q + \beta_2 \frac{1}{2}(\ln Q)^2 + \beta_3 \ln L + \beta_4 \frac{1}{2}(\ln L)^2 + \beta_5 \ln K$$

$$+ \beta_6 \frac{1}{2}(\ln K)^2 + \beta_7 \ln L \ln K$$

where TC are total costs.

This function provides a U-shaped cost curve. The main thrust of this empiricism is to investigate whether there is evidence of economies of scale. The approach is partly static and only assesses the efficacy of mergers by examining whether there is scope for economies of scale, as banking firms grow larger through mergers. Introducing dummy variables for mergers does, however, introduce a dynamic element. Early evidence suggested that the average cost curve was relatively flat and that economies of scale were exhausted at a fairly early stage. The estimate of optimum scale varies between the studies, but is usually between $100m and $10bn in assets – see, for example, Hunter and Timme (1986) and Berger *et al.* (1987), among others. This suggests that only small banks will gain economies of scale through mergers, and then the measured efficiencies are of the order of 5%. More recent research has suggested a greater potential for scale economies. For example, Berger and Mester (1997) found economies of scale of up to 20% for bank sizes from $10bn to $25bn. This difference from earlier studies could arise from the growth of technological progress discussed earlier in this chapter.

A study of European banking by Altunbas and Molyneux (1996) also employed the translog cost function to a cross-section sample of banks in France, Germany, Italy and Spain for 1988 (sample size 850 banks). They found that economies of scale appear to exist for banks in each of the countries and over a wide range of outputs. They also checked for economies of scope, but these appear to exist only in the case of Germany, possibly reflecting the universal nature of banking in that country.

This leaves the question of potential economies of scale ambiguous from the point of view of cost studies. There is also the additional question as to whether the translog cost function is the best vehicle for analysing the behaviour of costs.

10.6.4 The Accounting Approach

The third approach to the evaluation of mergers is through the use of key financial ratios such as return on assets/equity (defined as net income generally before but sometimes after tax), loans or overhead costs to total asset cash flows.[13]

---

[13] *Note:* using accounting data poses problems because of valuation methods and creative accounting.

There have been a number of studies using accounting data. Cornett and Tehranian (1992) examined the performance of large-bank mergers in the USA over the period 1982–1987. The key variable used in this analysis was the ratio of cash flow[14] to the market value of assets. The combined cash flow of the acquiring and target banks was compared with that of the new unit post merger over the period from −3 to −1 years prior to the merger as against the period from +1 to +3 years after the merger. The average improvement in pretax cash flow for the period prior to the merger compared with the period after the merger came to 1.2%, after allowance for industry improvements.

Rhoades (1993) also surveyed 898 US bank mergers during the period 1981–1986 in relation to all other banks. The methodology involved regression analysis with the dependent variable being the change in the ratio of total expenses to total assets. A dummy variable was used to capture the effects of mergers and other explanatory variables including the number of branches and the degree of deposit overlap. Further independent variables were introduced as control variables to allow for other major influences on bank costs. These included variables such as bank size, the ratio of loans to assets, etc. The analysis was conducted for the individual years over the sample period by OLS. The coefficients for the dummy variable were rarely significant and in two cases were wrongly signed. Similar comments apply to the other type of merger variables (i.e. deposit overlap variables).

VanderVennet (1996) covered an examination of the mergers of 'banks' within Europe over the period 1988–1993 and used both accounting data and the efficient frontier approach. The accounting data consisted of a wide range of financial measures such as return on assets, return on equity and asset utilization, among others. The general conclusion reached was that domestic mergers between equal-sized partners did significantly increase the efficiency of the merged banks. This was not so for mergers where a smaller bank was acquired by a larger bank (where the result was insignificant but positive) or majority acquisitions. Cross-border acquisitions also showed evidence of a slight but insignificant improvement in performance. In contrast, in domestic majority acquisitions, the target banks exhibit an inferior performance, but the acquirers are unable to improve the situation. The result for unequal mergers is surprising, as it would have been thought that these offered the clearest potential for economies. VanderVennet suggests that these mergers may be motivated by defensive motives and managerial preferences.

10.6.5 The Efficient Frontier Approach

The volume of studies using the efficient frontier methodology has expanded dramatically over recent years.

The efficiency of a merger can be made by assessing the changes in relative performance after the merger as compared with pre-merger. Sensitivity analysis can be carried out using a window over, say, 3 years. The general nature of DEA was examined earlier in Box 10.2, and a good description of this method is contained in Yue (1992), including an application to 60 Missouri commercial banks.

---

[14] Cash flow was defined as earnings before depreciation, goodwill, interest on long-term debt and taxes, and assets were defined as the market value of common stock plus the book value of long-term debt and preferred stock less cash. Industry adjustment was carried out by subtraction of the industry mean performance from the data. Figures were also provided for individual years.

A number of other studies have been made to assess the efficacy of mergers using this broad methodology. Avkiran (1999) applied the DEA approach to banking mergers in Australia. This study suggested that, as far as the Australian experience is concerned (albeit on a small sample of four mergers), (i) acquiring banks were more efficient than target banks and (ii) the acquiring bank did not always maintain its pre-merger efficiency.

As mentioned above, Vander Vennet (1996) also employed the efficient frontier methodology. The precise methodology used was the stochastic frontier, i.e. a parametric approach. These results mirror quite closely the results obtained through use of accounting measures and therefore reinforce the earlier conclusions. De Young (1997) examined 348 bank mergers in the USA during the period 1987–1988 using the thick cost frontier, i.e. a parametric approach. He found that post-merger efficiency improved in about 75% of the banks engaged in multiple mergers but in only 50% of those engaged in a single merger. This led De Young to conclude that experience improved the bank's chances of securing the potential benefits of a merger. An international perspective was provided by Allen and Rai (1996) who used a global stochastic frontier for a sample of banks in 15 countries for the period 1988–1992 and found that X-inefficiencies of the order of 15% existed in banks where there was no separation between commercial and investment banking. Where there was separation, X-inefficiencies were higher – of the order of 27.5%.

10.6.6 Event Studies

The basis of this approach is to examine the returns derived from the share prices of the relevant firms both before and after the announcement of a merger. An abnormal return is defined as the actual return less the return predicted by the firm's beta[15] given the market return and the risk-free rate of interest. Normally, the firm's beta would be measured over a period prior to the merger announcement and the actual return would be measured over a short period around the merger; for example, 1 day prior to 1 day after the announcement. Existence of abnormal returns would suggest that the market views the merger as likely to lead to increased profitability in the future.[16]

One interesting study using the event methodology was that carried out by Siems (1996) covering 24 US bank megamergers carried out during 1995.[17] This showed that the shares of the target bank rose by 13.04% but those of the acquirer fell by 1.96% (both results were significant at the 1% level). Market concentration seemed to be irrelevant.[18]

Event studies suffer from the defect that they consider only the movement in share prices adjacent to the announcement of the merger. Hence, they represent how the market views

---

[15] The beta represents the relationship between the return of an individual firm and that of a market index. As such it represents how the return of an individual firm should vary as the market return varies.

[16] *Note:* this approach assumes an efficient market, which is the subject of controversy.

[17] A megamerger was defined as a deal exceeding $500m.

[18] Event studies assess the level of abnormal returns to shareholders and hence could be the result of monopoly power rather than increased efficiency. This conclusion suggests that this was not so for the study under consideration.

the merger at the time it is announced.[19] It would be interesting to see how the share price of the merged firm moved relative to the index for the financial sector in the years following the merger.

Consequently, share performance of 19 of the 'Siems' sample of banks was examined over subsequent years. The base for calculation of the gains/losses was the average price of the share over a period of 28 days with a lag of 28 days following the announcement of the merger. This was then compared with the average prices 1, 2 and 3 years later to derive growth rates. Allowance was made for the growth rates exhibited by the banking sector of the S&P 500 share index, so that a plus figure represents faster growth than the banking industry as a whole, and conversely for a negative figure. In fact, mean excess growth rates averaged -1.0% per year. The standard deviation of the individual returns was quite high, so this suggests that the best interpretation of these results is that the mergers failed to produce significant difference[20] between the pattern of share price movements for the sample banks and those of the banking industry as a whole.

10.7 SUMMARY

- The measurement of output for banks is difficult. Two approaches have been followed: the intermediation and production approaches.
- Bank efficiency has followed the methodology of benchmarking, comparing bank performance with that of best-practice banks.
- Reasons suggested for mergers include increased technical progress, improvements in financial conditions, excess capacity, international consolidation of financial markets and deregulation.
- The price of acquisition of a company can be assessed through its consideration as a 'real' option.
- Assessment of the efficacy of mergers can be considered in a number of approaches including (a) the production function, (b) the cost function, (c) accounting, (d) the efficient frontier and (e) event studies.

QUESTIONS

1 How may bank output be measured?

2 How is bank performance evaluated?

---

[19] It is worth noting in this connection that Cornett and Tehranian (1992) found: (i) negative abnormal stock returns for acquiring banks and positive abnormal stock returns for target banks with a positive-weighted combined average abnormal return for the two merger firms; (ii) a significant positive correlation coefficient between the announcement period abnormal gain and various subsequent performance indicators. This latter point suggests that the market is able to identify which mergers are likely to be profitable.

[20] The small size of the sample makes the results of any formal significance tests of dubious value.

3   In recent years there has been a growth of mergers and acquisitions in the banking industry. Why may this have occurred?

4   How may the estimation of cost and production functions assist in measuring the efficacy of bank mergers?

5   What accounting ratios may be used to measure changes in efficiency following a merger?

6   What is data envelopment analysis and how may it be used in judging whether mergers have increased efficiency?

7   How may event studies be used to assess whether mergers have been advantageous?

TEST QUESTIONS

1   Critically comment on the various methods for the evaluation of bank performance.

2   What are the problems in measuring the efficiency of a bank's operation?

$\Large 11$

Banking Competition

MINI-CONTENTS

11.1 Introduction
11.2 Concentration in banking markets
11.3 Structure–conduct–performance
11.4 Competition analysis
11.5 Competition in the UK banking market
11.6 Summary

11.1 INTRODUCTION

Chapter 1 has shown that the result of the three trends in international banking, namely deregulation, financial innovation and globalization, has prompted a strong trend to consolidation in the banking industry. This consolidation has been partly a reaction to competitive pressure leading to downsizing, branch closure and cost reduction, and partly the result of defensive merger activity reviewed in the previous chapter. One of the dangers of consolidation is the implication for competition. Can the competitive pressure from deregulation lead to consolidation with bigger and stronger banks swallowing up smaller and weaker banks, resulting ultimately in a worsening of competition?

In this chapter we examine the competitive structure of the banking market and relate it to the profit performance of banks. The chapter begins by examining measures of market concentration and reviews a popular model in industrial economics known as the structure–conduct–performance model. In this model, market structure is defined as the interaction of demand and supply factors. Conduct is influenced by factors such as the number of competing firms and customers and barriers to entry. The combination of these two factors influences the performance/output of banking firms. The chapter goes on to examine empirical models of competitive conditions in banking and review the empirical findings. Finally, it examines the state of competition in the UK banking market.

11.2 CONCENTRATION IN BANKING MARKETS

How is market power measured? Does it have any relation to the number of banks in the market? We examine these questions in the context of the rising trend towards consolidation in banking markets globally. Many antitrust regulators across a number of countries define market power in terms of the concentration in the market. The importance of market concentration has its justification in the so-called structure–conduct–performance paradigm of Bain (1951). In a nutshell, the SCP hypothesis is that fewer and larger firms (high concentration) are more likely to engage in anticompetitive behaviour.

The most common measure of concentration and the one used by financial regulators is the Herfindahl–Hirschman Index (HHI), which is defined as the sum of the squared market shares of the banks in the market. Box 11.1 explains how the index is calculated. The upper bound for the index is 10 000, which indicates a monopoly, and the lower bound is zero in the case of an infinite number of banks (perfect competition). The US Department of Justice considers a market with a result of less than 1000 to be a competitive marketplace, a result of 1000–1800 to be a moderately concentrated marketplace and a result of 1800 or greater to be a highly concentrated marketplace. As a general rule, mergers that increase the HHI by more than 100 points in concentrated markets raise antitrust concerns. Should the threshold be breached, the regulators will first look for mitigating factors that would show the merger to be not anticompetitive. The regulators also balance the potential loss of consumer welfare from an increase in market power associated with a merger against wider issues such as preserving the stability of the banking market by consolidating a failed or weak bank. Figure 11.1 describes the theoretical link between the HHI index and market power.[1]

An alternative measure of concentration is the n-bank concentration ratio (CR_n), which stands for the percentage of the market controlled by the top n banks in the market. Popular measures in studies of banking markets have been the three-bank concentration ratio and the five-bank concentration ratio.[2] The measure takes the share of deposits (or assets) of the three (or five) largest banks in the market. The hypothesis is that, the larger the concentration ratio, the greater will be the potential for anticompetitive behaviour.

However, the empirical evidence of a link between concentration and market power is mixed. For example, Berger and Hannan (1989) analysed a cross-section of banking markets in the 1980s and found that deposit rates were significantly lower in highly concentrated markets. Nonetheless, in his review of the Berger and Hannan results, Jackson (1992) found a U-shaped relationship between concentration and market power, suggesting that low deposit rates were associated with low and highly concentrated markets but not intermediate concentrated markets. Such a finding directly contradicts the SCP hypothesis, as shown by the expected theoretical relationship depicted in Figure 11.1 and discussed below in Section 11.3.

---

[1] It is possible to derive a relationship between market concentration and market power on the basis of optimizing strategy under restrictive assumptions that banks act as Cournot oligopolists. However, under more general and realistic assumptions, the link is less obvious. See Cetorelli (1999).

[2] A number of studies have employed the concentration ratio to examine the effect of concentration on profit performance of banks. See, for example, Lloyd-Williams *et al.* (1994) and Molyneux and Forbes (1995).

BOX 11.1   Calculation of the *HHI* index

The formula for the *HHI* index is given by

$$HHI = \sum_{i=1}^{n} s_i^2$$

where s is the market share of the ith bank
     Consider a market that has five banks, with the market share for deposits (it could equally be loans) as follows:

Bank	Deposit share (%)
1	30
2	25
3	20
4	16
5	9

The $HHI = 30^2 + 25^2 + 20^2 + 16^2 + 9^2 = 2262$. Suppose that banks 3 and 5 merge. The *HHI* index after the merger is 2622. Because the banking market is already concentrated and $\Delta HHI = 360$, this merger may be rejected by the regulatory authorities.[3] The *HHI* index has an upper bound of 10 000 (100^2) in the case of a monopoly, and *HHI* tends towards zero as the market tends towards perfect competition.[4]

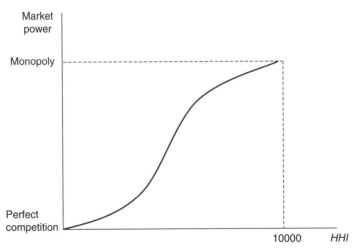

FIGURE 11.1 The Theoretical Relationship Between Market Concentration and Market Power.

[3] Note that the index has increased even though the arithmetic total of the values has remained the same. This is due to the fact that the percentages are squared.

[4] The proportions are sometimes calculated as decimals rather than percentages. In this case the maximum value is 1, although the minimum value remains the same.

11.3 STRUCTURE–CONDUCT–PERFORMANCE

Economic theory predicts that monopoly will lead to higher prices and a loss of efficiency compared with a competitive environment. Hence, theory predicts that the degree of monopoly and the scale of the banking industry will influence its performance. The influence is not unidirectional, as performance will also influence the conduct and structure. For example, an efficient firm with lower prices will affect the conduct of other firms. Similarly, excessive profits will induce new entrants into the industry.

This model can be summarized as

$$\textit{Structure} \leftrightarrow \textit{Conduct} \leftrightarrow \textit{Performance}$$

The SCP hypothesis states that greater concentration along with barriers to entry lowers the cost of collusion between banks, resulting in above-normal profits for all the banks in the market. The traditional model of SCP specifies a bank profit function for π_i for a market of $\{i\}$ banks of the form

$$\pi_i = \alpha_0 + \alpha_1 CR_n + \sum_{j=2}^{k} \alpha_j Z_{i,j} + \varepsilon_i \tag{11.1}$$

The variables Z are a set of $\{k\}$ control variables for the $\{i\}$ banks, CR_n is the n-bank concentration ratio (or, as an alternative, the *HHI* index is used to proxy market power) and π_i is profit measured either by ROA or by ROE (or even by NIM) for the ith bank. Support for the SCP hypothesis occurs if α_1 is found to be statistically significant and positive.

This specification has been challenged by Demsetz (1973) and others on the grounds that concentration is not a random event but an endogenous variable. Demsetz argued that concentration is the result of the efficiency of the leading firms, and consequently any observed relationship between concentration and profitability is spurious. Concentration is the outcome of strong competition and is referred to as the efficient structure hypothesis (ESH).

An extension to the SCP hypothesis recognizes that individual banks may have informational advantages relating to their clients that give them localized market power independently of what could be obtained from collusion. This is known as the relative market power hypothesis (RMPH) which states that banks with large market shares can exert market power directly, whereas concentration exerts indirect market power through collusion. To include this possibility, researchers have included market share $\{s_i\}$ of each bank as an independent control variable in (11.1):

$$\pi_i = \alpha_0 + \alpha_1 CR_n + \alpha_2 s_i + \sum_{j=3}^{k} \alpha_j Z_{i,j} + \varepsilon_i \tag{11.2}$$

However, market share could also reflect efficiency according to the Demsetz (1973) thesis, and a positive relationship ($\alpha_2 > 0$) could indicate that market share is a good proxy either for efficiency or for market power. Hence, the empirical investigation would have to control for efficiency as one of the control factors, otherwise the RMPH specification may only be testing the ESH model (the two models are observationally equivalent).[5]

Several papers have tested the ESH (or RMPH) model for banking. Smirlock (1985) and Evanoff and Fortier (1988) found evidence of a positive relationship between market share and profitability. However, these results cannot distinguish between the two competing hypotheses (ESH vs RMPH) because of observational equivalence. Lloyd-Williams *et al.* found that market share was either negatively related to profit or insignificant when included with the three-bank concentration ratio, which was positively related to profit, in their study of Spanish banks in the 1980s. They came down in favour of the SCP hypothesis, but in fact even their study can be interpreted as observationally equivalent to the ESF model. The survey by Gilbert (1984) on an earlier generation of SCP studies in banking concluded that the empirical results suffered from inconsistencies and methodological flaws in being unable to distinguish between two competing hypotheses. In the survey, it was noted that nearly 50% rejected the SCP hypothesis. Later studies by Lloyd-Williams and others, while attempting to distinguish between the two hypotheses, still fail to produce identifying restrictions that could reject one hypothesis against another. The effect of barriers to entry and restrictions on interstate banking in the USA was examined by Scott-Frame and Kamerschen (1997) in their study of rural Georgia banks in 1994. They include an independent estimate of inefficiency, using the cost function approach to estimate relative inefficiency (see Chapter 10, equation (10.2) and Figure 10.1). If the inclusion of an efficiency measure makes market share insignificant, then market share is a proxy for efficiency and the RMPH model is rejected. If, on the other hand, the inclusion of efficiency does not affect the statistical significance of market share, then the ESH hypothesis is rejected. Scott-Frame and Kamerschen (1997) reject the ESH model but conclude that the relative market power was created by legal and possible market barriers to entry given restrictions in interstate banking (now abolished in the USA).

As noted by Gilbert (1984), the policy implications of the SCP (or RMPH) model against the ESH model are starkly different. According to the SCP hypothesis, dominant banks in the market should be broken up by competition legislation, whereas the ESH model suggests that the banking market should be left alone.

If barriers to entry buttress the existence of market power in banking, the removal of such barriers in the context of the deregulatory trend of the 1980s suggests that market concentration is not an impediment to competition. Indeed, it can be argued that banking represents a 'contestable market'. Baumol (1982) defined a contestable market as one where 'an entrant has access to all production techniques available to the incumbents, is not prohibited from wooing the incumbent's customers and entry decisions can be reversed without cost'. The conditions of contestability are that there should be no legal restriction to enter the market, that the entrant has the right to use the best available technology and that there be an absence of 'sunk costs'.

Sunk costs are irrecoverable costs that the entrant bank faces in setting up the business. It is not obvious that banks have 'sunk costs'. They have fixed costs, but these are not irrecoverable. A branch network may be seen as a barrier to entry, but that does not stop a new

---

[5] An estimated model is said to be observationally equivalent to another model where the same variables appear in both models, in this case the variable market share appearing with the same signed coefficient.

entrant taking over an incumbent bank, including its branch network, as indeed Bank Santander did with Abbey National in the UK. It is also not clear, in the age of Internet banking, how important a branch network is, as Egg Banking plc has demonstrated.[6] The implication of market contestability is that incumbent banks act as if they are in a competitive market and price competitively so as to deter entry. In the following section we examine the theoretical basis for the testing for competition in banking markets.

11.4 COMPETITION ANALYSIS

The shortcomings of the SCP and ESH approaches have been addressed by the *new empirical industrial organization* (NEIO), which assesses the strength of market power by examining deviations between observed and marginal cost pricing, without explicitly using any market structure indicator. One of the most popular methods is the Rosse and Panzar (1977) reduced-form revenue model. Specifically, the Rosse–Panzar method proposes the estimation of a bank specific revenue function in terms of the bank factor prices. The sum of the elasticities of revenue with respect to factor prices is known as the *H*-statistic. The *H*-statistic reveals the effect on revenue of an equiproportionate rise in factor prices. Clearly the effect on revenue will depend on the slope of the demand curve.

Let profit for the $\{ith\}$ bank be given by revenue less costs:

$$\pi_i = R_i(q_{i,j}, n, z_{i,s}) - C_i(q_{i,j}, w_{i,h}, x_{i,s}), \ i = 1, 2, K, n \tag{11.3}$$

where R_i and C_i refer to the revenue and costs of the ith bank, q_j denotes a vector $\{m\}$ of the outputs of that bank, n represents the number of banks in the industry, $z_{i,s}$ is a vector of exogenous variables that influence demand for the bank's output, $x_{i,t}$ is a vector of control variables that affect the supply of the bank's output and $w_{i,h}$ is a vector of $\{k\}$ input prices. Formally, banks maximize profits (π) where marginal revenue equals marginal cost, so that

$$\frac{\partial R_i}{\partial q_i}(q_i, n, z_i) - \frac{\partial C_i}{\partial q_i}(q_i, w_i, x_i) = 0, \ i = 1, 2, k, n \tag{11.4}$$

At the market level, in equilibrium, the zero profit condition implies that

$$R_i^*(q_i^*, n_i^*, z) - C_i^*(q_i^*, w, x) = 0 \tag{11.5}$$

where $\{*\}$ denotes equilibrium values for the industry as a whole. Market power is measured by the extent to which the revenue of the bank is affected by a change in factor prices.

---

[6] Figure 1.2 in Chapter 1 shows the decline in the number of branches for five major banks in the UK. The sharp decline is suggestive of evidence that the importance of a large branch network has declined in recent years.

TABLE 11.1 The discriminatory power of the *H*-statistic

Estimated *H*	Competitive environment
$H \leq 0$	Monopoly equilibrium: each bank operates independently as a monopoly
$H = 1$	Perfect competition or natural monopoly in a perfectly contestable market or sales-maximizing bank subject to a break-even constraint
$0 < H < 1$	Monopolistic competition free entry

The Panzar–Rosse method defines the sum of the input price elasticities (H) as the measure of competition:

$$H = \sum_{h=1}^{k} \frac{\partial R_i^{\star} \, w_{i,h}}{\partial w_{i,h} \, R_i^{\star}} \tag{11.6}$$

Rosse and Panzar (1977) and Panzar and Rosse (1982, 1987) show that, when the H-statistic is negative ($H \leq 0$) the structure of the market is a monopoly, a perfectly colluding oligopoly or a conjectural variation short-run oligopoly, as under these conditions an increase in input prices will increase marginal costs, reduce equilibrium output and subsequently reduce total firm revenue. In contrast, the H-statistic is equal to 1 ($H = 1$) when there is perfect competition, as any increase in input prices increases both marginal and average costs without altering the optimal output of any individual firm. H is also unity for a natural monopoly operating in a perfectly contestable market, and also for a sales-maximizing firm subject to break-even constraints. If $0 < H < 1$, this is a case of monopolistic competition.[7] Table 11.1 above summarizes the interpretation of the H-statistic for the competitive state of the banking market.

The perfect competition and monopoly cases can be explained easily with the aid of a diagram. Consider the effect of an equiproportionate rise in factor prices in the perfect competition case shown in Figure 11.2. For the firms in the industry, average and marginal cost curves shift up equiproportionately, as the cost function is homogeneous of degree 1 in factor prices. Output will not change, and the output price rises equiproportionately. Thus, revenue rises equiproportionately. In Figure 11.2, if all factor prices rise by 10% from w_0 to w_1, the AC curve rises by 10% and the price of output rises from P_0 to P_1, where $P_1 = 1.1(P_0)$.

From Figure 11.2 we can see that the increase in unit costs caused by the equiproportionate increase in factor prices is measured by the vertical distance between AC_0 and AC_1, which is $P_1 - P_0$. Total costs rise by $(P_1 - P_0)q_0$. The increase in revenue from the subsequent rise in the output price is also given by $(P_1 - P_0)q_0$.

---

[7] It should be stated that the validity of the Rosse–Panzar approach hinges on the demonstration that the market is in equilibrium. A subsidiary test is carried out for long-run equilibrium when a reduced-form function, where the dependent variable is the profit (ROA) of the ith bank, is regressed on the input prices and control variables. The test that the sum of the elasticities of input prices to profit be equal to zero is taken as a test for long-run equilibrium. See Matthews *et al.* (2007).

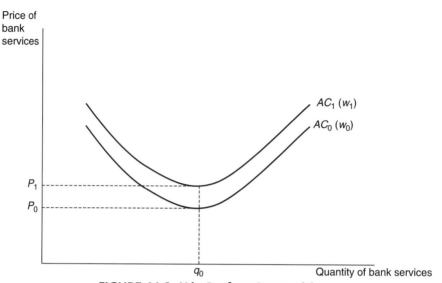

FIGURE 11.2 *H* in Perfect Competition.

Figure 11.3 describes the other extreme case which is the case of monopoly. The equilibrium position is defined as the quantity of bank services being produced is q_0 at the price P_0.

Total revenue is given by $P_0 q_0$. An equiproportionate increase in all input prices pushes
the AC curve up and the MC curve up to the left. Since the monopoly produces on the
price elastic part of the demand curve, the rise in MC will result in a lower production than
q_0 and a higher price than P_0. Because the price elasticity of demand is greater than unity,
total revenue declines, and hence $H < 0$.

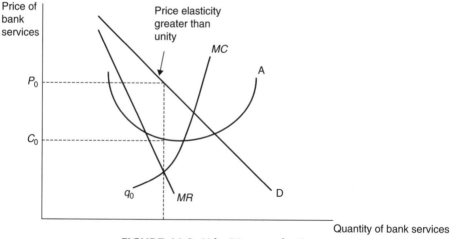

FIGURE 11.3 *H* in Monopoly Case.

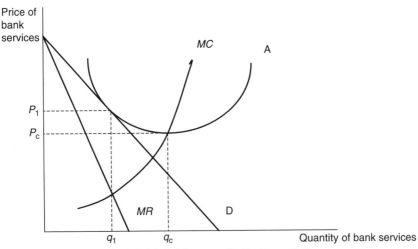

FIGURE 11.4 Monopolistic Free Entry.

The monopolistic competition case is where free entry takes place until the zero profit condition is satisfied and price equals average cost for each bank. Alternatively, industry behaviour is seen as being constrained by the threat of entry, as in the contestable markets case of Baumol *et al.* (1982) discussed earlier. The intermediate case when $1 > H > 0$ is the monopolistic competition case of Chamberlin (1929) and is described in Figure 11.4. Equilibrium in this case exhibits excess capacity where banks are producing at a point where average cost is higher than the minimum average cost point. Also, price $\{P_1\}$ exceeds marginal cost and is above the competitive equilibrium price $\{P_c\}$.

In equilibrium, supernormal profits are not earned, as banks price their services at average cost. However, market power exists, as measured by the price-marginal cost margin (the Lerner index).[8] The degree of price competition implied by the monopolistic competition model depends on how close the equilibrium price $\{P_1\}$ is relative to the competitive equilibrium price $\{P_c\}$.

A large number of empirical studies using the Rosse–Panzar approach have been used to study the banking markets of various countries. The consensus is that banking markets exhibit monopolistic competition, as confirmed by Table 11.2. However, Molyneux *et al.* (1996) found evidence of monopoly situations in Japan in 1986–1988, and De Bandt and Davis (2000) found that large banks in France, Germany and Italy faced monopolistic competition whereas small banks behaved as monopolists. In contrast, Bikker and Haaf (2002) found that, when they segmented the banking market into small-, medium- and large-sized banks for 23 countries (European and non-European), they were unable to reject perfect competition in the large bank market segments for some of the countries. This suggests that competition is tougher in the large bank market segment than in the smaller, perhaps more specialized, banks.

Clearly, the empirical results are themselves not without controversy. Whether the Panzar–Rosse *H*-statistic can definitively identify the competitive conditions of a banking

---

[8] See footnotes 8 and 9 of Chapter 6.

TABLE 11.2 Panzar–Rosse results in empirical studies

Study	Period	Countries	Results
Shaffer (1982)	1979	US (New York)	Monopolistic competition
Nathan and Neave (1989)	1982–1984	Canada	Mostly monopolistic competition
Lloyd-Williams et al. (1994)	1986–1988	Japan	Monopoly
Molyneux et al. (1994)	1986–1989	France, Germany, Italy, Spain, UK	Mostly monopolistic competition
Vesala (1995)	1985–1992	Finland	Mostly monopolistic competition
Molyneux et al. (1996)	1986–1988	Japan	Monopoly
Coccorese (1998)	1988–1996	Italy	Monopolistic competition
Rime (1999)	1987–1994	Switzerland	Monopolistic competition
Bikker and Groeneveld (2000)	1989–1996	15 EU countries	Monopolistic competition
De Bandt and Davis (2000)	1992–1996	France, Germany and Italy	Large banks monopolistic competition. Small banks monopoly
Bikker and Haaf (2002)	Various mostly 1991–1998	23 OECD countries	Mostly monopolistic competition, but large banks in some countries in perfect competition
Casu and Girardone (2006)	1997–2003	EU	Monopolistic competition
Matthews et al. (2007)	1980–2002	UK	Monopolistic competition

market is not an unchallengeable proposition. A more interesting case may be to examine the evolution of the banking market in the light of the global forces that have led to a state of continuous change. In an important study of the banking markets across a wide range of countries, Claessens and Laeven (2004) estimated the H-statistic for 50 countries over 1994–2001. The distribution of H-statistics was then explained by a set of country-specific factors. They found that, the higher the concentration of foreign banks in a banking market, the higher was the level of competitiveness as measured by the H-statistic. They also found that concentration was positively related to competitiveness, which rejects the SCP hypothesis in favour of contestability. Similarly, restrictions on entry and banking activity reduced competitiveness.

In the next section we shall examine the competitive conditions in the UK banking market.

11.5 COMPETITION IN THE UK BANKING MARKET

The growth of deregulation and competition in the UK market was briefly summarized in Chapter 1.2 but is discussed more fully below. The process of banking deregulation in the UK began in late 1971 with the creation of competition and credit control (CCC). Prior to CCC the UK banking system worked under a cartel agreement. Quantitative controls existed on loans in the form of external credit rationing, and interest rates on loans and deposits were regulated by a cartel agreement. The cash reserve ratio was 8% and the liquid assets ratio was 28%. Following CCC, the cash reserve ratio was reduced by 1.5%, which involved only the commercial bank deposits at the Bank of England, and the liquid assets ratio was reduced to 12.5%. Quantitative controls on bank lending were supposed to be replaced by a market-based solution. Credit growth and the monetary aggregates were to be controlled by the Bank rate of interest. The new environment prompted a rapid rise in bank lending and therefore a sharp increase in the money supply. The increase in the money supply was viewed as excessive, and a new instrument of control was created in the form of the supplementary special deposit scheme in late 1973 (also known as the 'corset'). Under this scheme, the Bank of England set guidelines for the growth of deposits which reintroduced quantitative controls on the commercial banks.[9] Interest rate ceilings were introduced between 1973 and 1975. Additionally, lending guidelines and informal controls (quaintly referred to as 'moral suasion') were introduced as a means of controlling the growth of bank lending in 1973 and 1975. Thus, the deregulation of CCC was short lived.

Deregulation began again in earnest with the 1981 reforms. The cash ratio was reduced further to 0.5% and the reserve asset ratio was abolished.[10] Exchange controls that existed during CCC were abolished in 1979. Exchange controls meant that banks were constrained in taking foreign currency deposits and making foreign currency loans. The removal of exchange controls amounted to the removal of a type of protection from international competition for the banking industry. Another form of quantitative credit control was hire purchase control, which was abolished in 1980.

The Banking Act of 1979 regularized banking supervision by extending the supervisory authority of the Bank of England to all deposit-taking institutions except for building societies. Deposit-taking institutions were separated into 'recognized banks' and 'licensed deposit takers', but, more significantly, the Banking Act of 1987 provided a mechanism by which non-bank institutions could enter the retail banking market, removing a former barrier to

---

[9] SSDs were levied as a progressively rising proportion of the excess of 'interest-bearing eligible liabilities' (IBELs). These SSDs were non-interest-bearing deposits with the Bank of England, which acted as a reserve ratio tax on the excess growth of deposits.

[10] Most commercial banks in the UK operate with liquidity ratios of 2−3% of assets, which also helps explain why the UK has higher ROE than other EU banks because loans and advances have been expanded dramatically to fill the gap created by the proportionately smaller low-interest liquid assets held on their balance sheets.

entry.[11] A further important concession to clearing bank competitors was access to the clearing house system and the widening market for retail demand deposits. Competition increased further with the break-up of the building society cartel in 1983. The Building Societies Act of 1987 created room for more competition in banking, with the provision for banking services, unsecured lending, credit cards and commercial loans of up to 10% of assets.

The deregulatory trend was extended to the Stock Exchange, with the deregulation of the financial markets. After 1986, the banks became more aggressive in the marketing and positioning of their off-balance-sheet products and services. Many banks entered the securities business, acquiring stockbroking and jobbing firms, while non-banking financial institutions, such as insurers, retailers and building societies, challenged the banks on their traditional balance sheet activity. The rest of the period from 1987 to 2003 saw a number of demutualizations, consolidations, mergers, acquisitions and diversifications that affected the banking sector. Abbey National was the first building society to convert to plc status in 1989. Banks took over building societies (Lloyds with Cheltenham and Gloucester). After 1995, there were a number of demutualizations of building societies (Halifax, Alliance and Leicester, Northern Rock, Woolwich and Bradford and Bingley) and building society acquisitions by banks (Bristol and West by the Bank of Ireland Group and Birmingham and Midshires by Halifax). Lloyds and TSB merged in 1995 to form the Lloyds-TSB group, Barclays took over Woolwich in 2000 and the Royal Bank of Scotland acquired National Westminster in the same year. The Bank of Scotland and Halifax merged in 2001 to form the HBOS group, and the Spanish bank Santander acquired Abbey National in 2004.

The number of mergers, consolidations and acquisitions that occurred in the UK during the 1990s and in the new century may give the impression that there was an increase in concentration and, with it, a worsening of competition. However, Matthews *et al.* (2007) point out that the asset-based two-bank concentration ratio, the five-bank concentration ratio and *HHI* showed, if anything, a modest decline in the second half of the 1990s compared with the earlier period (Table 11.3). Nevertheless, all the *HHI* ratios fall within the US Department of Justice's category of a moderately concentrated industry (see Section 11.2).

Because London is a centre for international banking, there is a presumption that the UK has an open and competitive banking market. However, there have been very few studies that have examined the UK banking market in detail. Sheila Heffernan examined competition in the retail banking market in the 1980s (Heffernan, 1993) and in the 1990s (Heffernan, 2002). She examined deposit rate, loan rate, mortgage rate and credit card rate setting behaviour of individual banks and building societies on the basis of econometric models of interest rate equations using monthly data. The tests involved regression analysis of interest rates of the form

$$r_{it} = \alpha + \sum_{j=1}^{k} \beta_j r^*_{t-j} + \gamma T + \delta_i D_i + \eta N + \varepsilon_{it} \tag{11.7}$$

where r_{it} is the rate of interest {deposit rate, saving rate, mortgage rate, credit card rate, personal loans, other rates}, r^* is the London interbank offer rate (LIBOR), T is a time trend,

---

[11] The 1987 Act effectively removed the distinction. While the conversion from licensed deposit taker to retail bank has not been rapid following the legislation, the number of retail banks in 1984 was 140 and the most recent statistics from the British Banking Association suggest a membership of 250 institutions (see www.bba.org.uk).

TABLE 11.3 Concentration ratios and HHI for the biggest two and biggest five banks

Year/Measure	CR2	CR5	HHI
1986	0.421	0.767	1428.470
1991	0.441	0.738	1423.817
1996	0.316	0.630	1051.831
2002	0.383	0.688	1249.696

Source: Reprinted from Matthews, K., Murinde, V. and Zhao, T. (2007). Competitive conditions among the major British banks. *Journal of Banking and Finance,* **31,** 2025–2042. With permission from Elsevier.

N is the number of banks in the market for that particular financial product, D is a dummy variable for bank $i = 1, 2, \ldots, N - 1$, where D takes the value 1 for the ith bank and 0 for all others, and the Nth bank is the benchmark, and ε is an error term. In the 2002 study, the data is monthly 1993–1999. Equation (11.7) can be interpreted as a spread (between the rate of interest in question and a market rate of interest (LIBOR)) if the restriction $\sum_{j=1}^{k} \beta_j = 1$ is applied. The time trend can be interpreted as the trend in the spread, which, if significant, can indicate rising (or falling) risk or increased (or decreased) market power, depending on the sign of $\{\gamma\}$. If η is significant, that would indicate Cournot pricing behaviour in that, the larger the number of banks in the market, the lower is the loan rate $\eta < 0$ or the higher the deposit rate $(\eta > 0)$.[12] The interpretation of the dummy variable can be viewed as a statement of market power based on imperfect information. A negative value of δ indicates that the bank in question underprices loans (and deposits). A positive value means that the bank overprices loans (and deposits).

Heffernan's results indicated an increase in competition in the mortgage market and low-interest checking accounts, but showed the existence of price discrimination behaviour in other products. Her findings suggested that the retail banking sector in Britain is best described as monopolistic competition based on imperfect information, particularly in the case of unsecured loans and credit card rate setting behaviour. Cournot-type behaviour was evident in the credit card market as interest rate setting was sensitive to the number of suppliers. The imperfect information result was based on the empirical finding that the dummy variable that identified each bank was in general significant, which indicated a difference with the benchmark bank (Royal Bank of Scotland). One possible reason for the differences is that banks may deliberately underprice some products as a loss-leader and use overpriced products as a cross-subsidy. This is a common practice in banking, which means that banks undertake strategic competition by charging for a bundled price rather than for individual products. In this scenario it is difficult to test for competition by just looking at the pricing behaviour of particular products.

[12] Chapter 6, Section 6.5.

A government enquiry into competition in UK banking was conducted by Don Cruickshank and published in March 2000 (Cruikshank, 2000). The Cruikshank report concluded that, while the market for personal retail banking was consistent with monopolistic competition as evidenced by sustained abnormal return, there were signs of 'new entry and increased competition' that would improve information flows and result in a convergence of pricing. The report recognized that banking involves 'joint products' or 'bundled' services that can lead to overpricing and underpricing on different products. However, new entrants target specific banking products, and, even though they may be part of a larger banking group, they often specialize in such products as mortgages, unsecured loans and credit cards, which have dynamic effects on improving competition in those niche markets. Will the entrance of new banks lead to a reduction in the over- and underpricing given that they will probably target areas where overpricing exists?

The difficulty with examining competition in the UK banking market by focusing on individual banking products is that the practice of bundled pricing or strategic competition makes such tests difficult to administer. Studies that focus on the total revenue of the bank may have a better prospect of identifying the competitive nature of the market.

Other studies of the UK bank market have been conducted in the context of wider studies of international bank competition using the Rosse–Panzar approach explained above.[13] These studies typically use a panel set of data and include a large number of banks in a country irrespective of specialist practice (in the case of the UK, many individual banks are either wholly owned or partially owned by larger parent banks that constitute the major British banks).

Using the Rosse–Panzar methodology, Matthews et al. (2007) examine interest and non-interest revenue of the banks. They conclude that the banking market in Britain over the period 1980–2002 was one of monopolistic competition. Their finding is surprising in that, following the number of mergers and acquisitions by banks and newly converted banks in this period, the competitive conditions on the core business of banking (balance sheet business) has remained roughly the same in the 1990s and 2000s, as in the 1980s. However, they find that, on examining non-interest revenue, there has been a significant worsening of competition. Non-interest earnings amounted to between 30 and 35% of gross revenue for banks, which represents a significant source of income.

How is it possible for competitiveness to be unchanged in some products but to worsen in others? The answer, according to Llewellyn (2005), is through the mechanism of 'bundling'. The purchase of one bank service may be conditional on the purchase of another, which may deter the customers from searching for the best individual product when in reality they purchase a bundle of products. The lack of competitiveness in the non-interest income segment of bank earnings has seen British banks making a strategic decision to develop capital-free business to raise ROE and the removal of assets from the balance sheet through securitization if they do not meet target ROE. Llewellyn (2005) argues that this is a deliberate strategy of economic value added (EVA) by maximizing shareholder value. However, economic theory suggests that the refocusing of British banks in the non-interest earnings capacity of their enterprise will eventually attract competition from new entrants or create the potential for the threat of entry.

---

[13] For example, Molyneux et al. (1994), Bikker and Haaf (2002), Claessens and Laeven (2004) and Casu and Girardone (2006).

11.6 SUMMARY

- This chapter has posed the question as to whether the consolidation in the banking sector has led to a worsening of competitiveness in banking? At a superficial level, economic theory suggests that, the larger the number of suppliers, the lower will be the likelihood of anticompetitive behaviour. Cournot oligopolistic behaviour would indicate that the number of banks in the market influences the price of individual financial products and the spread on intermediation.
- The empirical evidence for the existence of market power from the SCP literature is mixed and is challenged by the efficient structure hypothesis. The Rosse–Panzar model of testing for bank competitiveness has been examined, and the empirical findings for a wide area of banking markets have been reviewed. The consensus finding from the Rosse–Panzar model is that banking markets are consistent with monopolistic competition or contestable markets. Contestability and monopolistic competition result in prices being driven down to average costs to eliminate supernormal profits, but recognize that the specific informational nature of banking endows individual banks with market power, as described by a downward-sloping demand curve for its products.
- This chapter has examined the empirical evidence relating to the testing for competitiveness in the UK banking market. There is some evidence of Cournot pricing behaviour, but the evidence is also consistent with strategic competition and bundled pricing. The most recent study of the UK banking market suggests that banking in the new century is as competitive as in the 1990s and 1980s in the business of intermediation (loans and deposits), but there is evidence of a worsening competitiveness in off-balance-sheet and fee-income-generating product markets.

QUESTIONS

1   How is concentration measured in the banking market?

2   What information does the *HHI* statistic provide about the nature of a banking market?

3   What is the SCP hypothesis, and is the empirical evidence consistent with this hypothesis?

4   What has been the main empirical finding concerning the competitive state of banking markets in developed economies?

5   Explain how the *H*-statistic from the Rosse–Panzar methodology indicates the competitive nature of the banking market.

TEST QUESTIONS

1   Do bank mergers necessarily lead to anti-competitive behaviour? Explain your answer.

2   It is often said that British banking is highly competitive but paradoxically the banks report increasing profit performance each year. How is this paradox explained?

12

Bank Regulation

MINI-CONTENTS

12.1 Introduction
12.2 The case for regulation
12.3 Regulation
12.4 The case against regulation
12.5 Summary

12.1 INTRODUCTION

'Bank failures around the world in recent years have been common, large and expensive. While they were, perhaps, larger than generally appreciated, their existence does not of itself, necessarily justify the attention currently being given to the reinforcement of financial regulation and supervision'. So begins a recent study of financial regulation published in association with the Bank of England.[1]

It is commonplace to think of bank failure as something that happens in emerging economies and countries with unsophisticated banking systems, but there have been some spectacular failures of banks and banking systems within the developed economies in recent decades. In France, 8.9% of total loans in 1994 were non-performing. The French government rescue package for Credit Lyonnais amounted to $27bn. The Scandinavian bank crisis in 1991–1992 ($16bn) showed that, in Finland, non-performing loans reached 13% of total bank lending in 1992, following a liquidity crisis in September 1991. Heavy losses and insolvency in Norway led to a crisis in 1991 in which 6% of commercial bank loans were non-performing. In 1990–1993, 18% of total bank loans in Sweden were reported lost, and two main banks were assisted. The most spectacular record of banking system crisis was the failure of the Saving and Loan (S&L) associations in the USA. In the period 1980–1992, 1142 S&L associations and 1395 banks were closed. Non-performing loans amounted to 4.1% of commercial bank loans in 1987.

---

[1] Goodhart *et al.* (1998).

The scale and frequency of bank failures and banking crises have raised doubts about the efficacy of bank regulation and raised questions as to whether the regulation itself has created an iatrogenic[2] reaction.

The responses to the widespread banking failures around the world have been twofold. One response has been that market discipline does not work, because depositors are unable adequately to monitor banks. Rumour and imperfect information can lead to bank runs that can generate more widespread bank failures and systemic risk. A second reaction has been, in contrast to the first reaction, inadequate market discipline. Market forces are the best way of assessing and pricing bank risk.

This chapter addresses three issues. Firstly, drawing from the theories of market failure, it examines the arguments for regulation. Secondly, it examines the existing state of bank regulation and proposed changes. Thirdly, it critically examines the regulatory system from the perspective of the free banking school.

12.2 THE CASE FOR REGULATION

The strongest case for regulation of activities arises in cases where physical danger is involved, such as, for example, firearms or road safety regulations. Clearly, financial regulation does not fall into this category. In fact, the case for regulation of banks and other financial institutions hinges on the Coase (1988) argument that unregulated private actions create outcomes whereby social marginal costs are greater than private marginal costs. The social marginal costs occur because bank failure has a far greater effect throughout the economy than, say, failure of a manufacturing concern because of the widespread use of banks (a) to make payments and (b) as a store for savings. In contrast, the private marginal costs are borne by the shareholders and the employees of the company, and these are likely to be of a smaller magnitude than the social costs. Nevertheless, it should be borne in mind that regulation involves real resource costs. These costs arise from two sources:

(a) Direct regulatory costs.
(b) Compliance costs borne by the firms regulated.

These costs are not trivial and have been characterized by Goodhart (1995) as representing 'the monstrous and expensive regiment of regulators'.[3] Some estimate of category (a) in the UK can be derived from the Financial Services Authority (FSA) projected budget for 2007/2008, which forecast an expenditure of £301.7m for mainline regulatory activities, although it should be remembered that in the UK the FSA is responsible for supervision of other financial institutions as well as banks. An assessment of the importance of category (b) can be derived from a survey carried out by the Financial Services Practitioners Panel (FSPP, 2004) in which it is reported that the total cost (i.e. including both categories (a) and (b)) amounted to more than 10% of total operating costs for 44% of respondents and more than 5% of total operating costs for 72% of respondents. This level of cost is quite onerous,

---

[2] When the medicine for an illness creates worse problems for the patient than the illness itself.

[3] This is, of course, an intentional misquote of John Knox's famous polemic against Mary, Queen of Scots.

so that, consequently, the presumption is that the free market is preferable unless it can be shown that the benefits of regulation outweigh the costs involved. It should also be mentioned that one of the hidden costs of excessive regulation is a potential loss of innovation dynamism (Llewellyn, 2003). In the following sections we examine why regulation of banks may be desirable.

The main reasons for regulation are threefold. Firstly, consumers lack market power and are prone to exploitation from the monopolistic behaviour of banks. Secondly, depositors are uninformed and unable to monitor banks and, therefore, require protection. Finally, we need regulation to ensure the safety and stability of the banking system.

The first argument is based on the premise that banking continues to have elements of monopolistic behaviour. To some extent this is correct. Banks are able to exploit the information they have about their clients to exercise some monopolistic pricing, but to think that this is the reason for the differences in the pricing of loans and deposits would be to ignore elements of risk (Chapter 7) and the strong contestability of the banking market that has contributed to the decline in interest margins (Chapters 1 and 6). The second two arguments are linked. The support for regulation is based on three propositions:

1. Uninsured depositors are unable to monitor banks.
2. Even if depositors have the sophistication to monitor banks, the additional interest rates banks would pay on deposits to reflect risk would not deter bank behaviour.
3. Uninsured depositors are likely to run rather than monitor.

The first proposition is challengeable at least as far as wholesale banking, as opposed to retail banking, is concerned. Casual observation would suggest that users of wholesale (investment) banks have the sophistication and information to monitor such banks. The evidence on analysing stock prices of banks also produces mixed results. The decline in real-estate values in the 1980s and the rise in oil prices hit New England and South Western banks in the USA, particularly. There is some evidence that supports the view that bank stocks provide an early warning of bank problems. Where the evidence was mixed, it was largely due to 'unexpected' turns (news) in the market affecting stock prices. On the second proposition, there is evidence that certificate of deposit (CD) rates paid by S&Ls in the 1980s in the USA responded to perceptions of market risk.[4]

The argument that uninsured bank depositors are likely to cause a bank run when faced with information of an adverse shock to bank balance sheets has two supporting features. Firstly the argument can appeal to history, and secondly it can appeal to theory.

The USA has the best examples of bank failures caused by bank panics. The most infamous period was the era of 'free banking', which began in 1837. During this period many banks lasted only a short period and failed to pay out their depositors in full. In the period 1838–1863, the number of unregulated banks chartered in New York, Wisconsin, Indiana and Minnesota was 709. Of these, 339 closed within a few years and 104 failed to meet all liabilities.[5] The National Banking Act 1863 was an attempt to create a stable banking

---

[4] If market participants thought that the Federal Deposit Insurance Corporation (FDIC) would insure deposits at S&Ls, then CD rates would not be at a premium. The fact that some premium was found reflects uncertainty of a full insurance cover and bail-out.

[5] Rolnick (1993).

environment and a uniform currency. If a banking crisis is defined as widespread bank runs and bank failures accompanied with a decline in deposits, there were four such occurrences: 1878, 1893, 1908 and the Great Depression in the 1930s. The Federal Reserve system was established in 1913. In the decade of the 1920s, 6000 of 30 000 banks failed, but, in the period 1930–1933, 9000 banks failed. The experience of the 1930s led to the setting up of the Federal Deposit Insurance Corporation (FDIC) in 1934. Over the years the FDIC coverage widened as more and more depositors chose to bank with insured banks. The results were that, in the first 5 years of the FDIC being formed, bank failures averaged only 50 a year, and in the next 5 years the average fell to 17 a year. Indeed, bank failures in the USA never rose to more than 12 a year until 1982 with the advent of the S&L crisis.

The evidence certainly appears to support the argument that a deposit insurance scheme reduces the danger of bank runs and the systemic effects a run on one bank can cause to other banks and the banking system. The supporters of bank regulation also have theory as well as history on their side. The most influential theory of preventing bank runs is the analysis of Diamond and Dybvig (1983). The model consists of a large number of identical agents who live for three periods, so $T = \{0, 1, 2\}$. Each agent is endowed with one unit of a good and makes a storage or investment decision in period 0. In period 1, some agents are hit by an unpredictable liquidity demand and forced to consume in period 1 and receive one unit of goods. These are called *type-1* agents. The rest consume in period 2 and they receive R units of goods, where $R > 1$. These are *type-2* agents. One solution is that there will be trades in claims for consumption in periods 1 and 2. The problem with this solution is that neither type of agent knows *ex ante* the probability that funds will be required in period 1. However, they can opt for an insurance contract, which may be in the form of a demand deposit. This would give each agent the right either to withdraw funds in period 1 or hold them until the end of period 2, which provides a superior outcome. An alternative scenario occurs with both types of agent withdrawing funds in period 1; in other words, there is a run on the bank. Two policy initiatives can prevent this outcome:

1. Suspension of convertibility, which prevents the withdrawal of deposits.
2. Provision by the authorities of a deposit insurance scheme which removes the incentive for participation in a bank run because the deposits are 'safe'. The authorities can finance the deposit insurance scheme by levying charges on the banks. Given that a bank run does not occur, these will be minor after the initial levy to finance the required compensation fund.

This model and its predictions are set out more formally in Box 12.1.

The argument that deposit insurance eliminates bank runs has some validity.[6] But an important side effect is the development of moral hazard on the part of the insured bank. Once depositors are insured, they no longer have an incentive to monitor the bank they keep their deposits in. In return, riskier banks do not have to pay higher rates to their depositors to compensate them for riskier deposits. Rolnick (1993) illustrates how deposit insurance distorts banks' behaviour and creates moral hazard.

The balance sheet of the bank and Mr Smith is shown below. Let a new bank be chartered by Mr Smith who has $200k. He sets up the bank by passing $100k to the bank in return for $100k equity. Note he is the sole stockholder. The bank becomes a member of

---

[6] Although questioned fiercely by the proponents of the free banking school (Dowd, 1993).

BOX 12.1   A model of bank runs

The consumption choices made in period 1 for periods 1 and 2 are $(0, R)$ or $(1, 0)$. Table 12.1 shows the consumption choice for the two types.

TABLE 12.1

Type	$T = 1$	$T = 2$
1	1	0
2	0	R

Each agent has a state-dependent utility function of the form

$$U = U(C_1, C_2; \theta) \tag{12.1.1}$$

If the agent is type 1 in state θ, the utility function is $U = U(C_1)$. If the agent is type 2 in state θ, the utility is $U = \rho U(C_1 + C_2)$, where $1 \geq \rho > R^{-1}$.

The *competitive (autarky) solution* is one where there will be trades in claims on goods for consumption in $T = 1$ and 2. If we denote the consumption of agent type k in time t as C_t^k, then agents choose the following:

$$C_1^1 = 1; C_2^1 = C_1^2 = 0; C_2^2 = R$$

Now, let us assume that the probability of any given agent being type 1 is known *ex post* (after period 1) but not *ex ante* (in period 0). Then it is possible to design an optimal insurance contact in period 0 that gives an optimal sharing of output between both types. Both types recognize their individual condition in period 1 when they know whether they are type 1 or type 2. However, since neither of the types knows this in period 0, they opt for an insurance contract. The solution to this is $C_1^1 > 1; C_2^2 < R$, but $C_2^2 > C_1^1$, which is superior to the competitive (autarky) solution. The optimal insurance contract allows agents to insure against the outcome of being type 1. This contract can be made by banks in the form of a demand–deposit contract. The demand–deposit contract gives each agent withdrawing in period 1 a fixed claim r_1 per unit deposited in period $T = 0$. Withdrawals are serviced sequentially (the bank exists only until $T = 3$):

$V_1 =$ Period 1 payoff per unit of deposit withdrawn (depends on the agent's place in the queue)

$V_2 =$ Period 2 payoff

The payoff functions are described by the following expressions:

$$V_1(f_j, r_1) = \begin{cases} r_1, & \text{if}, f_j r_1 < 1 \\ 0, & \text{if}, f_j r_1 \geq 1 \end{cases}$$

$$V_2(f_j, r_1) = \max \left\{ \frac{R(1 - r_1 f)}{(1 - f)}, 0 \right\}$$

(continued)

where f_j is the number of withdrawals of deposits by agent j as a fraction of total deposits, and f is the total number of deposits withdrawn.

The payoff function for period 1 says that the withdrawal per depositor is 1 up until the point when all reserves held by the bank have been exhausted and remaining depositors get 0. The payoff function for period 2 says that depositors who do not withdraw in period 1 get R or 0 depending on whether or not the bank has been exhausted of reserves in period 1 from withdrawal.

There are two types of equilibrium in this model with the demand–deposit contract. Firstly, type-1 agents withdraw in period 1 and type-2 agents wait until period 2. Secondly, there is a bank run when all agents attempt to withdraw in period 1.

There are two policy conclusions from this analysis:

1. Suspension of convertibility. Removes incentives for type 2 to withdraw deposits. This is the same as the previous contract, except agents will receive nothing in $T = 1$ if they try to withdraw beyond a fixed limit.
2. In the case of a government deposit insurance scheme, type-2 agents never participate in the run. The government can tax to impose insurance but never needs to because there will not be a run.

the FDIC and is opened with $100k of reserves and $100k equity. The balance sheet of the bank and Mr Smith following these transactions is shown below:

Smith National Bank

Assets	Liabilities
Reserves $100k	Equity $100k

Smith's balance sheet

Assets	Liabilities
Cash $100k	
Bank stock $100k	Net worth $200k

Assume that the Smith Bank offers a deposit rate greater than his competitors' (say, 10%) and this attracts deposits of $900k. The balance sheet of Smith National Bank is now as follows:

Smith National Bank

Assets	Liabilities
Reserves $1000k	Deposits $900k
	Equity $100k

Smith's balance sheet is unchanged; however, he invests the bank's funds on the roulette table. He bets the bank's $1000k on *black* and hedges his investment by betting $100k of his own money on *red*. The balance sheets are now as follows:

Smith National Bank

Assets	Liabilities
Bet on black $1000k	Deposits $900k
	Equity $100k

Smith's balance sheet

Assets	Liabilities
Bet on *red* $100k	
Bank stock $100k	Net worth $200k

If *red* comes up, the bank fails and the bank's stock is worthless. Depositors are protected by the FDIC. Smith has a perfect hedge as his net worth is $200k, i.e. the original $100k plus the $100k profit on the bet, the bank stock value now being zero.

If *black* comes up, Mr Smith loses the bet and $100k, but the bank gains $1000k. The bank has to pay interest on deposits (10% of $900k). The balance sheets then become:

Smith National Bank

Assets	Liabilities
Cash from bet less $90k interest paid on deposits = $1910k	Deposits $900k
	Equity $1010k

Smith's balance sheet

Assets	Liabilities
Bet on *red* $0	
Bank stock $1010k	Net worth $1010k

This example illustrates the incentive for the bank owners to take on much more risk than would be prudent since there is a chance of a substantial gain in Smith's net worth ($910k) against the chance of zero loss. This illustrative example assumes that bank owners are able to hedge their positions perfectly or, equivalently, are risk neutral.

While it may be argued that bank owners may wish the bank to take on extra risk, the counterargument is that bank managers are risk averse and would value their employment. This argument is questionable. The board of directors of a bank can design incentive contracts

TABLE 12.2   Bank deposit insurance schemes

Country	Level of protection per deposit
United States	$100 000
Canada	C$100 000
United Kingdom	100% protected to max £2000 and 90% to £35 000
Japan	¥10 000 000
Switzerland	SFr30 000
France	€60 980
Germany	90% protected, 20 000
Hong Kong	HK$100 000

for bank managers to extend credit to risky borrowers. Targets for credit managers were common in East Asian banking, and the 1980s is replete with examples of UK banks overextending credit, particularly to real-estate lending. Rolnick (1993) cites the S&L crisis as an example of deposit insurance creating moral hazard in the S&L industry. By 1982, virtually all deposits of S&Ls became insured. In less than 6 years, S&Ls were in serious trouble. By 1988, nearly one-half of all S&Ls were close to bankruptcy. Once the policy of 100% deposit insurance was set in place, the problems of moral hazard extended to the commercial banks as well. Prior to the 1980s, relatively few banks failed in the post-war period. In 1982–1983, 45 banks failed per year. In the period 1984–1988, the average annual bank failure was 144. By 1990, the FDIC was estimated to be in negative net worth to the tune of $70bn.

The recognition that deposit insurance or the existence of a central bank that can act as a lender of last resort to the banking system creates the need for bank regulation is a well-established argument. Bhattacharya *et al.* (1998) argues that, because of the existence of deposit insurance, banks are tempted to take on excessive asset risk and hold fewer reserves (Table 12.2 lists the cover of deposit insurance in selected countries known at the time of writing this book). One way to deal with excess asset risk is to link banks' shareholder capital to the risk of the bank. Support for regulation on reserve ratios and capital adequacy is provided by this argument.

12.3 REGULATION

Economists are divided on the need for regulation of banks. Bhattacharya *et al.* (1998) argue that it is the existence of deposit insurance that provides the motivation for regulation. Dewatripont and Tirole (1994) emphasize the protection of small depositors who do not have the sophistication (e.g. to interpret bank accounts) or the incentive to monitor banks. The incentive problem arises because each depositor is a small holder of the bank's liabilities. Since the monitoring of banks requires both technical sophistication as well as resources, no individual depositor would be willing to exert the resources to monitor and, rather, free-ride on somebody else doing the monitoring. Regulation, therefore, is required to mimic the control and monitoring that would exist if depositors were coordinated and well informed.

The philosophy of current UK regulation is to allow for healthy competition in banking while improving prudential discipline through capitalization. Prior to the 1979 Banking Act, there were no specific banking laws in the UK. The 1979 Act also created a depositors' protection fund to which all banks contribute. The fund allows for an insurance cover of 90% of a maximum insurable deposit of £20 000. The current cover is a maximum payout of £33 500 – full payment of the first £2000 and 90% of the next £35 000.[7] See Table 12.2.

Central banks and other regulatory agencies have typically used two measures of capital adequacy:

1. The gearing ratio.
2. The risk capital–asset ratio.

The gearing ratio is formally the ratio of bank deposits plus external liabilities to bank capital and reserves. It is an indicator of how much of deposits is covered if a proportion of the bank's borrowers default. Let the balance sheet be described as

$$A = D + E \tag{12.1}$$

where A represents total assets, D is deposits and E is equity. The gearing ratio is $g = D/E$. If μ is the default rate, then max $\mu = 1/(1 + g)$. If μA of assets is lost from default, then all bank capital is lost but deposits are covered.[8]

The other common measure used by central banks and regulatory agencies is the risk capital–asset ratio of the Basel Accord 1988 (BIS, 1988). This capital adequacy ratio, commonly known as the 'Cooke ratio',[9] sets out a common minimum risk capital–asset ratio for international banks. The regulation was applied in 1993 and is set at a minimum of 8%, which is made up of tier-1 (at least 4%) and tier-2 capital. Tier-1 capital is essentially paid-up capital, retained earnings and disclosed reserves (general provisions to cover unidentified risks). Tier 2 includes other elements and hybrid debt instruments such as re-evaluation of premises (when real-estate values change), hidden reserves (these appear when there are excessive bad debt provisions on specific loans), 45% of unrealized gains on securities (when the market values of securities differ from book value) and subordinated debt (capped at 50% of tier 1). The latter protects ordinary depositors who are primary debt holders in case of bank default.

The Basel Accord considered only credit risk. The risk-adjusted assets are the weighted sum of assets explicit and implicit for both on-balance-sheet and off-balance-sheet items. On-balance-sheet items were assigned to one of five risk buckets and appropriately weighted. Off-balance-sheet items had to be first converted to a credit equivalent and then appropriately weighted.

---

[7] At the time of writing, the Chancellor of the Exchequer had mooted the idea of extending deposit protection to £100 000 following the collapse of the Northern Rock bank in the UK.

[8] From (12.1), $A = (g + 1)E$. If max $\mu A = E$, then, by substituting for E and eliminating A, $1 = (g + 1)\mu$. Or max $\mu = 1/(g + 1)$.

[9] Peter Cooke was the first chairman of the Basel Committee. See Cooke (1990).

The formal risk-weighted assets and solvency requirements as described by Dewatripont and Tirole (1994) are:

$$
\text{Capital} \geq 0.08 \left\{ \left[\sum_i \alpha_i \text{ on-balance assets of type } i \right] \right.
$$

$$
+ \left[\sum_{i,j} \alpha_i \beta_j \text{ off-balance assets of type } i,j \right]
$$

$$
\left. + \left[\sum_{i,k} \alpha_i \gamma_k \text{ off-balance exchange or interest rate contracts of type } i,k \right] \right\}
$$

where i represents the nature of the borrower, and j and k the nature of the operation. The risk buckets are:

$\alpha_1 = 0.0$ for cash loans to member states of the OECD, their central banks and loans backed by them, as well as loans in national currencies to other states and central banks.

$\alpha_2 = 0.1$ for short-term government bills, Treasury bills.

$\alpha_3 = 0.2$ for loans to – or backed by – international organizations, regions and municipalities from the OECD, OECD banks and those of other countries for maturities less than a year.

$\alpha_4 = 0.5$ for residential mortgage loans that are fully backed by the mortgaged asset.

$\alpha_5 = 1.0$ for all other loans and equity holdings.

Table 12.3 provides an illustration. For off-balance-sheet assets, the weight of the borrower is multiplied by a weight to convert them to on-balance-sheet equivalences: $\beta_j \in \{0.0, 0.2, 0.5, 1.0\}$ expresses the riskiness of the activity. For interest rate or foreign exchange operations (swaps, futures, options, etc.), the weight of the borrower is that described above for $\hat{\alpha}$ except in the case of α_5 where a weight of 0.5 is applied (i.e. $\hat{\alpha}_i = \alpha_i$, except for $i = 5$ where $\hat{\alpha}_i = 0.5$). The notional (implicit) principal is then multiplied by the weight (γ_k) to derive the risk-adjusted value of the asset. The weight (γ_k) increases with the duration of the activity and is higher for operations that involve foreign exchange risk than for interest rate operations.

The Accord of 1988, while hailed as a laudable attempt to provide transparent and common minimum regulatory standards in international banking, was criticized on a number of counts:

1. Differences in taxes and accounting rules meant that measurement of capital varied widely across countries.
2. The Accord concentrated on credit risk alone. Other types of risk, such as interest rate risk, liquidity risk, currency risk and operating risk, were ignored.
3. There was no reward for banks that reduced portfolio risk because there was no acknowledgement of risk diversification in the calculations of capital requirements.
4. The Accord did not recognize that, although different banks have different financial operations, they are all expected to conform to the same risk capital–asset ratio.

TABLE 12.3   Risk–asset ratio – an illustrative calculation

Asset	£m	Weight fraction	Weighted (£m)
Cash	25	–	–
Treasury bills	5	0.1	0.5
Other eligible bills	70	0.1	7.00
Secured loans to discount market	100	0.1	10.00
UK government stocks	50	0.2	10.00
Other instruments – government	25	0.2	5.00
– company	25	1.0	25.00
Commercial loans	400	1.0	400.00
Personal loans	200	1.0	200.00
Mortgage loans	100	0.5	50.00
Total assets	1000		*707.50*
Off-balance-sheet risks			
Guarantees of commercial loans	20	1.0	20.00
Standby letters of credit	50	0.5	25.00
Total risk-weighted assets			*752.50*
Capital ratio 8%			*60.2*

Source: Bank of England 'Banking Supervision' Fact Sheet, August 1990.

5. It did not take into account the market value of bank assets – except in the case of foreign exchange and interest rate contracts. It created a problem of accounting lags because the information required to calculate capital adequacy lagged behind the market values of assets.

However, the Basel conditions were only a *minimum*. Banks were also subject to additional supervision by their own central banks or regulatory agencies. The US regulators expect a higher capital adequacy standard to be regarded as 'well capitalized'. The Federal Reserve expects banks that are members of the Federal Reserve System to have a tier-1 capital–asset ratio of 5%. The Federal Deposit Insurance Corporation Act 1991 introduced a scale of premia for deposit insurance according to capitalization. A well-capitalized bank is one that has a total risk capital–asset ratio greater than or equal to 10%, with a tier-1 capital–asset ratio greater than or equal to 6%. However, well-capitalized banks are just as likely to require regulatory action as less well-capitalized banks. In a recent study, Peek and Rosengreen (1997) found that, during the New England banking crisis of 1989–1993, of the 159 banks that required regulatory action, only five had capital–asset ratios of less than 5%, and 77 had ratios exceeding 8%.

The Accord was continuously amended to take into account new risks that emerged from financial innovation. In 1996 the Accord was amended to require banks to allocate capital to cover risk of losses from movements in market prices. The Basel Committee produced a

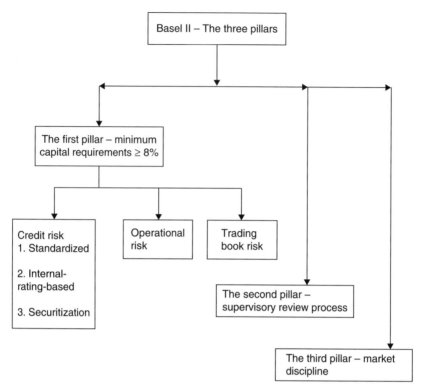

FIGURE 12.1 The Basel II Approach.

new and revised set of proposals on capital standards for international banks.[10] This report was the outcome of a consultative process that began in June 1999. The proposals were expected to be implemented by the end of 2006 and in some circumstances by the end of 2007.[11] The purpose of the new accord, dubbed Basel II, was to address some of the criticisms of Basel I and develop more risk-sensitive capital requirements. The key features of Basel I relating to the capital adequacy framework (8% risk capital–asset ratio) and the 1996 amendments for market risk are to be retained, but the major innovation in Basel II is to allow banks to use internal risk assessments as inputs to capital calculations. The stated purpose of Basel II is to allow banks to retain the key features of Basel I, but to provide incentives to adopt new innovations in risk management, thereby strengthening the stability of the financial system. This objective is to be achieved by three reinforcing pillars. Figure 12.1 describes the structure of the Basel II process and the three pillars.

Pillar 1 involves the assessment of minimum capital requirements to cover credit risk but, unlike Basel I, is carried over to include operational risk and market risk on the trading book of the bank. With credit risk, there are three approaches specified to suit different levels of risk and sophistication according to the operations of the bank. Firstly, the standardized

---

[10] BIS (2004).

[11] The current timetable for implementation is 1 January 2008, with the US having a delay until 1 January 2009.

TABLE 12.4   Total capital requirements for credit risk

Credit rating	Risk weight under Basel II	Capital under Basel II (%)	Risk weight under Basel I	Capital under Basel I (%)
AAA to AA− (%)	20	1.6	100	8
A+ to A− (%)	50	4	100	8
BBB+ to BB− (%)	100	8	100	8
Below BB− (%)	150	12	100	8
Unrated (%)	100	8	100	8

Source: Bank for International Settlements *www.bis.org*

approach is an extension of the Basel I approach of assigning risk weights to specific assets, with the addition of the risk weights being ordered according to external rating agencies.[12] Table 12.4 illustrates the differences between the capital requirements for the differing risk categories under Basel I and Basel II.

Secondly, banks that are engaged in more sophisticated risk-taking controls can, with the permission of their regulatory authority, apply their own internal ratings. These internal models are to be used to determine capital requirements subject to strict validation and data operational conditions. The third strand to credit risk is the securitization framework. Banks are expected to hold regulatory capital for positions of securitization transactions. The risk weights can either be derived from the standardized approach (with appropriate external rating) or the internal-ratings-based approach. The risk-weighted asset amount of a securitization exposure is computed by applying the risk weight shown in Table 12.4 in the case of the standardized approach.

A capital charge for operational risk is included in pillar 1, where operational risk is defined as the risk of loss resulting from inadequate or failed internal processes, people, systems or external events. There are three methods for calculating operational risk capital charges:

1. The basic indicator approach – calculates a percentage (known as alpha) of a 3-year average of gross income.
2. The standardized approach – divides bank activities into eight business lines, and the capital charge is the 3-year average of gross income applied to specific percentages for each line of business.
3. The advanced measurement approach – the risk measure obtained from the banks' own internal risk measurement system.

Box 12.2 describes the capital charges that apply on the basic indicator approach and the standardized approach.

Trading book risk stems from potential losses from trading. A trading book consists of positions in financial instruments and commodities held with an intention to trade or for

---

[12] For example, Standard & Poor's credit ratings.

BOX 12.2　Capital charges for operational risk

The capital charge for banks using the basic indicator approach must hold capital equal to the average of the previous 3 years of a fixed proportion (alpha – recommended as 15% by the Basel Committee) of positive annual gross income, where gross income is defined as net interest income plus non-interest income (gross of provisions). Negative income is excluded from the calculation. So

$$K_{BIA} = \alpha \left(\frac{\sum_{i=0}^{2} \pi_{t-i}}{3} \right) \tag{12.2.1}$$

The standardized approach is a little more sophisticated and requires the bank to collect data about gross income by line of business. The total capital charge is calculated as the fixed proportion (beta) of the three-year average of the gross income of each business line. As with the BIA, negative income is excluded:

$$K_{SA} = \frac{\sum_{i=0}^{2} \max [\beta_j \pi_{j,t-i}, 0]}{3} \tag{12.2.2}$$

The beta factors for each business line are as follows:

Business line	Beta factors (%)
Corporate finance	18
Trading and sales	18
Retail banking	12
Commercial banking	15
Payment and settlements	18
Agency services	15
Asset management	12
Retail brokerage	12

---

the purposes of hedging other entries in the trading book. Holding financial instruments on the book with intent means that they are held for short-term resale or to benefit from expected short-term price movements. Again, the bank can adopt the standardized approach or use internal models. This latter aspect is examined further in Chapter 13.

The second pillar gives regulatory discretion to national regulatory authorities to fine-tune regulatory capital levels. So, they can impose higher capital charges than provided for in pillar 1. The second pillar also requires banks to develop internal processes to assess their overall capital adequacy. The third pillar compels the bank to make greater disclosure to financial markets with the objective of strengthening market discipline and making risk management practices more transparent.

The publication of the new Basel guidelines for capital adequacy generated much comment from regulators, practitioners and academics in the next few years. In a number of cases, criticisms flew in at the consultative stages. Altman and Saunders (2001) criticized the use of external rating agencies on the grounds that these would produce cyclically lagging capital requirements, leading to greater financial instability, not less. Daníelsson *et al.* (2001) criticized the common use of value-at-risk models for a bank's internal risk assessments. Market volatility is the endogenous interaction of market participants. But this volatility is treated as exogenous in the calculation of risk by each bank. In reality, the endogeneity of market volatility may matter in times of stress, particularly if common models are being used. This could increase rather than decrease volatility. Clearly, the implications of the new guidelines have yet to be worked through, and comment will come in thick and fast. What has been presented in this chapter is a broad perspective.

Basel II recognizes the use of sophisticated risk-modelling techniques by banks to deal with the fast-changing world of banking, but, at the same time, the new requirements are voluminous and prescriptive. Regulations are often nullified by financial innovation and regulatory arbitrage. Regulators have to dream up further regulations to deal with the ever-evolving boundaries of banking and finance. A question that has to be asked is: Should these regulations with all their complexity be imposed on a banking system or a simple system arise out of a market system? This is the subject of Section 12.4.

12.4 THE CASE AGAINST REGULATION

The starting point for the case against regulation begins with a review of central banks' performance in monitoring and averting banking crises. A study by the International Monetary Fund (IMF, 1998) shown in Table 12.5 indicates the widespread nature and cost of the banking crisis around the world. A reasonable question to pose is: If central bank supervision produces problems in banking, as shown in Table 12.5, would 'free banking' be any worse?

The case for free banking begins with the argument by analogy. If free trade and free competition are considered to be welfare superior to restricted trade and competition, why is free banking not better than central banking? The second argument stems from distrust of the central bank management of the currency, through its monopoly power and political interference from the government. History has shown that central bank financing of government borrowing has led to the devaluation of the currency through the mechanism of inflation.

The first argument was the basis of much debate in the early and mid-nineteenth century.[13] The development of central banks was not, according to Smith (1936), the product of natural market development but through government favour and privileges. These privileges subsequently led to the monopoly of the note issue and to their responsibility for the soundness of the banking system. Free banking is a situation in which banks are allowed to operate freely without external regulation and even to issue bank notes, subject to the normal

---

[13] For the historical arguments for the free banking case, see Goodhart (1990) and Smith (1936).

TABLE 12.5 Bank crises and estimated costs

Country	Years	Costs as % of GDP
Argentina	1980–1982, 1985	13–55
Brazil	1994–1996	4–10
Chile	1981–1985	19–41
Colombia	1982–1987	5–6
Finland	1991–1993	8–10
Indonesia	1994	2
Japan	1990–	3
Malaysia	1985–1988	5
Mexico	1994–1995	12–15
Norway	1988–1992	4
Philippines	1981–1987	3–4
Spain	1977–1985	15–17
Sri Lanka	1989–1993	9
Sweden	1991–1993	4–5
Thailand	1983–1987	1
Turkey	1982–1985	3
USA	1984–1991	5–7
Uruguay	1981–1984	31
Venezuela	1980–1983, 1994–1995	17

Source: World Economic Outlook (IMF, 1998).

restrictions of company law. In essence, a bank has the same rights and responsibilities as any other business enterprise. Notes issued by any bank will be redeemable against gold. The gold standard is important to Smith's argument as it acts as a break on the incentive to overissue notes and create an inflationary spiral.[14] The mechanism of control works through a clearing house system. Banks that issue more notes than warranted by reserves will have their notes returned to them by other banks who will want them redeemed in gold. This will cause the overissuing bank's reserves to run down faster than the other banks in the clearing system. Uncleared notes in the clearing mechanism will signal the overissuing bank to the other banks, which can be used as a basis for sanctions. The signal of overissue would weaken the reputation of the bank, both within the banking community, which would have a strong incentive to distance itself from the rogue bank, and with the public. The argument that 'bad' banks would drive 'good' banks to emulate their behaviour is counter to intertemporal profit-maximizing behaviour (Dowd, 2003). On the contrary, good banks would want to distance themselves from the bad banks and to build up their financial strength so as to

---

[14] The gold standard is not a general requirement. Any commodity or basket of commodities that has unchanging characteristics would suffice. See Hayek (1978).

attract the bad bank's customers and increase market share when confidence in that bank evaporates.

Free bank managers understand that their long-term survival depends on their ability to retain depositors' confidence. They would pursue conservative policies, ensure that depositors have full information about the bank's investments and so on. A signal of conservativeness is the proportion of capital held by the bank. The more the owners of the bank (shareholders) are willing to invest in the bank, the greater will be the confidence in the bank. History certainly supports the notion that capital ratios would be higher under free banking than under central bank regulation. The US banks in the early nineteenth century had no federal regulations but had capital ratios in excess of 40%. At the turn of the twentieth century, US banks had ratios of 20%, and average capital ratios were 15% when the FDIC was established.

Government intervention in the form of deposit insurance has the opposite effect on capital ratios. The moral hazard created by deposit insurance will drive even conservative banks to take on extra risk when faced with competition from bad banks. The free banking school argue that it is the 'bad' effects of depositor protection in the form of moral hazard that creates the need for regulation. Once the government, or a government-backed agency, has offered deposit protection, it is politically impossible to withdraw it or to restrict it to a subset of banks. The evidence for the USA shows that the pressure to extend deposit insurance to all banks comes from small bank units that fear a haemorrhage of deposits to large insured banks. Therefore, the pressure for regulation follows from the existence of deposit insurance. If deposit insurance is a political reality and is a necessary evil, as Benston and Kaufman (1996) suggest, the types of regulation that should be considered are:

1. Prohibition of activities that are considered excessively risky.
2. Monitoring and controlling the risky activity of banks.
3. Requiring banks to hold sufficient capital to absorb potential losses.

Of these three, the first two would be overprescriptive, bring regulation into disrepute and stifle innovation (Llewellyn, 2003). The last recommendation is the only one that is operational and is the basis of the Basel I and II capital adequacy recommendations.

The second argument in favour of free banking is the poor record of central banks in maintaining the value of the currency. The free banking school argue that monetary stability is a necessary prerequisite for bank stability (Benston and Kaufman, 1996), and the loss of purchasing power incurred by depositors from unexpected inflation is much greater than losses from bank failures in the USA (Schwartz, 1987). However, the argument that central banks and a regulated banking system are financially less stable than a free banking system has lost force with the development of independent central banks, in combination with strict inflation targets.

An intermediate position taken by a number of economists is to argue that the current regulated system should be redesigned so as to allow market discipline to counteract the moral hazard problems created by deposit insurance. A popular suggestion is the use of subordinated debt in bank capital regulation. The existence of deposit insurance results in underpriced risk due to moral hazard. Wall (1989) proposes the use of subordinated debt aimed at creating a banking environment that functions as if deposit insurance did not exist. The Wall proposal is that banks issue and maintain 'puttable' subdebts of 4–5% of risk-weighted assets. If debt holders exercise the put option by redeeming the debt, the bank would have 90 days to make the appropriate adjustment, which would be:

1. Retire the debt and continue to meet the regulatory requirement.
2. Issue new puttable debt.
3. Reduce assets to meet the regulatory requirement.

The advantage of the put characteristic of the subdebt is that the bank would always be forced continuously to satisfy the market of its soundness. Holders of subdebt are not depositors and do not expect to be underwritten by deposit insurance; hence, they have strong incentives to monitor the bank. Benston (1993) highlights a number of advantages of using subdebt. First-ly, subdebt holders cannot cause a run; hence, there will not be any disruptive effects of runs from holders if the authorities decide to close a bank. Secondly, subdebt holders have an asym-metric payout. When the bank does well, subdebt holders can expect the premium interest promised. However, if a bank does badly, subdebt holders absorb losses that exceed equity. Thirdly, the risk premium on subdebt yields will be an indicator of a risk-adjusted deposit insurance premium. Fourthly, subdebt is publicly traded and the yield will be an advanced sig-nal of excess risk taking by the bank, as will be any difficulty in reissuing maturing debt.

A modification to the Wall (1989) proposal is that of Calomiris (1999) who proposes a min-imum of subdebt of 2% of assets and the imposition of a specified yield spread over the riskless rate of, say, 50 basis points. Banks would not be permitted to roll over the debt once the max-imum spread is reached and would be forced to reduce their risk-weighted assets. This would have the effect of using market discipline as a risk signal more effectively. Debt would have a 2 year maturity, with issues staggered to have equal tranches due in each month. This would limit the required monthly asset reduction to a maximum of approximately 4% of assets.[15]

An alternative proposal is the narrow banking scheme put forward by Tobin (1985) and strongly supported by the *Economist* (27 April 1996). This proposal is that deposit insurance and lender-of-last-resort facilities should be restricted to banks involved in the payments mechanism. These would be exclusively retail banks that would be required to hold only safe liquid assets such as Treasury and government bonds. Thus, the banking market would be segmented into a protected retail banking sector and a free banking sector catering to corporate clients and sophisticated investors. The problem is that the protected banking sec-tor would earn low return on assets (ROA) compared with the free banks. There is also the potential of time inconsistency if sufficient numbers of small depositors invest in the free banks directly or indirectly through mutual fund arrangements. Any crisis in the free bank-ing sector would create political pressure to bail out weak banks to protect small depositors who directly or indirectly will have a stake in the free banking sector (Spencer, 2000).

At the end of the day, the choice between the current, regulated banking system and free banking can be reduced to a cost–benefit type of calculus. Under free banking and in the absence of a lender-of-last-resort facility, we can expect individual bank reserves and capi-tal ratios to be higher than under regulated banking. A corollary is that interest rate spreads would be higher under free banking than under a regulated banking system with central banks (Box 12.3 demonstrates this).

---

[15] One concern of this proposal is the potential for adverse incentives. If banks cannot reissue subdebt at a low enough premium, they are likely to liquidate safe assets and increase the riskiness of the remainder of the portfolio. See Evanoff and Wall (2000).

BOX 12.3 The effect of higher capital ratios on interest rate spreads

Let us take the competitive model as the basis of this argument. The balance sheet of the banks is given by

$$L + R = D + E \tag{12.3.1}$$

where L is loans, R is reserves, D is deposits and E is equity. Let the capital–asset ratio (E/L) be given by e and the reserve–deposit ratio be given by k. The balance sheet constraint can be re-expressed as

$$L(1 - e) = D(1 - k) \tag{12.3.2}$$

The objective function of the bank (ignoring costs) is described by the profit function

$$\pi = r_L L - r_E E - r_D D \tag{12.3.3}$$

where r_E is the required return on equity.

Substituting from (12.3.2) into (12.3.3) and using the definition of E gives

$$\pi = r_L L - r_E e L - r_D \left(\frac{1 - e}{1 - k} \right) L$$

Differentiating π with respect to L and setting to zero gives

$$\frac{d\pi}{dL} = r_L - r_E e - r_D \left(\frac{1 - e}{1 - k} \right) = 0$$

$$\Rightarrow r_L(1 - k) - r_E e(1 - k) - r_D(1 - e) = 0$$

$$\Rightarrow r_L - r_D = r_E e(1 - k) + k r_L - r_D e$$

Let the spread be given by $s = r_L - r_D$. Then, we can see that

$$\frac{\partial s}{\partial e} = r_E(1 - k) - r_D > 0$$

provided that the required return on equity (adjusted for the reserve ratio) is greater than the deposit rate. The required return on equity will always be greater than the return on deposits in a steady state; otherwise, no investor will hold bank shares over bank deposits.

With deposit insurance and the existence of a lender of last resort, reserves and capital ratios and the level and spread of interest rates would be considerably lower. Higher interest rates would entail a welfare loss shown by the shaded area in Figure 12.2. Lower interest rates would have the benefit of creating liquidity (an important benefit in developing economies) but at the cost of increased risk and bank crisis.

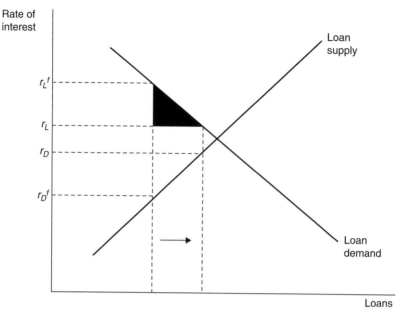

FIGURE 12.2 Welfare Loss from Higher Interest Rates.

12.5 SUMMARY

- This chapter has examined the arguments for bank regulation, the type of regulation that exists and the arguments for deregulation.
- As with many areas of economics, the balance of the argument is one that has to be evaluated on the basis of a cost–benefit calculus.
- Regulation may be justified on the grounds that the social costs of bank failure are large. On the other hand, costs of regulation (both direct and compliance) can be large.
- The benefits of a banking system free of central bank or regulatory control have to be balanced against the potential of externalities that may arise from individual bank failure and disruption to the payments mechanism.
- The benefits of the existence of deposit insurance and lender of last resort in terms of operating with high leverage (debt–equity ratio) have to be balanced against central bank (and government) interference and periodic banking crises generated by imprudent banking.

QUESTIONS

1 What are the real resource costs of regulation?

2 What are the main reasons for bank regulation?

3   What are the arguments in favour of a government-backed deposit insurance scheme?

4   What is the main regulatory condition of Basel I? What are the standard criticisms of Basel I?

5   How does Basel II differ from Basel I?

6   What measures have been suggested to increase the degree of market discipline on banks' risk taking and capital adequacy?

TEST QUESTIONS

1   'Deposit insurance weakens the incentive to maintain capital adequacy' (K. Dowd). Comment.

2   'Banks cannot be trusted to regulate themselves and therefore prudential regulations are a necessary evil'. Discuss.

13

Risk Management

MINI-CONTENTS

13.1   Introduction
13.2   Risk typology
13.3   Interest rate risk management
13.4   Market risk
13.5   Credit risk
13.6   Operational risk
13.7   Conclusion
13.8   Summary

13.1 INTRODUCTION

The business of banking involves risk. Banks make profit by taking risk and managing risk. The traditional focus of risk management in banks has typically arisen out of their main business of intermediation – the process of making loans and taking in deposits. These are risks relating to the management of the balance sheet of the bank and are identifiable as *credit risk*, *liquidity risk* and *interest rate risk*. In Chapters 4 and 5 we have already examined bank strategies for dealing with credit risk and liquidity risk. This chapter will concentrate on understanding the problems of measuring and coping with interest rate risk and further elaboration of the problems of credit risk management.

The advance of off-balance-sheet activity of the bank (see Table 1.7 for the growth of non-bank income) has given rise to other types of risk relating to its trading and income-generating activity. Banks have increasingly become involved in the trading of securities, derivatives and currencies. These activities give rise to *position* or *market risk*. This is the risk caused by a change in the market price of the security or derivative in which the bank has taken a position. While it is not always sensible to isolate risks into separate compartments, risk management in banking has been concerned with the risks on the *banking book* as well as the *trading book*.

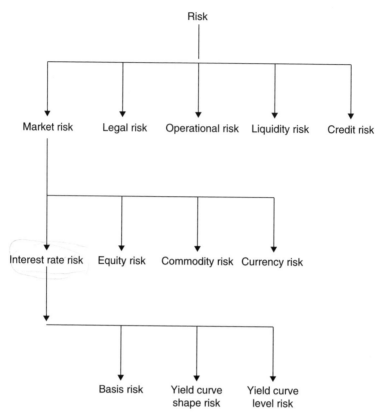

FIGURE 13.1 Types of Risk.

This chapter provides an overview of risk management by banks. Figure 13.1 describes a taxonomy of the potential risks the bank faces.

13.2 RISK TYPOLOGY

Credit risk is the possibility of loss as a result of default, such as when a customer defaults on a loan, or generally any type of financial contract. The default can take the form of failure to pay either the principal on maturity of the loan or contract or the interest payments when due. Essentially, there are three ways a bank can minimize credit risk. Firstly, the price of the loan has to reflect the riskiness of the venture. But bear in mind the problems of loading all of the price on to the rate of interest charged in the context of credit rationing, which were examined in Chapter 8. Secondly, since the rate of interest cannot bear all of the risk, some form of credit limit is placed. This would hold particularly for firms that have little accounting history, such as start-ups. Thirdly, there are collateral and administrative conditions associated with the loan. Collateral can take many forms, but all entail the placing of deed titles to property with the bank so that the property will pass to the bank in the event of default. Administrative arrangements include covenants specifying certain behaviour by the borrower. Breach of the covenants will cause the loan to be cancelled and collateral liquidated.

The price of a loan will equal the cost of funds, often the London interbank offer rate (LIBOR – see Box 4.1 for a discussion of LIBOR), plus risk premium plus equity spread plus costs mark-up. The cost of funds is the rate of interest on deposits or borrowing from the interbank market. The bank manager obtains the risk premium from a mixture of objective and subjective evaluation. The equity spread is the margin between the cost of funds and the interest on the loan that satisfies a given rate of return to shareholders. Cost mark-up represents the overhead costs of maintaining bank operations, such as labour, rent, etc.

The evaluation of the risk premium will involve a combination of managerial judgement, as in traditional *relationship banking*, plus objective analysis obtained from *credit-scoring* methods. Credit scoring is a system used by banks and other credit institutions to decide the band of riskiness to which a borrower belongs. It works by assigning weights to various characteristics, such as credit history, repayment history, outstanding debt, number of accounts, whether you are a householder and so on.[1] Other factors that are used in evaluating the risk premium would include historical and projected cash flow, earnings volatility, collateral and wealth of the borrower. The score is obtained by separating historical data on defaulters from non-defaulters and statistically modelling default using discriminant analysis or binary models of econometric estimation (logit, probit) to predict default. We shall examine the management of credit risk in greater detail later in this chapter.

Liquidity risk is the possibility that a bank will be unable to meet its liquid liabilities because of unexpected withdrawals of deposits. An unexpected liquidity shortage means that the bank is not only unable to meet its liability obligations but also unable to fund its illiquid assets.

Operational risk is the possibility of loss resulting from errors in instructing payments or settling transactions. An example is fraud or mismanagement.[2] Banks tend to account for this on a cost basis, less provisions.

Legal risk is the possibility of loss when a contract cannot be enforced because the customer had no authority to enter into the contract or the contract terms are unenforceable in a bankruptcy case.

Market risk is the possibility of loss over a given period of time related to uncertain movements in market risk factors, such as interest rates, currencies, equities and commodities. The market risk of a financial instrument can be caused by a number of factors, but the major one is interest rate risk. Net interest income is the difference between what the bank receives in interest receipts and what it pays in interest costs. The main sources of interest risk are (a) volatility of interest rates and (b) mismatch in the timing of interest on assets and liabilities. These risks can be further separated into the following three categories. *Yield curve level risk* refers to an equal change in rates across all maturities. This is the case when interest rates on all instruments move up or down equivalently by the same number of basis points. *Yield curve shape risk* refers to changes in the relative rates for instruments of different maturities. An example of this is when short-term rates change a different number of basis points to long-term

---

[1] Equal opportunities legislation precludes the use of racial and gender profiling to determine credit scores.

[2] The collapse of Barings and the Daiwa affair are good examples. In the case of Barings, trader Nick Leeson lost £827m through illegal derivative trading and covered up his losses by fraudulent methods. Similarly, the Daiwa trader Toshihide Iguchi lost $1.1bn and also covered up the losses by fraud.

interest rates. *Basis risk* refers to the risk of changes in rates for instruments with the same maturity but pegged to a different index. For example, suppose a bank funds an investment by borrowing at a 6-month LIBOR and invests in an instrument tied to a 6-month Treasury bill rate (TBR). The bank will incur losses if the LIBOR rises above the TBR.

Additional risks are currency and equity risk. In the case of foreign currency lending (including bonds), the bank faces currency risk in addition to interest rate risk. Currency risk in this case arises because of changes in the exchange rate between the loan being made and its maturity. Banks also engage in swaps where they exchange payments on the basis of a notional principal. One party pays/receives payments based on the performance of the stock portfolio, and the other party receives/pays a fixed rate. In this case the bank is exposed to both equity risk and interest rate risk.[3]

13.3 INTEREST RATE RISK MANAGEMENT

When a bank makes a fixed rate for a duration longer than the duration of the funding, it is essentially taking a 'bet' on the movement of interest rates. The larger the 'bet', the greater is the risk and the greater the amount of capital the bank should have to hold. Unexpected changes in the rate of interest create interest rate risk. An unexpected rise in interest rates will lead to loss of profit.

At its simplest level, the bank will use *gap analysis* to evaluate the exposure of the banking book to interest rate changes. The 'gap' is the difference between interest–rate–sensitive assets and liabilities for a given time interval:

$$\text{Negative gap} = \text{interest-sensitive liabilities} > \text{interest-sensitive assets}$$
$$\text{Positive gap} = \text{interest-sensitive liabilities} < \text{interest-sensitive assets}$$

The gap will provide a measure of overall balance sheet mismatches. The basic point of gap analysis is to evaluate the impact of a change in the interest rate on the net interest margin. If the central bank discount rate were to change tomorrow, not all the rates on the assets and liabilities could be changed immediately. Interest rates on fixed-rate loans will have to mature first before they can be repriced, whereas the majority of deposits will be repriced immediately. In reality, many medium–duration loans are negotiated on a variable-rate basis (LIBOR + margin), and many if not most large loans based on LIBOR are subject to adjustment at specified intervals. Furthermore, competition and financial innovation have created a strong impetus for banks to adjust deposit rates within a few days of the central bank changing interest rates.

The bank deals with interest rate risk by conducting various hedging operations. These are:

1. Duration-matching of assets and liabilities.
2. Interest rate futures, options and forward rate agreements.
3. Interest rate swaps.

---

[3] There are many good texts on derivatives (i.e. futures, options and swaps), which can be referred to for further discussion of swaps. One such text is Kolb (1997).

Duration-matching is an internal hedging operation and therefore does not require a counterparty. In the use of swaps and other derivatives, the bank is a hedger and buys insurance from a speculator. The purpose of hedging is to reduce volatility and thereby reduce the volatility of the bank's value. We will examine the concept of duration and its application to bank interest rate risk management. Box 13.1 provides a brief primer to the concept of duration.

Since banks typically have long-term assets and short-term liabilities, a rise in the rate of interest will reduce the market value of their assets more than the market value of their liabilities. An increase in the rate of interest will reduce the net market value of banks. The greater the mismatch of duration between assets and liabilities, the greater will be the *duration gap*.

If V is the net present value of the bank, then this is the difference between the present value of assets (PV_A market value of assets) less the present value of liabilities (PV_L market value of liabilities). As shown in Box 13.1, the change in the value of a portfolio is given by the initial value multiplied by the negative of its duration and the rate of change in the relevant rate of interest. Consequently, the change in the value of the bank is equal to the change in the value of its assets less the change in the value of its liabilities as defined above. More formally, this can be expressed as

$$dV \approx [(PV_A)(-D_A)]dr_A - [(PV_L)(-D_L)]dr_L \qquad (13.1)$$

where r_A is the rate of return on assets and r_L is the rate of interest on liabilities.

We can see from expression (13.1) that, if interest rates on assets and liabilities move together, the value of assets matches that of liabilities and the durations of assets and liabilities are the same, then the bank is immunized from changes in the rate of interest. However, such conditions are highly unrealistic. The repricing of assets, which are typically long term, is less frequent than the repricing of liabilities (except in the case of variable-rate loans). Solvent banks will always have positive equity value, so $PV_A > PV_L$, and the idea of duration-matching goes against the notion of what a bank does, which is to borrow short and lend long. However, a bank is able to use the concept of duration gap to evaluate its exposure to interest rate risk and conduct appropriate action to minimize it.

By definition, the duration gap (DG) is defined as the duration of assets less the ratio of liabilities to assets multiplied by the duration of liabilities. This is shown by the equation

$$DG = D_A - \left(\frac{PV_L}{PV_A}\right)D_L \qquad (13.2)$$

where D_A and D_L are the durations of the asset and liability portfolios respectively.

As demonstrated in Box 13.2, combining equations (13.1) and (13.2) links the duration gap to the change in the value of a bank:

$$dV = -DG\left[\frac{dr}{(1+r)}\right]PV_A \qquad (13.3)$$

Equation (13.3) says that, when the duration gap is positive, an increase in the rate of interest will lower the value of the bank. If the gap is negative, the opposite happens. The smaller the gap, the smaller will be the magnitude of the effect of an interest rate change on the value of the bank.

BOX 13.1   Duration

Duration is the measure of the average time to maturity of a series of cash flows from a financial asset. It is a measure of the asset's effective maturity, which takes into account the timing and size of the cash flow. It is calculated by the time-weighted present value of the cash flow divided by the initial value of the asset, which gives the time-weighted average maturity of the cash flow of the asset. The formula for the calculation of duration D is given by

$$D = \sum_{t}^{n} \frac{C_t/(1 + r)^t(t)}{P_0}$$

(13.1.1)

or

$$D = \frac{C}{P_0} \sum_{t}^{n} \frac{t}{(1 + r)^t}$$

(13.1.2)

where C is the constant cash flow for each period of time t over n periods, r is the rate of interest and P_0 is the value of the financial asset. An example will illustrate. Consider a 5-year commercial loan of £10 000 to be repaid at a fixed rate of interest of 6% annually. The repayments will be £600 a year until the maturity of the loan, when the cash flow will be interest £600 plus principal £10 000.

Table 13.1 shows the calculations.

TABLE 13.1

Period (t)	Cash flow	Discount factor	Present value of the cash flow	Present value of the cash flow times t
1	600	1.06	566.038	566.038
2	600	1.06^2	533.998	1067.996
3	600	1.06^3	503.772	1511.316
4	600	1.06^4	475.256	1901.024
5	10 600	1.06^5	7920.937	39 604.685
Sum				44 651.059

Duration years $D = \frac{44\,651.059}{10\,000} = 4.47$ years < 5 years. Such a measure is also known as the *Macaulay duration*. An extended discussion of the use of duration in bank strategic planning can be found in Beck *et al.* (2000). However, in reality, the cash flow figures will include the repayments of principal as well as interest, but the simple example above illustrates the concept.

(*continued*)

Duration can also be thought of as an approximate measure of the price sensitivity of the asset to changes in the rate of interest. In other words, it is a measure of the elasticity of the price of the asset with respect to the rate of interest. To see this, the value of the loan (P_0) in (13.1.1) and (13.1.2) is equal to its present value, i.e.

$$P_0 = \sum_{t=1}^{t=n} \frac{C_t}{(1 + r)^t} \tag{13.1.3}$$

Differentiating (13.1.3) with respect to $(1 + r)$ and assuming a constant C gives

$$\frac{\partial P_0}{\partial (1 + r)} = -C \sum_{t=1}^{t=n} \frac{t}{(1 + r)^{t+1}} \tag{13.1.4}$$

Multiplying both sides of (13.1.4) by $(1 + r)/P_0$ gives

$$\frac{\partial P_0 / P_0}{\partial (1 + r)/r} = -\frac{C}{P_0} \sum_{t=1}^{t=n} \frac{t}{(1 + r)^t} \tag{13.1.5}$$

The left-hand side is the elasticity of the price of a security (the loan in this case) with respect to one plus the interest rate, and the right-hand side is equal to the negative of its duration. Consequently, duration provides a measure of the degree of interest rate risk. The lower the measure of duration, the lower will be the price elasticity of the security with respect to interest rates and, hence, the smaller will be the change in price and the lower the degree of interest rate risk. To clarify this, consider the example at the beginning of this box and assume that the rate of interest rose from 6% per annum to 7% per annum. The change in price of the debt is approximately given by rearranging (13.1.5), with the discrete change Δ substituted for the continuous change ∂ and noting that the right-hand side is equal to the negative of duration, to arrive at

$$\Delta P_0 = -D \left\{ \frac{\Delta (1 + r)}{1 + r} \right\} P_0$$

so

$$\Delta P_0 = (-4.47) \left\{ \frac{0.01}{1.06} \right\} 10\,000 = -421.70$$

This calculation is an approximation which can be verified by recalculating the PV using a 7% interest rate. Clearly, as stated above, the smaller the duration, the smaller will be the change in price.

It should be noted that the above example for the change in the value of an individual security can easily be extended to the change in value of a portfolio. Here, the relevant portfolio duration is the average of the durations of the individual securities in the portfolio weighted by their value in the composition of that portfolio.

BOX 13.2   Duration and change in value

By definition

$$dV = dPV_A - dPV_L \tag{13.2.1}$$

Using the concept of elasticity explored in Box 13.1, we know that the change in the value of assets is given by

$$dPV_A = \frac{-D_A}{(1 + r_A)}dr_A PV_A \tag{13.2.2}$$

Similarly, the change in the value of liabilities is given by

$$dPV_L = \frac{-D_L}{(1 + r_L)}dr_L PV_L \tag{13.2.3}$$

Assuming for purposes of illustration that $dr_A = dr_L$ (no basis risk) and $r_A = r_L$, substituting (13.2.2) and (13.2.3) into (13.2.1) and rearranging gives

$$dV = -[D_A PV_A - D_L PV_L]\left(\frac{dr}{(1 + r)}\right) \tag{13.2.4}$$

Defining the duration gap (DG) as

$$DG = D_A - \left(\frac{PV_L}{PV_A}\right)D_L$$

expression (13.2.4) can be rewritten as

$$dV = -DG\left[\frac{dr}{(1 + r)}\right]PV_A \tag{13.2.5}$$

Equation (13.2.5) says that, when the duration gap is positive, an increase in the rate of interest will lower the value of the bank. If the gap is negative, the opposite happens. The closer the gap, the smaller will be the magnitude of the effect of an interest rate change on the value of the bank.

Box 13.3 illustrates the calculation of the duration gap for E-First bank's balance sheet. The bank has assets of £10 000 in commercial loans (5-year maturity at 6%), £1000 in cash reserves and £4000 in liquid bills (1-year maturity at 5%). For its liabilities it has 1-year maturity £9000 deposits costing 3%, £3000 of 4-year maturity CDs costing 4.5% and

BOX 13.3   Bank E-First's balance sheet

Asset	Value	Rate (%)	Duration	Liability	Value	Rate (%)	Duration
Cash	1000	0	0	Deposits	9000	3	1
Loan	10 000	6	4.47*	CDs	3000	4.5	3.74
Bills	4000	5	1	T deposit	2200	4	1.96
				Total	14 200		1.73
				Equity	800		
Total	15 000		3.25		15 000		

* This figure is that derived in the numerical example in Box 13.1, Table 13.1.

Consider the hypothetical balance sheet of an imaginary bank E-First. The duration of a 1-year maturity asset is the same as the maturity. The duration of 4-year CDs is 3.74 (you should check this calculation yourself – interest is paid annually) and a 2-year T deposit is 1.96, the weighted average of the duration of assets (weighted by asset share) is 3.25 and the weighted average of the duration of liabilities is 1.73 (note equity is excluded from the calculations as it represents ownership rather than an external liability).

The duration gap

$$DG = \left(3.25 - \frac{14\,200}{15\,000}(1.73) \right) = 1.61$$

Interest rate risk is seen in that there is a duration mismatch and a duration gap of 1.61 years. The value of assets will fall more than the value of liabilities if interest rates rise because the weighted duration of assets is larger than the weighted duration of liabilities. As an approximation, if all interest rates rise by 1% (0.01), then

$$dV = -1.61 \left(\frac{dr}{(1+r)} \right) 15\,000 = -£227.8 \text{ or } 1.5\% \text{ of its value}$$

To immunize the bank from fluctuations in value, the risk manager will have to shorten the asset duration by 1.61 years or increase the liability duration by

$$\left(\frac{14\,200}{15\,000} \right) 1.73 = 1.64 \text{ years}$$

The risk manager can increase the liability duration by reducing the dependence on deposits and hold long-dated zero-coupon bonds (you should confirm that the maturity of a zero-coupon bond is the same as its duration) or increasing capital adequacy.

£2200 of 2-year maturity time deposits costing 4%, plus £800 of shareholders' capital. The calculations show the duration gap and how the gap can be reduced.

In reality, a risk manager would not be able perfectly to immunize a bank from interest rate fluctuations. In practice, the risk manager would simulate a number of interest rate scenarios to arrive at a distribution of potential loss and then develop a strategy to deal with the low likelihood of extreme cases.

We now move on to consider the role of financial futures markets in managing interest rate risk. Financial derivatives can be defined as instruments whose price is derived from an underlying financial security. The price of the derivative is linked to the price of the underlying asset and arbitrage maintains this link. This makes it possible to construct hedges using derivative contracts so that losses (gains) on the underlying asset are matched by gains (losses) on the derivative contract. In this section we examine how banks may use derivative markets to hedge their exposure to interest rate changes. This discussion can only survey the methods available, and for more detail the interested reader is referred to Koch and MacDonald (2003). First of all, however, it is necessary to discuss briefly the nature of financial derivatives.[4]

Derivatives can be categorized in two ways. The first is according to type of trade, the main ones being futures, forward rate agreements, swaps and options. We will discuss the first three types in this section as vehicles for risk management. The second depends on the market where the transactions are carried out. Here, standardized trades (both quantities and delivery dates) are carried out on organized markets such as Euronext.liffe or the Chicago Board of Trade or, alternatively, over the counter (OTC), where the transaction is organized through a financial institution on a 'bespoke' basis. On organized markets, payments between the parties to the transaction are made according to movement in the futures price.

13.3.1 Futures

A future is a transaction where the price is agreed now but delivery takes place at a later date. We will take an interest rate contract on Euronext.liffe to illustrate the approach to hedging, but noting that the underlying principles would apply to other securities, although the administrative detail will differ.

The particular contract in which we are interested is the short-sterling contract. This represents a contract for a 3-month £500 000 deposit. The pricing arrangements are that the contract is priced at 100 – the rate of interest to apply. The price can move up or down by 0.01%, known as a tick or basis point. Each tick is valued at £12.50 $\left(500\ 000 \times \frac{0.01}{100} \times \frac{1}{4}\right)$. As a hypothetical example, suppose the settlement price[5] for Thursday 14 October for next March delivery is £95.04, implying an annual rate of interest equal to 4.96%. At the same

---

[4] A fuller description of financial futures is contained in Buckle and Thompson (2004).
[5] The settlement price is the price at the end of the day against which all margins are calculated.

time, the end-of-day 3-month LIBOR was 4.90% per annum. The gap between the two rates is basis and is defined by

$$\text{Basis} = \text{cash price} - \text{futures price}$$

If the bank is adversely affected by falling interest rates, as in the following example, it should purchase futures. To hedge an individual transaction, the bank can use the futures markets in the following manner. Suppose a bank is due to receive £1 m on 1 February which it intends to invest in the sterling money markets for 3-months expiring 30 April, and wishes to hedge against a possible fall in interest rates. Hence, the bank purchases two short-sterling contracts at 95.04.

If the rate of interest on 1 February has fallen to 4.46% per annum and the futures price has risen (with basis unchanged) to 95.48, then the bank's receipts at 30 April will be

	£
Interest received $\left(1\,000\,000 \times \dfrac{4.46}{100} \times \dfrac{1}{4} \right)$	11 150
Profit from futures trade	
Two contracts 44 × 12.5 per basis point per contract	1100
(purchased at 95.04 and sold at 95.48)	
Total	*12 250*

It should be noted that the total receipts are equal to 4.90% per annum $\left(\frac{12\,250}{1\,000\,000} \times 100 \times 4 \right)$, i.e. equal to the 4.90% available on 14 October.

If, on the other hand, the rate of interest had risen to 5%, then the bank's receipts on 30 April would be (again assuming no change in basis):

	£
Interest received $\left(1\,000\,000 \times \dfrac{5.00}{100} \times \dfrac{1}{4} \right)$	12 500
Loss from futures trade	
Two contracts 10 × 12.5 per basis point per contract	250
(purchased at 95.04 and sold at 94.94)	
Total	*12 250*

As before, the total return is 4.90% per annum, but in this case there is a loss on the futures contracts so that the bank would have been better off not hedging in the futures markets. This brings out the essential point that hedging is to provide certainty (subject to the qualification below), not to make a profit or loss.

Both these examples assume that the basis remains unchanged. If basis does change (i.e. the relationship between the futures price and the spot price changes), the hedge will be less than perfect. The effect of change in basis is illustrated by the following expression:

$$\text{Effective return} = \text{initial cash rate} - \text{change in basis}$$

In other words, the bank is exchanging interest rate risk for basis risk, which it is hoped will be smaller. The basis risk will be smaller when the hedge is carried out using a security that is similar to the cash instrument. If no close futures security exists, the basic risk is much higher.

Finally, with respect to the hedging of a single transaction, if the bank is adversely affected by rising rates of interest, it should sell future. An example of this situation is a bank selling a security in the future to finance, say, a loan. In this case the rise in interest rates would reduce the receipts from the sale of a security.

Futures markets can also be used to reduce duration. If we assume that the duration of a futures contract is 0.25, then solving the following equation for the quantity of futures will set duration = 0, so that the portfolio is immunized against interest rate changes:

$$PV_A D_A - PV_L D_L + FD_A = 0 \tag{13.4}$$

where F is defined as the value of futures contracts, with purchase of a futures contract shown by a positive sign and sale by a negative sign. Filling in the values in the example given in Box 13.3 gives

$$15\ 000(3.25) - 14\ 200(1.73) + 0.25F = 0$$

The solution to this equation suggests the bank should sell £96 736 of future. Note in this example that, for pedagogical purposes, we are abstracting from the fact that interest rate futures are denominated in fixed amounts.

13.3.2 Forward Rate Agreements

Interest rate risk can also be managed using forward rate agreements (FRAs). FRAs are in respect of an interest rate due in the future – say, 3 months. They are based on a notional principal, which serves as a reference for the calculation of interest rate payments. The principal is not exchanged, just the interest payment at the end of the contract. One such example would be a 3-month LIBOR with a fixed exercise price, say 8% per annum, operating in 3 months' time. If, at the maturity of the contract, LIBOR has risen above the fixed rate, say to 9%, the purchaser would receive the gap between the two rates. Assuming a notional principal of £1 000 000, in this example the receipt of funds (π) at the expiry of the contract would be as follows:

$$\pi = (0.09 - 0.08)(1/4) \times 1\ 000\ 000 = £2500$$

Conversely, if the rate had fallen to, say, 7%, then the purchaser would pay £2500.

In effect, the purchaser of the contract has fixed the rate of interest at 8%. It would seem, therefore, that forward rate agreements are very similar to interest rate futures. There is one important difference. Interest rate futures are conducted through an organized market, which stands behind the contract. There is, therefore, no counterparty risk. This is not true for FRAs, which are OTC contracts and thus entail some, albeit slight, risk of counterparty failure – normally, a bank. However, this should not be overemphasized, as the risk is the interest rate payment not the notional principal.

13.3.3 Swaps

A basic swap (or 'plain vanilla' swap, as it is often called) exists where two parties agree to exchange cash flows based on a notional principal. As in the case of FRAs, the principal itself is not exchanged. The usual basis of the transaction is that party A pays party B a fixed rate based on the notional principal, while party B pays party A a floating rate of interest. Thus, the two parties are exchanging fixed rates for floating rates, and vice versa. An intermediary will arrange the transaction for a fee.

Swaps can be used to adjust the interest rate sensitivity of specified assets or liabilities or the portfolio as a whole. Reductions can be obtained by swapping floating rates for fixed rates and, conversely, to increase interest rate sensitivity, fixed rates can be swapped for floating rates.

There are, however, dangers with regard to the use of swaps. If there is a large change in the level of rate, a fixed-rate obligation will become very onerous. One particular example of this concerned the US thrift institutions. They swapped floating rates for fixed rates at the beginning of the 1980s, but interest rates fell dramatically during the 1980s, leaving the thrifts with onerous fixed-rate liabilities.

13.3.4 Options

An option confers the right to purchase a security (a 'call' option) or to sell a security (a 'put' option), but not an obligation to do so at a fixed price (called the 'strike' price) in return for a fee called a 'premium'. The other feature of an option is that it is bought/sold for a fixed period. The risks/benefits in option trading are not symmetrical between the buyer and the seller (termed the 'writer').

In order to demonstrate the role of options in risk management, it is useful to look at the payoff of an option if held to maturity. We use an option on the short-sterling futures contract to illustrate the process. We assume a strike price of £95.00 and a premium of 20 basis points. In the case of the purchase of a call option, the option will only be exercised if the price rises above £95, because otherwise he/she can buy the security more cheaply in the market. Conversely, for a put option the put will only be exercised if the price falls below £95. Where it is profitable to exercise an option, the option is said to be 'in the money'. If the option is not exercised, the maximum loss to the buyer of the option is £0.20. The contrast for the seller of the option is marked. In return for a small profit, he/she faces a large degree of risk if the price of the underlying security moves against him/her.

The payoffs are illustrated further in Figures 13.2A and B. From these figures it can be clearly seen that selling options is not a risk management policy. It is a speculative policy. The basic point of buying an option on the relevant futures contract provides the same opportunities for risk management, as does a futures contract. There are two differences:

1. The purchaser benefits from any gain if the option moves into the money.
2. In return for this benefit, the purchaser pays a fee, i.e. the option premium. In financial markets with many traders the premium would be expected *ex ante* to reflect the degree of risk.

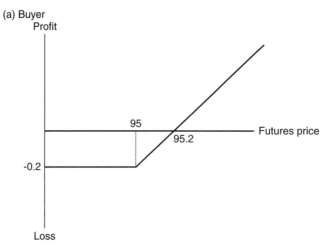

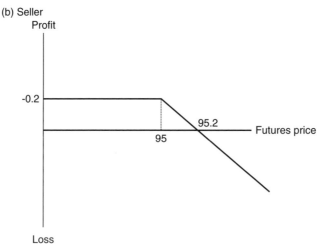

FIGURE 13.2A Call Option.

13.4 MARKET RISK

The industry standard for dealing with market risk on the trading book is the value–at–risk (VaR) model. Pioneered by JP Morgan's Riskmetrics™ (JP Morgan, 1995), the aim of VaR is to calculate the likely loss a bank might experience on its whole trading book. VaR is the maximum loss that a bank can be confident it would lose over a target horizon within a given confidence interval. In other words, VaR answers the question: How much can I lose with x% probability over a given time horizon?[6] The statistical definition is that VaR is an

---

[6] JP Morgan (1995).

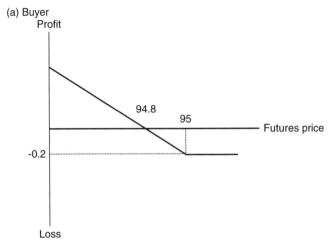

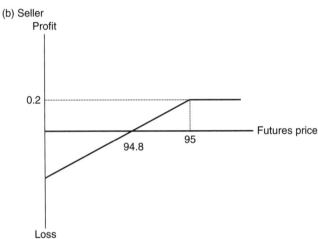

FIGURE 13.2B Put Option.

estimate of the value of losses (ΔP) that cannot be exceeded, with confidence $\alpha\%$ over a specific time horizon, i.e.

$$\Pr[\Delta P \, \Delta t \leq \text{VaR}] = \alpha \qquad (13.5)$$

The methodology of VaR is based around estimation of the statistical distribution of asset returns. Parametric (known as 'delta-normal') VaR is based on the estimate of the variance–covariance matrix of asset returns from historical time series. Returns are calculated as

$$R_t = \left(\frac{P_t - P_{t-1}}{P_{t-1}} \right) \times 100$$

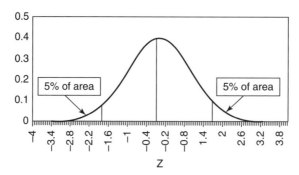

FIGURE 13.3 Standard Normal Distribution.

where P is the value of the asset and t defines the time period in consideration – usually daily in relatively liquid markets, but institutions that adjust their positions over a longer period such as pension funds might work on a monthly horizon.

The underlying assumption is that the asset returns are normally distributed. A normal distribution is defined in terms of the first two moments of its distribution – the mean μ and the standard deviation σ. The mean of the asset return defines its expected return, and the standard deviation is taken as a measure of risk. If the returns are normally distributed as in Figure 13.3, then we know that we can be 90% sure that the actual returns will lie within $\pm 1.65\sigma$ of the expected return. That is, actual return will be $\pm 1.65\sigma$. If we were only concerned with downside risk, then we would be 95% sure that the actual return would not be less than $\mu - 1.65\sigma$. Therefore, if the net position of a single asset were £100m and the standard deviation of the returns on the asset were 2%, then the VaR would be $100 \times 1.65 \times 0.02 = £3.3$m. The VaR states that the asset holder can expect to lose more than £3.3m in no more than 5 out of every 100 days.

The advantage of VaR is that it provides a statistical measure of probable loss on not just a single asset but a whole portfolio of assets. In the case of a portfolio, the VaR calculation incorporates the benefits of risk reduction from diversification. Note, as before, that risk (or portfolio volatility) is measured by the standard deviation of the portfolio returns.

For a two-asset portfolio, return and riskiness are defined by (13.6) and (13.7)[7] respectively:

$$R_p = \alpha_1 R_1 + \alpha_2 R_2 \tag{13.6}$$

$$\sigma_p \sqrt{(\alpha_1^2 \sigma_1^2 + \alpha_2^2 \sigma_2^2 + 2\rho_{1,2}\alpha_1\alpha_2\sigma_1\sigma_2)} \tag{13.7}$$

where $\rho_{1,2}$ is the correlation coefficient between the returns of assets 1 and 2, and α_1 and α_2 are the share of the assets in the portfolio and sum to 1.

---

[7] See Box 7.4 for a fuller discussion of the two-variable portfolio.

More generally, for a multivariable portfolio the riskiness is defined by

$$\sigma_p \sqrt{\sum_{i=1}^{n} (\alpha_i \sigma_i)^2 + \sum_{i=j} \sum_{i=j} \alpha_i \alpha_j \rho_{i,j} \sigma_i \sigma_j} \tag{13.8}$$

Let the value of a portfolio of n assets of value V_i be described by

$$V_p = \sum_{i=1}^{n} V_i \tag{13.9}$$

If the value of each asset V_i depends on the price of an underlying asset P_i, then the change in the value of a portfolio is

$$dV_p = \sum_{i=1}^{n} P_i \left(\frac{\partial V_i}{\partial P_i} \right) \left(\frac{dP_i}{P} \right) \tag{13.10}$$

where (dP_i/P_i) is the percentage return on the asset. The above expression says that the *change in value of the portfolio* = (*sensitivity of the portfolio to a price change*) × (*change in the price of the underlying asset*). This is known as the delta valuation method.

To illustrate the application of VaR, let us take a single asset case of a Treasury bill futures contract. Let us calculate the VaR of a position consisting of a November 2006 Treasury bill futures contract purchased in October 2006. The closing futures price was £110. Each Treasury bill futures contract is for the delivery of £100 000 in face value of bills, and each £1 change in the futures price results in £1000 change in the value of the position. The mean of Treasury futures returns is zero and the standard deviation is 0.546%. If returns are normally distributed, then 95% of all returns will fall within 1.96 standard deviations of the mean return. That is, in the range ±1.07%. If we are interested in downside risk only, then only 5% of returns will be less than −0.898 = 1.645(0.546). The 1-day VaR at 5% probability is

$$\left(\frac{0.898}{100} \right) \times 110 \times £1000 = £987.8$$

The daily loss on this position will exceed £987.8 no more than 5 days out of 100. If a 1-day holding period is considered too short and a 1-week holding period is more appropriate, then the calculation is modified to include time. The standard deviation is modified by multiplying it by the square root of time (in this case, five working days). So the modified standard deviation is 0.546($\sqrt{5}$) = 1.220. Box 13.4 illustrates the case for a portfolio of assets.

VaR can be estimated by the variance−covariance method, which we have described above, but it can also be evaluated using the method of historical simulation, which allows for all types of dependency between portfolio value and risk factors, as well as Monte Carlo simulation, which uses randomly generated risk factor returns. While this appears to give greater flexibility in estimating VaR, as Beder (1995) has shown, the three methods

BOX 13.4   VaR portfolio of assets

There are two ways to calculate VaR for a portfolio of assets. Both give the same results. Our starting point is portfolio theory. In the case of a two–asset portfolio, the return on the portfolio can be written as

$$R_p = \alpha_1 R_1 + \alpha_2 R_2$$
$$\alpha_1 + \alpha_2 = 1$$

The riskiness of the portfolio is given by

$$\sigma_p = \sqrt{(\alpha_1^2 \sigma_1^2 + \alpha_2^2 \sigma_2^2 + 2\rho_{1,2}\sigma_1\sigma_2)}$$

where $\rho_{1,2}$ is the correlation coefficient between the returns of assets 1 and 2. The per cent VaR can be stated as $1.65\sigma_p$ and the £ value of VaR is $V_0 1.65\sigma_p$, where V_0 is the £ value of the portfolio. We can also calculate the individual £ value of VaR for each asset. So, $VaR_1 = 1.65\sigma_1 V_1$ and $VaR_2 = 1.65\sigma_2 V_2$, and the value of the portfolio VaR is then

$$VaR_p = \sqrt{(VaR_1^2 + VaR_2^2 + 2\rho_{1,2}VaR_1 VaR_2)}$$

When there is a portfolio of more than two assets, VaR calculation is more easily done using matrix algebra:

$$VaR_p = [ZCZ']^{\frac{1}{2}}$$

where $Z = [VaR_1, VaR_2, \ldots, VaR_n]$

An example of this is the following. A $-based corporation holds $100m of US Treasury bills and $50m in corporate bonds. The standard deviation of returns of the US 10-year bonds, calculated on a daily basis, is 0.605%, and the standard deviation of the corporate bonds is 0.565%. The correlation between the returns on the US bonds and corporate bonds is 0.35. What is the VaR over a 1-day horizon, given that there is a 5% chance of understating a realized loss?

$$VaR_1 = \$100m(1.65)(0.00605) = \$998\,250$$

$$VaR_2 = \$50m(1.65)(0.00565) = \$466\,125$$

$$VaR_p^2 = [Var_1, VaR_2]\begin{bmatrix} 1 & 0.35 \\ 0.35 & 1 \end{bmatrix}\begin{bmatrix} VaR_1 \\ VaR_2 \end{bmatrix}$$

$$\therefore VaR_p = \sqrt{(VaR_1^2 + VaR_2^2 + 2(0.35)VaR_1 VaR_2)} = \$1.241m$$

(continued)

The alternative method of calculation is given below. It would be useful to look back to equation (7.4.2) in Chapter 7 and Box 7.4. Since the portfolio is made up of a total of \$150m, of which two-thirds (\$100m) is held in Treasury bills and one-third (\$50m) in corporate bonds, the weights on the individual components of the portfolio are 2/3 and 1/3 respectively:

$$\sigma_p = \sqrt{((\tfrac{2}{3})^2(0.00605)^2 + (\tfrac{1}{3})^2(0.00565)^2 + 2(\tfrac{2}{3})(\tfrac{1}{3})(0.35)(0.00605)(0.00565))} = 0.005013$$

$$VaR_p = \$150m(1.65)\sigma_p = \$150m(1.65)(0.005013) = \$1.241m$$

give different risk estimates for different holding periods, confidence intervals and data windows.

The assumptions of VaR are as follows:

1. Returns are normally distributed.
2. Serially uncorrelated returns.
3. Standard deviation (volatility) is stable over time.
4. Constant variance–covariance of returns.

These are questionable assumptions, and considerable research has gone into examining alternative distributions and assumptions. The most contentious assumption is that returns are normally distributed. The remaining assumptions have been shown to be invalid in times of financial stress when markets behave in an extreme or volatile fashion (e.g. the 1987 stock market crash, the 1997 Asian financial crisis, the 1998 Russia crisis). From a regulatory point of view, parameters of market return, which may appear stable to a single institution in normal times, will become highly volatile when a large number of financial institutions employ the same risk assessment methods and react to a shock in a concerted and common way. What can be taken as parametric for a single bank in normal market conditions will not be so when all banks react in a common way to a market shock. As Daníelsson (2000) has suggested, forecasting risk does change the nature of risk in the same way as Goodhart's law, which states that any statistical relationship will break down when used for policy purposes, and any risk model will break down when used for its intended purpose. For this reason, Basel II standards for the use of internal models have been set at strongly conservative levels. On the confidence level, the Bank for International Settlements (BIS) has recommended the 99th percentile rather than the Riskmetrics™ recommendation of the 95th percentile. Furthermore, the VaR calculation obtained is to be multiplied by a factor of 3 to obtain the capital adequacy level required for the cover of trading risk. Box 13.5 sets out Basel II minimum standards for the application of VaR to capital adequacy.

BOX 13.5   Basel II minimum standard for the use of VaR to calculate market risk for the assignment of regulatory capital adequacy

1. VaR must be computed on a daily basis, using a 99th percentile, one-tailed confidence interval.
2. A minimum 'holding period' of ten trading days must be used to simulate liquidity issues that last for longer than the 1-day VaR holding period. (The 'square root of time' may be applied to the 1-day VaR estimate, however, to simplify the calculation of this VaR measure.)
3. A minimum of a one-business-year observation period (250 days) must be used, with updates of data sets taking place every day, and reassessments of weights and other market data should take place no less than once every 3 months.
4. Banks are allowed discretion in recognizing empirical correlations within broad risk categories, i.e. interest rates, exchange rates, equity prices and commodity prices.
5. Banks should hold capital equivalent to the higher of either the last day's VaR measure or an average of the last 60 days (applying a multiplication factor of at least 3).
6. The bank's VaR measure should meet a certain level of accuracy upon 'back-testing', or else a penal rate will be applied to its charges (i.e. a plus factor). If the model fails three consecutive times, the institution's trading licence may be revoked.

13.5 CREDIT RISK

We now return to the subject of credit risk for a more detailed examination. Credit risk is the principal risk that a bank faces on its balance sheet, and we have devoted a complete chapter (i.e. Chapter 8) to one of the means by which banks minimize this risk, that is, by rationing loans. The riskiness of a loan is also reflected in the price of the loan. We showed in Box 8.2 in Chapter 8 that, if the loan rate is given by r_L, the funding rate is given by r_F and the repayment rate is μ, then a general loan pricing formula is given by

$$r_L = \left(\frac{1 + r_F}{1 - \delta} \right) - 1 \qquad (13.11)$$

where $\delta = 1 - \mu$ is the default rate. This expression says that the price of a risky loan is the cost of funds plus a risk premium that accounts for default risk. A more general loan pricing formula was derived in Box 9.1 in the chapter on securitization. This expression accounted for not only the expected default on loans (risk premium) but also the return on capital required from the loan to compensate shareholders (required return on capital), the cost of funds including the costs of meeting regulatory requirements and deposit insurance and the administrative costs (overheads). Risk management of the loan book is about the risk manager attempting to quantify (however imperfectly) the risk of default and include it in the pricing of loans so that it minimizes the effect of risk on the bank's balance sheet and on shareholders' capital. The recognition of risk in the loan decision enables the bank to assign capital to its specific business activities in line with the associated risk. Different activities with specific risk categories have different levels of capital associated with the activity. Capital provides protection against unexpected losses, whereas expected losses should be covered by appropriate risk premia on loan pricing and provisions. The recognition of risk and the potential of unexpected losses give rise to the concept of risk-adjusted capital or *CAR*. In turn, the allocation of *CAR* to specific bank activity gives rise to the concept of risk-adjusted return on capital (*RAROC*).

RAROC is a technique first introduced by Bankers Trust in the 1970s that is used extensively as a management performance tool to evaluate the economic profit generated from a particular activity or cost centre. In particular it is a useful tool for the loan officer to decide to accept or reject a loan application if the expected *RAROC* is less than, equal to or greater than some benchmark rate. A common measure of *RAROC* is given by

$$RAROC = \frac{R - C - E(l)}{CAR} + r_f \qquad (13.12)$$

where R is revenues generated from the loan, C is costs, $E(l)$ is expected losses, CAR is the capital allocated to the activity and r_f is the risk-free rate of return. Revenue could include expected fee income from the account as well as the expected loan interest payments. Costs could include operational and maintenance costs as well as the funding cost of the loan. The inclusion of the risk-free rate provides the return beyond which the loan transaction must reach, and represents the opportunity cost for shareholders.[8]

The decision to grant credit is based on a mixture of subjective and objective information. In the past, bankers relied entirely on subjective evaluations based on the characteristics of the borrower. Altman and Saunders (1998) describe these as the four Cs of credit, namely *character* (reputation), *capital* (leverage), *capacity* (volatility of earnings) and *collateral*. However, over the past 30 years, technical methods have been developed to help the loan officer in the evaluation of risk of default.

One of the simplest and favourite methods of assigning loans to different risk classes is through the method of credit scoring.[9] Credit scoring is a technical method of assigning a score that classifies potential borrowers into risk classes (both consumers and companies), which determines whether a loan is made, rejected or lies in an area that requires additional scrutiny, further conditions or higher risk premia. Basically, the history of loans is divided into two groups: those that have defaulted ($Z = 1$) and those that have repaid ($Z = 0$). These observations are then related to a number of observable borrower characteristics to generate a Z-score which classifies loan applications into a bankrupt group, into a non-bankrupt group and into an in-between 'zone of ignorance'. The modelling framework based on the work of Altman (1968) and Altman *et al.* (1977) is called multiple discriminant analysis which has the objective of identifying a set of variables that can discriminate between the two principal groups.[10] Altman *et al.* (1977) found that seven key discriminating factors helped to identify

[8] Alternatively, the risk-free rate could be replaced by the weighted average cost of capital for the bank.

[9] Mester (1997) finds that, in the USA, 97% of banks use credit scoring methods to approve credit card applications, and 70% of banks use them for small business loans.

[10] Other researchers have applied the methodology to consumer loans and commercial loans. For example, Orgler (1970) applies the model to commercial loan defaults.

the bankruptcy risk of companies. The model, which is known as the ZETA® discriminant model, is a linear relationship between the Z-score and the seven factors:

$$Z_i = \sum_{i=1}^{7} \alpha_i X_i \qquad (13.13)$$

The seven factors are:

1. Return on assets (measured as net profit divided by total assets).
2. Stability of earnings (measured by the reciprocal of the standard deviation of ROA over a 10-year moving period).
3. Debt service (measured by net profit divided by total interest payments).
4. Cumulative profitability (measured by retained earnings divided by total assets).
5. Liquidity (measured by liquid current assets divided by liquid current liabilities).
6. Capitalization (measured by a 5-year average market value of the firm's common stock divided by long-term capital).
7. Size (measured by the firm's total assets).

More sophisticated statistical techniques have been employed by researchers and specialist credit analysis companies (such as the linear probability model, logit and probit), but basically it involves the use of accounting-based information of borrower characteristics.

While these models have been successful in classifying borrowers into different categories based on data that exist for the past, and they can be a good aid for loan officers, the problem is that they depend on very up-to-date accounting information which is usually not immediately available, or the predictions are based on data that are out of date.

Timely information is not the only problem with the credit scoring framework. Its unashamedly statistical approach is 'black box' in the sense that it offers no theoretical explanation as to why loans should be risk classified in this way. An alternative class of model that has a theoretical underpinning is the 'risk of ruin' approach, which bears a resemblance to the option pricing models of Black and Scholes (1973) and Merton (1974). Basically, the model states that a firm goes bankrupt when the market value of its assets fall below its debt obligations. In the option pricing model, the probability of bankruptcy depends on the beginning-period market value of a firm's assets (A) relative to its short-term debt (D) and the volatility of the market value of the assets (σ_A). A commercial application of this is Moody's KMV model of distance to default.[11] The KMV model estimates the probability of default from A, D and σ_A, as is shown in equation (13.14) below.

Firstly, the value of the equity is viewed as a call option on the value of the firm's assets. Secondly, a theoretical link is made between the observed volatility of the value of equity and the unobserved volatility of the firm's value of assets. Thirdly, given initial values of A and D and a value for the diffusion of asset values given by σ_A, an expected default frequency (EDF) is calculated for each borrowing firm. In practice the KMV framework takes an empirically based 'distance from default' measure based on how many standard deviations A is from D. Crosbie and Bohn (2003) provide an example of the distance to default and

---

[11] See Crosbie and Bohn (2003) and other papers on *http://www.moodyskmv.com*

the calculation of the expected default frequency. The basic formula for the calculation of distance to default (*d*) is given by

$$d = \frac{(A - D)/A}{\sigma_A} = \frac{A - D}{A\sigma_A} \tag{13.14}$$

which is another way of asking the question as to the statistical significance of the difference between the firm's marketable assets and its short-term debts. Consequently *d* is equivalent to a 'Z' score in the standard normal distribution. Box 13.6 provides a graphical illustration and an example of the calculation. The main problem with the KMV model is that the volatility of the firm's stock price may not be a good proxy for the volatility of the firm's asset value. Even if it were, the model would work only with publicly traded companies that had the capability of raising funds on the capital market. Small- and medium-sized companies are usually not listed, and even fewer efficacious proxies will need to be used to measure the volatility of asset values.

The methodology of value at risk has been extended to evaluating the risk on the balance sheet with JP Morgan's Creditmetrics™ (1997). Unlike the KMV model, which uses an equity-driven evaluation of distance to default, the Creditmetrics approach utilizes external credit ratings. The Creditmetrics model is based on a transition matrix of probabilities that measures the probability that the credit rating of a loan or any debt security will change over the term of the loan or maturity of credit instrument. The transition matrix covers the entire range of possibilities including upgrades of credit rating as well as downgrades. Since loan prices and volatilities of values are unobservable, Creditmetrics uses the migration probabilities to estimate a loan's loss distribution.

A loan has eight possible credit ratings and correspondingly eight credit rating migration assumptions. The eight credit ratings are: AAA, AA, A, BBB, BB, B, CCC and default. If a loan is initially rated as BBB, the loan's value in the first year following its advance is calculated under different potential scenarios. Either the loan will remain at its initial credit rating or be upgraded or downgraded. As discussed in Allen *et al.* (2004), the probabilities of transition in the first year of the advance, as calculated by JP Morgan's Creditmetrics™, are shown in Table 13.2.

Creditmetrics aims to do for credit risk what Riskmetrics does for market risk. Creditmetrics asks the question: If tomorrow is a bad state, by how much does the value of my loan portfolio fall? In other words, what is the probability of the bank's loan portfolio falling below a certain level or what is the worst-case scenario for the loan portfolio at the given level of significance? The information needed to conduct this evaluation is as follows:

- The borrower's external or internal credit rating.
- The transition probabilities (Table 13.2).
- The recovery rates for defaulted loans.
- The credit risk premium associated with each risk class.

Consider the following example of a loan of £100m of a maturity of 5 years. The risk classification of the loan is BBB and the risk premium for this class is 1% per year. The risk-free rate of interest is 6% a year, and therefore the fixed rate of interest on the loan is 7%. The risk premium rises (or falls) for each fall (or rise) in credit class by 25 basis points per credit rating. The recovery rate on defaulted loans is 80% but at the maturity date. The

BOX 13.6 Distance to default

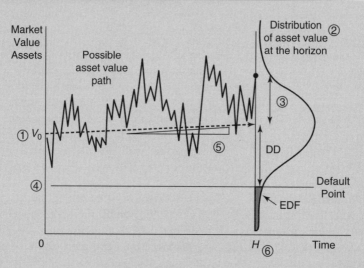

The current marketable asset value is V_0, shown by (1) on the diagram. The distribution of the asset value at time horizon H is shown by the normal distribution (2). The volatility of the future asset value at time H is shown by the gap (3). The default point, which represents the level of short-term debt, is shown by (4). The trend growth in asset values over the time horizon H (shown by the dotted line) is (5) and the length of the time horizon H is shown by (6). Table 13.3 illustrates for two companies AB and CC.

TABLE 13.3 Market value of assets and default point

Variable	Company AB	Company CC
Market value of assets (A)	44.1	43.3
Value of short-term debt (D)	5.3	13.2
Market net worth ($A - D$)	38.8	30.1
Asset volatility σ_A	21%	39%
Distance to default	4.19	1.78
Default probability	0.001%	3.6%

Given the asset volatility for each company, the distance to default is 4.19 for company AB and 1.78 for company CC. On a one-tailed test (downside risk) there is only a 0.001% chance that the market value of assets of company AB will be less than its short-term debt. Similarly, there is only a 3.6% chance that company CC will see the market value of its assets fall below its short-term debts (assuming a normal distribution).

Source: Crosbie and Bohn (2003).

TABLE 13.2 1-year transition probabilities for BBB-rated borrower

Rating	Probability	
AAA	0.02%	
AA	0.33%	
A	5.95%	
BBB	86.93%	← Most likely to stay in the same risk class
BB	5.30%	
B	1.17%	
CCC	0.13%	
D Default	0.18%	

Source: JP Morgan's Creditmetrics (1997).

discounted flow of income and balloon payment of £100m in the fifth year is constructed for each credit class. Think of the loan as a purchase of a fixed-coupon 5-year bond at 7%, so that the present value of the cash stream and balloon payment is given by

$$P = \frac{7}{(1 + r_{f1} + \rho_j)} + \frac{7}{(1 + r_{f2} + \rho_j)^2} + \frac{7}{(1 + r_{f3} + \rho_j)^3} + \frac{7}{(1 + r_{f4} + \rho_j)^4}$$

$$+ \frac{107}{(1 + r_{f5} + \rho_j)^5} \tag{13.15}$$

where r_{fi} represents the forward risk-free rate of interest in year (i), and ρ_j is the risk premium for the jth risk class. Table 13.4 shows the calculations for the value of the loans in each credit class and the transition probabilities. Box 13.7 shows how the calculations for Table 13.4 were obtained. In this exercise we assume a flat term structure of interest rates, so that $r_{f1} = r_{f2} = \ldots = r_{fn}$. Box 13.8 shows how the forward risk-free rate of interest can be backed out of the current spot rate and the term structure of interest rates. The recovery rate on the defaulted case is calculated for the year of maturity and at the risk-free rate of interest (once defaulted, there is no further associated risk).

The expected value and standard deviation are given by the following formula:

$$\text{Mean} = \mu = \sum_{i=1}^{8} p_i V_i \tag{13.16}$$

$$\text{Standard deviation} = \sigma = \sqrt{\sum_{i=1}^{8} p_i (V_i - \mu)^2} \tag{13.17}$$

You can see from Table 13.4 that the expected value of the BBB-rated loan is £99.92m (close to its par value of £100m). The standard deviation is £1.76m. If we assume that the distribution is normal (it is not!), then there is a 1% chance that the loan value will fall to £95.82m (= £99.92m − (2.326 × £1.76m)). This figure understates the true VaR

TABLE 13.4 VaR calculations for a hypothetical BBB-rated loan

Rating	PV of loan (£m)	Transition probability (%)	Weighted value (£m)
AAA	103.14	0.02	0.0206
AA	102.08	0.33	0.3369
A	101.03	5.95	6.0114
BBB	100.00	86.93	86.93
BB	98.98	5.30	5.2460
B	97.98	1.17	1.1464
CCC	96.99	0.13	0.1164
D default	63.97	0.18	0.1152
Expected value (mean)			99.92
Standard deviation			1.59

Source: JP Morgan's Creditmetrics (1997).

owing to the negative skewness of the actual distribution, but the purpose of this exercise is to illustrate the application of the VaR methodology to the loan book. However, staying with the assumption of a normal distribution, the mean value of the loan is £99.92m, and, if the loan had retained its BBB rating, its value would have been £100m. Therefore, the expected losses on the loan are £100m − £99.92m = £0.08m. The unexpected losses are the VaR calculation (£99.92m − £96.22m = £3.7m). Creditmetrics calculates that the loan's unexpected losses will be no more than £3.7m 1% of the time.

The calculation of a VaR to a specific loan is extended to the whole loan portfolio of the bank by recognizing the existence of correlations between loan values from different obligors. These correlations are calculated from the equity returns of the industries from which the respective obligors companies come. Given the correlations, Creditmetrics calculates a matrix of joint migration probabilities for all possible pairs of credit migration possibilities, and the process can be applied to all the loans on the bank's loan book.

The use of value-at-risk methodology to market risk and credit risk management gives the impression that risk management in banks has reached the levels of technology associated with the natural sciences. Nothing could be further from the truth. The information required for the application of Creditmetrics is often unavailable and the assumptions used in the calculation of VaR are certainly questionable.[12] Modern risk management methods should be seen as complements to and not substitutes for good judgement, experience and practice. The role of the risk manager in banks is to use both judgement (expert systems) and technical knowledge in risk management. The computer will never replace the loan officer and the risk manager.

---

[12] To some extent the proponents of VaR have recognized the problems associated with the simple application of value at risk and gone into further sophisticated extension of the VaR methodology. See, for example, Pearson and Smithson (2002).

BOX 13.7

The income stream from the 7% coupon bond (loan) with a par value of £100m is discounted at the risk-free rate and risk premium for its term to maturity of 5 years with a balloon payment of the principal plus interest in the fifth year. If a credit event occurs immediately after the loan has been made, the value of the loan will fall if the rating is downgraded, or raised if the rating is upgraded.

The risk-free rate of interest is assumed to be 6% and the risk premium for a BBB rating is 1%. The premium changes by 25 bp per rating class.

	D	CCC	B	BB	BBB	A	AA	AAA
$R_f + \rho$	6%	7.75%	7.50%	7.25%	7%	6.75%	6.50%	6.25%
$T = 1$	0	6.49652	6.51162	6.52680	6.54205	6.55737	6.57277	6.58823
$T = 2$	0	6.02925	6.05732	6.0856	6.11407	6.14274	6.17161	6.20069
$T = 3$	0	5.5959	5.63472	5.67422	5.71408	5.75432	5.79494	5.83594
$T = 4$	0	5.19313	5.24160	5.29064	5.34026	5.39046	5.44136	5.49265
$T = 5$	63.976	73.6711	74.5317	75.4045	76.2895	77.1870	78.0972	79.0203
PV	63.976	96.9856	97.9770	98.9817	100	101.031	102.077	103.137

The hypothetical distribution of loan values is shown in the figure below (not drawn to scale).

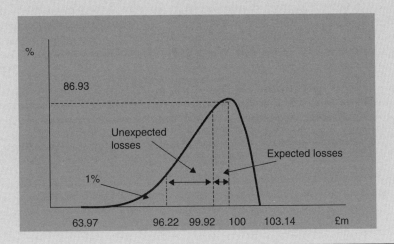

BOX 13.8

The interest rates in Creditmetrics are assumed to be deterministic. Therefore, the risk-free rates for each period are obtained by decomposing the yield curve with the current spot rate to construct the 1-year forward rate. For example, if the current risk-free spot rate for 1-year maturity bonds is $\{_1r_f\}$ and the 2-year maturity spot rate is $\{_2r_f\}$, from the expectations theory of the yield curve we have

$$(1 + {_2r_f})^2 = (1 + {_1r_f})(1 + {_1r_{f,1}})$$

For example, if the 1-year rate is 6% per annum and the 2-year rate is 7% per annum, the above equation becomes

$$(1 + 0.07)^2 = (1 + 0.06)(1 + {_1r_{f,1}})$$

solving $(1 + {_1r_{f,1}}) = \frac{1.07^2}{1.06}$ so that ${_1r_{f,1}} = 0.08$, where $\{_1r_{f,1}\}$ is the forward risk-free rate expected 1 year from now. The forward rate can be backed out from the above expression as the 1-year and 2-year maturity risk-free rates are observable.

The generalization of the expectations theory of the yield curve enables the 1-year forward rates to be backed out for any future period to be used in the discounting of the income flow from a specific loan.

Finally, we noted in Chapter 9 that one of the means of reducing the risk on the portfolio is by offloading risk on to the capital market through the process of securitization. An alternative to the process of securitization is to insure the bank asset by a credit default swap. A credit default swap (CDS) is, in essence, an insurance policy where the safety of a loan is guaranteed, subject, of course, to counterparty risk. It is a contract between two parties. The party buying credit protection pays a periodic fee to another party who agrees to reimburse the purchaser of credit protection in the event of failure to repay either the capital value of the debt or related interest within a specified time period. This is represented graphically in Figure 13.4.

In return for the periodic payment normally expressed as basis points, the protection seller would make payment designed to mirror the loss to the protection buyer over a fixed

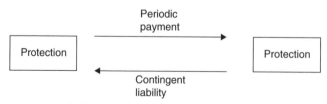

FIGURE 13.4 Credit Default Swap.

time period in the case of a credit event as defined below. For example, if the protection buyer purchases protection on a £100m debt over a period of 5 years at a price of 200 basis points paid quarterly, then the periodic payment would be $£m\frac{100(0.02)}{4} = £0.5m$ per quarter. The contingent liability to the protection seller is £100m, which would be paid over the course of the next 5 years in the event of a credit event normally defined as any of the following:

1. Failure to meet payment obligations.
2. Bankruptcy or moratorium in the case of sovereign debt.
3. Repudiation.
4. Material adverse restructuring of the debt.

Clearly, then, this process has a lot in common with securitization discussed in Chapter 9. Both processes permit the bank to sell (i.e. short) credit risk. There are, however, two salient differences between the role of CDS and securitization, namely:

1. The original borrower is not involved in the CDS, unlike in the case of securitization where the debt itself is transferred so the borrower owes an obligation to a new party.
2. The debt is not removed from the balance sheet, so there are no reserve ratio benefits.

A picture of the extent of the credit derivatives market is provided by the annual survey carried out by *Risk Magazine*. In 2003 the total market was estimated to be in the region of $2306bn of which single-name CDS formed 73%.[13] In a breakdown by end-users, banks were the largest users (just under 50% of the total). The market is an OTC market composed of a few major players. It is also a wholesale market, with transactions ranging between a few million to billions of dollars.

13.6 OPERATIONAL RISK

The Bank for International Settlements defines operational risk as the risk of loss resulting from inadequate or failed internal processes, people and systems or from external events. This definition includes legal risk but excludes strategic and reputational risk. In the previous chapter we introduced the concept of operational risk as part of the Basel II regulatory framework, and the capital adequacy charges were shown in Box 12.3. In this section we present some introductory aspects of operational risk.[14] Operational risk can be categorized by various sources, as defined by Rachlin (1998) and listed in Table 13.5.[15]

---

[13] Basket default swaps are also available.

[14] Anything more than an introduction would be beyond the scope of this book. For a detailed examination, see Allen *et al.* (2004).

[15] Quoted in Allen *et al.* (2004).

TABLE 13.5 Operational risk categories

Process risk

Pretransaction: marketing risks, selling risks, new connection, model risk
Transaction: error, fraud, contract risk, product complexity, capacity risk
Management information
Erroneous disclosure risk

People risk

Integrity: fraud, collusion, malice, unauthorized use of information, rogue trading
Competency
Management
Key personnel
Health and safety

Systems risk

Data corruption
Programming errors/fraud
Security breach
Capacity risks
System suitability
Compatibility risks
System failure
Strategic risks (platform/supplier)

Business strategy risk

Change management
Project management
Strategy
Political

External environment risk

Outsourcing/external supplier risk
Physical security
Money laundering
Compliance
Financial reporting
Tax
Legal (litigation)
Natural disaster
Terrorist threat
Strike risk

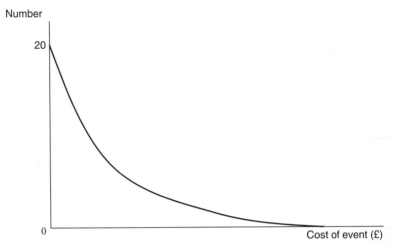

FIGURE 13.5 Frequency and Severity of Loss Events.

The problem in assessing operational risk is that it can be separated into high-frequency low-severity (HFLS) events, which occur regularly and for which data can be found, and low-frequency high-severity (LFHS) events, which are rare. Measuring operational risk will need to account for both types. Figure 13.5 illustrates the distribution.

The figure illustrates the case where high-risk events are quite rare and individual banks use case experiences from other banks, whereas low-risk events are quite frequent and each bank will have experienced some such events. To calculate the expected operational loss $E(L)$, the bank needs to have a probability (ρ), which is often subjective, of the operational loss event and the cost of the operational loss event (θ), so that expected loss is

$$E(L) = \rho\theta \tag{13.18}$$

Unexpected losses can then be modelled using the VaR methodology described in the earlier section. One of the problems of obtaining measures of expected operational losses is that each bank would be reluctant to provide information about HFLS events that may be useful to a competitor. Typically, LFHS events are made public when a bank cannot keep such an event hidden from the market and the media. A source of information is the experience of the managers and the 'gossip in the market'. Both LFHS and HFLS events are the gossip of the banking fraternity long before official information seeps out into the media and the attention of regulators. Subjective probabilities can be assigned to each of the events listed in Table 13.5 on the basis of educated guesses and scenario analysis.

13.7 CONCLUSION

This chapter has provided a glimpse into risk management techniques applied by banks to the banking book and trading book. A number of market-hedging techniques and operations have not been reviewed. Much ink has been consumed on the reviewing and critique of internal model risk management techniques in financial institutions. Banks have been gearing up to put in place VaR models, which in turn have been the subject of considerable academic interest and criticism. It is a subject worthy of more than is covered here, but what has been covered provides sufficient insight for the student to take any interest further.

13.8 SUMMARY

- Banks cannot function without taking risk. Risk management involves the maintenance of losses and the value of the bank to within accepted margins. Types of risk include: market risk, legal risk, operational risk, liquidity risk and credit risk.
- Risks occurring through interest rate changes can be managed by consideration of the duration gap.
- Derivatives can also be used to manage risk.
- Market risk can be managed through the value-at-risk (VaR) model.
- The assumptions of the VaR model are quite restrictive.
- VaR modelling is part of Basel II risk assessment but with a 99% confidence interval.
- Creditmetrics is a method applying the VaR framework to the loan book of the bank.
- Operational risk deals with the expected operational loss from high-frequency low-severity events and high-frequency low-severity events.

FURTHER READING

See Allen *et al.* (2004), Bessis (1998), Cuthbertson and Nitzsche (2001, Chapter 22), Dowd (1998), Hendricks and Hirtle (1997) and Koch and MacDonald (2003).

QUESTIONS

1 Why do banks need to manage risk?

2 What are the main risks that banks manage?

3 What is interest rate risk? How do banks manage interest rate risk?

4 What is value at risk and how is it used to manage market risk?

5 What is the advantage to the investor from diversification?

6 How is VaR used to evaluate capital at risk?

7 What is Creditmetrics and how is it used to manage credit risk?

8 What is operational loss? How would a risk manager begin to evaluate the expected losses from operational events?

TEST QUESTIONS

1   A bank is trading on its own account \$10m of corporate bonds and \$5m of Treasuries. The daily volatility of corporate bonds is $\sigma_1 = 0.9\%$, and the daily volatility of Treasuries is $\sigma_2 = 0.6\%$. Calculate the variance of the portfolio and the
   Basel-recommended VaR if the correlation between the returns of the two assets is:
   (a) $\rho = 1.0$;
   (b) $\rho = -0.5$.

2   What is your dollar VaR when holding a UK portfolio of £100m if the current
   exchange rate is \$1.5 per £, the correlation between the return on the UK port-
   folio and the exchange rate is $\rho = 0.5$, the standard deviation of the UK portfolio is $\sigma_1 = 1.896\%$ and the standard deviation of the exchange rate is $\sigma_2 = 1.5\%$?

14

The Macroeconomics of Banking

MINI-CONTENTS

14.1   Introduction
14.2   The economics of central banking
14.3   Financial innovation and monetary policy
14.4   Bank credit and the transmission mechanism
14.5   Summary

14.1 INTRODUCTION

This chapter examines the implications of a developed banking system for the workings and controllability of the macroeconomy through the application of monetary policy. The control of the macroeconomy through the operation of monetary policy is the domain of a central bank. The modern central bank has the remit of maintaining the value of the currency by maintaining a low rate of inflation, stabilizing the macroeconomy and ensuring the stability of the financial system. The conduct of monetary policy also has effects on the banking system itself in its role as the provision of finance and, hence, the money supply. Thus, the relationship between monetary policy and banks is a two-way one, with the banks affecting the conduct of monetary policy and the conduct of monetary policy affecting the banks.

This chapter has three main sections. Section 14.2 examines the role of the central bank in the macroeconomy. It poses the questions: 'What are the proper functions of the central bank?' and 'What type of central bank will deliver the tasks given to it by the government?'. As a preliminary to this analysis, it is important that students remind themselves of the time inconsistency issue in macroeconomic policy design and of 'credibility and reputation' in the design of anti-inflation policy.[1] Section 14.3 examines the implications of financial innovation and

---

[1] The problem of 'time inconsistency' is easily illustrated by a non-financial examination. Large department stores offer sales at various times of the year, and queues of people waiting for bargains build up long before the official opening time. One simple short-term policy would be for the store unexpectedly to open early, in which case the queue would disappear. This would, however, be unsatisfactory (i.e. time inconsistent) in the long run because the shoppers would know that the store tended to open early and would respond by arriving earlier still.

the existence of a developed banking system for the efficacy of monetary policy. We will also examine the tools of monetary policy and the use of the central bank rate of interest in setting monetary policy. Section 14.4 examines the implications of the banking system for the transmission mechanism.

Two schools of thought are examined: the credit channel, which emphasizes the role of bank credit in supporting the corporate sector, and the monetary buffer stocks model, which also lays great emphasis on the flow of bank credit but emphasizes the role of money in the transmission mechanism.

14.2 THE ECONOMICS OF CENTRAL BANKING

14.2.1 Background

Central banks are a relatively modern phenomenon. One of the oldest central banks is the Bank of England. It was chartered in 1694 as a joint stock company, following a loan of £12m by a syndicate of wealthy individuals to the government of King William and Queen Mary. The creation of the Bank of England formalized the process whereby the syndicate lent to the government in return for the right to issue bank notes. Between 1688 and 1815, Britain was involved in a number of wars that needed funding. Bank notes were issued from the year of charter, but it was not until 1709 that the Bank obtained a virtual monopoly on note issue. At the outset the Bank was meant to handle the accounts of the government and help in funding its activities. A rise in gold prices at the beginning of the nineteenth century sparked a debate about the role of the Bank. There were two schools of thought: the currency school and the banking school. The currency school argued that stabilization of the value of the currency could only be ensured by strictly linking note issue to the Bank's gold deposits. The banking school argued that currency stability depended on all of the Bank's liabilities and not just its gold deposits. The currency school was the precursor of modern-day monetarists, and the banking school was the precursor of the Keynesian–Radcliffe view.

The 1844 Bank Charter Act split the Bank into the issue department and the banking department. The role of the issue department was to ensure convertibility by backing currency issue by gold. The banking department carried on as a normal commercial bank. The Act also gave the Bank of England de facto monopoly of the note issue. As a result, the Bank of England became the bank to the banks and resolved to act as the *lender of last resort* to the banking system. It was often argued by the commercial banks that the Bank of England's role as bank to the banking system, particularly the lender-of-last-resort role, ran counter to its own commercial interests. Over the years the Bank's commercial business was reduced. The Bank of England Act of 1946 brought the Bank into public ownership, with the aim of assisting the government to achieve the goal of full employment. Yet, convertibility[2] remained an important issue under the Bretton Woods system. The Bank attempted to meet

---

[2] The Bretton Woods system required countries to fix their exchange rates relative to the dollar, which in turn had a fixed gold value. There was also the requirement that non-residents could convert their holdings of sterling into foreign currency, and the central bank was required to carry out this conversion.

the dual goal of assisting the target of full employment and maintaining the exchange rate to the US dollar by imposing quantitative controls on bank lending. Often the full employment objective overrode the exchange rate objective defined by the Bretton Woods system, and it was the exchange rate that lost out. When the system of fixed exchange rates broke down in the early 1970s, the Bank was pushed into an even closer relationship with the government. The Bank of England Act of 1998 gave the Bank operational independence in meeting the inflation targets set by the government. The government inflation target was set at an upper bound of 2.5% and a lower bound of 1% (this has recently been adjusted to an upper bound of 2%).

14.2.2 Monetary Policy

The textbook explanation of monetary policy assumes that the central bank controls the supply of base money, as shown in Box 6.1. Through the money multiplier, the control of the stock of base money is supposed to translate into the control of the money supply. This description of the actual mechanism by which the money supply is controlled is quite remote from reality.

In principle, central banks can alter the required reserve ratio to control bank lending and, thereby, the money supply. An increase in the required reserve ratio means that the central bank creates a shortage of reserves for the banking system, which forces banks to raise interest rates to reduce loan demand. As noted in Chapter 4, different central banks have different required reserve ratios, and some have different reserve ratios for different types of deposit. While the central bank can use required reserves in principle, in practice central banks rarely use the reserve ratio as an instrument of monetary control.

In reality, central banks use the discount rate to control the money supply. The discount rate is the rate of interest at which the central bank is willing to lend reserves to the commercial banks – the detail of this process as regards the Bank of England is contained in Box 14.1. The central bank exercises control on the banking system by exploiting the scarcity of reserves. Commercial banks need to hold reserves to meet withdrawals of deposits and maturing loans from the central bank. One simple way for the commercial banks to meet their liquidity needs is to run down any excess reserves they hold.

In reality, the amount of excess reserves is small (in most countries there is an opportunity cost of holding non-interest bearing reserves), and in the UK they are very small.[3]

In the main, the Bank of England provides reserves to the banking system by granting *repos* (sale and repurchase agreements) or buying 'eligible' assets (Treasury bills or approved bank bills). Repos are effectively short-term loans from the Bank of England to commercial banks. The Bank rate is the rate at which the Bank of England relieves shortages in the money market (the net amount of indebtedness of the commercial banks to the Bank of England is called the money market shortage). When there is a surplus caused by an injection of cash into bank deposits that has to be returned to the Bank of England because of an 'open-market sale' of government bonds from the Bank of England's own

---

[3] In the UK, the banks receive the official rate of interest on balances with the Bank of England, apart from the reserve ratio of 0.15%. If reserves go below the agreed level, there is a penalty that reduces the rate of return on balances.

BOX 14.1 Bank of England intervention in the money markets

Any payments to the government decrease banks' deposits at the Bank of England, and receipts from the government increase banks' deposits there. For example, a tax payment will involve the individual writing a cheque in favour of the government. Hence, the individual's bank account will be debited with the amount of the tax payment. Since both the government and the banks keep their deposits at the Bank of England, the final leg of the payment involves a transfer from the individual's bank's deposit to deposits of the government at the Bank so that the funds reach the government. The converse effect arises from payments by the government. Hence, variation in the respective flows affects the money market, and the Bank of England intervenes to ensure that the rate of interest in the market conforms to that fixed by the Monetary Policy Committee. We will now briefly describe how this is done – for a fuller reference see Clews (2005).

In 2006, the Bank introduced a new system for its operations in the money market. The banks will hold reserves at the Bank, and these will be remunerated at the official rate of interest set by the Monetary Policy Committee. Within limits, the banks are free to select the level of these reserves and are expected to achieve this level on average over the monthly accounting period. Penalties are applied if the average of these reserve balances over the month falls 1% outside the agreed level. The banks are also able to make use of standing facilities at the bank, but these involve a penalty in that the rate is above the official rate (normally a penalty of 25 basis points).

In addition, the bank will operate open-market operations in eligible assets (as defined by the Bank) at its volition to ensure that the market, in general, is subject neither to shortages nor to excesses of funds. Dealings are conducted through repo transactions[4] at the official rate, i.e. the Bank rate. A 'repo' is a transaction where one party, in this case the Bank of England, purchases a security for cash and agrees to resell it later at a price agreed now. The sale price is higher than the purchase price representing the interest cost. Hence, it is in essence a short-term loan backed by collateral.

---

account (Table 14.1), the Bank will accept deposits from banks at a rate linked to the Bank rate (i.e. the rate of interest as determined by the Monetary Policy Committee). With the Bank of England prepared to make repo loans as required at the stated repo rate, there is little need for the commercial banks to have large excess reserves to meet deposit withdrawals.

[4] Technically, it would be more correct to say reverse repos, as the Bank is the purchaser of the security.

TABLE 14.1 Balance sheet of the Bank of England, 17 October 2007

Assets (£m)		Liabilities (£m)	
Loans to HM government	13 370	Notes in circulation	40 529
Sterling market operations	41 490	Required reserves (cash ratio)	2716
Central bank and other securities	7691	Reserve balances	21 731
Other	29 127	Foreign currency public securities	4499
		Other	22 202
Total	91 678	*Total*	91 677

Source: Balance sheet of the Bank of England, 17 October 2007.

The Bank rate acts as the benchmark for interbank borrowing and lending, and market-determined interest rates like the London interbank offer rate (LIBOR) would normally be expected to match closely the Bank of England repo rate.

14.2.3 Central Bank Independence

The question then arises: How does the Bank of England (and, indeed, other central banks) choose the rate of interest? The answer to this depends on the relationship of the central bank to the government. The independence of central banks has two distinct facets. Goal independence means that the central bank sets the goals of monetary policy. Operational independence refers to a central bank that has freedom to achieve the ends which are themselves set by the government. A central bank that is not politically independent of the government tends to support government by financing its spending with little regard to the monetary consequences.

Nowadays, however, many central banks are operationally independent. The Federal Reserve in the USA is one of the few central banks that has both operational and goal independence. The Bank of England has been operationally independent since 1997, but in fact the 'Old Lady of Threadneedle Street' is a relative 'Johnny-come-lately' to the ranks of independent central banks. The Bundesbank and the Swiss central banks have the longest pedigree in terms of independence. The West German and Swiss economies have also had the best record of low inflation since World War II. The argument for an independent central bank is that monetary policy is cushioned from political interference and is removed from the temptation to cheat on a low-inflation environment by engineering some unexpected inflation prior to an election. An independent central bank gives credibility to an announced monetary policy that underpins low inflation.

In the UK, the Monetary Policy Committee[5] sets the rate of interest. Currently, the rate of interest is chosen to meet an inflation target of 2.0%. The European Central Bank (ECB) also has an inflation target of 2% a year. In reality, both the ECB and the Bank of England

[5] The Monetary Policy Committee consists of representatives from the Bank of England and outside representatives representing academia and the world of commerce.

adjust the rate of interest not just in response to inflation but also in response to real GDP. It is said that, in spite of the inflation target, the ECB follows a rule that looks strikingly like a Taylor rule (see Section 14.4). There is also evidence that the Bank of England responds to the real GDP gap and house prices. But what sort of targets should the central bank aim to meet if it were given goal independence (the right to choose the targets)?

14.2.4 What Type of Central Bank?

Should the sole goal of the central bank be the stabilization of inflation at a low rate (what the Governor of the Bank of England, Mervyn King, calls an 'inflation nutter'), or should it also try to stabilize the economy by aiming to keep real GDP as close as possible to capacity? The theory of central banking suggests that the central bank should have policy aims – i.e. objective functions – that include output stabilization but give output stability a lower weight than the government would wish and inflation a higher weight than the government would want. Therefore, the central bank should be conservative in the sense that it places a high priority on low inflation, but not completely to the detriment of output.

The argument for a not too conservative central bank can be shown by means of the following analytical aids. Let inflation be denoted by π and the GDP gap by x, where x is defined as the log of real GDP less the log of potential GDP. The government believes that there is a permanent positive gap (real GDP above potential), shown by $\bar{x}$, that can be sustained by monetary policy. Rogoff (1985) assumes that there is a wedge between the equilibrium $x = 0$ and the target $\bar{x}$.[6] A loss function of the following type describes the government and society's preferences:

$$L = \frac{1}{2}E[\pi^2 + b(x - \bar{x})^2]$$ (14.1)

This loss function describes quadratic isoloss curves, as shown in Figure 14.1. Each curve describes a trade-off where the government would be indifferent between combinations of inflation and output. The second term shows that the loss (L) increases as the output gap increases over its target, i.e. $b > 0$. In a similar way, L increases as inflation increases. Note the fact that it is π^2 that enters the loss function, thus implying that deflation also imposes a loss in the same way as inflation does. The government is willing to tolerate more inflation if output increases, but, because inflation is 'bad', output has to increase at an increasing rate for an indifference to be established. Hence, the curves are positively sloped. Shifts of the curve to the right are preferred to shifts to the left because this means that, for every level of inflation, society could buy more output.

Let the actual trade-off between inflation and output be described by the following simple, linear, rational-expectation 'Phillips curve', which specifies inflation as a function of the output gap (excess demand) and expected inflation:

$$\pi = x + \pi^e + \varepsilon$$ (14.2a)

---

[6] This is justified by the existence of various distortions in the labour market, taxes, unemployment benefits and restrictive practices. These distortions keep the level of employment and output below what would occur in a non-distorted economy.

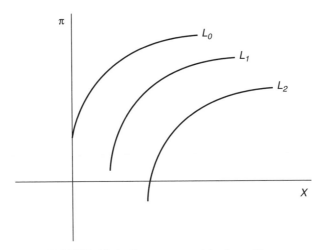

FIGURE 14.1 Government Isoloss Curves.

Note that, for ease of exposition, we have assumed the coefficient attached to x to be 1. Rearranging (14.2a), we obtain

$$x = (\pi - \pi^e) + \varepsilon \tag{14.2b}$$

where π^e is the expected inflation rate conditional on information prior to the shock, and ε is a random shock with mean zero. Figure 14.2 shows the equilibrium.

The tangency points to the family of Phillips curves for specific random shocks is described by the points A, B and C. Each Phillips curve describes the potential trade-off between inflation and output if the government engineers inflation conditional on the state

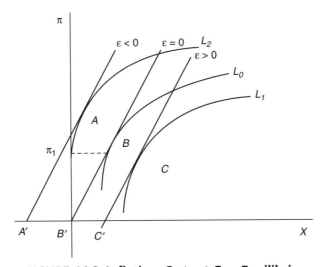

FIGURE 14.2 Inflation–Output Gap Equilibrium.

of inflation expectations. Position B represents the zero-shock equilibrium for the government and highlights the 'inflation bias' in its strategy. This point is also the time-consistent outcome, because rational agents expect the government to engineer this inflation. So, in a shock-free world a trade-off would not exist, the output gap would be zero actual inflation and expected inflation would be π_1. However, the central bank and the government observe the shock ε after wage setters have negotiated their wages, so there is an incentive to generate unexpected inflation. A negative shock shifts the Phillips curve up to the left, and a positive shock shifts it down to the right. Movement up the Phillips curve is possible only if actual inflation is greater than expected inflation.

If the government and, thereby, society thought nothing of the consequences on output from stabilizing inflation at, again, $\pi = 0$, the points of equilibrium would be A', B' and C'. This would be tantamount to setting $b = 0$ in the loss function of equation (14.1). You can see that the implied volatility on output as a result of placing a zero weight on output is greater than in the case where $b > 0$. In the face of shocks to the economy, the government would want also to stabilize output and choose points A, B and C.

The equilibrium points A, B and C highlight the time inconsistency problem. The average rate of inflation is non-zero, which is the inflation bias in the government's strategy. The first-best policy is to eliminate the inflation bias and stabilize output, but this would not be credible. The private sector knows that there is an incentive for the government to cheat, as $b > 0$ in (14.1). If $b = 0$, the inflation bias is eliminated but at the cost of not stabilizing output. The positions defined by the preferences of the government ($b = 0$ or $b > 0$) represent the two points on either side of the spectrum. What should the preferences of the central bank be if it were independent of the government? A conservative central banker would set $b = 0$. Rogoff (1985) shows that the optimal preferences of a central bank would lie in between the two positions of a conservative central banker and the preferences of the government. The central bank should be conservative but not too conservative, which means that it should also aim to stabilize output but give output stabilization a lower weight than the government does. This analysis is formally set out in Box 14.2.

BOX 14.2   The conservative central banker

The time-consistent policy is given by the agents minimizing L (equation (14.1) in the main text). Firstly, substitute for x from (14.2b):

$$L = \frac{1}{2}E[\pi^2 + b(\pi - \pi^e + \varepsilon - \bar{x})^2]$$

$$\frac{\partial L}{\partial \pi} = \frac{1}{2}E[2\pi + 2b(\pi - \pi^e + \varepsilon - \bar{x})] = 0$$

Taking expectations so that $E(\varepsilon) = 0$:

$$\pi^e + b\pi^e - b\pi^e - b\bar{x} = 0$$

$$\therefore \pi^e = b\bar{x}$$

(continued)

The government minimizes the same loss function, but they know ε:

$$\frac{\partial L}{\partial \pi} = \pi + b\pi - b\pi^e + b\varepsilon - b\bar{x} = 0$$

Plugging in the value of π^e from above, we have

$$\pi(1 + b) = \bar{x}b(1 + b) - b\varepsilon$$

$$\Rightarrow \pi = b\bar{x} - \frac{b\varepsilon}{1 + b} \tag{14.2.1}$$

Therefore, substituting for π and π^e in (14.2b), output is

$$x = \frac{1}{1 + b}\varepsilon \tag{14.2.2}$$

Equations (14.2.1) and (14.2.2) highlight the time consistency problem. The term $b\bar{x}$ implies that the average inflation rate is above zero. The first-best policy would eliminate the inflation bias without reducing the extent of output stabilization. So:

$$\pi' = -\left(\frac{b}{1 + b}\right)\varepsilon$$

but this lacks credibility.

The crucial parameter, which characterizes the trade-off balance between average inflation and variance of output, is b. Take, for instance, the variance of x:

$$\sigma_x^2 = \left(\frac{1}{1 + b}\right)^2 \sigma_\varepsilon^2$$

Clearly, if $b = 0$, the inflation bias is eliminated.

The government may prefer a conservative central banker, but this creates a deflationary bias in that output is not stabilized. The question is: What should b be?

What should the optimal set of preferences be for a central banker? Let the loss function reflecting the central bank's preferences be given by

$$L_B = \frac{1}{2}E[\pi^2 + \beta(x - \bar{x})^2] \tag{14.2.3}$$

where β replaces b and can be chosen by the central bank.

Optimizing (14.2.3) with respect to π for a given value of β following the same procedure as (14.2.1) gives

$$\pi = \beta\bar{x} - \left(\frac{\beta}{1 + \beta}\right)\varepsilon$$

(continued)

and

$$x = \left(\frac{1}{1 + \beta}\right)\varepsilon$$

Substituting this result into society's loss function (14.1) yields

$$L = \frac{1}{2}E\left[\left(\beta\bar{x} - \frac{\beta}{1 + \beta}\varepsilon\right)^2 + b\left(\frac{1}{1 + b}\varepsilon - \bar{x}\right)^2\right]$$

$$\Rightarrow \frac{1}{2}\left\{\beta^2\bar{x}^2 + \left(\frac{\beta}{1 + \beta}\right)^2\sigma_\varepsilon^2 + b\left(\frac{1}{1 + \beta}\right)^2\sigma_\varepsilon^2 + b\bar{x}^2\right\}$$

Optimizing L with respect to β yields

$$\frac{\partial L}{\partial \beta} = \frac{1}{2}\left[2\beta\bar{x}^2 + 2\left(\frac{\beta}{1 + \beta}\right)\frac{1}{(1 + \beta)^2}\sigma_\varepsilon^2 - 2b\left(\frac{1}{1 + \beta}\right)\left(\frac{1}{1 + \beta}\right)^2\sigma_\varepsilon^2 = 0\right]$$

$$\Rightarrow \beta\bar{x}^2 + \frac{\sigma_\varepsilon^2}{(1 + \beta)^3}(\beta - b) = 0$$

For this condition to hold, clearly $\beta < b$ but $\beta \neq 0$.

Therefore, Rogoff concludes that we would want a conservative central bank, but not too conservative.

14.3 FINANCIAL INNOVATION AND MONETARY POLICY

14.3.1 Financial Innovation and Monetary Policy

In 1985 the UK Chancellor of the Exchequer downgraded the monetary target on M3 (what was then the measure of broad money). One of his reasons was that *financial innovation* had destroyed the traditional links between the broad money supply and nominal income. Following a brief attempt to use the exchange rate mechanism of the European Monetary System to underpin monetary policy, the UK, in line with a number of other economies, began to target inflation, using the rate of interest as the instrument of control.

How does financial innovation alter the link between money and income and, therefore, weaken the effectiveness of monetary policy? Goodhart (1984) identified one of the major structural changes in the developed economies' banking system as being the switch from asset management to liability management.[7] The most recognizable form of financial innovation, which supports the commercial banks' liability management strategy, is the development of interest-bearing sight deposits. The conventional money demand function which

[7] This was discussed in Chapter 7, Section 7.3.

has as its determinants the price level, real income and the rate of interest on bonds or bills – would now also include the rate of interest on deposits. In other words, the conventional money demand function would be given by

$$M^d = f(P,y,R_b), \quad f_p > 0, \quad f_y > 0, \quad f_r < 0 \tag{14.3}$$

where M is the stock of money, P is the price level, y is real income and R_b is the rate of interest on short-term bonds. With the development of interest-bearing sight deposits, the demand for money function looks like

$$M^d = f(P,y,R_b - R_d), \quad f_p > 0, \quad f_y > 0, \quad f_r < 0 \tag{14.4}$$

The substitution between money and non-money liquid assets will depend on the margin between the interest on non-money liquid assets and deposits. When interest rates rise, in general, banks will also raise interest rates on deposits; consequently, the rate of interest on liquid assets will have to rise even more to generate a unit substitution from money to non-money liquid assets. The implication for monetary policy is twofold. Firstly, the slope of the LM schedule is steeper with respect to the rate of interest R_b. Secondly, the established relationship between income and money is altered. Control of the money supply becomes increasingly difficult for the central bank if banks compete with the government for savings, so that banks will raise interest rates on deposits in response to a general rise in interest rates caused by a rise in the central bank rate of interest. The reduction in the demand for money in response to a change in the rate of interest on non-money liquid assets can be thought of as a fall in the interest elasticity of demand for money. We can illustrate the argument that a financial-innovation-induced fall in the interest elasticity of demand for money alters the relationship between money and income by using the results of Poole (1970), who first showed that an economy that is dominated by IS shocks should target the money supply, and an economy that is dominated by monetary shocks should target the rate of interest. We will argue that the powerful results of Poole (1970) also explain why central banks have gradually moved away from monetary targets to inflation targets, using the rate of interest as the primary instrument of control. This result is illustrated using the familiar IS/LM model in Figure 14.3. In Figure 14.3(a) the real demand shock causes the IS curve to shift outwards, increasing both income and the rate of interest. Holding the money supply constant produces a new equilibrium income at Y', whereas, in contrast, if

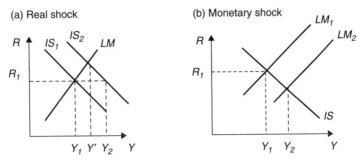

FIGURE 14.3 Differential Policy Responses to Real and Monetary Shocks.

the rate of interest were held constant at R_1, output would rise further to Y_2. It should also be noted that, the steeper the *LM* curve, the smaller is the increase in output in response to the original shock when the money supply is held constant. In Figure 14.3(b) the economy is subject to a monetary shock. If the money supply is held constant, the equilibrium level of income will increase to Y_2. In contrast, if the rate of interest is held constant, the equilibrium level of income will return to Y_1, its original position. This analysis is set out formally in Box 14.3.

At this stage we can bring in the insights of Poole (1970). In a world of dominant monetary shocks and low money demand sensitivity to the rate of interest, an interest rate target stabilizes nominal income better than a monetary target. Box 14.3 outlines the technical argument. An interest rate target can be described by a money supply response function of the form

$$M^s = M^\star + \lambda(R - \overline{R}) + v \tag{14.5}$$

If λ is set to a large value, then a rise in the rate of interest above the target level $\overline{R}$ will result in an increase in the money supply, which will have the effect of lowering the rate of interest.

The Bank for International Settlements' report on financial innovation (BIS, 1986) identified that, as a result of financial innovation, the money supply figures would be an unreliable guide to monetary conditions. It also argued that the effectiveness of the rate of interest as the instrument of monetary policy is greatly increased. The above analysis provides a theoretical foundation for this conclusion.

14.3.2 Inflation Targeting

In reality, no central bank actually targets the rate of interest. The rate of interest is an intermediate target used for the purpose of targeting inflation. Central banks such as the Federal Reserve and the ECB follow a rule for the rate of interest that looks like a Taylor rule. A Taylor rule is an interest rate response function that reacts to inflation deviating from its target and real output deviating from some given capacity level of output, as shown in the equation[8]

$$R - \pi^\star = \phi(\pi - \pi^\star) + \gamma(y - y^\star) \tag{14.6}$$

The Taylor rule function (equation (14.6)) describes the behaviour of the central bank. The rate of interest is raised above the target rate of inflation $\pi^\star$ if actual inflation is above target or if real output is above capacity $y^\star$. The coefficients ϕ and γ show the power of reaction to the two determinants of government policy. An inflation 'nutter' would allocate a high value to ϕ and a low value to γ. To understand how inflation-targeting helps stabilize the economy, we need to add further ingredients to a simple macroeconomic model. Once inflation is introduced into the model, we have to distinguish between the nominal rate of interest and the real rate of interest. We also need to have an equation that

---

[8] For the sake of ease of exposition, we assume that the real rate of interest is zero at full equilibrium when $\pi = \pi^\star$ and $y = y^\star$.

BOX 14.3   Financial innovation and the volatility of output

For simplicity we will abstract from the effects of the price level in the analysis.[9] To examine the implications of decreasing money demand sensitivity to the rate of interest, we start out with a stochastic version of the *IS/LM* model:

$$Y = Y_0 - \beta R + u \tag{14.3.1}$$

$$M^d = Y - \alpha R \tag{14.3.2}$$

$$M^s = M^* + v \tag{14.3.3}$$

where Y is nominal income, R is the rate of interest, M^d is the demand for money, M^s is the supply of money, Y_0 and M^* are fixed constants and u and v are stochastic terms with the following properties: $E(u) = E(v) = 0; E(u)^2 = \sigma_u^2 = E(v)^2 = \sigma_v^2$.

The solution to (14.5) – (14.7) is given by

$$Y = Z + \varepsilon$$

$$Z = \left(\frac{\alpha}{\alpha + \beta}\right)\left[Y_0 + \frac{\beta}{\alpha}M^*\right] \tag{14.3.4}$$

$$\varepsilon = \left(\frac{\beta}{\alpha + \beta}\right)v + \left(\frac{\alpha}{\alpha + \beta}\right)u$$

We can think of the first term Z as the deterministic part and the second term ε as the stochastic part. The stochastic part is a weighted average of the two shocks v and u. A monetary shock ($v > 0$) increases nominal income by $\left(\frac{\beta}{\alpha + \beta}\right)$, a real shock ($u > 0$) increases nominal income by $\left(\frac{\alpha}{\alpha + \beta}\right)$. If the interest elasticity of the demand for money declines because of liability management and financial innovation, then α gets smaller and, in the limit when $\alpha = 0$, all of the monetary shock is translated into nominal income, and none of the real shock. Furthermore, it is fair to say that the frequency of monetary shocks increases as a result of financial innovations, so that monetary shocks dominate real shocks.

The stochastic variance of Y from (14.3.4) is

$$\sigma_Y^2 = \left(\frac{\beta}{\alpha + \beta}\right)^2\sigma_v^2 + \left(\frac{\alpha}{\alpha + \beta}\right)^2\sigma_u^2 \tag{14.3.5}$$

As α gets smaller, the variance of Y is going to be dominated by the variance of v. Further, we can also expect, with financial innovation, that $\sigma_v^2 \gg \sigma_u^2$, which adds to the dominance of the monetary shocks.

Solving for the rate of interest by equating (14.5) with (14.3.2) gives

$$R = \left(\frac{1}{\lambda + \alpha}\right)\left[\lambda\bar{R} - M^*\right] + \left(\frac{1}{\lambda + \alpha}\right)(Y - v) \tag{14.3.6}$$

(continued)

[9] This means that we will not need an extra equation to determine the price level.

Plugging (14.3.6) into (14.3.1) gives

$$Y = \Psi + \left(\frac{\lambda + \alpha}{\lambda + \alpha + \beta}\right)u + \left(\frac{\beta}{\lambda + \alpha + \beta}\right)v \qquad (14.3.7)$$

where ψ represents all the deterministic terms. The variance of Y is given by

$$\sigma_Y^2 = \left(\frac{\beta}{\lambda + \alpha + \beta}\right)^2 \sigma_v^2 + \left(\frac{\lambda + \alpha}{\lambda + \alpha + \beta}\right)^2 \sigma_u^2 \qquad (14.3.8)$$

The limit variance of Y as α gets smaller and λ gets larger ($\lim \alpha \to 0$, $\lim \lambda \to \infty$) is shown by

$$\lim \sigma_y^2 \to \sigma_u^2 \qquad (14.3.9)$$

By assumption $\sigma_u^2 \ll \sigma_v^2$, therefore (14.3.9) is the best the central bank can do to stabilize output.

determines the rate of inflation. The macroeconomic model requires an *IS* schedule and a 'Phillips curve' schedule:

$$y = y_0 - \alpha(R - \pi^\star) + u \qquad (14.7)$$
$$\pi = \delta(y - y^\star) + \pi^\star + \eta \qquad (14.8)$$

The *IS* schedule shows an inverse relationship between the real output and the real rate of interest where the expected rate of inflation is given by the target rate of inflation. The Phillips curve shows that, when inflation is above the expected rate of inflation, output is above capacity and η is a supply-side random shock. Substituting (14.6) into (14.7) and (14.8) into the resulting equation, we have

$$y = Z_1 + \left(\frac{u - \alpha\phi\eta}{1 + \alpha\phi\delta + \gamma}\right) \qquad (14.9)$$

where Z_1 is the deterministic component and the expression in parentheses represents the stochastic component. The stochastic variance is

$$\sigma_y^2 = \left(\frac{1}{1 + \alpha\phi\delta + \gamma}\right)^2 \sigma_u^2 + \left(\frac{\alpha\phi}{1 + \alpha\phi\delta + \gamma}\right)^2 \sigma_\eta^2 \qquad (14.10)$$

In the case of an 'inflation nutter', we can set ϕ to be very large. We can see that, as ϕ approaches infinity, $\sigma_y^2 \to \sigma_\eta^2/\delta$, which means that the variance of output is independent of demand shocks and only dependent on the variance of supply shocks (the same result is shown in Figure 14.2).

14.4 BANK CREDIT AND THE TRANSMISSION MECHANISM

A summary of the transmission mechanism is shown in Table 14.2. More detailed discussion follows. The textbook view of the monetary transmission mechanism separates the effect of monetary policy on the economy into an *indirect route* and a *direct route*. The direct route concerns the direct effect of money on spending. It works through the real balance effect of Patinkin (1965) and the *wealth effect* of Pigou (1947). The rationale of these two approaches is that consumption not only depends on disposable income. The Patinkin approach includes the real value of money (i.e. real balance) in the determinants of consumption, whereas the Pigou effect includes wealth, of which the real value of money is just one component. An increase in the supply of money, in excess of the level demanded, as implied by some equilibrium level of real balances, generates an increase in spending.[10]

The indirect route works through the effect of interest rates and asset prices on the real economy. A fall in the rate of interest (both real and nominal) and/or an increase in asset price inflation results in a fall in the cost of capital (Tobin's q) and an increase in investment and consumer durables spending (including real-estate purchases).[11]

It has been argued that a further transmission effect of monetary policy comes from the 'expectations effect', particularly rational expectations. However, this is more of an enhancement effect as it is not independent of monetary policy. Rational expectations work by speeding up the effect of monetary policy. An anticipated tightening of monetary policy by either a rise in the central bank rate of interest or a decrease in the money supply will have faster ultimate effects on the economy than an unanticipated tightening of monetary policy. The real effects are weaker in the case of an anticipated change in monetary policy than in the case of an unanticipated one.

A complementary channel to the conventional one is known as the *credit channel*. This also is not an alternative to the orthodox transmission mechanism but is a mechanism for enhancing and amplifying the effects of the textbook monetary channel. The credit channel works by amplifying the effects of interest rate changes by endogenous changes in the

TABLE 14.2   Transmission mechanism of monetary policy

Direct effect	Real balance effect	
Indirect	Pigou effect	
Credit channel	External finance premium	Balance sheet Lending

[10] See Archibald and Lipsey (1958).

[11] For a clear statement of the indirect route and the development of the monetary transmission mechanism, see Tobin (1969).

external finance premium. The external finance premium is the gap between the cost of funds raised externally (equity or debt) and the cost of funds raised internally (retained earnings). The reason for the gap is because a lender fears that a borrowing firm possesses inside knowledge and the existence of costs to enforce the loan contract in the event of default. Changes in monetary policy change the external finance premium. It works through two channels:

1. The balance sheet channel.
2. The bank lending channel.

The balance sheet channel is based on the notion that the external finance premium facing a borrower should depend on the borrower's net worth (liquid assets less short-term liabilities). In the face of asymmetric information, the supply of capital is sensitive to shocks that have persistence on output. Bernanke and Gertler (1989) show that the net worth of entrepreneurs is an important factor in the transmission mechanism. A strong financial position translates into higher net worth and enables a borrower to reduce dependence on the lender. A borrower is more able to meet collateral requirements and/or self-finance.[12]

The bank lending channel recognizes that monetary policy also alters the supply of bank credit. If bank credit supply is withdrawn, medium or small businesses incur costs in trying to find new lenders. Thus, shutting off bank credit increases the external finance premium. The implication of the two channels is that the availability of credit or otherwise has short-term real effects. For example, a negative monetary shock to the economy can reduce the net worth of businesses and reduce corporate spending, shifting the *IS* curve to the left. In the context of the macroeconomic *IS/LM* model, Bernanke and Blinder (1988) argue that negative shocks to net worth as a result of adverse monetary shocks cause reinforcing shifts in the *IS* curve. Blinder (1987) suggests that this also causes additional constraints on supply, which leads to a reinforcing contraction in aggregate supply.

While it is arguable that small firms will face a more disproportionate cost on their balance sheets from a negative monetary shock than large firms and, consequently, a stronger reduction in net worth and collateral capability, the credit channel model is observationally equivalent to the monetarist-type buffer stocks model which allows for a real balance effect. Figure 14.4 shows the effect of a positive monetary shock in the credit channel framework. A positive monetary shock (a relaxation in monetary policy from LM_1 to LM_2) results in a strengthening of corporate balance sheets which causes a reinforcing rightward shift of the *IS* curve (from IS_1 to IS_2). The converse would apply in the case of a negative monetary shock.

The Northern Rock crisis that broke out in September 2007 in the UK was one of the outcomes of the credit crunch that began with the troubles in the subprime loans market nearly a year earlier in the USA. Box 14.4 describes how the crisis in the subprime loans market in the USA had the effect of raising the cost of credit and the external finance premium. Large blue-chip firms would be able to absorb a rise in the cost of credit more easily than small- and medium-sized enterprises. If sustained, the credit crunch would result in the reverse of what is shown in Figure 14.4.

---

[12] This is counter to the neoclassical theory of investment, which offers no role for net worth.

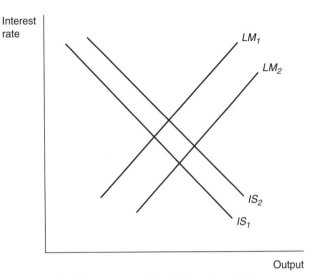

FIGURE 14.4 Positive Monetary Shock.

BOX 14.4   The 2007 credit crunch

The story begins with the rapid rise in house prices in the USA. House prices in the USA and across the developed economies have risen spectacularly in the decade to 2006.

Country	House price inflation 1997–2006 (%)
USA	124
UK	194
Spain	180
Ireland	253

Matched against the gains in house prices in the UK and elsewhere, house price inflation in the USA appeared moderate. However, what was different in the USA was the ability of borrowers with poor credit history to take out mortgages, lured by low 'teaser' mortgage rates for an initial period before market rates emerged. Once these market-based rates emerged, the default rate on subprime mortgages began to rise sharply. These mortgages had been securitized (Chapter 9) and sold as collateralized debt obligations (CDOs). Collateralized debt obligations are a portfolio of fixed-income asset-backed securities. The CDOs were given good credit ratings by the rating agencies and as a result had been bought up by pension funds, insurance companies and hedge funds. Furthermore, because of their good credit rating, they were able to be used as collateral for loans. A BBC radio commentator flippantly described CDOs much like compiler

(continued)

musical CDs. The music company wants to sell a load of bad musical tracks so it makes a CD and throws in a few popular tracks at the beginning to lure you into thinking the rest of the CD has similarly good songs. In the same way, a CDO has a good rating, even though it includes subprime loan mortgages, because of the good-quality paper that is mixed in with it. In the summer of 2007, hedge funds managed by affiliates of major investment banks in the USA and Europe had begun to record losses on portfolios heavily exposed to subprime loans. The rating agencies responded by cutting the ratings on securities backed by subprime mortgages. The result was that banks that held CDOs backed by subprime mortgages began to demand cash or collateral calls on borrowers who had used the CDOs to obtain funds at low interest rates. In the capital markets, the price of CDOs and other asset-backed commercial paper began to fall. The banks' 'off-balance-sheet' subsidiaries (known as structured investment vehicles or conduits) found that they were unable to sell ABSs at the prices they expected, which raised the prospect of these assets reappearing on the parent bank's balance sheets, with the associated Basel I capital adequacy requirement. The response of the commercial banks was not to lend to each other. This was done for two reasons. Firstly because they were unsure which counterparties would turn out to be bad risks. Secondly, they conserved cash to meet capital requirements in case they had to bring the assets of their own subsidiaries back onto their balance sheets. The outcome was that the interbank market and the spread between the sterling LIBOR and the Bank of England bank rate soared to over 100 basis points, raising the cost of borrowing to households and firms alike. Figure 14.5 shows the turmoil that hit the interbank market during the summer of 2007.

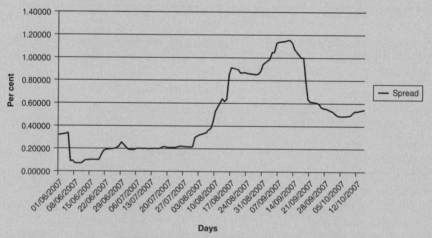

FIGURE 14.5 Interest Rate Spread.

By October 2007, the markets had calmed down, but the spread was still twice as wide as that which existed before the crisis broke. A test of the credit channel hypothesis would be that the economy slows down in 2008 more than expected by economic forecasters before the crisis broke. On 16 June 2007, the *Economist* magazine poll of forecasters predicted that GDP growth for the UK would be 2.5% in 2008.

The money buffer stocks model also allows for bank credit to play a part in the transmission mechanism, but the transmission mechanism works through money. The basic mechanism is that disequilibrium between the supply of real balances and the demand for real balances drives real output away from capacity output:

$$\left(\frac{Y_t - Y_t^*}{Y_t^*}\right) = \alpha\left(\frac{M_t^s}{P_t} - \frac{M_t^d}{P_t}\right)$$ (14.11)

where Y is real output, Y^* is capacity output, M^s is the money supply, M^d is money demand, P is the price level and subscript t stands for time. The supply of money is driven by the flow of funds, which is obtained by the interaction of the bank's balance sheet and the public sector financing constraint. A simplified aggregated banking system balance sheet would look like

$$L + R = D + E$$ (14.12)

where L is loans, R is bank reserves, D is deposits and E is bank capital (equity). The government financing constraint is

$$G - T = \Delta H + \Delta B + \Delta F$$ (14.13)

which says that government spending (G) in excess of tax revenue (T) is financed by an increase in base money (H) or an increase in sales of government bonds to the public (B) or an increase in borrowing from foreigners (F) or a combination of all three. The measure of money is currency in circulation (C) plus bank deposits (D), and the measure of base money is currency plus bank reserves.

Eliminating R from (14.12) by plugging in the definition of base money produces

$$L + H - C = D + E$$ (14.14)

Eliminating D from (14.14) by plugging in the definition of money gives

$$L + H - C = M - C + E$$
$$L + H = M + E$$ (14.15)

Taking differences and plugging (14.15) for the change in base money in (14.13) gives $G - T = \Delta M + \Delta E - \Delta L + \Delta B + \Delta F$. Rearranging the expression gives the money supply counterparts to the flow of funds:

$$\Delta M = [(G - T) - \Delta B] + \Delta L - \Delta E - \Delta F$$ (14.16)

The term in the square brackets is the public sector funding requirement. If the budget deficit is greater than the sales of bonds, the budget is underfunded and the public sector contributes to the increase in the money supply. If the budget deficit is smaller than the sale of bonds to the public, the deficit is overfunded. You can see from (14.16) that the increase in bank lending has a direct link to increase in the money supply. This is nothing but an alternative way of looking at the credit multiplier and money multiplier discussed in

Chapter 6. Table 14.3 shows that in 2006 the budget deficit was underfunded by £12.8bn, but the largest contribution to the increase in the money supply in the UK is bank lending.

The monetary buffer stocks theory argues that, if the money supply implied by the counterparts is in excess of the long-run demand for money, there will be an increase in expenditure that drives the economy above capacity. The above-capacity growth in the economy will ultimately generate inflation, which in turn will increase the demand for money. The increase in the demand for money will cause a convergence of the demand for money to the supply of money. Equilibrium is restored when the demand for money rises to meet the supply of money, when the economy is back at full capacity and the price level is raised to restore real balances to their equilibrium value. The price level must rise by the same proportion as the increase in the money supply – as predicted by equation (14.11). The point about the buffer stocks disequilibrium money model is that, because of liability management, an increased demand for bank credit is met by the expansion of bank liabilities. However, it is not the increase in bank credit that is driving real expenditure but the increase in money implied by the increase in bank liabilities (deposits).

While attempts have been made to test for the credit channel,[13] aggregate data using money supply and bank credit are unable to distinguish between a conventional monetary transmission mechanism and a bank credit channel. The evidence for the existence of a bank credit channel can only be confirmed from microeconomic data. Kashyap *et al.* (1993) predict that, if a bank credit channel exists, a monetary tightening should be followed by a

TABLE 14.3 M4 counterparts in the UK (£m)

Year	Budget deficit $G - T$	Purchases of public sector debt by UK private sector $-\Delta B$	External and foreign currency counterparts $-\Delta F$	Lending to the UK private sector ΔE	Net non-deposit sterling liabilities ΔL	Change in money stock ΔM
1996	24 778	−19 241	7 032	41 591	−12 214	59 395
1997	11 851	−16 121	22 429	68 311	−6 187	80 287
1998	−6 395	1 517	8 957	63 929	−7 905	60 095
1999	−1 792	−1 263	−38 544	78 088	−3 101	33 386
2000	−37 337	14 587	10 699	111 230	−30 949	67 231
2001	−2 809	−11 905	1 937	82 446	−10 787	58 885
2002	17 090	−8 032	−22 477	107 654	−25 293	68 941
2003	38 391	−32 051	−41 260	126 062	−21 880	69 262
2004	41 303	−31 928	1 971	156 084	−67 477	100 014
2005	40 998	−11 247	598	158 086	−37 567	150 868
2006	33 059	−20 278	−30 170	218 446	−30 688	170 159

Source: http://www.statistics.gov.uk/statbase/. Numbers do not add up to $\Delta M4$ because of rounding.

[13] Mixed evidence from King (1986) for the USA and weak evidence from Dale and Haldane (1993) for the UK.

decline in the supply of bank loans more than in other types of debt (commercial paper, finance company loans). The evidence from microeconomic data is mixed. What evidence there is shows that there is a reallocation of all types of debt from small firms to large firms, which is consistent with a credit channel.[14]

14.5 SUMMARY

- Central banks have evolved from commercial institutions that had special relationships with the government to guardians of the financial system and operators of monetary policy.
- An independent central bank insulates monetary policy from the interference of the government, which may have short-term objectives that differ from medium-term stabilization of the economy.
- An independent central bank should give a higher priority to inflation stabilization than the government, but also give some weight to the stabilization of output.
- Financial innovation and, in particular, the development of liability management by the commercial banks have altered the traditional relationship between money and nominal income. Combined with a higher frequency of monetary shocks than real shocks, central banks have abandoned monetary targets and adopted inflation targets, using the central bank rate of interest as the instrument of policy.
- It is claimed by the credit channel school that bank credit has a unique role to play in the monetary transmission mechanism by enhancing the effect of monetary shocks. The evidence for this claim is mixed, but the monetary disequilibrium buffer stocks theory also argues that, through the process of liability management, the demand for bank credit is the main driver of the money supply, but it is the money supply and not bank credit that is the principal driver of the economy.

QUESTIONS

1   How does the Bank of England influence the level of interest rates in the market?

2   In the context of central banking, explain the difference between the terms 'operational independence' and 'goal independence'.

3   What are the macroeconomic objectives of a central bank? How do they differ from the macroeconomic objectives of the government?

4   How does financial innovation reduce the effectiveness of domestic monetary policy?

5   Review the mechanisms by which monetary policy affects the economy.

6   What is the credit channel?

---

[14] See Gertler and Gilchrist (1994) for a discussion of some of the evidence and a survey by Oliner and Rudebusch (1996) for some evidence relating to small firms.

TEST QUESTIONS

1 Critically evaluate the argument that an independent central bank should be 'conservative' but not 'too conservative'.

2 Is it possible to distinguish between the credit channel transmission mechanism and the monetarist notion of the credit channel? Explain how the global credit crunch of 2007 may help to distinguish between the two mechanisms.

REFERENCES

Allen, L. and Rai, A. (1996). 'Operational efficiency in banking: An international comparison'. *Journal of Banking and Finance*, **20**, 655–672.

Allen, L., Boudoukah, J. and Saunders, A. (2004). *Understanding Market, Credit and Operational Risk*. Oxford, UK: Blackwell.

Altman, E. I. (1968). 'Financial ratios discriminant analysis and the prediction of corporate bankruptcy'. *Journal of Finance*, **23**(4), 589–609.

Altman, E. I. and Saunders, A. (1998). 'Credit risk measurement: Developments over the last 20 years'. *Journal of Banking and Finance*, **21**, 1721–1742.

Altman, E. I. and Saunders, A. (2001). 'An analysis and critique of the BIS proposal on capital adequacy and ratings'. *Journal of Banking and Finance*, **25**, 25–46.

Altman, E. I., Haldeman, R. and Narayanan, P. (1977). 'Zeta analysis: A new model to identify bankruptcy risk of corporations'. *Journal of Banking and Finance*, **1**, 29–54.

Altunbas, Y. and Molyneux, P. (1996). 'Economies of scale in European banking'. *Applied Financial Economics*, **6**, 367–375.

Amel, D., Barnes, C., Panetta, F. and Salleo, C. (2004). 'Consolidation and efficiency in the financial sector: A review of the international evidence'. *Journal of Banking and Finance*, **28**, 2493–2519.

Archibald, G. C. and Lipsey, R. G. (1958). 'Monetary value theory: A critique of Lange and Patinkin'. *Review of Economic Studies*, **26**, October, 1–22.

Avkiran, N. K. (1999). 'The evidence of efficiency gains: The role of mergers and the benefits to the public'. *Journal of Banking and Finance*, **23**, 991–1013.

Bain, J. S. (1951). 'Relation of profit rate to industry concentration: American manufacturing, 1936–1940'. *Quarterly Journal of Economics*, **65**, 293–324.

Baltensperger, E. (1980). 'Alternative approaches to the theory of the banking firm'. *Journal of Monetary Economics*, **6**, 1–37.

Baltensperger, E. and Dermine, J. (1987). 'Banking deregulation in Europe'. *Economic Policy*, **4**, April, 61–110.

Bank of England (1987). *Sterling Business Analysed by Maturity and Sector* (March).

Bauer, P. W., Berger, A. N., Ferrier, G. D. and Humphrey, D. B. (1998). 'Consistency conditions for regulatory analysis of financial institutions: A comparison of frontier efficiency methods'. *Journal of Economics and Business*, **50**, 85–114.

Baumol, W. (1982). 'Contestable markets: An uprising in the theory of industry structure'. *American Economic Review*, **72**, 1–15.

Baumol, W., Panzar, J. and Willig, R. (1982). *Contestable Markets and the Theory of Industry Structure*. San Diego, CA: Harcourt Brace Jovanovich.

Beck, K. L., Goldreyer, E. and Antonio, L. D. (2000). 'Duration gap in the context of a bank's strategic planning process'. *Journal of Financial and Strategic Decisions*, **13**(2), 57–71.

Beder, T. S. (1995). 'VAR: Seductive but dangerous'. *Financial Analysts Journal*, **51**, 12–24.

Benston, G. J. (1993). 'Market discipline: The role of uninsured depositors'. In: R. Randall (ed.), *Safeguarding the Banking System in an Environment of Financial Cycles* (Conference Series No. 7). Boston, MA: Federal Reserve Bank of Boston.

Benston, G. J. (1994). 'Universal banking'. *Journal of Economic Perspectives*, **8**(3), 121–143.

Benston, G. J. and Kaufman, G. G. (1996). 'The appropriate role of bank regulation'. *Economic Journal*, **106**(436), 688–697.

Benston, G. and Smith, C. W. (1976). 'A transaction cost approach to the theory of financial intermediation'. *Journal of Finance*, **31**, 215–231.

Berg, S. A., Førsund, F. R., Hjalmarsson, L. and Suominen, M. (1993). 'Banking efficiency in the nordic countries'. *Journal of Banking and Finance*, **17**, 371–388.

Berger, A. N. and Hannan, T. (1989). 'The price–concentration relationship in banking'. *Review of Economics and Statistics*, **71**, 291–299.

Berger, A. N. and Humphrey, D. B. (1991). 'The dominance of inefficiencies over scale and product mix economies in banking'. *Journal of Monetary Economics*, **28**, 117–148.

Berger, A. N. and Humphrey, D. B. (1997). 'Efficiency of financial institutions: An international survey and directions for future research'. *European Journal of Operations Research*, **98**, 175–211.

Berger, A. N. and Mester, L. (1997). 'Inside the black box: What explains difference in efficiencies of financial institutions'. *Journal of Banking and Finance*, **21**, 895–947.

Berger, A. N., Demester, R. S. and Strahan, P. E. (1999). 'The consolidation of financial services industry: Causes, consequences and implications for the future'. *Journal of Banking and Finance*, **23**, 135–194.

Berger, A. N., Hanweck, G. A. and Humphrey, D. B. (1987). 'Competitive viability in banking, scale, scope and product mix economies'. *Journal of Monetary Economics*, **20**, 501–520.

Berger, A. N., Hunter, W. C. and Timme, S. G. (1993). 'The efficiency of financial institutions: A review and preview of research past, present and future'. *Journal of Banking and Finance*, **17**, 221–249.

Bernanke, B. S. and Blinder, A. (1988). 'Credit, money, and aggregate demand'. *American Economic Review, Papers and Proceedings*, **78**, 435–439.

Bernanke, B. S. and Gertler, M. (1989). 'Agency costs, net worth and business fluctuations'. *American Economic Review*, **79**, 87–114.

Bessis, J. (1998). *Risk Management in Banking*. Chichester, UK: John Wiley & Sons.

Bester, H. (1985). 'Screening versus rationing in credit markets with imperfect information'. *American Economic Review*, **75**(4), 850–855.

Bhattacharya, S., Boot, A. W. A. and Thakor, A. V. (1998). 'The economics of bank regulation'. *Journal of Money, Credit and Banking*, **30**(4), 745–770.

Bikker, J. A. and Groeneveld, J. M. (2000). 'Competition and concentration in the EU banking industry'. *Kredit und Kapital*, **33**, 62–98.

Bikker, J. A. and Haaf, K. (2002). 'Competition, concentration and their relationship: An empirical analysis of the banking industry'. *Journal of Banking and Finance*, **26**, 2191–2214.

BIS (1986). *Recent Innovations in International Banking*. Basel, Switzerland: Bank for International Settlements.

BIS (1988). *International Convergence of Capital Measurement and Capital Standards* (July). Basel, Switzerland: Basel Committee on Banking Supervision, Bank for International Settlements.

BIS (2004). *International Convergence of Capital Measurement and Capital Standards* (June). Basel, Switzerland: Basel Committee on Banking Supervision, Bank for International Settlements.

Black, F. and Scholes, M. (1973), 'The pricing of options and corporate liabilities'. *Journal of Political Economy*, **81**(3), 637–659.

Blinder, A. (1987). 'Credit rationing and effective supply failures'. *Economic Journal*, **97**, 327–352.

Boyd, J. and Gertler, M. (1994). 'Are banks dead? Or are the reports greatly exaggerated?' *Federal Reserve Bank of Minneapolis Quarterly Review*, Summer.

Bruggeman, A. and Donnay, M. (2003). 'A monthly monetary model with banking intermediation for the euro area'. *ECB Working Paper Series*, No. 264.

Buckle, M. and Thompson, J. L. (2004). *The UK Financial System: Theory and Practice* (4th edn). Manchester, UK: Manchester University Press.

Cable, J. (1985). 'Capital market information and industrial performance: The role of West German banks'. *Economic Journal*, **95**, 118–132.

Calomiris, C. W. (1999). 'Building an incentive compatible safety net'. *Journal of Banking and Finance*, **23**, 1499–1519.

Canals, J. (1997). *Universal Banking*. Oxford, UK: Oxford University Press.

Canhoto, A. and Dermine, J. (2003). 'A note on banking efficiency in Portugal, new vs old banks'. *Journal of Banking and Finance*, **27**, 2087–2098.

Casu, B. and Girardone, C. (2006). 'Bank competition, concentration and efficiency in the single European market'. *Manchester School*, **74**, Special Issue, 441–468.

Cetorelli, N. (1999). 'Competitive analysis in banking: Appraisal of the methodologies'. *Economic Perspectives*, Federal Bank of Chicago, **1**, 2–15.

Chamberlin, E. (1929). 'Duopoly: Value where sellers are few'. *Quarterly Journal of Economics*, **43**, 371–382.

Charnes, A., Cooper, W. W. and Rhodes, E. (1978). 'Measuring efficiency of decision making units'. *European Journal of Operational Research*, **1**, 429–444.

Claessens, S. and Laeven, L. (2004). 'What drives bank competition? Some international evidence'. *Journal of Money, Credit and Banking*, **36**, 563–584.

Claessens, S. and Van Horen, N. (2007). 'Location decisions of foreign banks and competitive advantage. *World Bank Policy Research Working Paper*, WPS4113.

Clark, J. (1988). 'Economies of scale and scope at depository financial institutions: A review of the literature'. *Federal Reserve Bank of Kansas City*, *Economic Review*, September, 16–33.

Clews R. (2005). 'Implementing monetary policy: reforms to the Bank of England's operations in the money market'. *Bank of England Quarterly Bulletin*, summer, 211–220.

Coase, R. H. (1988). *The Firm, The Market and The Law*. Chicago, IL: University of Chicago Press.

Coccorese, P. (1998) 'Assessing the competition conditions in the Italian banking system: Some empirical evidence'. *BNL Quarterly Review*, **205**, 171–191.

Coccorese, P. (2004). 'Banking competition and macroeconomic conditions: A disaggregated analysis'. *International Financial Markets, Institutions and Money*, **14**, 203–219.

Cooke, P. (1990). 'International convergence of capital adequacy measurement and standards'. In: E. P. Gardener (ed.), *The Future of Financial Systems and Services: Essays in Honour of Jack Revell*. New York, NY: St Martin's Press.

Cornett, M. M. and Tehranian, H. (1992). 'Changes in corporate performance associated with bank acquisitions'. *Journal of Financial Economics*, **31**, 211–234.

Crosbie, P. and Bohn, J. (2003). 'Modeling default risk', 18 December, Moody's KMV White Paper, http://www.moodyskmv.com/.

Cruikshank, D. (2000). *Competition in UK Banking: A Report to the Chancellor of the Exchequer*. London, UK: HMSO.

Cumming, C. (1987). 'The economics of securitization'. *Federal Reserve Bank of New York Quarterly Review*, Autumn, 11–23.

Cuthbertson, K. and Nitzsche, D. (2001). *Financial Engineering*. Chichester, UK: John Wiley & Sons.

Dale, S. and Haldane, S. (1993). 'Bank behaviour and the monetary transmission mechanism'. *Bank of England Quarterly Bulletin*, 478–490.

Daníelsson, J. (2000). 'The emperor has no clothes: Limits to risk modelling'. Available at *www.RiskResearc.org*

Daníelsson, J., Embrechts, P., Goodhart, C., Keating, C., Muennich, F., Renault, O. and Shin Hyun Song (2001). 'An academic response to Basel II'. *LSE Financial Markets Group Special Paper*, No. 130.

De Bandt, O. and Davis, E. P. (2000). 'Competition, contestability and market structure in European banking sectors on the eve of the EMU'. *Journal of Banking and Finance*, **24**, 1045–1066.

De Grauwe, P. (1982). 'The exchange rate in a portfolio balance model of the banking sector'. *Journal of Money and Finance*, **1**, 225–239.

De Meza, D. and Webb, D. (1987). 'Too much investment: A problem of asymmetric information'. *Quarterly Journal of Economics*, **102**, 281–292.

Demsetz, H. (1973). 'Industry structure, market rivalry and public policy'. *Journal of Law and Economics*, **16**, 1–9.

Dermine, J. (1986). 'Deposit rates, credit rates and bank capital: The Monti–Klein model revisited'. *Journal of Banking and Finance*, **10**, 99–114.

Dermine, J. (2003). 'The new world of euro banking'. In: A. W. Mullineux and V. Murinde (eds), *Handbook of International Banking*. Cheltenham, UK: Edward Elgar.

Dermine, J. (2006). 'European banking integration: Don't put the cart before the horse'. *Financial Markets, Institutions and Instruments*, **15**(2), 57–106.

Dewatripont, M. and Tirole, J. (1994). *The Prudential Reputation of Banks*. Cambridge, MA: MIT Press.

De Young, R. (1997). 'Bank mergers, X-efficiency and the market for corporate control'. *Managerial Finance*, **23**, 32–46.

Diamond, D. W. (1984). 'Financial intermediation and delegated monitoring'. *Review of Economic Studies*, **51**, 728–762.

Diamond, D. W. (1996). 'Financial intermediation as delegated monitoring: A simple example'. *Federal Reserve Bank of Richmond Economic Quarterly*, **82**, 51–66.

Diamond, D. W. and Dybvig, P. (1983). 'Bank runs, deposit insurance and liquidity'. *Journal of Political Economy*, **91**, 401–419.

Dowd, K. (1993). *Laissez-faire Banking*. London, UK: Routledge.

Dowd, K. (1998). *Beyond Value at Risk: The New Science of Risk Management*. Chichester, UK: John Wiley & Sons.

Dowd, K. (2003). 'Free banking'. In: A. W. Mullineux and V. Murinde (eds), *Handbook of International Banking*. Cheltenham, UK: Edward Elgar.

Dunis, C. L. and Klein, T. (2005). 'Analysing mergers and acquisitions in European financial services: An application of real options'. *European Journal of Finance*, **11**(4), 339–355.

ECB (2000). *Mergers and Acquisitions Involving the EU Banking Industry: Facts and Implications*. Frankfurt, Germany: European Central Bank.

Evanoff, D. D. and Fortier, D. (1988). 'Reevaluation of the structure–conduct–performance in banking'. *Journal of Financial Services Research*, **1**, 277–294.

Evanoff, D. D. and Wall, L. D. (2000). 'Subordinated debt as bank capital: A proposal for regulatory reform'. *Economic Perspectives, Federal Reserve Bank of Chicago*, Qtr 2, 40–53.

Favero, C. A. and Papi, L. (1995). 'Technical efficiency and scale efficiency in the Italian banking sector: A non parametric approach'. *Applied Economics*, **27**, 385–395.

Focarelli, D. and Pozzolo, A. (2000). 'The determinants of cross-border bank shareholdings: An analysis with bank-level data from OECD countries'. *Federal Reserve Bank of Chicago, Proceedings*, May, 199–232.

Freixas, X. and Rochet, J.-C. (1997). *Microeconomics of Banking*. Cambridge, MA: MIT Press.

Fried, J. and Howitt, P. (1980). 'Credit rationing and implicit contract theory'. *Journal of Money, Credit and Banking*, **12**, 471–487.

FSPP (2004). *Third Survey of the FSA's Regulatory Performance*. London, UK: Financial Services Practitioners Panel.

Fukuyama, H. (1993). 'Measuring efficiency and productivity growth in Japanese banking: A non-parametric frontier approach'. *Applied Financial Economics*, **5**, 95–117.

Galindo, A., Micco, A. and Serra, C. (2003). 'Better the devil that you know: Evidence on entry costs faced by foreign banks'. *Inter-American Development Bank Working Paper*, No. 477.

Gertler, M. and Gilchrist, S. (1994). 'Monetary policy, business cycles and the behaviour of small manufacturing firms'. *Quarterly Journal of Economics*, **109**(2), 309–340.

Gilbert, R. A. (1984). 'Bank market structure and competition: A survey'. *Journal of Money, Credit and Banking*, **16**, 617–645.

Goodhart, C. A. E. (1984). *Monetary Theory and Practice: The UK Experience*. London, UK: Macmillan.

Goodhart, C. A. E. (1989). *Money, Information and Uncertainty* (2nd edn). London, UK: Macmillan.

Goodhart, C. A. E. (1990). *The Evolution of Central Banks*. Cambridge, MA: MIT Press.

Goodhart, C. A. E. (1995). 'Some regulatory concerns'. *LSE Financial Markets Group Special Paper*, No. 79.

Goodhart, C. A. E., Hartmann, P., Llewellyn, D. T., Rojas-Suárez, L. and Weisbrod, L. S. (1998). *Financial Regulation*. London, UK: Routledge.

Gowland, D. H. (1991). *Financial Innovation in Theory and Practice* (Surveys in Monetary Economics, Vol. 2, edited by C. J. Green and D. T. Llewellyn). Oxford, UK: Blackwell.

Gurley, J. and Shaw, E. (1960). *Money in a Theory of Finance*. Washington, DC: Brookings Institute Press.

Hansen, R. S. and Thatcher, J. G. (1983). 'On the nature of credit demand and credit rationing in competitive credit markets'. *Journal of Banking and Finance*, **7**, 273–284.

Hayek, F. A. (1978). *Denationalising Money*. London, UK: Institute of Economic Affairs.

Haynes, M. and Thompson, S. (1999). 'The productivity effects of bank mergers: Evidence from the UK building societies'. *Journal of Banking and Finance*, **23**, 825–846.

Heffernan, S. A. (1993). 'Competition in British retail banking'. *Journal of Financial Services Research*, **7**, 309–322.

Heffernan, S. A. (2002). 'How do UK financial institutions really price their products?'. *Journal of Banking and Finance*, **26**, 1997–2016.

Hendricks, D. and Hirtle, B. (1997). 'Bank capital requirements for market risk: The internal models approach'. *Federal Reserve Bank of New York Economic Policy Review*, **3**(4), 1–12.

Hirschleifer, J. (1958). 'On the theory of optimal investment analysis'. *Journal of Political Economy*, August, 329–352.

Hodgman, D. (1960). 'Credit risk and credit rationing'. *Quarterly Journal of Economics*, **74**, 258–278.

Holmström, B. and Tirole, J. (1993). *Financial Intermediation, Loanable Funds and the Real Sector* (Mimeo). Toulouse, France: IDEI, Toulouse University.

Hoshi, T., Kasyhap, A. and Scharfstein, D. (1991). 'Corporate structure, liquidity and investment: Evidence from Japanese industrial groups'. *Quarterly Journal of Economics*, **106**, 33–60.

Hunter, W. C. and Timme, S. G. (1986). 'Technical change, organisational form and the structure of bank productivity'. *Journal of Money, Credit and Banking*, **18**, 152–166.

IMF (1998). *World Economic Outlook*. Washington, DC: International Monetary Fund.

Jackson, W. (1992). 'Is the market well defined in bank merger and acquisition analysis'. *Review of Economics and Statistics*, **74**, 655–661.

Jaffee, D. M. and Modigliani, F. (1969). 'A theory and test of credit rationing'. *American Economic Review*, **59**(5), 850–872.

Jaffee, D. M. and Russell, T. (1976). 'Imperfect information, uncertainty and credit rationing'. *Quarterly Journal of Economics*, **90**, 651–666.

Jensen, M. C. (1986). 'Agency costs of free cash flow, corporate finance and takeovers'. *American Economic Review*, **76**, 659–665.

JP Morgan (1995). *RiskMetrics™: Technical Document* (3rd edn). New York, NY: JP Morgan Securities.

Kashyap, A. K., Stein, J. C. and Wilcox, D. (1993). 'Monetary policy and credit conditions: Evidence from the composition of external finance'. *American Economic Review*, **3**, 78–98.

Keynes, J. M. (1930). *A Treatise on Money*. London, UK: Macmillan.

Keynes, J. M. (1936). *The General Theory of Employment, Interest and Money*. London, UK: Harcourt Brace.

Kim, T. (1993). *International Money and Banking*. London, UK: Routledge.

King, S. R. (1986). 'Monetary transmission through bank loans or bank liabilities'. *Journal of Money, Credit and Banking*, **19**, 290–303.

Klein, M. (1971). 'A theory of the banking firm'. *Journal of Money, Credit and Banking*, **3**, 205–218.

Koch, T. W. and MacDonald, S. S. (2003). *Bank Management* (5th edn). South-Western, OH: Thomson.

Kolb, R. W. (1997). *Futures, Options and Swaps* (2nd edn). Oxford, UK: Blackwell.

Kumbhakar, S. C. and Lovell, C. A. K. (2000). *Stochastic Frontier Analysis.* Cambridge, UK: Cambridge University Press.

Lerner, A. (1934). 'The concept of monopoly and the measurement of monopoly power'. *Review of Economic Studies*, **1**(3), 157–175.

Lewis, M. (1991). 'Theory and practice of the banking firm'. *Surveys in Monetary Economics* (Vol. 2, edited by C. J. Green and D. T. Llewellyn). Oxford, UK: Blackwell.

Leyland, H. E. and Pyle, D. H. (1977). 'Informational asymmetries, financial structure and financial intermediation'. *Journal of Finance*, **32**, 371–387.

Llewellyn, D. T. (1996). 'Banking in the 21st century: The transformation of an industry'. In M. Edey (ed.), *The Future of the Financial System.* Sydney, Australia: Reserve Bank of Australia.

Llewellyn, D. T. (2003). 'Some lessons for bank regulation from recent financial crises'. In: A. W. Mullineux and V. Murinde (eds), *Handbook of International Banking.* Cheltenham, UK: Edward Elgar.

Llewellyn, D. T. (2005). 'Competition and profitability in European banking: Why are British banks so profitable?'. *Economic Notes*, **34**(3), 279–311.

Llewellyn, D. T. (2006). 'Globalisation and convergence on the shareholder value model in European banking'. *Bank for International Settlements Papers*, No. 32, December.

Lloyd-Williams, D. M., Molyneux, P. and Thornton, J. (1994). 'Market structure and performance in Spanish banking'. *Journal of Banking and Finance*, **18**, 433–443.

Markowitz, H. M. (1959). *Portfolio Selection: Efficient Diversification of Investments.* New York, NY: John Wiley & Sons.

Matthews, K., Murinde, V. and Zhao, T. (2007). 'Competitive conditions among the major British banks'. *Journal of Banking and Finance*, **31**, 2025–2042.

Mayer, C. (1990). 'New issues in corporate finance'. *European Economic Review*, **32**, 1167–1189.

McCauley, R. N., Ruud, J. S. and Woodridge, P. D. (2002). 'Globalising international banking'. *BIS Quarterly Review*, March, 41–51.

Merton, R. (1974). 'On the pricing of corporate debt'. *Journal of Finance*, **29**, 449–470.

Mester, L. J. (1987). 'Efficient production of financial services'. *Federal Reserve Bank of Philadelphia, Business Review*, January, 15–25.

Mester, L. J. (1996). 'A study of bank efficiency taking into account risk-preference'. *Journal of Banking and Finance*, **20**, 1025–1045.

Mester L. (1997). 'What's the point of Credit Scoring?'. *Federal Reserve Bank of Philadelphia Business Review*, September/October, 3–16.

Molyneux, P. and Forbes, W. (1995). 'Market structure and performance in European banking'. *Applied Economics*, **27**, 155–159.

Molyneux, P., Lloyd-Williams, D. M. and Thornton, J. (1994). 'Competitive conditions in European banking'. *Journal of Banking Finance*, **18**, 445–459.

Molyneux, P., Thornton, J. and Lloyd-Williams, D. M. (1996). 'Competition and market contestability in Japanese commercial banking'. *Journal of Economics and Business*, **48**, 33–45.

Monti, M. (1972). 'Deposit, credit and interest rate determination under alternative bank objectives'. In: G. P. Szego and K. Shell (eds), *Mathematical Methods in Investment and Finance.* Amsterdam, The Netherlands: North-Holland.

Mullineux, A. W. and Murinde, V. (eds) (2003). 'Globalization and convergence of banking systems'. *Handbook of International Banking.* Cheltenham, UK: Edward Elgar.

Murinde, V. and Ryan, C. (2003). 'Globalization, the WTO and GATS: Implications for the banking sector in developing countries'. In A. W. Mullineaux and V. Murinde (eds), *Handbook of International Banking.* Cheltenham, UK: Edward Elgar.

Nathan, A. and Neave, E. (1989). 'Competition and contestability in Canada's financial system: Empirical results'. *Canadian Journal of Economics*, **22**(3), 576–594.

National Economic Research Associates (1990). An evaluation of the loan guarantee scheme. *Department of Employment Research Paper*, No. 74.

Nickell, S. J. (1996). 'Competition and corporate performance'. *Journal of Political Economy*, **104**, 724–746.

Niehans, J. (1978). *The Theory of Money*. Baltimore, MD: Johns Hopkins University Press.

Niehans, J. and Hewson, J. R. (1976). 'The Eurodollar market and monetary theory'. *Journal of Money, Credit and Banking*, **5**(8), 1–27.

Oliner, S. D. and Rudebusch, G. D. (1996). 'Is there a broad credit channel for monetary policy?'. *Federal Reserve Board of San Francisco Economic Review*, **1**, 3–13.

Orgler, Y. E. (1970). 'A credit scoring model for commercial loans'. *Journal of Money, Credit and Banking*, **2**(4), 435–445.

Panzar, J. and Rosse, J. (1982). 'Structure, conduct and comparative statistics'. *Bell Laboratories Economic Discussion Paper*, No. 248.

Panzar, J. and Rosse, J. (1987). 'Testing for monopoly equilibrium'. *Journal of Industrial Economics*, **35**, 443–456.

Patinkin, D. (1965). *Money, Interest and Prices: An Integration of Monetary and Value Theory* (2nd edn). New York, NY: Harper & Row.

Pearson, N. D. and Smithson, C. (2002). 'VaR the state of play'. *Review of Financial Economics*, **11**, 175–189.

Peek, J. and Rosengreen, E. S. (1997). 'How well capitalised are well capitalised banks?'. *New England Economic Review*, **42**, September/October.

Pennacchi, G. G. (1988). 'Loan sales and the cost of bank capital'. *Journal of Finance*, **43**, 375–396.

Pigou, A. C. (1947). *The Veil of Money*. London, UK: Macmillan.

Pilloff, S. J. and Santomero, A. M. (1998). 'The value of bank mergers and acquisitions'. In: Y. Amihud and G. Miller (eds), *Bank Mergers and Acquisitions*. Boston, MA: Kluwer Academic, 59–78.

Podolski, T. (1986). *Financial Innovation and the Money Supply*. Oxford, UK: Blackwell.

Poole, W. (1968). 'Commercial banks reserve management in a stochastic model: Implications for monetary policy. *Journal of Finance*, **23**(5), 769–791.

Poole, W. (1970). 'Optimal choice of monetary policy instruments in a simple stochastic macro model'. *Quarterly Journal of Economics*, **84**, 2.

Prisman, E., Slovin, M. and Sushka, M. (1986). 'A general model of the banking firm under conditions of monopoly, uncertainty and recourse'. *Journal of Monetary Economics*, **17**, 293–304.

Pyle, D. H. (1971). 'On the theory of financial intermediation'. *Journal of Finance*, **26**, 737–747.

Rachlin C. (1998). 'Operational risk in retail banking' in *Operational Risk and Financial Institutions*, Arthur Andersen Risk Books, 113–127.

Rhoades, S. A. (1993). 'Efficiency effects of horizontal (in market) bank mergers. *Journal of Banking and Finance*, **17**, 411–422.

Rime, B. (1999). 'Mesure de degré de concurrence dans le système bancaire Suisse à l'a ide du modèle de Panzar et Rosse'. *Revue Suisse d'Economie Politique et de Statistique*, **135**, 21–40.

Rogoff, K. (1985). 'Optimal degree of commitment to an intermediate monetary target'. *Quarterly Journal of Economics*, **100**, 1169–1189.

Rolnick, A. J. (1993). 'Market discipline as a regulator of bank risk'. In: R. Randall (ed.), *Safeguarding the Banking System in an Environment of Financial Cycles* (Conference Series No. 7). Boston, MA: Federal Reserve Bank of Boston.

Rosse, J. and Panzar, J. (1977). 'Chamberlin vs Robinson: An empirical test for monopoly rents'. *Bell Laboratories Economics Discussion Paper*, No. 90.

Saunders, A. and Walter, I. (1993). *Universal Banking in America: What Can We Gain? What Can We Lose?* New York, NY: Oxford University Press.

Schwartz, A. (1987). 'The lender of last resort and the federal safety net'. *Journal of Financial Services Research*, **1**, 1–18.

Scott-Frame, W. and Kamerschen, D. (1997). 'The profit–structure relationship in legally protected banking markets using efficiency measures'. *Review of Industrial Organization*, **12**, 9–22.

Sealey, C. W. and Lindley, J. T. (1977). 'Inputs, outputs and a theory of production and cost at depository financial institutions'. *Journal of Finance*, **32**, 1251–1277.

Shaffer, S. (1982). 'A non-structural test for competition in financial markets'. In: *Bank Structure and Competition, Conference Proceedings*. Chicago, IL: Federal Reserve Bank of Chicago, 225–243.

Sherman, H. D. and Gold, F. (1985). 'Bank branch operating efficiency: Evaluation with Data Envelope Analysis'. *Journal of Banking and Finance*, **9**, 297–315.

Siems, T. S. (1996). 'Bank mergers and shareholder wealth: Evidence from 1995's megamerger deals'. Federal Reserve Bank of Dallas, Financial Industry Studies, August, 1–12.

Smirlock, M. (1985). 'Evidence on the (non) relationship between concentration and profitability in banking. *Journal of Money, Credit and Banking*, **17**, 69–83.

Smith, V. C. (1936). *The Rationale of Central Banking and Free Banking Alternative*. Reprinted by Liberty Press, Indianapolis, IN, in 1990.

Spencer, P. (2000). *The Structure and Regulation of Financial Markets*. Oxford, UK: Oxford University Press.

Stiglitz, J. E. (1985). 'Credit markets and the control of capital'. *Journal of Money, Credit and Banking*, **17**(2), 133–152.

Stiglitz, J. E. and Weiss, I. (1981). 'Credit rationing in markets with imperfect information'. *American Economic Review*, **71**(3), 393–410.

Tobin, J. (1958). 'Liquidity preference as a behaviour towards risk'. *Review of Economic Studies*, **25**(77), 75–87.

Tobin, J. (1969). 'A general equilibrium approach to monetary theory'. *Journal of Money, Credit and Banking*, **1**, 15–29.

Tobin, J. (1985). 'Financial innovation and deregulation in perspective'. *Bank of Japan Monetary and Economic Studies*, **3**(2), 15–29.

Vander Vennet, R. (1996). 'The effect of mergers and acquisitions on the efficiency and profitability of EC credit institutions'. *Journal of Banking and Finance*, **20**, 1531–1558.

Vesala, J. (1995). 'Testing for competition in banking: Behavioural evidence from Finland'. *Bank of Finland Studies*, E:1.

Vives, X. (1991). 'Banking competition and European integration'. In: A. G. Giovannini and C. Mayer (eds), *European Financial Integration*. Cambridge, UK: Cambridge University Press.

Vives, X. (2001). 'Competition in the changing world of banking'. *Oxford Review of Economic Policy*, **17**(4), 535–547.

Wall, L. D. (1989). 'A plan for reducing future deposit insurance losses: Puttable subordinated debt'. *Economic Review, Federal Reserve Bank of Atlanta*, July/August, 2–17.

Walter, I. (1988). *Global Competition in Financial Services*. Cambridge, MA: Ballinger.

Walter, I. (2003). 'Universal banking and shareholder value: A contradiction?'. In: A. W. Mullineux and V. Murinde (eds), *Handbook of International Banking*. Cheltenham, UK: Edward Elgar.

Wilson Committee (1979). *The Financing of Small Firms* (Interim Report of the Committee to Review the Functioning of the Financial Institutions, Cmnd. 7503). London, UK: HMSO.

Wolfe, S. (2004). 'Equity toxic waste in asset-backed securitisation'. University of Southampton School of Management Discussion Paper, AF04-22.

Wolfe, S. (2007). 'A tripartite primer on securitization'. MMF Workshop, University of Essex, Colchester, UK, 9 November.

Yue, P. (1992). 'Data envelopment analysis and commercial bank performance: A primer with applications to Missouri banks'. *Federal Reserve Bank of St Louis Review*, January/February, 31–45.

INDEX

Abbey National plc 4, 176, 182
abnormal returns 167
ABSs *see* asset backed securities
accounting data, mergers 162, 165–6
acquisitions *see* mergers and acquisitions
ACs *see* average costs
adverse incentives
    credit rationing 119–23
    see also moral hazard
adverse selection
    asymmetric information 42–3, 46, 119–25
    credit rationing 119–23
agency problems 58–9, 125, 162
Allen, L. 156, 167, 231
Alliance and Leicester 182
allocative efficiency 151–2, 162
alternative banking models 93–114
Altman, E. I. 201, 229–30
Altunbas, Y. 165
antitrust concerns 172
arbitrage opportunities
    eurocurrency markets 68–9
    interest rate differentials 100
    risk management 218–40
Argentina 202
Asian crisis (1997) 227
asset allocation processes 102–7
asset and liability management, concepts
    94, 107–13, 252–7
asset backed securities (ABSs)
    concepts 7, 62, 131, 136–45
    credit crunch 260
    economic effects 143–5
    gains 138–45
    processes 138
    see also securitization
asset management, concepts 5–6, 52, 94,
    102–7, 116
asset risk, concepts 54–5, 58
assets 5–8, 35–49, 51–75, 94, 102–4, 116,
    131, 136–45, 190–4, 211–40

CDs 36, 57, 135, 189, 216–18
financial intermediation 35–49, 101–2,
    107–13, 131–2
negative 100
risk-free 80–2, 100–10, 118–19, 125–8,
    163, 167
see also loans
Association of Payment Clearing Services
    Information Office 56
asymmetric information
    concepts 41, 42–6, 119–25, 189–94
    credit rationing 119–25
ATMs *see* automated teller machines
Australia 160, 167
autarky process, concepts 23, 24, 27, 32,
    191–2
automated teller machines (ATMs) 6, 56,
    148, 160
availability doctrine, credit rationing
    115–16
average costs (ACs) 12, 65, 81–7
    H-statistic 177–8
Avkiran, N. K. 167

Bain, J. S. 172
balance sheets 2–18, 37–8, 51–60, 69, 70,
    71, 93–114, 116, 138, 141, 142, 149,
    150, 190–201, 212–18, 245–7, 258–61
Baltensperger, E. 80
Bank Charter Act 1844 244
bank credit, transmission mechanism
    243–4, 257–63
Bankers Trust 229
Bank for International Settlements (BIS)
    64–7, 68–9, 195–205, 237, 254
Bankhaus Herstatt 54–5
banking 3–4, 9–12, 31–2, 35–49, 101–2,
    107–13, 131
    alternative banking models 93–114
    asymmetric information, 41, 42–6,
    119–25, 189–94

banking (*Continued*)
  barriers to entry 2, 175, 181–2
  building societies 36, 164
  changes 1–19
  competition 171–85
  concentration 172–3
  consolidation 171
  contract 17, 18
  demand/supply curves 6, 10–12, 109–13, 116–28, 205–6
  deregulation trends 2–4, 9, 14, 160–1, 175
  direct borrowing 47–8, 134–6
  domestic banking 1–19
  economic theory 77–91
  economies of scale/scope 12, 41, 45, 59, 65, 147–69
  efficiencies 147–69
  failures 16, 37, 55, 187–90, 195, 199, 201–4
  financial innovation trends 2–3, 4–6, 9, 134, 160–1, 252–7
  free 189–90, 201–5
  future 14–18
  general features 52–5, 77–8
  globalization trends 2–3, 6–8, 160–1
  historical background 47, 61, 116, 244–5
  imperfect competition model 87–90
  information-sharing coalitions 38, 43
  internationalization 'push/pull' factors 6
  investment 4, 6–7, 13–14, 52, 58
  lender-of-last-resort role 14, 16, 77–8, 190–4, 204–5, 244–5
  liquidity insurance 36–7, 41–2
  macroeconomics 243–64
  multifaceted operations 1–3
  needs 31–2, 35–49, 51–5, 77–8, 101–2
  net interest income 2, 9, 56, 81–90, 99–100, 107–13, 117–19, 204, 211–12
  output measures 147–9
  overlending problems 125
  payment mechanisms 47, 54–6, 77
  perfectly competitive banks 80–2
  performance measures 149–59
  profitability 8–14, 47–8, 100, 108–13, 117–28

  regulations 6–7, 59, 65–6, 97–8, 134, 142, 187–207
  relationship banking 45–6, 58–9, 107, 125, 143, 211
  reputation factors 48
  restructuring exercises 12–14
  risk management 14–16, 56–8, 197–201, 209–41
  roles 14, 31–2, 35–49, 51–5, 77–8
  runs 37, 55, 98–9, 187–94
  structural issues 61–76, 147–69
  technological developments 4–6, 12, 41, 134, 160, 161–2
  theory of the banking firm 141
  transaction costs 38–41, 90, 117
  transformation concepts 36–8, 41, 51–60, 69–74
  trends 1–19, 55–6, 160–8
  types 51–2
  see also central banks; international banking; monopoly banks; net interest income; retail banking, concepts; universal banking; wholesale banking
Banking Act 1979, UK 195, 181
Banking Act 1987, UK 181–2
banking book risk, concepts 209
Banking School, central banks 244
banking system
  balance sheet 245–7, 258–61
  transmission mechanism 243–4, 257–63
Bank of America 6
Bank of England 3, 9, 53–4, 57, 98–9, 127, 143, 181, 197, 244–52, 260
  balance sheet 245–7
  independence issues 247–8
  money markets 244–52
  repos 245–6
  roles 244–52
  see also central banks
Bank of England Act 1946 244
Bank of England Act 1998 245
Bank of Ireland Group 182
Bank of Japan 53
bank risk 188
bankruptcies
  banking 37

default costs 45
   risk 230
   see also failures
Bank Santander 176, 182
Bankscope Stats 56
Barclays Group 7, 9–10, 12, 48, 52, 58, 161, 182
Barings 211
barriers to entry, banking 2, 175, 181–2
Basel agreements 7, 66, 67, 142, 195–205, 277–8, 237, 260
base money, concepts 78–80, 245–6, 261
basis
   definition 219–20
   risk concepts 210–39
Bauer, P. W. 159
Baumol, W. 175, 179
BCCI 45, 135
Beck, K. L. 214
Beder, T. S. 225
Belgium 160
Benston, G. J. 38, 59, 203, 204
Berg, S. A. 156
Berger, A. N. 152, 156, 159, 161, 165, 172
Bernanke, B. S. 258
Bester, H. 124
beta 163, 167
Bhattacharya, S. 194
Bikker, J. A. 179
bilateral determination of lending terms 107
bills of exchange 47
Birmingham and Midshires 182
BIS *see* Bank for International Settlements
Black and Scholes option pricing model 163, 230
black box approach, credit scoring 230
Blinder, A. 258
Bloomberg Markets 143
blue-chip companies, low-risk factors 106
Bohn, J. 230, 232
bonds 21, 29–32, 41, 116, 136–45, 212, 217
   see also securities
borrowers 14, 21–33, 35–49, 64, 67–76, 131–46

asymmetric information 41, 42–6, 119–25, 189–94
CHL 131–2
credit rationing 115–29
creditworthiness checks 43–5, 48, 131–2
direct borrowing 47–8, 131, 134–6
interest rates 27–33, 99–100
international banking 64, 67–76
investments 22–7, 39–41
monitoring considerations 38, 42–6, 131–2
moral hazard 14, 42–3, 46, 119–23, 194, 203
requirements 22–7, 36–8, 41–2, 47–8, 107–13
securitization 7, 36, 37–8, 131–46, 199
syndicated loans 69
welfare-superior agents 21–32, 40–1
   see also deficit units; loans
Bowie, David 136
Boyd, J. 1
BP 69
Bradford and Bingley 182
branch networks 175–6
   closures 12, 14, 47
   globalization 7
Brazil 202
Bretton Woods System 244–5
Bristol and West 139, 182
British Banking Association 53, 55
broad money, concepts 78–80, 252–7, 262
buffer stocks, monetary policy 258–63
building societies
   banking 36, 164
   UK 3–4, 36, 135, 136, 164, 181–2
Building Societies Act 1986, UK 3, 4
Building Societies Act 1987, UK 182
Bundesbank 247
bundled services 17, 47, 184
business plans, loans 44
business strategy risk 238

Cahoot 4
call options 162–3, 221, 222, 230
   see also options
Calomiris, C. W. 204

Canada 160, 194
Canals, J. 7
Canhoto, A. 156
capital
  adequacy 14, 53–4, 97–8, 138–45,
    194–206, 217, 227–8, 237, 245, 260
  concepts 51–60, 195–201, 261–3
  definition 51–2
  risk capital–asset ratio 195–201, 204–5
capital charges for operational risk 200
capital controls, relaxation 7, 65
capitalization, credit risk 230
capital markets 7, 10, 21–33, 39–41, 43,
    47–8, 59, 101–7, 127, 131–6
  benefits 21, 27, 135
  concepts 7, 10, 21–33, 127, 131–6
  contract banking 17
  credit-rationing effects 127
  definition 21
  direct borrowing 47–8, 131, 134–6
  disintermediation processes 7, 10, 41
  equilibriums 22–7, 39–41
  financial intermediation 21–33, 35–49,
    131–2
  impact 21–33
  interest rates 21–2, 27–33
  microeconomic theory 22–7
  optimal investment analysis 22–7, 39–41,
    43, 59, 101–7
  risks 16
  roles 22–7, 31–2, 134–6
  syndicated loans 69
  theory 21–33
  welfare-superior agents 21–32, 40–1
car loans, ABSs 7, 136–45
cartel agreement, UK banking system 181,
  182
cash balances, concepts 51–2
cash flows
  definition 166
  duration concepts 212–20
cash management technology 5, 6
cash reserve ratio, UK 181
CBOs see collateralized bond obligations
CCC see competition and credit control
CCR see Charnes, Cooper and Rhodes

CDOs see collateralized debt obligations
CDs see certificates of deposit
CDSs see credit default swaps
central banks 51–4, 77–8, 90, 97, 190–4,
    197–205, 212–13, 243–64
  conservative 252
  consolidation trend 16
  discount rates 245–6
  foreign currency role 243–5
  full employment role 244–5
  GDP 247–52
  historical background 244–5
  independence considerations 247–8
  inflation targets 243, 244–5, 247–57
  interest rates 247–63
  lender-of-last-resort role 14, 77–8,
    190–4, 204–5, 244–5
  monetary policy 115–29, 143–64
  money markets 245–6
  political interference 201–2, 247
  regulations 190–4, 197–205, 212
  roles 14, 77–8, 190–4, 204–5, 244–52
  schools of thought 244–5
  types 248–52
  see also individual central banks
certificates of deposit (CDs) 36, 57, 135,
    189, 216–18
Chamberlin, E. 179
Chancellor of the Exchequer, UK 252
Charnes, A. 153, 154–6
Charnes, Cooper and Rhodes (CCR)
    154–6
Cheltenham and Gloucester 182
cheques 6, 36, 47, 56
  clearing costs 6, 56
  cost-free accounts 17
  payment mechanisms 47, 56
Chicago Board of Trade 218
Chile 202
China 67
chip-and-pin cards 55
CHL see cost of holding loans
CI see cost–income ratio
Citibank 6
Citigroup 7, 56, 58, 149
Claessens, S. 180–1

Clark, J. 161
classical theory of saving and investment
    27–33
clearing houses 6, 56, 182, 202
Clews, R. 246
CLNs *see* credit linked notes
CLOs *see* collateralized loan obligations
Coase, R. H. 188
Cobb–Douglas production function 163
collateral 38, 43, 107, 120, 123–8, 210–11
    credit rationing 123–8
    default risks 38, 43, 107, 120, 123–5,
        210–11
collateralized bond obligations (CBOs)
    136–45
collateralized debt obligations (CDOs)
    136–45, 259
collateralized loan obligations (CLOs)
    136–45
Colombia 202
commercial banking 4, 116, 181, 244–5
commercial paper 29, 41, 134, 263
commitment mechanisms, banks 45–6
commodities trading 15
commodity risk 210
comparative advantages, international
    banking 65
competition and credit control (CCC) 181
Competition and Credit Control Act 1971,
    UK 3, 6
competition factors 1–19, 80–9, 109–13,
    160–1
    analysis 176–81
    banking 171–85
    consolidation 12
    diversification 13–14
    excessive 16
    NBFIs 9–11
    profitability 8–14, 108–13
    UK 181–4
computer technology, technological waves
    4–5, 41
concentration in banking markets 172–3
concentration ratio 172, 174, 182, 183
confidentiality 13
conservative central banks 252

consolidation in banking 171
consolidation risks 16
consumption, capital markets 22–7, 39–42
contestable markets 175–6, 181
contingent claims 15
contract banking 17, 18
Cooke ratio 195–201
    see also capital, adequacy
Cooperative Bank 56, 149
core competencies, separation from
    delivery 17
Cornett, M. M. 166
corporate governance 59
'corset' controls, UK 3, 181
cost efficiency 150–2
cost functions
    mergers 158–9, 162, 164, 165
    specification 158–9
cost–income ratio (CI) 150
cost inefficiency 158
cost of holding loans (CHL) 132
cost/return structures, transaction costs
    38–41
costs
    ACs 12, 65, 81–7, 177–8
    bank failures 188
    CHL 132
    economies of scale/scope 41, 45, 59, 65,
        147–69
    information 43
    long-run cost curves 65
    MCs 12, 81–9, 95–9, 113, 178
    monitoring 38–41, 44
    operating expenses 2, 9, 82–7, 108–9
    opportunity costs 94–9, 245
    reductions 11–12, 47, 56
    regulations 134, 188–9
    restructuring exercises 12–14
    social costs 188, 201–2, 205
    sunk costs 175
    transaction costs 38–41, 90, 117
    translog cost function 159, 164, 165
    types 38–9
Cournot imperfect competition 87–90
Cournot pricing behaviour 183
covariance, stochastic returns 102–4, 223–8

credit cards 6, 55, 136–45, 183
credit channels, concepts 257–63
credit controls 3–4, 115–29
credit crunch 258, 259–60
credit default swaps (CDSs) 236–7
credit lines 10, 15
Credit Lyonnais 187
Creditmetrics 16, 231, 233, 234, 236
credit ratings 14–16, 44, 134–8, 139, 143,
    199, 260
credit rationing 115–29
    adverse incentives 119–23
    adverse selection 119–23
    asymmetric information 119–25
    availability doctrine 115–16
    collateral 123–8
    concepts 115–29
    existence critique 125–8
    historical background 116
    interest rates 116–28
    profitability issues 117–28
    screening alternative 123–5
    self-rationing outcomes 126–7
    SMEs 127
    sticky interest rates 117–19
    theories 115–28
    types 115–23
credit risk, concepts 195–201, 209–12,
    228–37
credit-scoring methods 14–16, 211,
    229–34
creditworthiness checks 43–5, 48, 131–2
crises 37, 55, 187–94, 197–9, 201–2,
    203–4
    Northern Rock 98–9, 143, 182, 258
'crony' capitalism 46
Crosbie, P. 230, 232
cross-border functions, international
    banking 64–76
cross-subsidization in banking 17, 183
Cruickshank Review (2000) 127, 184
Cumming, C. 131
currency school, central banks 244
customers
    demands 5, 109–13, 116, 205–6
    feedback 5

information files 5
    see also borrowers; lenders
customs, credit rationing 119

Daiwa 211
Daníelsson, J. 201, 227
data envelopment analysis (DEA) 152–7
Davis, E. P. 179
DBS 145
DEA see data envelopment analysis
De Bandt, O. 179
debit cards 6, 47
    clearing costs 6, 56
    payment mechanisms 47, 56
debt–equity ratios, banking 77–8, 206
decision-making units (DMUs) 154–6
deconstruction in banking 17
default
    CDSs 236–7
    distance to 230–1, 232
    risk 38, 43, 107, 120, 123–5, 210–11,
        229, 230–1
deficit units
    capital markets 21–33, 35–49
    financial intermediation 31–2, 35–49
    see also borrowers
De Grauwe, P. 110
delegated monitoring 38, 42–6
demand/supply curves
    banking 6, 10–12, 109–13, 116–28,
        205–6
    eurocurrency markets 72–4
    interest rates 28–32, 109–13, 116, 205–6
    securities 29–32
De Meza, D. 125
Demsetz, H. 174
Department of Justice, USA 172, 182
deposit insurance 134, 189–205
depositors' protection fund, UK 195
deposits 35–49, 51–60, 62–76, 94–114,
    131–2, 148, 188–206, 261–3
    eurocurrency markets 64–76
    financial intermediation 35–49, 101–2,
        107–13
    historical background 47
    imperfect competition model 87–90

international banking 61–76
liquidity risk 54–6, 94–5, 209
maturity transformation 37–8, 41, 51–60, 69–74
monopoly banks 82–7, 93, 109–13, 119
negative assets 100
net interest income 2, 9, 56, 81–90, 99–100, 107–13, 117–19, 204, 211–12
opportunity costs 94–9, 245
payment mechanisms 47, 54–6
perfectly competitive banks 80–2
regulatory needs 188–206
reserve asset ratios 53–4, 67, 70–2, 78–90, 112–13, 142, 194–206, 227–8, 245–6
retail banking 55–6, 204
securitization 131–46, 199
sight deposits 51–3, 56, 107–13, 252–7
time deposits 51–3, 72, 107–13
withdrawals 37, 55–6, 94–9
see also liabilities; savings
deregulation
    banking trends 2–4, 9, 14, 160–1, 175
    building societies 3–4
    concepts 2–4, 9, 14, 160–1, 175
    credit controls 3–4
    financial intermediation 4, 9
    government impositions 3
    interest rates 2, 3
    mortgage market 3–4
    new entrants 4
    phases 3–4
    self-imposed restrictions 3
    surveys 3
    types 3
    UK 3–4, 181–2
derivatives 15, 160, 162–3, 212–40
    categorizations 218
    definition 218
    risk management 212–40
    see also forward rate agreements; futures; options; swaps
Dermine, J. 156
Deutsche Bank 7, 58
Dewatripont, M. 193, 196
De Young, R. 167

DFA *see* distribution free approach
Diamond, D. 42, 45
direct borrowing, capital markets 47–8, 131, 134–6
direct replacement, securitization 134–6
direct route, monetary policy 257–63
disclosure laws 13
discount rates, central banks 245–6
disintermediation processes, concepts 7, 10, 41
distribution-free approach (DFA) 157
diversification
    competition factors 13–14
    mergers 161
    portfolios 13, 37–8, 41, 45, 66, 93, 99–114, 224–8
dividend yield, concepts 29–30, 163
DMUs *see* decision making units
domestic banking
    barriers to entry 2
    changes 1–19
    international banking 61
    see also banking
dominance risk 16
downsizing exercises 12
Dunis, C. L. 162, 163
duration
    futures 220
    primer 213–15
Dybvig, P. 42, 190

earnings on asset (EOA) 149
e-cash 5
ECB *see* European Central Bank
economic efficiency, definition 162
economics
    asset and liability management 94, 252–7
    theory 77–91
    see also macroeconomics
economic value added (EVA) 184
economies of scale/scope, banking 12, 41, 45, 59, 65, 147–69
Economist 260
EDF *see* expected default frequency
Edward III, King of England 61
efficiencies, banking 147–69

efficiency, SCP hypothesis 175
efficient capital markets *see* perfect capital
    markets
efficient frontiers, mergers 156, 163, 166–7
efficient structure hypothesis (ESH) 174–5
EFT *see* electronic funds transfer
Egg 4, 176
elasticity of the price of assets, duration
    concepts 214–20
electronic funds transfer (EFT) 6
electronic payment methods, technological
    waves 5
employees
    downsizing exercises 12
    expenses 108
    international banking 65
    migration issues 65
    multiskilled personnel 1–3
end-of-day net settlements, interbank
    balances 54
endowment effect, formula 9
enforcement costs, concepts 38–41
EOA *see* earnings on asset
equities *see* shares
equity funds, private 16
equity risk 211–12
equity tranche 139
ESH *see* efficient structure hypothesis
EU *see* European Union
eurocurrency markets 2, 4–6, 61, 64–76
    arbitrage 68–9
    balance sheets 69, 70, 71
    concepts 2, 4–6, 61, 64–76
    consequences 70–4
    definitions 64
    demand/supply curves 72–4
    deposits 64–76
    growth 67–8
    historical background 2, 4–6, 65–8
    institutional aspects 68–9
    interest rates 68–9
    liquidity issues 72–6
    money supply effects 70–4
    operational illustration 70–2
    uncertainty issues 68–9
eurodollar market 2, 4–6, 61, 65–6, 67

Euronext.liffe 218
European call options 163
European Central Bank (ECB) 53–4, 160,
    247–8, 254
    see also central banks
European Monetary System 252
European Union (EU)
    ABSs 137–8
    deregulation 3
    mergers 159
    reserve asset ratios 53–4
    ROE 181
    Second Banking Directive 7
    single market 7
    USA expansion 6
EVA *see* economic value added
Evanoff, D. D. 175
event studies, mergers 163, 167–8
exchange controls 3
    see also foreign currency positions
exchange rate mechanism 252
exercise prices, options 163
expected capital gains, securities 29–30
expected default frequency (EDF) 230
export–import services 15
external environment risk 238
external finance premiums, concepts 258

failures
    banking 16, 37, 55, 187–90, 195, 199,
        201–4
    costs 188
Favero, C. A. 156
Federal Deposit Insurance Corporation
    (FDIC) 190, 192–4, 197, 203
Federal Reserve 53, 67, 144, 190, 197, 247,
    254
    see also central banks
feedback, customer demands 5
fee income 14, 48, 54, 62–76
    see also non-interest income
FILs *see* financial investment opportunities
    lines
finance-raising methods, firms 59
financial derivatives *see* derivatives
financial innovation

banking trends 2–3, 4–6, 9, 134, 160–1,
    252–7
competition 13
concepts 2–3, 4–6, 9, 134, 160–1, 243–4,
    252–7
definitions 4
financial instability 4–6
forces 4–5
interest-bearing demand deposits 6, 9
liability management 5, 252–7
monetary policy 243–4, 252–7
process 5
profitability effects 8
regulations 4–6
surveys 3
technological developments 4–6, 41, 134,
    160–2
variable interest rates 2, 4, 5, 6
see also technological developments
financial instability, financial innovation
    4–6
financial institutions see institutional
    investors
financial intermediation
    asymmetric information 41, 42–6,
        119–25
    banking 4, 9, 31–2, 35–49, 101–2,
        107–13, 131–2
    capital markets 21–33, 35–49, 131–2
    categories 35–6
    concepts 4, 9, 21–33, 35–49, 57, 94
    deficit/surplus unit flows 31–2, 35–49,
        57, 94
    definition 35–6
    delegated monitoring 38, 42–6
    deregulation 4, 9
    distinguishing criteria 35–6
    liquidity insurance 36–7, 41–2
    needs 31–2, 35–49, 77–8, 101–2
    roles 31–2, 35–49
    transaction costs 38–41, 90
financial investment opportunities lines
    (FILs) 23–7, 39–41
financial services, OBS activities 14, 15, 48,
    52, 56, 58, 160, 195–6, 209
Financial Services Authority (FSA) 188

Financial Services Practitioners Panel
    (FSPP) 188–9
Financial Times 138, 143, 144, 145
Finland 187, 202
firms
    economic theory 77–91
    finance-raising methods 59
    reputation factors 48
    SMEs 106, 127, 258–63
Fitch 144
fixed-rate mortgages 4
floating-rate loans 57
floating-rate notes (FRNs) 134
forecasts, risks 227
foreign currency positions 7–8, 54–5, 56,
    64–76, 243–5
    Bretton Woods system 244–5
    eurocurrency markets 2, 4–6, 61, 74–76
    globalization 7–8
    UK 7, 8, 244–5
    see also exchange controls
foreign currency risk, concepts 54–5, 210,
    212
Fortier, D. 175
forward markets 68–9, 212–40
forward rate agreements (FRAs) 212–40
    definition 220
    OTCs 220
    risk management 212–40
France
    bank failures 187
    competition 179
    deposit insurance 194
    foreign currency positions 8
    mergers 160, 165
    OBS statistics 14, 16
    profitability statistics 8
FRAs see forward rate agreements
fraud risk 16
free banking 189–90, 190, 201–5
free services 47
Freixas, X. 89, 90
FRNs see floating-rate notes
FSA see Financial Services Authority
FSPP see Financial Services Practitioners
    Panel

Fukuyama, H. 156
futures 15, 212–40
    concepts 218–40
    duration 220
    risk management 212–40

gap analysis, interest rate risk 212–40
Garn–St Germain Act 1982, USA 4
GATS *see* General Agreement on Trade in
    Services
GDP
    capacity gaps 248–9
    central banks 247–52
    UK growth 260
gearing ratio, concepts 195–201
GE Capital 4
General Agreement on Trade in Services
    (GATS) 7
General Electric 4
General Motors 4
Germany
    Bundesbank 247
    deposit insurance 194
    foreign currency positions 8
    mergers 160, 165
    OBS statistics 12, 16
    OE statistics 12, 13
    profitability statistics 8
    relationship banking 45–6, 58–9
    subprime market 145
    universal banking 58, 165
Gertler, M. 1, 258
Gilbert, R. A. 175
gilts 245
    see also government securities
Glass–Steagall Act 1933, USA 4
global banking contrasts, international
    banking 64–5
globalization
    banking trends 2–3, 6–8, 160–1
    branch networks 7
    concepts 6–8, 160–1
    foreign currency positions 7–8
    mergers 7, 160–1
    profitability effects 8
    regulations 7

securitization 7
strands 7
strategic alliances 7
gold standard 202, 244–5
Goodhart, C. A. E. 5, 124, 127, 187, 188,
    201, 227, 252
goodwill constraints, credit rationing 119
government impositions, deregulation 3
government securities 54, 80–2, 116,
    196–7, 204, 212, 225, 245–6, 261
Gowland, D. H. 4
Great Depression, USA 190
guarantees 10, 15, 47, 54, 138, 197
Gurley, J. 38

Haaf, K. 179
Halifax 182
Hannan, T. 172
Hansen, R. S. 125–6, 127
harmonization trends, regulations 7
Haynes, M. 164
HBOS 182
hedge funds 16
hedging 4, 15, 193, 212–40
    certainty benefits 219–20
    interest rate risk 212–40
    purposes 212, 219–20
Heffernan, S. 182–3
Herfindahl–Hirschman Index (HHI) 172,
    173, 174, 182–3
Herstatt risk (risk of settlement), concepts
    54–5
HHI *see* Herfindahl–Hirschman Index
high-frequency low-severity (HFLS) events
    239
hire purchase 181
Hirschleifer, J. 22
historical background
    banking 47, 61, 116, 244–5
    central banks 244–5
    credit rationing 116
historical simulations, VaR 225–7
Hodgman, D. 117, 118
Holmström, B. 48
home banking 5
Hong Kong, deposit insurance 194

horizontal structures, international banking 61–76
Hoshi, T. 46
housing loans
  lifespan 37
  see also mortgages
HSBC 12
H-statistic 176–81
Humphrey, D. B. 161
Hunter, W. C. 165

IBELs *see* interest-bearing eligible liabilities
IKB 145
IMF *see* International Monetary Fund
imperfect competition model, concepts 87–90
income
  net interest income 2, 9, 56, 81–90, 99–100, 107–13, 117–19, 204, 211–12
  non-interest 10, 14, 16, 47–8, 52, 55, 56, 58, 160, 196–7, 209
income statements 149, 150
independence considerations, central banks 247–8
indifference curves 22–4, 123–5
indirect route
  monetary policy 257–63
  see also interest rates
Indonesia 202
industrial organization economic approach (I-O approach) 77–91, 93–114
inflation 6, 9, 70, 202, 243, 245, 24–57
  central banks 243, 244–5, 247–57
  equilibrium 249–52, 262
  house prices 259
  macroeconomics 6, 9, 70, 202, 243, 245, 247–57, 262
  nominal/real rates 254–6
  targets 243, 245, 247–57
  Taylor rule 248, 254–7
information
  asymmetric properties 41, 42–6, 119–25, 189–94
  costs 43
  perfect capital markets 22, 38, 41, 42–3, 45, 59, 119–23, 189–94

regulatory needs 189–94
information-sharing coalitions 38, 43
institutional aspects, eurocurrency markets 68–9
institutional investors 29, 36, 134–6
  growth statistics 136
  statistics 136
  see also insurance companies; pension funds
insurance
  bank failures 134, 189–205
  bankruptcy protection 37
  deposit insurance 134, 189–205
insurance companies 29, 36, 135, 136
insurance services 4, 10, 14, 58
interbank market
  concepts 54, 56–8, 70–4, 94–9, 110–13
  end-of-day net/real-time gross settlements 54
  liquidity risk 57, 94–9
  UK 99
interest-bearing demand deposits, financial innovation 6, 9
interest-bearing eligible liabilities (IBELs) 181
interest rate risk
  concepts 209–41
  gap analysis 212–40
  hedging operations 212–40
  risk management 209, 212–14
  sources 211–12
interest rates 2, 3, 6, 21–33, 67–8, 99–114, 116–28, 209–41
  capital markets 21–2, 27–33
  ceilings 3, 6, 67, 181
  central banks 247–63
  concepts 27–32, 99–100
  Creditmetrics 236
  credit rationing 116–28
  demand/supply curves 28–32, 109–13, 116, 205–6
  deregulation 2, 3
  determination 27–32, 99–100, 109–13
  differentials 100, 119
  equilibrium 28–32, 80–2, 83–90, 107–13, 119–23

interest rates (*Continued*)
  eurocurrency markets 68–9
  financial innovation 2
  imperfect competition model 87–90
  inflation targets 243, 245, 247–57
  loanable funds theory 27–32
  monopoly banks 82–7, 109–13, 119
  net interest income 2, 9, 56, 81–90,
    99–100, 107–13, 117–19, 204, 211–12
  perfectly competitive banks 80–2
  securities prices 29–32
  sticky interest rates 117–19
  Taylor rule 248, 254–7
  UK 181
  unsecured loans 123–5
  variable 2, 4, 5, 6
interest rate swaps *see* swaps
intermediation approach, banking
    performance measurement 152
internal-ratings-based approaches, capital
    adequacy 198–201, 227
international banking 52, 61–76
  categories 64
  changes 1–19
  comparative advantages 65
  concepts 1–19, 52, 61–76
  cross-border functions 64–76
  definition 64–5
  domestic banking 61
  employees 65
  global banking contrasts 64–5
  growth 65–6
  historical background 61
  liability statistics 61–76
  location considerations 61–76
  nature 62–5
  regulations 65–6
  salary levels 65
  statistics 62, 66–7
  trends 1–19
  UK 66, 70
  see also banking; eurocurrency markets
internationalization 'push/pull' factors,
    banking 6
International Monetary Fund (IMF) 201
Internet 4, 5, 12, 17, 41, 176

intertemporal maximizing processes 22–7
investment banking 4, 6–7, 13–14, 52, 58
investment brokerage, OBS activities 13,
    15, 48, 52, 56
investments 22–7, 32, 36–8, 39–41, 51–2,
    115–29, 257–63
  capital markets 22–7, 32, 39–41
  FILs 23–7, 39–41
  law of diminishing returns 32
  macroeconomics 257–63
  optimal investment analysis 22–7, 39–41,
    43, 59, 101–7
  PILs 22–4
  savings 22–7, 36–8, 39–41
investment trusts 36
I-O approach *see* industrial organization
    economic approach
Ireland, Republic of 259
Italy 61, 160, 165, 179

Jackson, W. 172
Jaffee, D. M. 118–19, 120
Japan
  competition 179
  crises 202
  deposit insurance 194
  foreign currency positions 8
  mergers 160
  OBS statistics 12
  OE statistics 12, 13
  problems 59
  profitability statistics 8
  relationship banking 45–6, 58–9
  reserve asset ratios 53, 54
  universal banking 58
Jensen, M. C. 162
JP Morgan 222, 227, 231, 233

Kamerschen, D. 175
Kashyap, A. K. 262
Kaufman, G. G. 203
Keynes, J. M. 27–8, 115, 244
key ratios 1–2, 8–14, 53, 165–6
Kim, T. 62, 63
King, Mervyn 248
Klein, M. 82, 87–90, 93, 107–13

Klein, T. 162, 163
KMV model 230–1
Know Your Customer (KYC) laws 13
Knox, John 188
Koch, T. W. 218
Kohlberg Kravis Roberts 69
KYC laws 13

Laeven, L. 180–1
law of diminishing returns, investments 32
legal constraints, credit rationing 119
legal risk 210, 211–12, 237
lender-of-last-resort role, banking 14, 16,
    77–8, 190–4, 204–5, 244–5
lenders
    adverse selection 42–3, 46, 119–23
    asymmetric information 41, 42–6,
        119–25, 189–94
    eurocurrency markets 68–9
    requirements 36–8, 41–2, 107–13
    see also savings
Lerner index 86, 179
letters of credit 15, 197
leverage 51–2
Leyland, H. E. 43
liabilities 5, 35–49, 51–60, 61–76, 77–91,
    94, 107–13, 135, 190–4, 211–40
    financial intermediation 35–49
    international banking 61–76
    see also deposits
liability management, concepts 5–6, 57, 94,
    107–13, 252–7
LIBOR see London interbank offer rate
Lindley, J. T. 107
linear probability model, credit risk 230
linear programming 152–6
liquid assets ratio, UK 181
liquidity insurance, concepts 36–7, 38, 41–2
liquidity issues 36–7, 38, 41–2, 54–6, 57,
    72–6, 94–9, 107–13, 209–12
    borrowers'/lenders' requirements 36–7,
        41–2, 107–13
    credit risk 230
    eurocurrency markets 72–6
liquidity management, concepts
    94–9, 143

liquidity risk, concepts 54–6, 57, 94–9,
    209–12
liquid reserves, definition 51–2
Llewellyn, D. T. 184
Lloyds 12, 182
Lloyds-TSB 182
Lloyd-Williams, D. M. 175
loanable funds theory, concepts 27–32
loan origination, concepts 131–2
loans 4, 5–6, 7, 10–12, 14, 37, 38, 41, 42–3,
    46, 51–60, 61–76, 99–146, 148, 261–3
    alternatives 29, 41, 47–8, 131, 134–6
    asset allocation process 102–7
    bank failures 187–8
    bilateral determination of terms 107
    CHL 132
    credit ratings 231
    credit rationing 115–29
    credit risk 228–37
    crises 37, 55, 187–94, 197–9, 201–2
    demand/supply curves 6, 10–12, 109–13,
        116–28, 205–6
    granting processes 43–5
    imperfect competition model 87–90
    monopoly banks 82–7, 109–13, 119
    moral hazard 14, 42–3, 46, 119–23, 194,
        203
    mortgages 4, 6, 7, 37
    net interest income 2, 9, 56, 81–90,
        99–100, 107–13, 117–19, 204, 211–12
    perfectly competitive banks 80–2
    pooled loans 37–8, 42, 121
    portfolios 38, 41, 93, 99–114, 131–2, 138
    pricing issues 99–102, 107–13, 126–8,
        209–12, 228
    quality effects 125–8
    rationing 228
    retail banking 55–6
    securitization 7, 36, 37–8, 131–2, 143
    supply curves 6, 10–12, 107–13, 116–28
    syndicated loans 38, 56–8, 69
    see also borrowers
loan servicing, concepts 131–2
loan warehousing, concepts 131–2
location considerations, international
    banking 61–76

location cycle theory, international banking
63–4
logit analysis, credit risk 230
London interbank offer rate (LIBOR) 6,
57, 69, 99, 134, 182–3, 211–12, 219,
247, 260
long-run cost curves, flatness 65
Long-Term Capital Management (LTCM)
16
loss curves, GDP/inflation 248–9
low-frequency high-severity (LFHS) events
239
LTCM 16

M&As *see* mergers and acquisitions
Macaulay duration 213
MacDonald, S. S. 218
macroeconomics
bank credit/transmission mechanism
243–4, 257–63
banking 243–64
central banks 51–4, 77–8, 90, 97, 190–4,
197–205, 212–13, 243–64
financial innovation 243–4, 252–7
GDP 247–52
inflation 6, 9, 70, 202, 243, 245, 247–57,
262
investments 257–63
time inconsistency issues 243–4, 250–2
see also monetary policy
Malaysia 202
management issues
agency problems 58–9, 125, 162
liability management 5–6, 57, 94,
107–13, 252–7
risk management 14–16, 56–8, 197–201,
209–41
marginal costs (MCs) 12, 81–9, 95–9, 113,
178
H-statistic 178
margins 2, 9–10, 102, 109–13, 205
see also net interest spread
market power
concentration in banking markets 172–3
mergers 161
risk-taking activity 16

market risk 16, 198
concepts 210–41
risk management 222–40
VaR 16, 20, 222–40
see also interest rate risk
Markowitz model 93, 100–2
Marks & Spencer 4
Mary, Queen of Scots 188
Matthews, K. 182, 184
'maturity of funds borrowed or deposited'
57
maturity transformation, concepts 37–8, 41,
51–60, 69–74
Mayer, C. 45
MBSs *see* mortgage backed securities
McCauley, R. N. 64
MCs *see* marginal costs
mean, normal distribution 224–8
medium-of-exchange function, money 47,
77
mergers and acquisitions (M&As) 12, 59,
69, 147–68
accounting data 162, 165–6
branch networks 176
concepts 7, 12, 147–68
corporate governance 59
cost functions 162, 164, 165
downsizing exercises 12
dynamic studies 162–8
economies of scale 12
efficiencies 147, 160–8
efficient frontiers 156, 163, 166–7
empirical evidence 162–8
event studies 163, 167–8
globalization 7, 160–1
growth trends 160–8
HHI 172
international comparisons 160–1
motives 161–2
options analogy 162–3
pricing issues 162–3
production functions 162, 163–4
reasons 160–8
share prices 167–8
static studies 162–8
statistics 160–8

Merton, R. 230
Mester, L. 152, 156, 161, 165
metals 15
Mexico 202
microeconomic theory, capital markets
    22–7
Modigliani, F. 119, 120
Molyneux, P. 165, 179
monetarism, origins 244
monetary policy 115–29, 243–64
    buffer stocks 258–63
    concepts 115–29, 243–64
    financial innovation 243–4, 252–7
    rational expectations 248–52, 257
    transmission mechanism 243–4, 257–63
    see also macroeconomics
Monetary Policy Committee 246, 247
money
    multiplier model 78–9, 261–2
    purposes 47
money laundering activity 13
money markets
    central banks 245–6
    concepts 21, 57, 118–19, 245–6
    definition 21
money supply
    base money 78–80, 245–6, 261
    broad money 78–80, 252–7, 262
    buffer stocks 258–63
    concepts 70–4, 78–80, 243–64
    eurocurrency markets 70–4
    textbook model 78–80
monitoring 38–41, 42–6, 131–2, 189–205
    costs 38–41, 44
    delegated 38, 42–6
    regulatory needs 189–94, 201–2
    types 45
monopoly banks 16
    concepts 82–7, 93, 109–13, 119,
        189–94
    regulatory needs 189–94, 201–2
    UK 183
Monte Carlo simulation 225–7
Monti, M. 82, 87–90, 93, 109–13
Moody 44, 230
moral hazard

asymmetric information 42–3, 46,
    119–25, 194
consolidation 16
credit rationing 119–23
lender-of-last-resort role 14, 204–5
Northern Rock crisis 99
moral suasion 181
Morgan Grenfell 7
Morgan Guarantee 69
Morgan Stanley 56, 149
mortgage backed securities (MBSs)
    136–45
mortgages 3–4, 6, 7, 37, 52–3, 136–45
    ABSs 7, 136–45
    deregulation 3–4
    lifespan 37
    subprime market 143, 144–5, 258,
        259–60
    variable interest rates 4, 6
multifaceted operations, banking 1–3
multinational banks 62–5
    see also international banking
multiple discriminant analysis 229
multiplier model, money 78–9, 261–2
multiskilled personnel 1–3
mutual funds 6, 13, 28

narrow banking scheme, regulation
    alternatives 204
National Banking Act 1863, USA 189–90
National Economic Research Associates
    125
National Westminster 12, 182
n-bank concentration ratio 172, 174, 182,
    183
NBFIs see non-bank financial
    intermediaries
negative assets, deposits 100
NEIOs see new empirical industrial
    organizations
neoclassical theory of production and
    technical efficiency 150–2
Netherlands 160
net interest income 2, 9, 56, 81–90,
    99–100, 107–13, 117–19, 204,
    211–12

net interest margin (NIM) 2, 9–10, 81–7,
    99–102, 149, 150
  competition 174
  formula 2
  international comparisons 9–10
  statistics 9–10
net interest spread
  concepts 9, 99–102, 107–13, 204–5
  see also margins
new empirical industrial organizations
    (NEIOs) 176
new entrants 16
  deregulation 4
new ventures, riskiness factors 106, 210
Niehans, J. 110
NIFs see note issuance facilities
NIM see net interest margin
non-bank financial institutions see
    institutional investors
non-bank financial intermediaries
    (NBFIs)
  competition factors 9–11
  contract banking 17
non-interest income 10, 14, 16, 47–8, 52,
    55, 56, 58, 160, 196–7, 209
normal distributions, VaR 2s4–8
Northern Rock 98–9, 143, 182, 258
Norway 187, 202
note issuance facilities (NIFs) 134

OBS see off-balance-sheet (OBS) activities
OE see operating expense (OE) ratio
OECD 8–14, 109, 196
off-balance-sheet (OBS) activities 10, 14,
    15–16, 52, 54–5, 56, 58, 160, 195–7,
    209
  future 17
  international comparisons 14, 16
  risk 54–5, 195–7, 209
  statistics 14, 16, 48
  types 10, 14, 15, 47–8, 52, 56
  UK 182
online banking 4, 5, 12, 17, 41, 160, 176
operating costs 2, 9, 82–7, 108–9
operating expense (OE) ratio
  formula 2

international comparisons 12–13
statistics 9
operational risk 196–201, 211–12, 237–9
  capital charges for 200
  categories 238
  concepts 196–201, 211–12, 237–9
  definition 237
operational risk management 16
opportunity costs, reserves 94–9, 245
optimal investment analysis 22–7, 39–41,
    43, 59, 101–7
optimal reserve decisions 95–9
optimization problems, stochastic
    conditions 94–9
optimum consumption patterns, capital
    markets 24–7
optimum production plans, capital markets
    23–7
options 15, 162–3, 212–40
  Black and Scholes option pricing model
    163, 230
  definition 221
  M&As 162–3
  payoffs 221
  premiums 163
  risk management 212–40
  types 221–3
organizational risk 16
OTCs see over the counter (OTC)
    transactions
output measures
  banking 147–9
  GDP 247–52
overcapitalization in banking 17
overdrafts 53
overlending problems, banking 125
over the counter (OTC) transactions 218,
    220
owners, agency problems 58–9, 125, 162

Panzar, J. 176–7, 179–80, 184
Papi, L. 156
parametric VaR 223–4
Parmalat 138
Patinkin approach 257
payment mechanisms

clearing costs 6, 56
concepts 54–6, 77
free services 47
payments risk, concepts 47, 54–5
Peek, J. 197
pension funds 29, 36, 135–6
people risk 238
PEPs 28
perfect capital markets 22–7, 29–30, 38, 41,
    42–3, 45, 59, 119–23, 189–94
perfectly competitive banks, concepts 80–2
performance issues, banking 147–69
performance measures, banking 149–59
Philippines 202
Phillips curves 248–50, 256
physical investment opportunities lines
    (PILs) 22–4
Pigou approach 257
Pilloff, S. J. 161
PILs see physical investment opportunities
    lines
point-of-sale (POS) machines 6
political interference, central banks 201–2,
    247
Poole, W. 253–4
pooled loans 37–8, 42, 121
portfolios
    diversification 13, 37–8, 41, 45, 66, 93,
        99–114, 224–8
    loans 38, 41, 93, 99–114, 131–2, 138
    risk aversion 100–7
    securities 29
    VaR 224–8
portfolio theory
    concepts 66, 93, 99–114, 225–8
    conclusions 106–7
    primer 103–7
POS see point of sale (POS) machines
price equilibrium, demand/supply curves
    10–12, 109–13, 205–6
price-marginal cost margin 179
price risk, concepts 37
pricing issues
    loans 99–102, 107–13, 126–8, 209–12,
        228
    M&As 162–3

options 162–3
shares 59, 167–8
private equity funds 16
probit analysis, credit risk 230
process risk 238
production approach, banking performance
    measurement 152
production consumption processes, capital
    markets 24–7
production functions, mergers 162, 163–4
productivity increases 12
profitability
    banking 8–14, 47–8, 100, 108–13,
        117–28
    competition factors 8–14, 108–13
    credit rationing 117–28
    international comparisons 8–14
    statistics 8–14, 47–8
    see also return/cost structures, transaction
        costs; return on assets; return on
        equity; returns
profit and loss accounts, ratios 2, 8–14,
    165–6
Prudential 4
prudential control, regulations 3, 14, 55, 67,
    194–206
put options 221, 223
    see also options
Pyle, D. H. 41, 43, 100

quadratic isoloss curves, loss functions
    248–9

Rachlin, C. 237
Rai, A. 156, 167
random shocks, Phillips curves 248–50, 256
rating agencies 14
rational expectations, monetary policy
    248–52, 257
ratios, key 1–2, 8–14, 53, 165–6
real balance effects, concepts 257
real resource model, asset and liability
    management 107, 252–3
real-time gross settlements, interbank
    balances 54
reduced-form revenue model 176

regulation Q, USA 3, 6, 67
regulations
    Basel agreements 7, 66, 67, 142,
        195–205, 227–8, 237, 260
    benefits 188–94
    case against regulations 187–9, 194,
        201–5
    case for regulations 188–94
    central banks 190–4, 197–205, 212
    concepts 6–7, 59, 65–6, 97–8, 134, 142,
        187–207
    consolidation trend 16
    costs 134, 188–9
    critique 187–207
    financial innovation 4–6
    free banking alternatives 189–90, 201–5
    globalization 7
    harmonization trends 7
    international banking 65–6
    international comparisons 194–201
    internationalization 'push/pull' factors 6
    needs 188–206
    political interference 201–2, 247
    prudential control 3, 14, 55, 67, 194–206
    reserve asset ratios 97–8, 142, 194–206,
        227–8, 245–6
    universal banking 59
regulatory arbitrage 4
relationship banking 45–6, 58–9, 107, 125,
    143, 211
relative market power hypothesis (RMPH)
    174–5
repos 245–7
reputational risk 237
reputation factors, banking 48
reserve asset ratios
    concepts 53–4, 67, 70–2, 78–90, 97–8,
        112–13, 142, 194–206, 227–8, 245–6
    regulations 97–8, 142, 194–206, 227–8,
        245–6
reserve ratio, cash 181
reserves 53, 67, 70–2, 78–90, 94–9, 112–13,
    142, 194–206, 227–8, 245–6, 261–3
    deficiencies 94–9
    opportunity costs 94–9, 245
    optimal reserve decisions 95–9

restructuring exercises
    cost-cutting methods 12–14
    international comparisons 12
retail banking, concepts 52, 55–6, 181–2,
    204, 244–5
return/cost structures, transaction costs
    38–41
return on assets (ROA) 2, 8, 149, 165, 204
    competition 174
    credit risk 230
    formula 2
    international comparisons 8
    mergers 165
    Rosse–Panzar model 177
    statistics 8
return on equity (ROE) 2, 149, 165
    competition 174
    EU 181
    UK 181
returns 2, 8, 102–7, 117–25, 165, 167–8,
    204, 219–40
    abnormal 167
    covariance 102–4, 223–8
    credit rationing 117–19
    risks 102–7, 120–5, 224–8
reverse repos 246
Rhoades, S. A. 166
risk-adjusted assets
    Basel agreements 195–6
    securitization 143, 199
risk-adjusted capital 229
risk-adjusted return on capital 229
risk aversion
    concepts 93, 99–114, 123–5
    portfolios 100–7
risk capital–asset ratio, concepts 195–201,
    204–5
risk-free assets 80–2, 100–10, 118–19,
    125–8, 163, 167
risk-free rates 101–10, 118–19, 125–8, 163,
    167
Risk Magazine 237
risk management 14–16, 56–8, 197–201,
    209–41
    arbitrage opportunities 218–40
    concepts 56–8, 197–201, 209–41

derivatives 212–40
interest rate risk 209, 212–40
market risk 222–40
syndicated loans 56–8
VaR 201, 222–40
Riskmetrics, JP Morgan 222, 227, 231
risk of ruin approach, credit scoring 230
risk of settlement *see* Herstatt risk
risk premiums 93–114, 211, 228–9, 235
risks 14–16, 37–8, 42–3, 46, 54–5, 93–114,
    119–28, 194–206, 209–41
    Basel agreements 7, 66, 67, 142,
        195–205, 277–8, 237, 260
    business strategy 238
    credit rationing 119–28
    default 229, 230–1
    external environment risk 238
    forecasts 227
    interest rate risk 209–41
    moral hazard 14, 42–3, 46, 119–23, 194,
        203
    people risk 238
    portfolio theory 66, 93, 99–114
    process risk 238
    reputational risk 237
    returns 102–7, 120–5, 224–8
    standard deviation 163, 224–8
    strategic risk 237
    systems risk 238
    types 37–8, 54–5, 94, 195–201, 209–12
    VaR 201, 222–40
    variance 38
    yield curves 211–12
    see also individual risks
risk transformation, concepts 37–8, 41,
    69–74
R.J.R. Nabisco 69
RMPH *see* relative market power
    hypothesis
ROA *see* return on assets
Rochet, J.-C. 89, 90
ROE *see* return on equity
Rogoff, K. 248, 250
Rolnick, A. J. 190, 194
Rosengreen, E. S. 197
Rosse, J. 176–7, 179–80, 184

Royal Bank of Scotland 182, 183
rumours 188
runs, banks 37, 55, 187–94
Russell, T. 120
Russia 67, 227

S&Ls *see* Saving and Loan (S&L)
    associations
S&P 500 168
salary levels, international banking 65
Santander 176, 182
Santomero, A. M. 161
Saunders, A. 58, 201, 229
Saving and Loan (S&L) associations 187,
    189, 194
savings 21–33, 35–49, 64, 67–76, 131–46
    interest rates 27–33, 100
    international banking 64, 67–76
    investments 22–7, 36–8, 39–41
    requirements 22–7, 36–8, 41–2, 107–13
    securitization 7, 36, 37–8, 131–46, 199
    welfare-superior agents 21–32, 40–1
    see also deposits; lenders; surplus units
Scandinavian bank crisis 187, 202
Schumpeter, J. 4
Scott-Frame, W. 175
screening alternative, credit rationing 123–5
Sealey, C. W. 107
search costs, concepts 38–41
Sears Roebuck 4
securities 6, 15, 21–33, 47–8, 131–6
    government securities 54, 80–2, 116,
        196–7, 204, 212, 225, 245–6, 261
    loanable funds theory 29–32
    price/interest rate relationship 29–32
    underwriting services 15, 47, 58, 134–5
    yields 29–30, 163
    see also capital markets; demand/supply
        curves
securitization 7, 16, 17, 62, 131, 136–45,
    199
    balance sheets 7, 37–8, 138, 142
    concepts 36, 37–8, 131–46, 199
    credit default swaps 237
    definition 7, 131
    direct replacement 134–6

securitization (*Continued*)
 disintermediation processes 7, 10
 economic effects 143–5
 gains 138–45
 permission requirements 1, 143
 processes 138
 types 131–8
 underwritten replacement 134–5
 see also asset backed securities
self-imposed restrictions, deregulation 3
self-rationing outcomes, credit rationing
 126–7
sensitivity analysis 166
SFA *see* stochastic frontier analysis
shareholders, opportunity risk 229
shareholder value, maximization of 184
shares 21, 29–32, 41, 58, 59, 167–8
 mergers 167–8
 prices 59, 167–8
 see also securities
Shaw, E. 38
shocks
 monetary policy 248–50, 253–4,
 256–63
 Phillips curves 248–50, 256
 stochastic macro models 253–7
short-term deposits 37
Siems, T. S. 167, 168
sight deposits, concepts 51–3, 56, 107–13,
 252–7
Singapore 145
single market, EU 7
SIVs *see* structured investment vehicles
size transformation, concepts 36–8, 41
small- and medium-sized enterprises
 (SMEs) 106, 127, 258–63
 credit crunch 258
 credit rationing 127
 negative money shocks 258–63
 riskiness factors 106
smartcards 5, 55
SMEs *see* small- and medium-sized
 enterprises
Smirlock, M. 175
Smith, C. W. 38
Smith, V. C. 201

social costs, regulation needs 188, 201–2,
 205
Spain 160, 165, 175, 202, 259
SPCs *see* special-purpose companies
special-purpose companies (SPCs) 138
special-purpose entities (SPEs) 138
special-purpose vehicles (SPVs) 138, 139,
 143
speculators 213, 221
SPEs *see* special-purpose entities
SPVs *see* special-purpose vehicles
Sri Lanka 202
SSDs *see* supplementary special deposits
staff *see* employees
stakeholders, universal banking 52, 58–9
Standard & Poor 44, 139
standard deviation 163, 224–8
start-ups 210
sticky interest rates, credit rationing 117–19
Stiglitz, J. 120, 122–3, 125
stochastic condition, optimization problems
 94–9
stochastic frontier analysis (SFA) 157, 167
stochastic macro models 253–7
stochastic returns, covariance 102–4, 223–8
Stock Exchange, UK 182
stock market crash (1987) 227
store-of-value function, money 47, 77, 188
strategic alliances, globalization 7
strategic risk 237
structural issues
 banking 61–76, 147–69
 international banking 61–76
structure–conduct–performance model,
 concepts 171, 174–6, 180–1
structured investment vehicles (SIVs) 144,
 260
subdebts, regulation alternatives 203–4
subprime loans market, USA 143, 144–5,
 258, 259–60
sunk costs 175
supermarkets 4
supplementary special deposits (SSDs) 181
supply curves, banking 6, 10–12, 107–13,
 116–28
surplus units

capital markets 21–33, 35–49
   financial intermediation 31–2, 35–49, 57
   see also savings
surveys, deregulation/financial innovation 3
swaps 15, 212–40
   credit default (CDSs) 236–7
   dangers 221
   definition 221
   risk management 212–40
Sweden 160, 187, 202
Swiss National Bank 53
Switzerland
   central banks 247
   deposit insurance 194
   foreign currency positions 8
   mergers 160
   OBS statistics 16
   profitability statistics 8
   reserve asset ratios 53, 54
syndicated loans
   advantages 69
   concepts 38, 56–8, 69
   terms 69
systemic risk 14
systems risk 238

takeovers *see* mergers and acquisitions
taxation
   Basel agreements 196
   capital markets 22, 27
Taylor rule 248, 254–7
technical efficiency 150–2, 161–2
technocracy 14
technological developments 41
   competition 13
   computer technology 4–5, 41
   concepts 4–6, 12, 134, 160–2
   customer information files 5
   electronic payment methods 5
   financial innovation 4–6, 41, 134, 160–2
   productivity increases 12
   telecommunications technology 5
   waves 4–6
Tehranian, H. 166
telecommunications technology,
   technological waves 5

telephone banking 4, 12, 41
Tesco Finance 4
TFA *see* thick-frontier approach
Thailand 202
Thatcher, J. G. 125–6, 127
thick-frontier approach (TFA) 157
Thompson, S. 164
thrift institutions, USA 221
ticks, concepts 218
time deposits, concepts 51–3, 73, 107–13
time inconsistency issues, macroeconomics
   243–4, 250–2
time to maturity, duration concepts 212–20
Timme, S. G. 165
Tirole, J. 48, 194, 196
Tobin, J. 93, 100–2, 204, 257
trading book risk, concepts 199–200, 209
tranching 139
transaction costs
   concepts 38–41, 90, 117
   financial intermediation 38–41, 90
   types 38–9
transformation concepts, banking 36–8, 41,
   51–60, 69–74
translog cost function, concepts 159, 164,
   165
transmission mechanism, banking system
   243–4, 257–63
Treasury bills 80–2, 196–7, 212, 225, 245
trends
   banking 1–19, 55–6, 160–8
   international banking 1–19
TSB 12, 182
Tullas 138
Turkey 202

UK
   ABSs 137–8
   Bank of England 3, 9, 53–4, 57, 98–9,
      127, 143, 181, 197, 244–52, 260
   barriers to entry 181–2
   branch closures 12, 14, 47
   budget deficits 261–2
   building societies 3–4, 36, 135, 136, 164,
      181–2
   Chancellor of the Exchequer 252

UK (*Continued*)
  competition 171, 181–4
  'corset' controls 3, 181
  deposit insurance 194
  depositors' protection fund 195
  deregulation 3–4, 181–2
  eurocurrency markets 70
  fixed-rate mortgages 4
  foreign currency positions 7, 8, 244–5
  GDP growth 260
  house price inflation 259
  institutional investors 136
  interbank market 99
  international banking 66, 70
  maturity transformation statistics 37,
    52–3
  mergers 160, 176, 182
  Monetary Policy Committee 246, 247
  new entrants 4
  NIM statistics 9, 10
  OBS statistics 12, 14, 16
  OE statistics 12, 13
  profitability statistics 8, 48
  regulations 188–9, 195
  reserve asset ratios 53–4, 67
  restructuring exercises 12
  retail banking 55, 181–3
  ROA statistics 8
  ROE 181
unbundled services 17
uncertainty issues 41–2, 68–9, 90, 93–114
  eurocurrency markets 68–9
  liquidity insurance 41–2
  yields 93–114
  see also risks
underwriting services 15, 47, 58, 134–5
underwritten replacement, securitization
  134–5
unit trusts 13
universal banking 17
  advantages 58–9
  concepts 52, 58–9, 165
  finance-raising considerations 59
  regulations 59
  types 58
unsecured loans, interest rates 123–5

Uruguay 202
USA
  ABSs 137
  capital ratios 203
  concentrated markets 172, 182
  credit crunch 259–60
  crises 187–94, 197, 202, 203
  Department of Justice 172, 182
  deposit insurance 194
  deregulation 3–4
  eurodollar market 2, 4–6, 65–6, 67, 70–4
  European expansion 6
  FDIC 190, 192–4, 197, 203
  Federal Reserve 53, 67, 144, 190, 197,
    247, 254
  foreign currency positions 8
  Great Depression 190
  house price inflation 259
  international banking 66–7, 70–4
  interstate banking 175
  liability management 5–6
  mergers 160–8
  new entrants 4
  NIM statistics 9, 10
  OBS statistics 14, 16
  OE statistics 12, 13
  profitability statistics 8
  regulation Q 3, 6, 67
  reserve asset ratios 53–4, 70–2
  restructuring exercises 12
  ROA statistics 8
  subprime loans market 143, 144–5, 258,
    259–60
  thrift institutions 221
  variable-rate mortgages 4
usury laws 116, 117, 119
utility functions 24–7, 38, 39–41, 101, 107
utility maximization assumptions, capital
  markets 22–7, 39–41, 101, 107

value-at-risk models (VaR) 16, 201, 222–40
Vander Vennet, R. 161, 166, 167
variable interest rates 2, 4, 5, 6
variance 38, 223–8, 255–6
variance–covariance matrix, asset returns
  223–8

Venezuela 202
verification costs, concepts 38–41
vertical structures, international banking 61–76
Virgin 4
virtual banking 17
volatility 201–2, 211–40

Wall, L. D. 203–4
Walrasian equilibrium 32
Walter, I. 58
wealth effects, concepts 257
Webb, D. 125
Weiss, I. 120, 122–3, 125
welfare-superior agents, capital markets 21–32, 40–1
wholesale banking 38, 52, 56–8, 65, 68–9

Wilson Committee, The 127
withdrawals
    deposits 37, 55–6, 94–9
    risk 94
Wolfe, S. 139
Woolwich 182
World Trade Organization (WTO) 7

yield curves, risks 211–12
yields
    securities 29–30, 163
    uncertainty issues 93–114
Yue, P. 166

zero-coupon bonds 217
ZETA model 230
Z-score 229–30